AUTHOR'S ACKNOWLE

My good friend, Dr. Anna Kato, asked me over breakfast one morning, "What moved you to write this book?" In short, I replied, "How could I not write it? It's like I found a gift that needed to be shared. It's not mine to hoard." The evolution and creation of this book is and continues to be a collective process with man participating along the journey. Those who have participated in the ever growing "circle" have given the gift of knowledge that, I have discovered, has the gift to heal.

How did this publication and its' unique orientation come about? It was a developmental process in which a host of friends and allies have participated and for doing so deserve recognition. In my first year as an Assistant Professor at California State University, Sacramento, I sensed the polarized perceptions and sentiments of students in my graduate level classes that fell on either side of racial lines. I was perplexed by this as I was working diligently to introduce problem posing educational approaches but was encountering students who were reticent to engage in dialogue and when they did, often expressed anger and resentment across the racial divide. Subsequently, I enlisted Darcy Hall to engage her Euro-American classmates in a focus group discussion related to their experience in our required courses that were designed to enhance multicultural competence. They shared tremendous discord given that they often felt attacked and blamed for what had transpired in the history of the United States.

As a new professor, I knew I would have to address this issue by way of curriculum, the content of what they were learning, and by approach, the pedagogical orientation employed to enhance their competencies. Serendipitously, and as elaborated in the chapters that follow, I had the opportunity to meet Bob Shaw, a descendent of the famous Shaw family. He provided rich sources for me to develop a different approach to teaching multiculturalism from a social justice perspective. He prompted my journey in search of answers to questions related to the contributing factors that create the dispositions of people who possess what we call "Transcendent Identity" (Chapter 12). Who would have thought that this man from Boston would entrust this woman from California with as much as he did but he always responded to my never ending questions though, at times, we were physically 3,000 miles away from one another.

I found an Acquisitions Editor, Frank Forcier, who was willing to take a chance in publishing a book that had yet to be "field tested" and demonstrate its' efficacy. Having the power of the pen has allowed this approach to be shared with wider audiences in print form. It has been liberating to give voice to the humanists in this printed medium and to tell the stories of people who, historically and in modern times, are willing to take on prevalent inequities and injustices. The Kendall Hunt team which include Ryan Schrodt and Tammy Hunt attend to my every need as we attempt to put expanding knowledge to print and liberate people from cultural encapsulation and from the divisive forces that maintain "isms."

The humanists in this publication are from our "history" and modern times. Their modeling of what social justice looks like and their reflections about their own worldview give voice to not only the developmental aspects of self-awareness but also the challenges that one faces when embarking upon making needed changes that address inequities and injustice in our world. Their collective spirit provides a source of strength that urges me on, researching further, writing, reading, and revising even when I think I can't do more. Their lives are not only interesting and inspiring, but, more importantly, their existence on this earth has been vital to creating a nation and fostering a collective identity that would be very different had these individuals not been who they were and done what they did. Their lives serve as models for how to engage across the divides that separate us.

Two modern-day humanists, Courtenay Tessler and Elizabeth Johnson (pseudonym), whose voices are woven throughout the chapters of this publication spent long hours with me in 2007. At that time I was initially gathering data for the endeavor of putting together an approach to teaching multicultural competencies in a way that promotes positive identity development. We never imaged that their words would be repeated in conferences, presentations, and classrooms in New York, North Carolina, New Jersey, Palm Springs, and Sacramento. Their words resonated in conferences across international borders as I presented in Vancouver, British Columbia and Merida, Mexico. In all these venues; the response was always the same... inspiration and hope. These two women urged me on to write with courage, which meant writing from truth. The words of these two wise women compelled me, along with the historical humanists, to stay focused, to not back down, and to draw strength from those whose esteem we desire. Both these women remain a part of my circle and are people I consider, "friends."

Many joined me on this journey by, first, testing the "Prelim," and then providing input in the expanded 1st edition. Carissa Brehm Fleshman, my former teaching assistant, put in long hours at my home, reviewing data from classes and recognizing that this research had significance, that it meant something. Carissa went over and beyond the call of duty! Then, Tom Higgins carried the torch and often carried me through the next semester where we saw the same results from the curriculum. The various iterations of this endeavor would not be where it is today if it were not for the ongoing vision of Nancy Padrick who carried this work from the preliminary printed version that was initially tested in classrooms to the focus group endeavor that led to the Transcendent Identity Development Model.

Three faculty members, Dr. Lynn Wilcox, Teresa Rasor, and Deborah Senna, from my home campus were willing to test the Prelim and provide the opportunity for me to engage with students to hear directly from them as to whether or not the material even made sense. As I heard from students and faculty as to the impact the 1st edition had on their awareness of power and privilege, self-identity, and the development of cross cultural bridge building, I then sought to expand on the "isms" addressed within the storylines and also included contributions from more students and colleagues working in the field of counseling and education. The feedback from students continued to point to the strength of this publication in that the models of people who have enacted Social Justice provides a pathway that not only fosters self-awareness but that promotes the developmental domain of understanding the worldview of others.

A HUMANIST APPROACH TO DIVERSITY

Third Edition

WHAT IS THE COLOR OF YOUR

HEART?

Rose M. Borunda

with Rolla E. Lewis & Michael Mobley

Kendall Hunt
publishing company

Kendall Hunt
publishing company

www.kendallhunt.com
Send all inquiries to:
4050 Westmark Drive
Dubuque, IA 52004-1840

CONTENTS

Grappling with the Unpleasant: Critical Consciousness, Racial Identity, and the Discovery of Humanist Role Models
Dr. Diane Carlson

It's Never to Late to Advocate
Dr. Elisabeth Liles

Using the Power of Privilege to Transform and Heal in the Speech Classroom: Spitting in the Face of a Culture of Silence
Dr. Scott Kirchner

You Speak So Well For a Black Person
Dr. Lisa William-White

Mindfully Responding to Each and Every Client, Every Time
Dr. Chris Knisely

I was fortunate to dialogue with students from various institutions on the content of this orientation. For example, Dr. Rolla Lewis provided access to graduate students at California State University, East Bay. Dr. Thomas Easley and Dr. Barbara Metelsky hosted me at North Carolina State University. Dr. Michael Mobley, after we met at a presentation I gave at Columbia University, invited me to speak at Rutgers University. Dennis and Anna Kato hosted a gathering with faculty and students from University of California, Davis; Rebecca Rosa, Shannon Cannon, Ruth Santer, Ava Gilani, and Tricia Cowen. These visionaries added value to what would become an evolving and living work of art by providing constructive thoughts and suggestions on how to improve the reception of this work. Concurrently, I continued to expand on the lives of the historical humanists through my research at the Boston Public Library as well as the Massachusetts Historical Society. To add more of a "West Coast" orientation, I was provided by neighbors, Rich and Sue Kendall, with excellent books that addressed the (mis)treatment and exploitation of miners as well as learning about Mary Ellen Pleasant.

There were gentle souls with warrior hearts who came across my path in my effort to promote the model of humanism. These individuals were more angel than human as they cleared the pathway so I could do what I needed to do unencumbered and fully supported. Buyaadai Frolov reminded me that this topic is relevant to the issues of today and put me in touch with the work of Michelle Alexander. Karla Amanda Brown maintained composure and vision as the "work in progress" developed into a full publication. Jill McElroy helped me "keep it light" throughout the process and understand the nature of "the work" from the mind and the heart. Kim Ross, Crystal Lopez, and Truc Le provided a cushion of support and humor during the earlier years of writing at the office so I could stay focused. Peggy Bean of KVMR gave me my first radio interview on, of all days, February 14, 2011, Valentine's Day! This was appropriate for "What is the Color of Your Heart?"

Assistant Coach Betsy Yonkman of Rutgers University provided more than just access to Hall of Fame Coach Stringer (Chapter 11). She listened to my purpose for traveling across the country to secure the coach's perspective and input. Assistant Coach Yonkman provided a context for my first to New Jersey that set the stage for the dynamic and engaging dialogue during my visit to the Rutgers campus. I will be a Scarlet Knight fan forever and, more so, I know the formula of how Coach Stringer creates champions, on and off the court... she creates a circle of people around her team who have the vision of the eagle and hearts of the lion!

The Master of Science in Counseling students at CSUS have provided ongoing heartfelt reflection and growth. Evidence of transformation has been captured through discussions and journal writing and presentations that reveal the capacity for and willingness to grow. Our students inspire me to seek ways to address collective pain and to present constructive discourse that unites, rather than divides, and that fosters a more hopeful and harmonious way of being with one another. May the organic evolvement that led to the creation of this publication continue to generate the capacity to create the sacred space in the classroom, work space, community and in the lives of all.

Cohorts 3 and 4 from CSUS's Doctorate in Educational Leadership program provided inspiration in understanding how the tenets of social justice can be enacted by leaders who are grounded in humanist principles. The use of the humanist narratives in their papers and in their presentations resurrected the lives of people who, in some cases, died for causes that are now being adopted by many who are furthering these causes. My hope is that these courageous leaders, counselors, therapists, and agents of change be blessed with many allies while they strive to create more inclusive communities and relationships that promote safety and healing. Many of the stories added throughout this book and more so in Chapter 13 come from the direct experiences of these courageous leaders and healers.

The recent publication of the Multicultural and Social Justice Counseling Competences (MSJCC) (Butler, S.K. et al, 2015) examines how multicultural and social justice competence are vital in facilitating change while taking into account the sociocultural systems affect a client's well-being. These competencies calls us to do the work of developing our capabilities related to (1) counselor awareness, (2) client worldview, (3) counseling relationship, and (4) counseling and advocacy interventions. These competencies underscore the expectation that we not just work with clients from a one on one basis but that we extend our power and privilege in the realms beyond our office. The aspirational competencies of attitudes and beliefs, knowledge, skills, and action (AKSA) offer an expansive opportunity to move from one's own growth and development that takes place from critical introspection to applying one's knowledge and skill to enact positive change (pg. 3)

The language provided by the specific competencies set the stage for educators using this book in the classroom setting to contextualize the assignments and measure student learning outcomes and growth. For classes that are of an introductory or foundational level in developing one's cross cultural competence, instructors and students may want to focus on questions and activities focused on 1) counselor awareness and 2) client worldview. For more advanced courses or those in which students have addressed the first two competencies, then the focus can examine the developmental aspects of the final two competences; 3) counseling relationship and 4) counseling and advocacy interventions.

Chapter 14 is new to the third edition. This chapter expands upon the previously learned chapters and looks to challenge the student to developing his/her capacity related to advocacy in a wide range of contexts and realms. Since the end of the opening chapters provide discussion topics for the classroom, and self-reflection topics as homework assignments, there are also activities that take apply what students are learning beyond the classroom. Chapter 14 recaps and challenges the student to apply the MSJCC competences within a socioecological model that includes intrapersonal, interpersonal, institutional, community, public policy and international/global levels.

Finally, the roots of my own tree continue to be nourished by my life partner, Mike, who has consistently provided the love and support for me to write from the heart. My parents, Henry and Norma, my brother, Henry Martinez, Jr., remind me of the long lineage of relations who did what needed to be done during challenging times for me to have the privilege to do what I do. It is not for me to squander in my lifetime, my power and privilege, but to use it in ways that promotes equity when and where possible.

INTRODUCTION

Try bringing up the topic of racism, sexism, ablism, classism or any one of the known constructs of power and privilege to a room full of people and see what response you get. Think about the various contexts in which these topics might generate different responses. For example, think of the contrast in responses you might hear if you are in a room with only people of color talking about racism in modern times versus the response you would have heard if you were in a room with people who upheld the institution of slavery in the mid-1800s; same topic, diametrically different positions. Yet, these are topics that in times past and in the present generate polarizing debate and exacerbate intergroup dissonance.

Now, imagine you are a university professor, a school superintendent, a classroom teacher, a shift leader, a counselor or an agency diversity coordinator who is expected to lead constructive dialogue about the legacy of racism and all the other constructs of power and privilege with those you are charged with educating or leading in a way that moves them toward greater understanding. How difficult might this be? What might be the various perspectives of the people in your group? How would you facilitate such a dialogue without alienating yourself from people in the group who may have radically different understandings than you and of others in the group? How would you facilitate such a discussion with group members who have no conscious understanding by which to contribute and yet, their engagement is needed to arrive at conclusions that promote greater commitment to social justice principles?

Then, what do you do if the dialogue got heated and members of your group polarize into opposite camps? Polite yet guarded interactions suddenly turn into hostile looks and defensive or aggressive comments. Common ground escapes out the door; the mood is tense, emotions run high, and you wonder when such discussions will ever take place without ending in the dichotomous outcome of "us" and "them."

Let us entertain, for a moment, that you would facilitate this discussion with group members who see one another not with eyes that perceive skin color, gender, sexual orientation, ability level or any other marker that designates "difference" but rather with eyes that perceive the Color of our Hearts. To understand this viewpoint, we will examine how, in the 1800's, these topics were addressed by individuals with red hearts. From efforts that preceded us, we can determine what we have to gain from historical figures that may be relevant and of value for us today.

PART I
Lived Humanism

Red-Hearted Rebels and Misfits

South Carolina plantation society, during the period of Sara Grimké's childhood, represented a well-functioning social system, as attested by the increasing prosperity of the region, in which her family shared. Why, coming from such an environment, Sarah should become a rebel and a misfit, critical of what others accepted, unable to tolerate what others considered normal, has remained an open question. During Sarah Grimke's lifetime she provided an answer, which became part of the abolitionist rhetoric and myth. It consisted of a series of anecdotes of her childhood designed to show that she had always, instinctively, hated slavery. One incident concerns a very early experience: Sarah was four years old when, accidentally, she witnessed the whipping of a slave woman. She rushed out of the house, sobbing. A half hour later her nurse found her on one of the wharves, trying to convince a captain to take her away to someplace where such things did not happen (Lerner, 1998, pp. 16–17).

How is a child's worldview shaped when born into a reality in which mistreatment of human beings is not only legitimized but also is *normalized*? Does a child lose her capacity for compassion and care of others, or does the heart, over time and exposure, harden and become "accustomed" to systematized cruelty that has been socially and morally sanctioned? Evidence points to the fact that Sarah had much to gain *financially* by way of the "well-functioning social system" since the Grimké estate depended upon and benefited from the labor of enslaved people. Daily life for members of the Grimké family was replete with servants who, out of fear of physical punishment, responded to the most trivial commands. Sarah was born into a wealth consciously derived from willful exploitation of others, a wealth accumulated by the motivations of those with green hearts.

This child, a white child, was born in Charleston, South Carolina, on November 26, 1792. She inherited the birthright and the burden of a "well-functioning social system" founded on principles that falsely espoused the racial superiority of one group to enforce and rationalize the enslavement of another. Subsequently, racialized slavery sustained itself through structural, social, and psychological forces that granted advantages and privileges for one group, wealthy white elites, while denying basic human rights for other groups.

Sarah did not create this system. Instead, she retained her critical perspective of what was often referred to as the "peculiar institution." Furthermore, she abhorred the methods used to enforce it. When she knew that an enslaved person was to be punished, she was known to isolate herself in her room and pray that the punishment be averted. Invariably, her prayers for the beatings to cease went unanswered, and shutting herself in her room did nothing to stop the sounds and images of the cruelty inflicted upon fellow human beings. Her eventual self-imposed exile to the north did nothing to free her of what she had witnessed of this entrenched "well-functioning social system." Freeing herself would require much more.

Sarah, "rebel and a misfit," along with her younger sister and godchild, Angelina, encountered in their daily existence the habituated beliefs and dehumanizing behaviors of their family, community, and society. Yet, something in the Grimké sisters' nature made them not only intolerant of beliefs and behaviors considered normal by others but they were moved from prayer and aversion to committed activism. Uncovering the source of this nature can be found in the definition of a **"humanist,"** an individual whose values are grounded in "a concern with the needs, well-being, and interest of people" (Encarta Dictionary). The definition does not qualify "people" as being limited only to those of one's own racial category, sexual orientation, socio-economic class, gender, religious identification, physical or mental ability, or any other descriptor that separates people into categories. Rather, it pertains to *all* people. What factors then, drove the Grimké sisters, born into material wealth and privilege, to take their "concern" and "interest" of people to a level of committed activism and defiance of their family and their community's norms?

The Freedom of Choice

Sarah, and her younger sister by 13 years, Angelina, lived and behaved in ways that branded them as outcasts and contraries. In their life's work, they risked personal safety and sacrificed monetary wealth to dismantle the very system that ensured their financial security. For this, they were considered insane.

These two women detested what others commonly accepted; the practice of slavery. Even though the Grimké sisters were raised to uphold and benefit from the institution of slavery, they not only resisted participation in the mistreatment of the people owned by their family, they vehemently defended them against family members who were more intent on inflicting physical punishment. As a child, Angelina's "sympathies were with the cruelly treated race around her, and she was unspeakably shocked by the terrible punishments inflicted upon them. When a child, she had her little bottle of oil, and other simple medicaments, with which in the darkness she would steal out of the house to some wretched creature who had been terribly whipped, and do what she could to assuage his sufferings" (Weld, 1880, p. 10). These two women would sit at the same dining table, meal after meal, with family members and openly challenge their relatives on behalf of the people they owned. Their defiance started with their own southern slave-owning family and then extended to members of their community who owned slaves or who did nothing to speak against slavery. When their defiance did not affect change in their family, church, or community they took their firsthand accounts about the horrors of slavery to the citizens of the north. The Grimké sisters refused to be silent.

Humanistic behaviors such as those modeled by the Grimké sisters might be prevalent under "right conditions" when there is little to no risk in speaking out against injustice; but, what can be expected of human beings when they are subjected to the worst conditions? Psychotherapist Viktor Frankl (2006), as a prisoner in concentration camps during World War II, bore witness to the strength of the human spirit under the most extreme conditions of human cruelty. Frankl concluded, "In the concentration camps, for example, in this living laboratory and on this testing ground, we watched and witnessed some of our comrades behave like swine while others behaved like saints. Man has both potentialities within himself; which one is actualized depends on decisions but not on conditions" (p. 134).

In a world in which basic necessities of food, water, shelter, safe communities, respect for all faiths, and the opportunity to excel with our unique talents and abilities does not exist for all, we gain further insight into human behavior when tested by adverse conditions. Frankl (2006) poses:

> I may give the impression that the human being is completely and unavoidably influenced by his surroundings. (In this case the surroundings being the unique structure of camp life, which forced the prisoner to conform his conduct to a certain set pattern.) But what about human liberty? Is there no **spiritual freedom** in regard to behavior and reaction to any given surroundings? Is that theory true which would have us believe that man is no more than a product of many conditional and environmental factors—be they of a biological, psychological or sociological nature? Is man but an accidental product of these? ... The experiences of camp life show that

man does have a choice of action. There were enough examples, often of a heroic nature, which proved that apathy could be overcome, irritability suppressed. Man can preserve a vestige of spiritual freedom, of independence of mind, even in such terrible conditions of psychic and physical stress. We who lived in concentration camps can remember the men who walked through the huts comforting others, giving away their last piece of bread. They may have been few in number, but they offer sufficient proof that everything can be taken from a man but one thing: the last of the human freedoms-to choose one's attitude in any given set of circumstances, to choose one's own way (pp. 65–66).

The Grimké sisters and the other humanist subjects of this book "choose their own attitude" in response to circumstances they were subjected to in their lifetime. Their ability to enact their "spiritual freedom," reflects a high degree of "independence of mind" that defied the prescribed expectations of others. Their conscious "choice of action" drew from their "heroic nature." While these humanists could have distanced themselves from the misery of those for whom they sought justice, they choose, instead, to openly challenge the norms of their community and, at times, their religion and government. These individuals recognized that doing so meant, often, that they were putting themselves at risk. At the funeral services held for Angelina in 1879, famed abolitionist Wendell Phillips stated, "Listen to the fearful indictment she records against the system. And this was not slavery in its most brutal, repulsive form. It was slavery hid in luxury, when refinement seemed to temper some of its worse elements. But, with keen sense of right, even a child of a dozen years saw through the veil, saw the system in its inherent vileness, saw the real curse of slavery in the hardened heart of the slaveholder" (Weld, p. 31). In the case of the Grimké sisters, their confrontations began with members of their own slave holding family. The subsequent tensions informed their day to day realities. These individuals had nothing to personally or financially gain by their efforts, but, rather, had much to lose; they, nonetheless, responded to the motivations of their red hearts and risked it all.

A combination of external factors and internal forces converged to create the conditions to which these two humanists, Sarah and Angelina, responded. These are the same conditions that called upon them to draw from what Frankl calls their "spiritual freedom." To fully grasp the **existential reality** of their world, we must explore the "conditional and environmental factors" leading to the circumstances surrounding these two sisters who were considered "high-bred" Southern women. We will unearth the factors that fueled the massive departure of Europeans from all corners of the continent, but will first explore the circumstances that awaited them in the colonies. This wider view will provide greater context to understand why, despite horrendous conditions awaiting them on these shores, Europeans came to America anyway.

Misery Awaits in the Colonies

Journals of the House of Burgesses of Virginia, a document from 1619, reveals the first 12 years of the Jamestown Colony. Founded in 1607, Jamestown was the intended destination of the Mayflower. Before Jamestown, no fewer than 18 attempts were made to create a settlement whose sole purpose was to gain quick profit from gold mining for hopeful investors. This means that the initial European settlements in what is now known as the United States were capitalistically profit driven. This less-known truth about the initial European settlements lies in direct contrast to the more known and retold folklore surrounding the Mayflower, which centers primarily on a people fleeing England for religious freedom in 1620 (Middlekauff and Savelle, 1964). Conditions awaiting the passengers of the Mayflower were such that:

> The first settlement had a hundred persons, who had one small ladle of barley per meal. When more people arrived, there was even less food. Many of the people lived in cavelike holes dug into the ground, and in the winter of 1609–10, they were driven thru insufferable hunger to eat those things which nature most abhorred, the flesh and excrements of man as well as our own nation as of an Indian, digged by some out of his grave after he had lain buried three days and wholly devoured him; others, envying the better state of body of any whom hunger has not yet so much wasted as their own, lay wait and threatened to kill and eat them; one among them slew his wife as she slept in his bosom, cut her in pieces, slated her and fed upon her till he had clean devoured all parts saving her head ... (Zinn, 1999, p. 24).

Even so, the passengers of the Mayflower still came. Their voyage across the Atlantic Ocean was to be made on two ships. The other ship, the Speedwell, was suspected to be unseaworthy, so the passengers arranged themselves into the confines of one ship. The trials of the voyage meant crossing an ocean span of over 3,000 miles in 66 grueling days under inclement weather. On the Mayflower's initial voyage, two passengers died of disease, and the rest never arrived at the intended destination, the mouth of the Hudson River, which is now New York City. They landed; instead, in what is now Plymouth, Massachusetts, which is considerably removed from Jamestown.

These passengers spent their first winter on board the ship where 53 of the original 102 passengers and half the crew died of scurvy, tuberculosis, or pneumonia. Despite the heavy losses, the hostile weather, and their lack of the skill and knowledge needed to survive in their new environment, they stayed. The ship, however, returned to England, and a second ship, also called the Mayflower, brought more people over the course of four more voyages (1630, 1633, 1634, and 1639). A fifth voyage, in 1641, departed from England with 140 passengers but never arrived. And yet, Europeans continued to come.

The colonists' desperate conditions proved ripe for the birth and development of a psychological normative process explained by Zinn (1999) in that "cultures that are different are often taken as inferior, especially when such judgment is practical and profitable" (p. 26). Amid the acts of violence within their own community and the aggression committed against those who had no stake in the creation of the colonies, Frankl (2006) observes that human beings have freedom of choice even in the worst of conditions. This accounts for the evidence that not all of the colonists responded to the horrific conditions in the same way or viewed the indigenous people as "inferior." In fact, many sought sanctuary with Native American communities. Those who chose this course of action exacerbated the frustration and anger of colonists who resented the runaways due to the need for labor to sustain the colony as well as to secure profit from gold mining. Subsequently, deserters who were captured were not spared. They were put to death "by hanging, shooting and breaking upon the wheel ... of whom one for stealing two or three pints of oatmeal had a bodkin thrust through his tongue and was tied with a chain to a tree until he starved ..." (Zinn, 1999, p. 24). In particular, Europeans who came or were brought to the Americas as **indentured servants** had limited options in this hostile environment.

Those hungry for gold were motivated by Columbus's discovery of gold, though his discovery did not occur on his first search. Columbus did initially encounter indigenous people, the Arawaks of the Bahama Islands, who, much like the original inhabitants on the mainland, were described as, "remarkable (European observers were to say again and again) for their hospitality, their belief in sharing" (Zinn, 1999, p. 1). These people proved to be valuable, but not because of their "hospitable" nature. When gold was not initially found, Columbus found capital through the enslavement of indigenous people who were then sold in the European market. This marked the birth of the Trans-Atlantic slave trade that initially moved from west to east. Once this trade no longer proved profitable, indigenous people were forced to mine gold for Columbus, as well as for others who followed him. As native people died from disease or brutality, a new source of enslaved labor replaced them. This spawned the flow of slave ships from east to west and originated from the continent of Africa.

As previously addressed, options for colonists who abhorred their dreadful existence were limited. Britain was a major source for white slavery. It expelled vagrant children, convicts, and destitute women. These people worked, side by side, with the initial wave of Africans, and "were lucky to out live their terms of service. Of the 300 children shipped from Britain between 1619 and 1622, only 12 were still alive in 1624" (Painter, 2010, p. 41). Even before the "eighteenth-century boom in the African slave trade it was estimated that between 300,000 to 400,000 of Europeans in the British colonies came as unfree laborers" (p. 42). Those who attempted to escape, if captured, were returned to the colony and suffered severe punishment. Meanwhile, the ships that carried them to these shores returned to Europe only to bring more people. Why then, did the early voluntary colonists, encountering the harsh realities of life in their new environment, not just board ships and return to Europe? Was it solely the blind quest for material wealth? Did they fear punishment for abandonment? We can examine the motivations that drove them here from the other side of the shore that drew an initial wave of 400,000 to 1 million immigrants during the seventeenth and eighteenth centuries. This was followed by the next major flow of immigrants of over 30 million between 1836 and 1914; these people came despite the high risk in which one out of seven travelers died en route (Taylor, 1971).

Briefly explored were the factors that drew immigrants to these shores; the hope for material wealth, as modeled by Columbus, or for others, the promise of freely practicing their religious beliefs. Now we will examine conditions on the opposite shore that drove one of the greatest voluntary migrations (Ogbu & Simons, 1998) in history. In more depth, we will expand upon the conditions in Europe that compelled early colonists to leave their homelands under hazardous conditions, only to arrive at colonies where mistreatment and subhuman living conditions awaited them.

How Bad Could It Be?

Kelly's (2005), *The Great Mortality*, asserts that "the years between 1000 and 1250 were a period of great economic and demographic growth in the medieval West." These were years of enlightenment and prosperity. Circumstances changed after 1250, with oppressive weather, inter-nation conflict, and rampant religious persecution fueling a "stalled" economy. Kelly (2005) further explains:

> and while medieval Europeans were still able to feed, clothe, and house themselves, but because the balance between people and resources had become very tight, just barely. A worsening climate made the margin between life and death even narrower for tens of millions of Europeans. Between 1315 and 1322 the continent was lashed by waves of torrential rain, and by the time the sun came out again in some places 10 to 15 percent of the population had died of starvation. In Italy, especially, malnutrition remained widespread and chronic, right until the eve of the plague (p. 16).

War, of various scales and for diverse reasons, raged in every corner of Europe. In Italy, the papacy and the Holy Roman Empire fought for control. Mercenaries fought up and down the peninsula while maritime conflict raged on the waters.

> Scotland, Brittany, Burgundy, Spain, and Germany, the ports and plains and cities of northern France, the English and French were fighting the first battles of the Hundred Years' War. The European continent was a land in turmoil, devastation and chaos. Life within the cities where many flocked only added to the prelude of a devastating disease that would prove deadlier than the famines and the wars. A combination of people, rats, flies, waste, and garbage concentrated inside a few square miles of town wall also made the medieval city a human cesspool. By the early fourteenth century so much filth had collected inside urban Europe that French and Italian cities were naming streets after human waste.... Other Parisian streets took their names from the animals slaughtered on them. (pp. 16–17)

Life in large-scaled, overcrowded cities that lacked basic infrastructures such as sanitation taxed and challenged the sensibilities. The blood of slaughtered animals ran freely down the streets of cities where butchers practiced their trade without restrictions on how or where animal parts were discarded. The one sanitation ordinance by which medieval Europeans abided by was a requirement that homeowners shout, "Look out below!" three times before dumping a full chamber pot into the street (p. 17).

Environmental conditions in Europe were ripe for "what we call the Black Death—and what medieval Europeans called the Great Mortality, and medieval Muslims, the Year of Annihilation ... the greatest natural disaster in human history" (Kelly, p. xii). In the fourteenth century, the plague claimed from 30 to 60 percent of European lives, and it took the continent almost 150 years for the population to recover. The prevailing theme of death must have been compounded by the fact that even "dogs, cats, birds, camels, even lions" could not escape the rampant and endemic scourge of the plague. Accounts from that era proclaim, "This is the end of the world." Why would it not seem so when:

corpses packed like "lasagna" in municipal plague pits, collection carts winding through early-morning streets to pick up the previous day's dead, husbands abandoning dying wives and parents abandoning dying children—for fear of contagion—and knots of people crouched over latrines and sewers inhaling the noxious fumes in hopes of inoculating themselves against the plague. It was dusty roads packed with panicked refugees, ghost ships crewed by corpses, and a feral child running wild in a deserted mountain village (pp. xiii–xiv).

A succession of plagues besieged Europeans, with an estimated 100 outbreaks right up until the 1700s. Hopelessness in the midst of the high mortality rate compelled thousands to board ships and set sail for a new land that held unknown possibilities. While we have recognized the miserable conditions awaiting them, we can now also imagine why a European of that era would take a chance at survival in a different and unknown part of the world. Even though there were no assurances that life would be better, where they were headed, their frame of reference provides a sense of optimism in that they had hope for more promising possibilities.

The term "Land of Opportunity" derives from this backdrop in which people chose to be in the United States for the hope of improving their life circumstances. The determination to act upon this hope, despite the grave odds, gave this mass movement of expectant immigrants terms such as "pull yourself up by the bootstraps," which promotes a Euro-American value of self-determination and rugged individualism. Ogbu and Simon's (1998) **cultural-ecological theory** frames the experiential realities of **Voluntary Immigrants**, people who have chosen to move, voluntarily, to the United States with hope of a better future. Furthermore, these people do not perceive their presence in the United States as being forced upon them by the U.S. government or white Americans. For the vast majority of these European immigrants, once they boarded a ship, there was no turning back. They were committed to a life in this new land and would do whatever it took to ensure their survival. For some, the quest for survival took on a new form of existence, and they enacted whatever means necessary to sustain the quest.

Whatever Means Necessary

Painter (2010) states that "what we can see depends heavily on what our culture has trained us to look for" (p. 16). By the time Sarah and Angelina Grimké were born, exploitation of humanity was a fundamentally accepted method by some to sustain a thriving economic system. The "well-functioning social system" that justified gross mistreatment of "others" was rooted by the following contributing factors: 1) the need to survive, 2) incapacity to be self sufficient, 3) inability to sustain a workforce of other Europeans, and 4) the opportunity for capitalistic gain. In combination, these toxic factors fertilized an orientation that maintains a psychological and sociological grip on the way many still perceive racial "difference" to this day.

Even the concept of "race" is a construction devised over time. Painter, in her well researched publication entitled "The History of White People," poses,

> Were there "white" people in antiquity? Certainly some assume so, as though categories we use today could be read backwards over the millennia. People with light skin certainly existed before our times. But did anyone think they were "white" or

that their character related to their color? No, for neither the idea of race nor the idea of "white" people had been invented, and people's skin color did not carry useful meaning. What mattered was there they lived; were their lands damp or dry; were they virile or prone to impotence, hard or soft; could they be seduced by the luxuries of civilized society or were they warriors through and through? What were their habits of life? Rather than as "white" people, northern Europeans were known by vague names: Scythians and Celts, then Gauls and Germani. (p. 1)

The capacity to arrive at this place of extreme exploitation and dehumanization of people based on the superficial marker of skin color can be further explained by the mental adjustment known as "**cognitive dissonance**." Festinger (1957) posits that human beings find ways to justify their behavior, even when they know it to be wrong. Their attitude about the "other" is adjusted to rationalize the behaviors required to achieve their goals of exploitation. In the early development of the United States, we have two major outcomes from the formation of this psychological grip; one outcome was slavery, which guaranteed cheap labor, and the second was genocide and forced relocation that ensured access to land. This frame of thinking underscored the hypocrisy that Angelina commonly encountered when people not only justified slavery as righteous, but also defended it based on "Christian principles." Such was the polar contradiction in world views of those that profited by human exploitation verses the Grimké sisters who sought to change it.

Angelina, who had occasion to tutor the daughter of the "workhouse" master, often heard and saw the extreme horrors inflicted by fellow citizens who claimed to be "good Christians." The workhouse was where slave owners, unwilling to do their own dirty work, sent the people they owned to be punished by others.

> These are not things I have heard; no, my own eyes have looked upon them and wept over them.... No one can imagine my feelings walking down that street. It seemed as though I was walking on the very confines of hell. This winter being obliged to pass it to pay a visit to a friend. I suffered so much that I could not get over it for days and wondered how any real Christian could live near such a place (Lerner, 1998, p. 60).

The Grimké sisters and many others never made the "mental adjustment" to the cruelty of slavery or the mistreatment of Native Americans. They saw the attitudes and behavior of their own family, their community, and their government as aberrant and sinful. Despite being born into and living in a reality that normalized and justified slavery, these sisters openly challenged their family members in their homes, confronted their friends and larger community in public, and found a larger audience through publication and speaking venues throughout the United States to change the "well-functioning social system" that was imposed upon them. They did so even though it heightened the discord and tension in their family. Angelina's personal journal reveals a level of inherent discontentment in the very heart and soul of her slave-holding family. Dated June 29, 1829:

> Left the table today on account of a variety of unpleasant little things day after day and week after week am I tried in this way. There is such a spirit of finding fault, either the meal is given too late or things are too cold or they are badly cooked

or if they are not found fault with, then they are crass and rude to each other or the servants-so that I have often remembered with feeling what Solomon says-"a dinner of herbs where love is, is better than a stalled ox and hatred therewith." My daily experience causes me to say "Better is a little with the fear of the Lord, than great treasure & trouble therewith." So weary is my soul with the strife & contention that it seems to me I would willingly purchase peace, sweet peace, at the sacrifice of any earthly luxury or gratification (Wilbanks, 2003, p. 100).

This was a slave-owning home abundant with luxury. It was built on a land deplete of the native people who were removed or killed to establish it and eventually sustained by the enslaved labor of Africans to work it. Ogbu and Simons (1998) refer to people who were conquered, colonized or enslaved, and forced to be in the United States against their will as **Involuntary Immigrants**. The distinguishing features of this classification are that these people did not choose to become a part of the United States and that they usually interpret their presence in the United States as forced on them by white people.

The opposing developmental histories between "Voluntary Immigrants" and "Involuntary Immigrants" left strained relationships and outcomes at multiple levels. The aftermath of the violent origins espoused enmity and historical distrust, as reflected in the following statement from Chief Red Jacket of the Seneca tribe.

Library of Congress

Your forefathers crossed the great waters, and landed on this island. Their numbers were small. They found friends and not enemies. They told us they had fled from their own country for fear of wicked men, and come here to enjoy their religion. They asked for a small seat. We took pity on them, granted their request, and they sat down amongst us. We gave them corn and meat. They gave us poison in return. The white people had now found our country (Cleary, 1996, p. 36).

To reveal the clash of cultures that was taking place during the formation of the original thirteen colonies, Forbes (2008) explains the concept of wétiko, a term from the Cree, that refers to an evil person or spirit who terrorizes other creatures by acts that include cannibalism. Forbes applies the term to the imperialistic and exploitive acts committed upon people and resources. He states that

"Cannibalism, as I define it, is the consuming of another's life for one's own private purpose or profit" (p. 24). Angelina Grimké lived in the midst of a period in which this "raw consumption for profit" was evident. In a letter written to Catherine E. Beecher, an educator from the Northern states who was committed to gradual emancipation as opposed to immediate emancipation as the Grimké Sisters were, Angelina expands upon the nature of "wétiko." Grimke (1838) states,

> Northern Christians believe it is a sin to hold a man in slavery for 'mere purposes of gain:' as if this was the whole abolition principle on this subject ... our principle is, that no circumstances justify a man in holding his fellow man as property; it matters not what motive he may give for such a monstrous violation of the laws of God ... for myself, I believe that there are hundreds of thousands in the South, who do not hold their slaves, by any means, as much 'for purposes of gain' as they do for lust of power; this is the passion that reigns triumphant there, and those who do not know this, have much yet to learn (p. 7–8).

With this insight to the nature of wétiko we continue to examine "and learn about this violent clash...." of realities and motivations, in which these two sisters were, moved from avoidance and prayer for those who suffered to action on their behalf. They went on to provide voice, as did others, for those who were either forcibly silenced through force of whip, through genocide, or through forced relocation while opposing those who maintained it. It is the force from the "spiritual freedom" that Frankl speaks of that the following chapters address.

Where are we Today?

Many would say that laws have ended the conditions into which the Grimké sisters were born. The Emancipation Proclamation ended slavery, and Civil Rights legislation has further rectified the structural inequities of the laws that govern the United States. What has not changed is the legacy of intergroup tensions that are rooted in our historical discord as well as the numerous social constructions that define what traits, attributes, beliefs and status are given higher value and worth than others. To this day, habituated beliefs permeate and impact the very social and emotional distance between people of different racial groups. This aftermath is explored in Paxton's (2002) dissertation case study in which six European-Americans participated as co-inquirers in a Cooperative Inquiry group for nine months on the

Library of Congress

meaning of "whiteness." Paxton states, "While People of Color are often shocked with how little White people understand about racism and confirm their beliefs that White people, at best, don't care about People of Color, many White people often dismiss such difficulties by citing over-sensitivity and reverse discrimination." He refers to this distance in emotional and social reality and perception as a "**racial reality gap**" (p. 4).

Frederick Douglass provides a unique perspective on the causes of the gap that were later discussed in Paxton's study. Mr. Douglass came into this world in 1818 as a member of a multi-generational line of people born into slavery. He was the property of others for the first 20 years of his life. Finding his way to members of the Underground Railroad, Mr. Douglass gained freedom and committed the rest of his life to abolitionism. His autobiography chronicles the cruelties inflicted upon enslaved humanity, and his lectures provide insight to the cultural mores that sustained the U.S. system of slavery. In the winter of 1855, he spoke to the seeds of "human selfishness" that breeds, even today, oppressive policies and behaviors. He observes that to maintain an oppressive system such as slavery, "Every new-born white babe comes armed from the Eternal presence, to make war on slavery. The heart of pity, which would melt in due time over the brutal chastisements it sees inflicted on the helpless, must be hardened" (Douglass, 1994, p. 451).

Though Douglass never met the Grimké sisters in person, his reference to the "hardened" heart echoes their observations of slave-holders as cited earlier in this chapter. In contrast, Angelina, though refusing to succumb to the social forces of her community was described during her years speaking against slavery as one who "often spoke from a broken heart, with a pathos which melted and subdued those who listened to her" (Weld, p. 13). When the Euro-American child born today, observes a reality in which those who were previously deemed as "inferior" and "expendable" disproportionately living under depressed conditions, what does it do to his or her perception of the group's capacity and worth? If the Euro-American child is grounded in a cultural fabric that espouses meritocracy (Johnson, 2001) and does not understand how generational poverty is sustained by morbid inequities in opportunity structures, then she may come to narrow-minded conclusions that are not only groundless but are also prejudicial. A society that fosters absolute meritocracy absolves the Euro-American and every other child of his or her participation in addressing the inequities that may be grounded in ideologies that are racist, sexist, heterosexist, classist, or any of the other social constructions that maintain dominance of one group over another. The social forces promote emotional disassociation. The heart, as Mr. Douglass points out, becomes hardened to the realities of others.

When Angelina walked past the "workhouse" and heard the cries of people being whipped or subjected to some other cruel punishment, she "wept over them." When she expressed her isolation by saying "no one could imagine my feelings," it was not that no one else could hear or that no one else knew what was transpiring, it is that it seemed to her that nobody else *cared* about the mistreatment of people ... or, at least, *cared enough* to make the living "hell" end. She did not enact **cognitive dissonance** as her ancestors and her immediate family had done. She did not distance herself from her own emotional response to the realities of human beings who were grossly mistreated in her everyday existence. Rather, she retained her capacity to *feel* and did not divorce herself from her feelings. She did not disassociate.

If we follow the course of a culture rooted in its fostered capacity to distance itself from its emotions, its capacity to care, its capacity to feel for the suffering of humanity, then we have devolved to a place of detachment that Paxton further describes:

> As White people, I assume that we lead an unbalanced life. We spend a great deal of time trying to understand everything around us, but when it comes to self-reflection, emotion and feelings, we have little or no access or patience. We expect to control the world around us instead of participating consciously in evolution. We are good at doing things but have little patience for understanding the full implications of our actions (p. 33).

If our children are not encouraged to respond to and act upon this reality from their hearts, then active and engaged participation in improving the world will not occur. Our children will remain unengaged and distant observers of humanity and of the world, blind to the disparities that exist. The laws enacted since the founding of this nation will not change this ingrained dissonance, only enactments from the heart will—not green hearts, but hearts like those of the Grimké sisters and the subjects of this book.

The Euro-American child of today may not observe the extreme inequities that the Grimké sisters witnessed in their daily lives; but, if she is raised to be unengaged, then she will never realize that the starting line for her peers "of color" may be several leagues behind her own and that, in many cases, the unique "differences" of many other children mark them as targets of mistreatment. This child will not develop empathy for her peers when implicit and explicit messages about her peers' "differences" in language, culture, appearance, and belief systems are not only marginalized but maligned. The Euro-American child learns and accepts without question a history of the United States from the vantage of expansionists and extreme capitalists that justifies conquest and colonization (for the greater good of those who are like you) and that the cost for doing so is inevitable (though maybe not regrettable).

This child, and every other child, lacks the edification of prominent and not-so-prominent models that choose to behave differently under the same conditions as those who acted out of greed and self gain. As a nation, we continue to pay the price for fostering values that promote the quest for extrinsic rather than intrinsic rewards. As our children learn to devalue meaningful relationships with others we pay a higher price as they disassociate from their own heart. This book pays tribute to those who, under the same set of circumstances of family and community, choose to respond to gross inequities differently. While every other child in this nation is bombarded with models of people who continue to amass financial wealth at the expense of, and without consideration for the needs of, others, we are fortunate to have these unheralded models from our past to provide an alternate and more engaged way of fully *being* in the world.

Humanist Models

The following chapters present the lives of white historical and modern-day humanists who not only *felt*, but who *acted* on what they felt. These humanists provide models of advocacy for two main reasons: 1) They modeled selfless advocacy in what they attempted to accomplish, and

2) They used their power and privilege for the benefit of others. The central focus of this book is to elaborate on the common themes that emanate from the lives of these humanists. From these shared experiences, we can learn what conditions foster the nature of people who draw from their "spiritual freedom."

The data collected on these individuals come from a wide range of sources. It should be noted that much of the information uncovered here is from books no longer published and archived sources maintained in the Boston Public Library, the New York Historical Society, the Staten Island Historical Society and the Massachusetts Historical Society. Chapter 2 introduces the selected historical humanists and provides an overview of their lives and their adopted causes. When we consider what these very diverse individuals have in common and what compelled them to become humanists, certain themes arise. These common themes emanating from the lives of these individuals are further elaborated upon in the following chapters: Chapter 3 is entitled "Call It What It Is" and addresses the common theme of early exposure to racist behavior and attitudes. Chapter 4, "Who Is in Your Circle," expands upon our subjects' development of meaningful relationships with people across the racial divide and how these relationships, under different circumstances, strengthened their capacity to ground their efforts. Chapter 5, "Actions Speak (and Heal) Louder than Words," chronicles the active involvement of our subjects in deconstructing racism. Chapter 6, "Not for the Meek of Heart," addresses the difficult subject of fear. Testaments from the lives of our subjects provide examples of the price that humanists pay in having to come face to face with varying degrees of violence. The final theme that emanated from the qualitative research on the lives of our humanist subjects is addressed in Chapter 7, which is entitled "The World from the Eyes of Humanists." It presents the common theme of a "spiritually based identity" in the lives of the humanists.

The final chapters provide a forum by which to activate what we have learned from the historical humanists and even those humanists who live in our midst today. My colleague, Dr. Rolla Lewis, leads us in Chapter 8 in a discussion on "What is the Color of Your Heart? Personalizing and Activating Humanism." While we have, at this point, learned what common themes emanated from the lives of the historical humanists, how do we, in our own lifetimes, become champions from the heart and use our positions of power and privilege for good? Dr. Lewis' chapter prompts further exploration of the cultural forces that shape and inform the evolving identity of Euro-Americans. His chapter is followed by Chapter 9, "The Mis-Education of the Euro-American Child." The title of this chapter was inspired by Carter Woodson's book, "The Miseducation of the Negro." This particular chapter examines the forces that impede positive white identity development (Helms, 1994) with recommendations on bridging the racial reality gap.

Chapter 10, "Healing the Soul Wound," addresses the role of People of Color in understanding Whiteness, and the potential contributions of People of Color in racial bridge building. My colleague, Dr. Michael Mobley, facilitates this discussion. Chapter 11, "Grace ... Be the Eagle," provides thoughts and examples of how People of Color can preserve their well-being in the face of subtle and, sometimes not too subtle, micro-aggressions. Chapter 12 provides a model by which to visualize and speak about a space that lies above the constructs of race. The template and language derived from this model can be applied to other constructs of power and privilege that exist in our society and that serve to askew the way we perceive one another. This Transcendent

Identity model was developed after several focus group discussions with graduate students who read the 1st edition of "What is the Color of Your Heart?" Their names, thoughts, and experiences are provided within the chapter as they speak to the possibility, the struggles, and the joy in living and loving beyond divisive constructs. Chapter 13, "When We Care," provides a compilation of stories from a range of contributors. Each story captures the range and diversity in which humanism can be activated. From these courageous acts to thoughts on our language, we examine ways in which to transform our world.

Many who read this are formally engaged in the process to develop cross cultural competency as future counselors, social workers, teachers, educational leaders, health care providers or some other people oriented profession. The competencies delineated by the MSJCC (Butler, S.K. et al, 2015) provide specific domains by which to foster and measure development. Our growth begins with the *first domain* of **Self Awareness** which entails developing the aspirational competencies that address, a) exploring **attitudes and beliefs** related to one's social identities and how these identities reflect privileged or marginalized status, b) possessing **knowledge** of one's history and the values, beliefs, and biases that may come with one's privileged or marginalized status, c) Acquiring **skills** by which to communicate one's privileged or marginalized status, and d) taking **action** to increase one's self-awareness related to one's social identities. These four aspirational competencies of attitudes and beliefs, knowledge, skills, and action are also applied to the other three domains. The *second domain* of **Client Worldview** calls for us to "develop our understanding of the client's worldview, assumptions, attitudes, values, beliefs, biases, social identities, social group status, and experiences with power, privilege, and oppression" (p. 6). This requires a foundational understanding that we not assume a client's identity but that we continue to expand our knowledge related to differences in the realities and experiences of others. In the *third domain,* **Counseling Relationship**, "privileged and marginalized counselors are aware, knowledgeable, skilled, and action-oriented in understanding how client and counselor privileged and marginalized status influence the counseling relationship" (p. 9). It is incumbent upon the counselor to recognize how the client may perceive them based on their own histories and how this informs the counseling relationship. Often, these perceptions may be unspoken but, nonetheless, affect the relationship itself. Finally, in the *fourth domain* of **Counseling and Advocacy Interventions**, privileged and marginalized counselors intervene with and on behalf of clients at the intrapersonal, interpersonal, institutional, community, public policy, and international/global levels" (p. 11). This last domain is modeled by the individuals in this publication and numerous examples that run the gamut from intrapersonal to international/global levels provided throughout the chapters.

Questions and activities at the end of the chapters are provided under the subtitle of each of the four competencies. These can be utilized to stimulate thought, reflection, introspection, discussion and even suggestions for action. For more advanced classes in which student competency within the domains of Self Awareness and Client Worldview have already been addressed in previous courses, the domains of Counseling Relationship and Counseling and Advocacy Intervention can be addressed by focusing on the suggested activities under these action oriented domains. Chapter 14 encourages the reader to not only recap but to expand upon one's capacity to serve as an agent of change in a wide realm of situations as provided in Chapter 13.

The reader also has the option of applying problem posing and Advocacy Interventions to a situation that is relevant to our lives today.

All of us make decisions every day. We make decisions in our personal lives and in our professional lives. For those choosing to live a life of "spiritual freedom," there is much to be learned from historical humanists who drew from their "heroic nature" during a very challenging era of our nation's history. The path of a committed social justice activist is not easy; our contextualized reality can make "heart inspired decisions" difficult to make and act upon. For those in the field of education, social work, counseling, public health, or even those working in the private sector where the distinction of "haves and have-nots" may be apparent, the themes from the lives of these humanists can find relevance in the "well-functioning social systems" that we encounter in the present day. Many of you reading these words may already be free of wétiko in your heart but you are seeking, in your lifetime, to improve the quality of life for others who fall victim to oppressive forces. As a cancer researcher does not need to have cancer in order to study and eradicate it, those endeavoring to relieve human suffering of a psychological and/or sociological nature must also understand with their minds but see with their hearts.

While the systems that we live in today may be "well-functioning," we may also consider, just as the Grimké sisters did, whether a system that is considered *normal* is actually just. So, if you have felt the despair that drove Sarah Grimké to the docks at the age of four, if you would like to live freely but don't know how, if you acknowledge that a racial reality gap exists but don't know how to bridge it, if you have wondered about how your life can have more meaning, in ways big or small, but would like to understand how, or maybe you even question the color of your heart, then you will find inspiration in the chapters that follow. I encourage you to read on.

QUESTIONS FOR DISCUSSION OR SELF REFLECTION

SELF-AWARENESS

1. What is your family's place of origin, and how does their history affect you in the here and now?

2. How does the rendition of European migration you just read in this chapter differ from what you have previously learned?

3. Frederick Douglass (1994, p. 432) wrote, "America is false to the past, false to the present and solemnly binds herself to be false to the future." What does he mean in this statement and how does it apply today?

CLIENT WORLDVIEW

4. What are the histories of other people in your community?

5. What difference(s) would there be in the perceptions and realities of people who choose to be in the United States voluntarily versus those who are here involuntarily?

COUNSELING RELATIONSHIP

6. How does your family's place of origin and your history affect the way you perceive yourself and perhaps inform the way you perceive others?

7. How does the rooted nature of "cognitive dissonance" in this nation's development inform our intergroup and intra-group relations and perceptions today?

8. The author uses the term "enslaved humanity" rather than using the commonly used term of "slaves." How does this different reference change the perception of people in bondage? How would this shift in our words inform the nature of our relationships with one another?

COUNSELING AND ADVOCACY INTERVENTIONS

9. The Grimké sisters refused to be silenced. What are issues in our own communities that fall into the shadows of silence but that need to be addressed?

10. The Grimké sisters set about dismantling slavery, which was a flourishing, oppressive system in their lifetime. What structural inequities persist today?

NEW CONCEPTS AND VOCABULARY TO REVIEW

Humanism:

Spiritual Freedom:

Existential Reality:

Indentured Servants:

Cultural-Ecological Theory:

Voluntary Immigrant:

Cognitive Dissonance:

Involuntary Immigrant:

Racial Reality Gap:

Wétiko:

Activity

Self-Awareness and Client Worldview

Contributed by JoAnn Tennyson: Family Shield

Family Shield: draw on a large piece of paper and use symbols and pictures (no words) to describe the 5 quadrants of family information:

1. Neighborhood or Place of Origin,

2. Family Values & Beliefs,

3. Family Barriers & Challenges /Community Issues,

4. Family Successes & Triumphs, and

5. Personal Successes & Dreams.

Be colorful and creative and design as neatly as possible.

Share your shields in small groups. Afterward, tape your shields in a space in the front of the room that identifies which of the 5 areas in which there was consensus of similarity.

Discuss, as a class what differences are prevalent as well as what similarities cut across the differences.

References

Clearly, K. M. (1996). *Native American wisdom.* New York, NY: DoveTail Books.

Douglass, F. (1994). *Douglass autobiographies.* New York, NY: Penguin Books.

Festinger, L. (1957). *A theory of cognitive dissonance.* Evanston, IL: Row, Peterson.

Forbes, J. (2008) Columbus and other cannibals. New York, NY. Seven Stories Press.

Frankl, V. (2006). *Man's search for meaning.* Boston, MA: Beacon Press.

Grimké, A. (1838) Letters to Catherine E. Beecher. Boston MA. Printed by Isaac Knapp.

Helms, J. E. (1994). *The conceptualization of racial identity and other "racial" constructions.* In E. J. Trickett, R. J. Watts, & D. Birmen (Eds.), Human diversity: Perspectives on people in context (pp. 285–311). San Francisco, CA: Jossey-Bass.

Johnson (2001). *Power, privilege and difference.* Mountain View, CA: Mayfield Publishing Company.

Kelly, J. (2005). *The great mortality.* New York, NY: HarperCollins Publishers.

Lerner, G. (1998). *The Grimké sisters from South Carolina, pioneer for women's rights and abolition.* NY: Oxford University Press.

Middlekauff, R. & Savelle, M. (1964). *A history of colonial America.* NY: Holt, Rinehart and Winston, Inc.

Ogbu, J. & Simons, H. (1998). *Voluntary and involuntary minorities: a cultural-ecological theory of school performance with some implications for education.* In Anthroplogy & Edcation Quarterly 29(2):155–188. American Anthropological Association.

Painter, N. (2010). The history of white people. New York, NY. W.W. Norton & Company, Inc.

Paxton, D. (2002). *Facilitating transformation of white consciousness among Euro-American people: A case study of a cooperative inquiry.* Unpublished doctoral dissertation, California Institute of Integral Studies, San Francisco, CA.

Taylor, P. (1971). *The distant magnet.* Great Britain; Ebenezer Baylis & Son Ltd.

Weld, T. (1880). In Memory, Mrs. Angelina Emily Grimké Weld. Boston, MA. Press of George H. Ellis.

Wilbanks, C. (2003). *Walking by faith, the diary of Angelina Grimké, 1828–1835.* Columbia, SC: University of South Carolina Press.

Woodson, C. G. (2000). *The mis-education of the negro.* Chicago, IL. Associated Publishers.

Zinn, H. (1999). *A people's history of the United States.* New York, NY: HarperCollins Publishers, Inc.

Insane or Humanists?

At the trial which eventually ruled for his execution to be carried out by hanging, "Brown seemed the least interested person present. Most of the time he spent lying on his back, with his eyes closed, attentive to the procedures but apparently indifferent to their outcome. His sole desire was that the court recognize what he saw as the truth of the case: He had attacked Harpers Ferry for the noble purpose of liberating slaves, which he regarded as his divine, patriotic duty. He had treated his hostages well. The kills that occurred were regrettable but unforeseen by him. When the chance came for him to plead insanity, he refused to do so on the grounds that he believed such a plea would be false (Reynolds, 2005, p. 350).

It has been over ten years since we moved our daughter to Boston for her freshman year of college. I recall that after the flurry of parent orientations and dorm move in, we set out for sightseeing. A temperate fall day welcomed us through the historic streets, and we eventually arrived at the famous Boston Common, the oldest park in the United States. In the Common's north corner is a memorial dedicated to Colonel Robert Gould Shaw and the men of the 54th Regiment. It portrays a man on horseback in the midst of soldiers marching with muskets resting on their shoulders. The memorial lists the names of all the men who died in an ill-fated attempt to overtake Fort Wagner, South Carolina, during the Civil War. The Colonel died in this battle as well.

I had done well in my public education history classes, so I was dumbfounded as to why I knew nothing about the 54th Regiment and Colonel Shaw but I didn't give the monument a second thought until months later when I was back in California. My husband and I were visiting the home of our friends, Ray and Pat Johnson. Ray collects African American memorabilia and as I browsed his private collection of African American literature, my eyes fell upon a book entitled, "A Brave Black Regiment, History of the Fifty-Fourth Regiment of Massachusetts Volunteer Infantry." It was published in 1891. Ray saw that this book piqued my interest, so he placed it in a plastic wrapper and handed it over to me.

During my education as a doctoral student, I learned about the **"Culture of Silence"** (Freire, 1998). This term denotes the state of submersion in which the oppressed live in the reality and worldview of their oppressor. The oppressor relishes this state because an oppressed people who do not have critical awareness of their circumstances are more easily manipulated and controlled. One way by which those in power maintain compliance and control is by writing and teaching history from their own perspective. The power and privilege of the pen allows them to write history in a tone that generally reflects well on them. The men of the 54th and their colonel did not fit the description of any historical figure I had ever studied. That told me something.

I had no recollection of participating in engaging and animated discussions in my history classes where we, the students, challenged the merits of historical figures. We just accepted what we were taught. We received information, memorized it, and then repeated it on tests. I was good at this and "this," I learned, is the **Banking Method of Education** in which the teacher transmits information, known as "depositing," and the students passively receive, memorize, and repeat (Freire, 1998). I reached deep in my memory for any recollection of the Colonel and his famous regiment, but nothing came forth. So when Ray placed the book in my hand, I went on a humanizing journey to liberate myself by learning history from a point of view about which I was unaware.

Emerging from Submersion

This book led to a thread of inquiry and hours of research in archives far from the reach of most. I would hold in my hand letters penned by Sarah Shaw, the mother of the Colonel, and follow the trajectory of her hatred for slavery. Her son became the first white colonel to lead black troops, a social experiment advanced by abolitionists who believed that if black men fought in the battlefield like white men, they "would in turn prove that they were men and thus entitled to be free citizens" (Duncan, 1999, p. 20). Later, I was to hold the letter written by Ruth Thompson, John Brown's daughter. He had received and read this letter while he was held prisoner in a Virginia jail cell for attempting an insurrection that would liberate people from bondage. All of this intrigued me.

I learned that the Colonel initially rejected the appointment to the colonelcy of the 54th. He was already serving his nation during the Civil War in an all white regiment. He was comfortable there and saw no reason to step into the maelstrom of racial controversy. His disappointed mother, Sarah, told her son for refusing the appointment that he had "degenerated sadly from the principles" by which he was raised. The young man responded by way of confessing that he was just "an ordinary mortal" (p. 24). In the end, the mother's will prevailed. The Colonel accepted the appointment and went on to do what his mother called "God's work."

Sarah's disdain for slavery was unwavering. As I delved deeper into the lives of the Shaw family I came to learn more about the strength and influence of the famous Colonel's mother. I had a strong sense that, if allowed, she would have picked up a gun and fought against the institution of slavery as a soldier, but women in her day could not enlist. It was through her son that she saw that he "was her John Brown and she would fight the war vicariously through her son's body" (p. 37). I was drawn to the tension surrounding the Colonel and his regiment. More so, I was captivated by the tenacious woman behind them both so in my attempt to emerge from a state of **submersion**, more questions arose. The next being, "Who is John Brown? And, what was he doing that Sarah Shaw would be so fervently committed to completing *his* work at the cost of putting her one and only son in greater danger?"

Curiosity spurred me on to unearth names, voices, and actions that I had never before encountered. I uncovered people who, like the Grimké sisters though enjoying the comforts of power and privilege, were driven by forces beyond the quest for financial gain and personal wealth to act selflessly on behalf of others. The historical figures in my history books never provided this point of view or orientation. I was puzzled by this because while it was evident that the perspectives of these individuals are chronicled in varying degrees, such as the monument in Boston Common, their contributions are missing from the retelling of this nation's history. Nonetheless, these individuals fought on behalf of people who did not share the same status, power, or privilege. They fought with fervor to save the soul of the nation.

I concluded that these voices and lives deserve prominent casting in this nation's history. So, I share with you, the reader, the stories of, at minimum, six historical figures that lived by humanist principles. My inquiry also included research on two modern-day white humanists which uncovered the same **generative themes** as the historical humanists. These two modern-day Euro-American humanists were Courtenay Tessler, a counselor at Davis Senior High School, and Elizabeth Johnson (pseudonym), who had been employed as manager of a rice drying plant. The research on the modern-day humanists included two individually taped sessions, separate taped sessions in a graduate counselor education classroom where each presented as a guest speaker, followed by one joint session in which Tessler and Johnson discussed the challenges of humanist activism. Their voices, experiences, and perspective are integrated throughout the text of the chapters that follow.

Image courtesy of Courtenay Tessler

In addition, the modern day accounts of humanist endeavors from other contributors are woven throughout the following chapters and also contained in the final chapter. While we are able to identify by name, Courtenay Tessler who is one of the modern day humanists, the reader will note the use of a pseudonym and only a symbolic representation of Johnson. This is at her request due to the level of physical risk and threats that she endured related to the work she shared with us for this endeavor. The danger that comes from living and acting from the heart is discussed in Chapter 6.

The research on historical humanists focused on six primary individuals: John Brown, an abolitionist executed for his efforts to end the institution of slavery (Reynolds, 2005); Colonel Robert Shaw, the first white colonel of black troops in the Civil War (Emilio, 1891; Duncan, 1992); Colonel Shaw's mother, Sarah Shaw, an ardent abolitionist (Duncan, 1992; Gilchrist, 1995); William Lloyd Garrison, abolitionist and editor for the longest running abolitionist newspaper (Bordewich, 2005); Helen Hunt Jackson, advocate for Native Americans in the late 1800s (Jackson, 2003; Jackson, 1988; Odell, 1939); and Angelina Grimké, (Lerner, 1998; Wilbanks, 2003) who challenged the institution of slavery from across the dinner table in her southern plantation home, in the greater community, and finally as an outspoken abolitionist who provided firsthand accounts on the atrocities of slavery to a wide range of audiences. References are also made to Angelina's older sister and godmother, Sarah Grimké. These individuals served as allies for people of color during historical periods in which doing so meant risking social status and even loss of life.

I will leave it to the reader to discover and uncover the multitude of individuals whose names have dropped into the margins of United States history, despite their courageous efforts to remedy injustice. The inspiring and engaging narratives of others not commonly given just due will hopefully move from library archives to full view where the next generation may consider and learn from the values modeled by these humanists.

My initial research focus examined, in depth, but a handful of individuals. What came forth, however, was a web of relationships, across the racial divide, of courageous people who committed their lives to eradicating social structures and laws that exploited and oppressed humanity. I attempt to present some of these figures throughout the initial chapters as evidence to the fact that moral courage lives in hearts residing above social constructs. A true honoring of all those who committed their lives to causes so that I, a woman, a woman of color, can have the privilege to research, write, and publish on this topic would require a rewriting of the history books in our public education. My intentions related to this endeavor, however, is not to present a history book but instead, to focus on the shared qualities, dispositions and strategies employed by those who have changed the course of history in the United States. What we learn from those who came before us and who live in our midst even today provide valuable lessons to be employed today, as we face daunting challenges of our own.

There are countless examples of selflessness from those who were exploited in the quest for gold, land, and excessive wealth. As previously mentioned, the men of the 54th Regiment were led by Colonel Shaw, but there is further significance in the fact that these men were *free* men. They enlisted *voluntarily* with full knowledge that, if they were captured, they risked being executed or returned to slavery. Ultimately, many of them gave their lives in their effort to free others. Of the 600 men of the 54th who charged Fort Wagner, 272 were killed, wounded, or captured. These men were humanists.

This speaks to, once again, choices based on humanist principles. The sacrifices of *all* people, regardless of their stature in society or their power and privilege, should be valued. The men of the 54th Regiment typify the countless unheralded women, people of color, and those from other marginalized groups who have fought to rectify injustices but are not even granted a footnote in traditional historical discourse. It is my hope that written history will someday provide a centrist place for their stories as well. For now, I bring forth from the library archives and volumes of multiple books six individuals who lived in ways that bridged the "racial reality gap" and who used their power and privilege for gain immeasurable by capitalistic standards. The lessons to be gained from the forces that moved these humanists to action, as well as openly examining the challenges they faced, have direct bearing on those who endeavor to act, today, in ways that promote social justice.

Challenging Times, Courageous Hearts

The collective lives of the six historical humanists span just over a hundred-year period from the earliest birth of John Brown in 1800 to the passing of Sarah Shaw in 1902. During this period, the fixed reality for many people was one of enforced systemic oppression. As we read in Chapter 1, some colonists had, in the early development of what would eventually become the United States, declared slaves, "The strength and sinew of this western world" and the lack of them "the grand obstruction" here, as the settlements "cannot subsist without supplies of them" (DuBois, 1896,

p. 8). So dependent was the United States economy on enslaved labor that by 1860, the United States census reported 4 million enslaved people living in the United States.

During the lifetime of the historical humanists in this manuscript, the original inhabitants of this land, the **First Nations**, were systematically and violently removed from their homelands under the provisions of treaties that were broken, time and again. When they fought back, there were consequences. Helen Hunt Jackson wrote, "Early in our history was the ingenious plan evolved of first maddening the Indians into war, and then falling upon them with exterminating punishment" (Jackson, 2003, p. 40). President Andrew Jackson, known as the "Indian Fighter," pushed through Congress the Indian Removal Act of 1830. This systematized the United State's policy and intentions related to Native Americans. Essentially, the United States committed more money in support of military enforcement to remove Native Americans from their lands in the Southeast and open it for white settlement.

In the early part of the 1800s, children were expected to begin working as early as the age of five. Public education slowly became available over the course of this century, but more so for those from upper classes. Boys were expected to pick a trade by age 10, and girls were married at 15. Women were not allowed to vote, were denied access to education past grammar school, had no rights over inherited property or their earnings, could not sue or be sued, and had no guardianship rights over their children, even in cases of separation. The precepts of Manifest Destiny provoked a war against Mexico, and the new nation engulfed more land to be governed under a well-defined caste, class, and racialized system. This intensifying cultural identity welcomed, with varying degrees, and for various intentions a range of European ethnic groups fleeing famine and disease.

This was the reality in which the selected historical humanists chose to intervene. From their stories I gained a sense of healing that the counseling field calls the narrative approach. This orientation "contends that narratives are a reflection of the dominant culture and therefore must be challenged to ensure that they are sensitive to diversity issues" (Nystul, 2010, p. 275). Up until this point, I had only been exposed to this nation's "history" from a one-dimensional perspective. As a child and as a child of color, this dominant discourse never appealed to or included me, though I memorized the historical story lines and its content for my exams. The narratives of the historical humanists not only appealed to me but provided a contrast to the "master" narratives that I had been taught and that are most commonly considered representative of the "dominant culture." As an educator I had to ask myself if these contrasting narratives may be of benefit when introduced into the classroom where topics of diversity are discussed.

Narrative therapy further states that it "help(s) families deconstruct dysfunctional narratives (from the dominant culture) and re-author new, more functional narratives." For once, as I followed the thread of the lives of these individuals, I found myself not only engaged with *their* narratives, but I also found myself wanting to explore the multi-dimensional aspects of their lives and the impact they had on history. My own personal narrative never seemed congruent with the "master" narrative; but as I came to learn more about these historical figures, I began to have context for my own. Furthermore, as an educator who regularly teaches topics related to diversity, I could not help but consider the evolutionary implications of re-authoring the identity development of my students to a more functional path.

The Colonel on a horse, the men marching along his side, and the fervor of a mother whose force of will was behind their destiny seemed complex, rich, and remarkable. It made me want to learn more. The values and worldview of these humanists spoke to me more than any other self-serving and exploitive historical narrative I had learned thus far. In reading about the lives of the following historical figures, and the wider cast of active visionaries you may come to your own conclusion of whether these people were insane, rebels or misfits as they were often called, or were they simply humanists.

Colonel Robert Gould Shaw (1837–1863)

"Blue-Eyed Child of Fortune" (Duncan, 1992) is a fitting title for a book about Robert Gould Shaw. It speaks not just to the financial wealth into which he was born, but also the enrichment of a socially conscious circle of abolitionists in his life. These people had tremendous influence on his short life and played a major role in the staging of his prominent death. The son of Boston abolitionists, Francis and Sarah Shaw, his playmates included the children of William Lloyd Garrison, the abolitionist editor of *The Liberator*. One can imagine discussions Robert and his playmates overheard during family visits as their parents "discuss(ed) the immorality of slavery" (Duncan, p. 2).

Francis's and Sarah's associations worked collectively to address the conditions that led to poverty and shared a disdain for slavery. This circle of relationships provided strength and fervor to Francis's participation in the Boston Vigilance Committee, a collaborative effort of Bostonians who helped people who were escaping slavery to achieve freedom. Sarah, the guiding force in Robert's spiritual and career development, was a close friend of Lydia Maria Child, also a prominent abolitionist who communicated with John Brown during his imprisonment prior to his execution. Child edited Harriet Jacobs's narrative, entitled "Incidents in the Life of a Slave Girl," and was an active member of the American Anti-Slavery Society.

Library of Congress

From this who's who of associations in Robert's life, he was well aware of the political efforts of people who yielded their power to undo the establishment of slavery, as well as risk involvement by directly aiding people escaping captivity. His family's wealth afforded him a life of privilege; attending luxurious parties, traveling internationally, and studying abroad, but it also distanced him from the people for whom his parents' passionately advocated. This social distance is evident in his younger years when he learned about the plight of enslaved people but only through secondhand accounts and reading material.

Robert's youth was spent traveling to Berlin, Paris, Norway, Switzerland, and Naples. While studying for two years in Neuchâtel, Switzerland, he read Harriet Beecher Stowe's *Uncle Tom's Cabin*, which was written, his mother Sarah told him, "as a matter of conscience, after the passage of the **Fugitive Slave Law**." While traveling with his family in Europe, he met Frances "Fanny" Kemble, an abolitionist who had been married to Pierce Butler, one of the wealthiest slave owners in Georgia. From her, Robert learned about the brutality of slavery in the United States. He made mention in a letter to his mother of an article he had read of a "slave being burned alive in Alabama." His disbelief was summed up with the following commentary to his mother, "I didn't think that this ... would happen again" (Duncan, 1992, p. 9).

Despite the lack of direct contact with people who were enslaved, the influence of Robert's activist parents and their circle of friends served to mold his worldview. His mother persistently urged him to keep his mind and heart open to the cause for which she had committed her life. Robert's life of privilege and disconnect from the realities of slavery, however, did not recreate her zeal and commitment to the cause. His early awareness revealed more of a nationalistic stance in that he viewed slavery as "the only fault in America" and was embarrassed that the integrity of the northern states was wrongfully blamed for the "disgrace of all their (Southerners) shameful actions" (Duncan, 1992, p. 12).

For Robert, the undoing of slavery was a matter of honor rather than a matter of moral principle. His development as an active humanist was yet to take place. It was not until he witnessed the state of conditions in which people in bondage were held and, more so, until he forged his relationships with the men of the 54th Regiment that Sarah's passion for this cause became Robert's as well. The foundational values to which he was exposed in his youth, the guidance of his mother's determination, his father's modeling, and his willingness to accept the position of colonelcy of the first black regiment ultimately earned him a place in history.

Sarah Blake Shaw (1815–1902)

Five years before her death in 1902, Sarah witnessed the unveiling of the bronze memorial dedicated to her only son, Robert, and the men of the 54th Massachusetts Regiment. This was 1897. Her son, killed in battle at the age of 25, had already been dead for 34 years. Sarah, considered stoic in the wake of her son's death, expressed her grief to her friend, Elizabeth Gaskell. "I thought I was ready for the blow when it should come, but when can a mother be ready to give up her child? It has been a terrible struggle, and no relief comes to me but from prayer" (Gilchrist, p. 7).

This was a woman born into wealth. Like the Grimké sisters, she inherited a wealth that positioned her among the most prosperous families in Boston. Unlike the Grimkés, she did not witness the daily horrors and cruelty of slavery. What women of that era shared, regardless of living in the

Shaw's mother, Sarah Blake Sturgis Shaw, with grandson Frankie Curtis, 1863. Staten Island Institute of Arts and Sciences.

Library of Congress

"North" as the Shaw's did or the "South" of the Grimkés, was an inferior status. The *Public Ledger* of Philadelphia, as late as 1850 in an article ridiculing the advocates of equal rights for women, printed, "A woman is a nobody ... A wife is everything. A pretty girl is equal to 10,000 men and a mother is, next to God, all powerful. The ladies of Philadelphia therefore ... are resolved to maintain their rights as wives, belles, virgins and mothers and not as women" (Lerner, 1998, p. 5).

Nonetheless, Sarah's skin color and financial wealth ascribed her social standing in society. "She belonged to the seventh generation of a reputed and cultured family" (Cairnes, 1968, p. 49) and she used her status to affect change in the world to which she was born. In her role as a mother, she raised children who championed causes beyond the realm of her household. She influenced her son's decision to lead the first black troops in the Civil War, which positioned this regiment as the most visible model of cross-racial bridging and collaboration during that era. Her four daughters were devoted to philanthropic causes and charitable works. Josephine, the fourth child of the five, was mourned after her death in 1905 at the age of 61 as "a city's saint" for her devoted efforts in "education for black children, poor relief, women's rights, and the improvement of prison and mental hospital conditions—with particular attention to the treatment and provision of facilities for women" (Gilchrist, 1995, p. 8).

Sarah Shaw's legacy through her children defied conventional expectations of her day. She was a Unitarian by faith and, while doubling her financial wealth through her marriage to her half-cousin, Francis George Shaw, the two of them were known to share their prosperity and dedicated their lives to creating a more just society so that others living in poverty could have more opportunity. The standards of that era dictated that a "mannerly" woman of her status acquiesce to her husband; but Sarah had found a life partner not only committed to the same causes, but who also, in his own right, had promoted women's causes and supported Sarah's voice in the affairs of their finances and development of their children.

John Brown (1800–1859)

Sarah's inspiration and Colonel Shaw's symbolic predecessor was John Brown. While Colonel Shaw became the living extension of his mother's will to end slavery, it was John Brown's Calvinist father, Owen, who fueled his son's hatred of slavery. Owen Brown forbade his family to discriminate against people of color. In contrast to the life of a young Robert Shaw who grew up with privilege and was disconnected from the day-to-day realities of slavery, John, in his childhood, developed positive relationships with people of color. His father's lifestyle as a struggling farmer, tanner, and shoemaker availed John the opportunity to grow up in a community consisting of mostly Indians from the Hudson area. With forged positive relationships between the Browns and the original inhabitants of the land, John learned that "Indians were not savage 'others' to be conquered but were fellow humans to be respected" (Reynolds, 2005, p. 31). In contrast to many of the white settlers who settled in the surrounding area, John was raised by his parents to apply the Golden Rule to all, not just to other whites. This meant that from his worldview and orientation, slavery was evil (Reynolds, 2005).

The principles of equality with which John was raised provided a foundational belief system that grew into a disdain for slavery. At the age of 12, John befriended a boy of his own age who was owned by a family with whom John and his father were staying. John observed how he was given preferential treatment and praise while the boy, though intelligent and benevolent, was maltreated, beaten with household tools, and made to sleep in the cold in rags. John recognized "the wretched, hopeless condition, of Fatherless & Motherless slave children: for such children have neither Fathers nor Mothers to protect and provide for them" (Reynolds, p. 33).

John Brown shared the same goals of many of his contemporary abolitionists. He differed radically, however, in his tactics to achieve those goals. He was willing to fight fire with fire by using violence to end slavery. Brown developed and executed a plan to achieve his goal that was inspired by multiple uprisings of people in bondage as well as the resistance of Native Americans and escaped Africans. For example, in Haiti, Toussaint L'Ouverture led enslaved blacks in a long struggle for independence over French colonizers. He went on to abolish slavery and secured "native" control. In Florida, the Seminole tribe not only resisted capture, but also established communities despite the efforts of the United States to remove them, time and again.

JOHN BROWN.
LEADER OF THE HARPER'S FERRY INSURRECTION.

Library of Congress

In the United States, "the uprisings in New York City in 1712; a plot by a slave named Gabriel to seize Richmond, Virginia, in 1800; the large slave uprising near New Orleans in 1811; and Denmark Vesey's plan to take over Charleston, South Carolina, in 1820" (Reynolds, 2005, p. 52) were just a few of the most notable revolts and conspiracies enacted by enslaved people to gain their own freedom. Nat Turner's rebellion, August 1831, in southeastern Virginia generated the most fear for Southerners during Brown's lifetime and was also Brown's major source of inspiration. While unsuccessful, six cohorts under Turner's command moved from plantation to plantation, taking the lives of 55 white men, women, and children. In retaliation, hundreds of people of African descent were killed. Turner was captured after two months in hiding, but his death by hanging did not end the fear implanted in the minds of Southern slave owners.

The similarities of Turner's tactics to Brown's plan may not be coincidence given the same goal. Brown's plan was to:

> invade a Southern state with "at first twenty-five picked men" who would be stationed in separate groups of five in a southward line along the mountain range. Periodically, these groups would raid nearby plantations, liberate enslaved blacks,

arm them and retreat with them to the mountain hideaways. The more timid blacks would be sent north to freedom on what Brown called the Subterranean Pass Way. The rest would remain with the liberators, whose number would grow so that eventually a colony of free blacks would be living in the mountains (Reynolds, 2005, p. 104).

Brown targeted the Southern slave-holding state of Virginia to enact his plan. The specific town chosen was Harpers Ferry, a town of 5,000 that, as the home of a federal arsenal, produced weapons and munitions used by the United States military. Brown's attempt was ill-fated. He stormed Harpers Ferry with 18 men, black and white, leaving three additional men behind as a rear guard. From this small militia, 10 were killed, including his sons, Watson and Oliver, five escaped (including his son, Owen), and seven were captured. Of this latter group, all, including John Brown, were executed.

John Brown did not live to see the emancipation of humanity from bondage but only a few days before being hung for attempting to do so he received and read a letter from his daughter, Ruth Thompson. The letter was dated November 29, 1859. The letter contained a message from a minister who knew of Brown's efforts and who asked to be remembered "to all those *noble prisoners, colored* as well as white." Additionally, Ruth's son, Johny, communicated, "tell Grandfather that I know he is in prison because he tried to do good." Then, came a message from one of Brown's surviving sons, "tell Father, though your life may be taken, your deeds and influence will live to be remembered and do good." These are the words Brown carried with him as only a few days later, on December 2nd, he was executed at a remote site on the outskirts of Charlestown.

Wm. Lloyd Garrison.

William Lloyd Garrison (1805–1879)

Diametrically opposed to John Brown's tactics but in alignment with his goals was the pacifist, William Lloyd Garrison. While Brown had no reservations about the use of weapons and violence to eradicate the institution of slavery, Garrison sought a nonviolent solution by using moral principles to persuade the South to free enslaved people. Pushing for emancipation on moral grounds, Garrison and other pacifists even proposed dissolution of the Union as a way of confining the practice of slavery to the

South. This position changed, however, once the North and South witnessed Brown's ill-fated and self-sacrificing attempt to capture Harpers Ferry and secure weaponry to be used by freed black men. This not only inspired Garrison, but it also swayed him to a more militant position (Reynolds, 2005).

Garrison's pacifist roots were nourished by the parenting style of his Baptist mother, who raised him from the age of three as a single parent. His father, reportedly, an alcoholic seaman, deserted Garrison's mother, Frances Maria Lloyd, and left her with three small children to raise on her own. Born in Newburyport, Massachusetts, his mother took up the vocation of nursing, which forced Lloyd (as called by his mother) to work in whatever apprenticeship or trade he could to earn money to support himself and his family. He sold candy sticks, sawed and split wood, sold applies at a corner stand, was making shoes by the age of nine, and eventually learned cabinet-making in Haverhill, Massachusetts.

Homesickness drove him back to Newburyport where, at the age of 14, he was offered a seven-year apprenticeship at the printing-office of the *Herald*. Despite not having the presence of a parent in his life, he developed a sense of compassion from his own struggle with poverty. His mother took up residence in Baltimore where she contended with the ravages of yellow fever and a host of other illnesses. Although Frances and her son were separated during his childhood and early adolescence, they maintained written contact with one another. Frances acknowledged those who cared for her dependent son, as well as her gratitude, love, and respect for people of all races who cared for her during her convalescence. She expressed her sentiments to Garrison in great detail, which may have had bearing on his own views of "difference." Garrison's mother remained in Baltimore until her death at the age of 45. Garrison was 17 years old at the time.

A year later, Garrison left the apprenticeship of the *Herald* and embarked upon a career as publisher for a new paper called the *Free Press*, a paper devoted to politics, poetry, editorials, opinion pieces, and the like. Opposing political activists shut down the *Free Press*, which prompted Garrison's relocation to Boston where he became editor of *The Philanthropist*, a paper devoted to temperance but that also addressed "questions as lotteries, imprisonment for debt, peace, and the 'desecration of the Sabbath' by the transportation of mails and of passengers on that day" (Garrison, 1885, p. 84). The religious orientation of this paper may have further encouraged Garrison to take a moralistic view of the world. By the age of 23, he was using his position to challenge what he perceived to be the passivity, indifference, and hypocrisy of Christians to the subject of war. He also began revealing his indignation over proclaimed Christians' participation in the "Culture of Silence" (Freire, 1998) over the matter of slavery:

> They have been guilty of a neglect which no discouragement, no excuse, no inadequacy can justify. Why is it by far the larger portion of the professed followers of the Lamb have maintained a careless, passive neutrality? ... There are, in fact, few *reasoning* Christians; the majority of them are swayed more by the usages of the world than by any definite perception of what constitutes duty—so far, we mean as relates to the subjugation of vices which are incorporated, as it were, into the existence of society; else why is it that intemperance, and slavery, and war, have not ere this a measure been driven from our land? Is there not Christian influence enough

here, if properly concentrated, to accomplish these things? Skepticism itself cannot be at a loss to answer this question. (Garrison, pp. 84–85)

The pivotal incident in Garrison's life that moved his life to a committed social activist came with meeting Thomas Lundy, a Quaker. Thomas had moved to Wheeling, Virginia, at the age of 19 to apprentice as a saddler. During his four years of living in Virginia, he witnessed chained people being driven through the streets. "My heart was deeply grieved at the gross abomination; I heard the wail of the captive; I felt his pang of distress; and the iron entered my soul" (Garrison, 1885, p. 87). Similar to Angelina Grimké and her sister, Sarah, who acted upon what they felt, Lundy proceeded to tell all who would listen of the horrors of slavery. Garrison, a young man who was only 22 at the time he met Lundy, became one of 20 members of an anti-slavery committee in Boston. By 1831, Garrison went on to publish his own newspaper, *The Liberator*. Taking on a most unpopular position at the time, his paper was dedicated to the immediate emancipation of all slaves. It became the longest running anti-slavery newspaper in U.S. history.

Helen Hunt Jackson (1830–1885)

The plight of people in bondage and those subjected to relocation and genocide moved the sympathies of humanists who witnessed the toll inflicted by a nation built on capitalism and expansionism. Similarly, Helen Hunt Jackson, as John Brown, was witness to mistreatment of African Americans during her youth, but she did not participate in abolitionism during her lifetime. She lacked persistent relationship with people in bondage and remained somewhat emotionally distanced to their plight. Her evolvement as a humanist and as an activist seem to have taken

Library of Congress

place as she matured and after she had suffered personal losses of her own, including the loss of her first husband and the childhood deaths of her only two children. Hunt's development speaks to the potential for development from a submerged consciousness that is blind to the suffering of others to one of committed engagement in social advocacy.

Born in Amherst, Massachusetts, Helen Maria was the oldest of two children, the daughter of a professor and a mother who died when Helen was only 14. Her father passed away when she was 17. With resources provided to secure a proper education accorded to young women of that time, it was not uncommon for her to bear witness to rented maids or servants who were linked to the institution of slavery. Later in life, her husband feared she had been infected with the fever of abolitionism because she associated with activists such as Colonel Thomas Wentworth Higginson, Lydia Maria Child, and Samuel Howe. Still, she was silent to the practice. In fact, for a short period, she "had her own servant, a slave girl, whose master was glad to lease her services for five dollars a month, and Hunt found herself a little less intolerant of the institution of slavery, now that she had an opportunity to see its brighter aspect" (Odell, 1939, p. 52).

At this point in her life, we can see that the convenience of cheap labor outweighed any moral discomfort that she may have experienced. Even her initial contact with Native Americans was more tourist-like as when she visited an Indian camp located in the region behind Medford Hill. In describing her encounter with Native People, she wrote, "Some of them were very handsome, they were dressed very curiously, the women had a thing that looked very much like loose gowns except that they were not confined about the waist" (Odell, 1939, p. 28). From this statement, we bear witness to a woman who in the earlier years of her life was cognizant of the existence of "others" but who did not take notice of the substandard conditions in which they lived and how they arrived at these disparate conditions.

We can speculate that her experiences with oppression as a female writer may have incited a sense of empathy that was lacking in her earlier years. During Hunt's development as a writer, she had to use pseudonyms to have her material printed. Women writers who printed anything beyond romance and housekeeping were frowned upon during Hunt's lifetime; when she began to solicit pay for her writings, it was recommended that she write "'pleasant gossipy letters' on the very unpleasant subject of Boston" (Odell, 1939, p. 64). Having to restrict herself to gender-ascribed topics opened her awareness to the unequal status of women but, more so, provided the fodder for a growing consciousness of the inequities affecting the lives of others. Hunt's written observations about her surroundings reveal an emerging social consciousness not evident earlier in her life. For example, upon visiting New York, she noted, "We went through some of the lowest most miserable streets in the city, and never in my life did I see such misery, such degradation and wretchedness" (Odell, 1939, p. 43).

While Hunt began to make observations relevant to classism, her development as a writer was mentored by Colonel Higginson, a man described as her "champion" (Odell, 1939, p. 72). Colonel Higginson's influence and presence in Hunt's life must be recognized as he was a notable and progressive figure in U.S. history; He used his wealth to fund John Brown's failed mission to capture Harpers Ferry, he served as a commanding officer to a regiment of black soldiers during the Civil War and after the war, Colonel Higginson abolished separate schools for children of color which led to his removal as chairman of the school committee in the town of Newport. And, of foremost importance for Hunt, he was an advocate for **women's suffrage** (Odell, 1939). The influence of being mentored by another Euro-American humanist may have swayed her own development, but there was a stimulus above and beyond these associations that launched her efforts toward social advocacy.

In 1879, post Civil War, Hunt had the opportunity to hear a lecture from Ponca Chief Standing Bear and Bright Eyes, his wife and interpreter. It was their plight that moved Hunt to become an activist. Surrounded by the fervor of abolitionists who savored the satisfaction of having

achieved the ultimate goal of emancipation, Hunt witnessed how they now refocused their zeal and attention to the plight and mistreatment of Native Americans. Whether Hunt was caught up in the emotional response of her associates or personalized the plight of native people, their relocation, the constant manipulation and lies of the U.S. government, and genocide, she was moved until her death to make the cause of native people her own (Odell, 1939).

Hunt (2003) witnessed how the new "Americans" claimed "barbarous" behavior on part of the original Natives without bearing responsibility for their own cruel actions, which incited the behavior. The vilification of Native Americans was a constant theme the United States government employed to justify acts of aggression. Hunt had gone so far as to uncover and chronicle the United States Government's use of unsuspecting European immigrants as pawns to incite conflict with Native Americans. The conflict generally resulted in the death of many on both sides and in repeating a cycle of "**Divide and Rule**" (Freire, 1998).

Up until hearing the personal testimony of a Native American speaking to the atrocities being committed against his people, Hunt had never aligned herself with any particular movement, whether it was abolitionism or women's suffrage, despite her close association with other progressive individuals. Yet it was Hunt who "later persuaded Wendell Phillips to take the platform for the Indians as he had for the Negroes" (Odell, 1939, p. 157). Hunt had ample opportunities to utilize her skill of writing for social causes but it was the testimony of this delegation that prompted a turning point in her life. From here, Hunt moved from the passive voice of spectator of the world and embarked upon challenging the United States government to stop the mistreatment inflicted upon Native Americans.

Angelina Grimké (1805–1879)

Angelina and her older sister, Sarah, were daughters of a prominent South Carolina justice of the South Carolina Supreme Court, John Faucheraud. Their mother, Mary Smith, had a brother, Benjamin Smith, who was governor of North Carolina. The breadth of political connection and expansive wealth into which these sisters were born in Charleston, South Carolina, included two homes in Charleston and two plantations with a housekeeper, "parlormaids, laundresses, 'Mauma' in charge of the nursemaids (one for each child), personal servants for the master and mistress, the butler and footmen who were charged with the care of the dining room and table service; the cook and kitchen helpers, plus a host of servants' children. The family coaches and horses would be attended by several coachmen, stable boys and grooms (Lerner, 1998, p. 13).

A.E. Grimké

Library of Congress

By the time Judge Grimké died in 1819, he left behind 50 people in bondage to provide for the comfort and needs of the family.

Acts of resistance were evident early in the lives of Angelina and her sister, Sarah. They persistently questioned and challenged the laws that maintained the separation and differentiated power of the races. Sarah's defiance of these laws was evident even as a child when she secretly taught her "waiting-maid" how to read. Using the time that was to be used for the maid to comb and brush Sarah's hair, Sarah turned off the light in her bedroom, covered the keyhole, and by the light of the fire, proceeded to break the law. For this, she was severely scolded, and her maid barely escaped punishment.

The Grimké sisters saw their brothers go on to higher education with Thomas, the oldest, attending Yale. Sarah openly acknowledged her desire to become a lawyer, but she would never be able to pursue what her intellect desired. Even so, the sisters measured their limited privileges in light years above those whose sole purpose in life was to serve them. For the Southern belle, their relegated life was lived in contradictions. While the Southern woman was expected to live a life of purity and religious piety, the men lived a very different reality, which is best described by a contemporary of the Sisters:

> Ours is a monstrous system ... Like the patriarchs of old, our men live all in one house with their wives and their concubines; and the mulattoes one sees in every family partly resemble the white children. Any lady is ready to tell you who is the father of all the mulatto children in everybody's household but her own. Those, she seems to think, drop from the clouds (Lerner, p. 27).

Refused access to education and perhaps deterred by the prospect of marriage in such a "monstrous system," the options for women of their era were limited. The emergence of these two women from this reality demonstrates that rather than commit to its principles, they enacted what Freire (1998) calls **Conscientização**, the deepening of the attitude of awareness characteristic of all emergence. Paulo Freire (1998), a Brazilian educator, was known world wide for his theories that contextualize the nature of oppression, its causes and its consequences. His uncovering of the forces that maintain oppression were considered threatening to many and resulted in his being jailed and exiled from his home country. Banishment is a common outcome for those who speak openly and honestly about oppression.

Unable to acquire a formal education, the two sisters found another outlet for their lives and ultimately found purpose to their existence. Moved by the horrendous realities that they bore witness to every day, they acted upon the "limit-situations" that maintained an entire targeted group of people in bondage and the female gender in subservience. "**Limit situation**" refers to the specific conditions that serve some at the expense of others.

Though these women inherited financial wealth, they refused to embrace their family and community's dehumanizing practice. Angelina's personal journal chronicles multiple observations of dominance that are eloquently described by Freire (1998), "the oppressors do not perceive their monopoly on having more as a privilege which dehumanizes others and themselves. They cannot see that, in the egoistic pursuit of having as a possessing class, they suffocate in their own possessions and no longer are; they merely have" (p. 41). Angelina and Sarah rejected the opulence maintained by a maligned and enmeshed cultural system that was condoned by religious, economic, and legal structures. The contradictions and the tension within this cultural milieu are reflected in the following narrative by Allen V. Manning, who was born in 1850 and who lived to tell of his experience with enslavement in three states, Mississippi, Louisiana, and Texas. Interviewed when he was 87 years old, Mr. Manning provides firsthand insight to the tension derived from the extension of capitalistic motivations into the fabric of moral values.

> I was born in slavery, and I belonged to a Baptist preacher. Until I was fifteen years old I was taught that I was his own chattel-property and he could do with me like he wanted to, but he had been taught that way, too, and we both believed it.... He had been taught that they was just like his work hosses, and if they act like they his work hosses they git along all right. But if they don't-oh, oh! ... When the war come along, Old Master just didn't know what to do. He always been taught not to raise his hand up and kill nobody—no matter how come—and he just kept holding out against them that was talking about fighting, and he wouldn't go and fight. He had been taught that it was all right to have slaves and treat them like he want to, but he been taught it was sinful to go and fight and kill to keep them, and he lived up to what he been taught (Botkin, 1945, pp. 93–94).

As we have already seen, the Grimké sisters, even more detested the mistreatment required to maintain slaveholders' lavish lifestyle. After her self-imposed exile from the South where she was witness to the atrocities of slavery, Angelina wrote a letter to William Lloyd Garrison in support of abolitionists. Without her permission, Garrison published her letter in his newspaper, *The Liberator*. Her position was now made public. Many urged Angelina to retract her published letter, as well as to change her anti-slavery position, but she refused.

Instead, this act of assertion launched public-speaking tours on behalf of abolitionism and later, women's rights.

Revealing the "Limit-Situation"

The men of the 54th Regiment were handed weapons and directed to the battlefield as the stage on which they would prove their equal capacity to white men. The stakes were high because they had to demonstrate courage equal to if not beyond their white counterparts in other regiments. They succeeded, and their efforts were widely known. Less celebrated, however, were the accomplishments of African-Americans who gained their freedom by escape or by birth on free land and then went on to demonstrate intellectual capacity in realms that most white Americans of their era assumed to be impossible. One of these prominent intellectuals, John Rock, became a practicing doctor, lawyer, and dentist, despite being barred from medical school since none would admit him because he was black. Through apprenticeships and eventually enrolling in the American Medical College of Philadelphia, he earned a living using the intellect that many whites of his lifetime claimed he could not genetically possess.

As an active abolitionist, he assisted in the recruitment of men for the 54th and 55th Massachusetts Infantry Regiments. His speeches on behalf of enslaved people disputed the belief of racial inferiority as he shed light on the limit-situation that promulgated this ignorant belief. In 1860, Dr. John Rock stated:

> The unfortunate position which both the bond and the free colored people have been forced to occupy in this country, has not been favorable to the development of our higher faculties; ... we are not what we would have been under more favorable circumstances. Our enemies have taken every advantage of our unhappy situation, and attempt to prove that, because we are unfortunate, we are necessarily an inferior race, incapable of enjoying to a full extent the privileges of citizenship. The very unjust method of comparing the highest grades of Anglo-American intellect with the lowest forms of Negro sensuality is resorted to, to prove our inferiority, and that the blessings of citizenship have been specially reserved by our Heavenly Parent for those men who have white skins and straight hair.... It is not difficult to see that [this idea of Negro inferiority] is a mere subterfuge, which is resorted to to bolster up the infamous treatment which greets the colored man everywhere in this slavery-cursed land, where to us patriotism produces no honor, goodness no merit, and intellectual industry no reward ... we have both physical and moral courage. I believe in the equality of my race. We have always proved ourselves your equals, when placed in juxtaposition with you. We are the only oppressed people that advance in the country of their oppression (McPherson, 1965, p. 100).

The six primary humanists who we will further examine would have agreed with Dr. Rock. They understood the nature of limit-situations and recognized the forces of oppression enacted on people who suffered as a result. In their commitment to express their humanism, these

humanists challenged a wide range of boundaries. Beyond this, they attempted to humanize those of their own race who had lost their capacity to be fully human in their quest for power and wealth. As you read on to examine the common threads that bind these humanists, determine for yourself if their lives deserve greater accord in our renditions of written history and how the themes are relevant in today's "well-functioning social system."

QUESTIONS FOR DISCUSSION OR SELF REFLECTION

SELF-AWARENESS

1. Who have you learned most about when learning United States History?

2. How many of the humanists addressed in this chapter have you heard of before?

3. If there is a discrepancy in your knowledge related to the two previous questions, how do you account for this?

4. What narratives inform how "success" is defined in this nation? Is your definition of "success" congruent with this?

CLIENT WORLDVIEW

5. Some of these humanists were referred to as "insane." Why would they be considered "insane," "contrary," "misfits," and "rebels?"

6. What are values that your classmates or people in your community possess that may be different than your own?

COUNSELING RELATIONSHIP

7. In reflection of the challenges faced by Dr. John Rock, what might be privileges accorded to members of your own social group identity but not to others?

COUNSELING AND ADVOCACY INTERVENTIONS

8. What strategies were employed by the six humanist to activate their humanist principles?

9. Discuss how their intervention drew from the socioecological model of intrapersonal, interpersonal, institutional, community, public policy and international/global levels.

NEW CONCEPTS AND VOCABULARY TO REVIEW

Culture of Silence:

Banking Method of Education:

Submersion:

Generative Themes:

First Nations:

Narrative Therapy:

Fugitive Slave Law:

Divide and Rule:

Women's Suffrage:

Conscientização:

Limit situation:

Activity

Find and present orally in class pertinent information on one of the following "Isms" in the U.S.: Racism, Sexism, Religious Prejudice (Faithism), Heterosexism, Classism (Socio-Economic Status) or Ableism. What is the motivation behind the "ism"? What drives it? You may want to examine important areas, such as education, politics, religion, violence, health & health care, and working. What are the "limit-situations" related to each of these constructs and what are the biggest problems resulting from the "limit-situation" Present what the "experts" say as well as your own perceptions about the impact of these "isms."

References

Bordewich, F. (2005). *Bound for canaan*. New York, NY: HarperCollins Publishers, Inc.

Botkin, B. A. (1945). *Lay my burden down*. Chicago, IL: University of Chicago Press.

DuBois, W. E. B. (1896) *The suppression of the African slave trade to the United States of America by 1638–1870*. A Penn State Electronic Classics Publication. 2007. Originally Published in March 1896.

Duncan, R. (1992). *Blue eyed child of fortune*. Georgia: University of Georgia Press.

Emilio, L. F. (1891). *History of the fifty-fourth regiment of Massachussetts volunteer infantry, 1863–1865*. Boston, MA: The Boston Book Company.

Freire, P. (1998). *Pedagogy of the oppressed*. New York, NY: The Continuum Publishing.

Garrison, F. & Garrison, W. (1885). *William Lloyd Garrison, 1805–1879*, Volume 1. New York, NY: The Century Co.

Gilchrist, M. (1995). *The Shaw family of Staten Island: Elizabeth Gaskell's American friends*. University of Manchester; The Gaskell Society Journal, Vol. 9, 1995.

Jackson, H. H. (1988). *Ramona*. New York, NY: Signet Classic.

Jackson, H. H. (2003). *A century of dishonor*. New York, NY: Dover Publications, Inc.

Lerner, G. (1998). *The Grimké sisters from South Carolina, pioneer for women's rights and abolition*. NY: Oxford University Press.

McPherson, J. (1965). *The Negro's civil war*. New York: NY, Pantheon Books.

Nystul, M. (2010). *Introduction to Counseling, An Art and Science Perspective*. NJ: Pearson.

Odell, R. (1939). *Helen Hunt Jackson*. New York: NY: D. Appleton-Century Company.

Reynolds, D. (2005). *John Brown abolitionist*. New York: Random House, Inc.

Wilbanks, C. (2003). *Walking by faith, the diary of Angelina Grimké, 1828–1835*. Columbia, SC: University of South Carolina Press.

Call "It" what "It" is

CHAPTER 3

I came rather late into the assembly, and all the seats were occupied; but as soon as I was observed, effort was kindly made to procure me one; directly a colored sister came in; she was probably far more fatigued than I was, and how could you tell but that within that colored body there was a soul far more noble than mine— yet she was suffered to stand in the aisle. Angelina Grimké

From the Anti-Slavery Convention Report; Report of a Delegate to the Anti-Slavery Convention of American Women, Held in Philadelphia, May 1838 (p. 14)

Sitting among abolitionists, not slave holders, Angelina still witnessed inequitable treatment and she called it what it was. Racism can be as obvious as putting chains on people and calling them "inferior," or it can also be a slight micro-aggression in which one is left wondering ... is this, or is it not, racism?

We have already discussed how racism was economically constructed. Now let us define "it" so as not to confuse it with another word, prejudice, that holds similar but not the same meaning. Memmi (2000) provides a clear definition: "**Racism** is the generalized and final assigning of values to real or imaginary differences, to the accuser's benefit and at his victim's expense, in order to justify the former's own privileges or aggression." A racist worldview is grounded in a specified way of perceiving others that we will call "**habits of thought.**" In turn, these habituated thoughts give life to "**habituated behaviors**" (Bateson, 1972). Transmitted from one generation to the next, these habituated thoughts allow racism and other constructs of power and privilege to reinvent and manifest themselves in different forms.

Paxton's (2002) exploration on the construction of whiteness examines the impact of this construction on those who are not white. He chronicles the exhausting experience of being black in the United States, as related to him by an African American woman. Paxton's retelling of her reality provides context to Memmi's definition of racism:

> her work life is an uphill battle on every front, as she is constantly bombarded with Whiteness that at best ignores her Blackness but more often denigrates and attacks it. To be ignored when one is different is to be rendered invisible. To be seen, but be hated and feared because of one's skin color is a tragic consequence from which People of Color cannot escape in America today (p. 28).

This African American woman conveys the "assigning of value" to a "real or imaginary difference." In this case, the designated "difference" is skin color. The negative value associated with that skin color is revealed when she speaks to the "denigration" placed on her blackness. Finally, the element of being "attacked," "hated," and "feared" is the manifestation of aggression. This component of aggression to racism may be as fierce as the racially motivated lynchings that have taken place throughout the history of our nation to full-scale laws and policies such as the **Chinese Exclusion Act** of the 1800s or the **internment of United States citizens of Japanese descent** during World War II. It can also be as innocuous as the discourteous and inequitable treatment by Grimké's fellow abolitionists who simply did not extend, under the same set of circumstances, a kindness provided a white woman to a black woman.

The grounding of racism in "habits of thought" transfers to "habits of behavior" and distinguishes it from "prejudice," which means a preformed, unfavorable opinion of someone based on insufficient knowledge, irrational feelings, or inaccurate stereotypes. A prejudice can be inflicted on anyone by anyone. A person of color can hold prejudices about white people. The key difference between the terms is that "racism" holds affixed power that discharges various means of aggression to maintain privilege. It is important to recognize these distinguishing components of "racism" because racism, like heterosexism, sexism, classism, ablism, etc., are all socially *constructed* realities that can also be deconstructed. Humanists know this. The multiple ways in which to deconstruct these manifestations of negative associations to "difference" are addressed in later chapters.

Identification of Racism and Responding to One's Heart

The first and most prevalent theme that emanated from the lives of humanists was their exposure to racist attitudes and behavior. Several witnessed racism at an early age. All of them were aware of the negative value associated with "difference" in skin color. What sets humanists apart from many of their contemporaries is their understanding that 1) "difference in skin color" is not the reason for the inferior status of people of color, and 2) people of color are not at fault for the marginal conditions inflicted upon them. Humanists do, however, attribute prevalent, persistent, and structural forces as the cause for the negative conditions that impede the full expression and capacity of people of color. They also understand the profound impact that anyone of us can have on the life of another. In other words, they believe in their capacity to affect positive change. We can recall Sarah Grimké teaching, though it was against the law to do so, reading and writing to another child "owned" by her family. In short, humanists recognize that people are not "poor" or "uneducated" because their particular racial group is inherently inferior. They recognize that inferior status is *caused* and that the factors contributing to causation can be changed with intervention.

Freire (1998) espouses that humanist revolutionary leaders do not believe the myth that people are ignorant. Instead, humanists must understand the **anti-dialogical forces of Conquest, Divide and Rule, Manipulation, and Cultural Invasion** that act in concert to instill the illusion of ignorance in the people targeted for oppression. With this framework as our backdrop, we can examine the entrenchment of racism and other oppressive constructs in the lives, community, and culture in which humanists respond. Painfully obvious as we examine our modern day "well-functioning social systems" are the prevalent and tangible forces of overt and often-veiled violence by those invested in maintaining constructs of power and privilege. When humanists understand the structural elements of power and privilege whether it be racism, sexism, heterosexism, classism, ablism, etc., their capacity to focus their advocacy efforts to unravel the social structures that create marginalizing patterns is elevated. Principle to humanists perception of racism is their regard of injustices as acts of cruelty against *humanity*.

"Racism" and "Humanism"

The humanists we are examining provide a range of developmental models to consider. Some, even from childhood, never adopted racist beliefs, while others demonstrated transformation and evolvement during their lives. Regardless of their starting point or the background, these humanists invariably came to the same conclusion; oppressors use ill-founded justifications to deem a people "inferior" so they can exploit them. Then, they use various forms of violence in order to maintain control and subservience of those they exploit as well as using violence on those they want to silence.

The lesson in the capacity for transformation can be derived by contrasting the various starting points of our different humanists. One starting point to consider is Colonel Shaw who, we know, was born into a family of wealth and privilege. He was born in the North so was not exposed to the daily atrocities witnessed by the Grimké sisters. He also did not have day-to-day contact with people of color that would have availed the opportunity for relationship and bonds. On the other hand, the sisters had daily and intimate contact with people of color. They came to *know* the servants who were "objects" in the culture of their era, and yet the sisters regarded these same servants as *human beings*. One story relates how, as the custom would have it in Southern antebellum society, Sarah was:

> Given a slave girl to be her constant companion, to wait upon her, to serve her needs. But Sarah simply considered her as a playmate and treated her as an equal. When, a few years later, the girl died after an illness, Sarah was disconsolate. Her attitude puzzled her parents. After all, it was not as if the servant girl was irreplaceable; there were plenty of idle slave children in the Grimké household among whom she might choose. But Sarah refused (Lerner, p. 17).

Clearly, Sarah grieved the loss of this child whom she valued as a friend and as a human being. She did not accord a negative association to the color of the child's skin. She accepted this child as her "*equal.*" Her parents perceived the child as an object of no worth, other than as a replaceable material possession. Similarly, Sarah's sister, Angelina, never lost her empathy and compassion for humanity. The persistent exposure to racism's aggression deepened the resolve of this humanist that moved her from despairing observer to committed activist. Several incidents have already been cited, and the one that follows is from her childhood.

While Angelina was attending Charleston Seminary, she fainted at school. Her sister, Sarah, alarmed about the condition of her godchild asked Angelina what caused the fainting spell. This is what the child revealed:

> A little boy, a slave child of their school mistress, had been called in during class time to open the window. He was small, and moved with an uncertain, shuffling gait so awkward that he could barely accomplish the task demanded of him. When his back was turned toward the class, the reason for his awkwardness became clear-his back and legs were scarred by whip-marks, the injuries so recent they were still encrusted with blood and scabs. At the sight, Angelina had fainted. Now, in the telling, she wept (Lerner, p. 30).

Angelina witnessed the use of aggression on a regular basis. She also discerned the hypocrisy of her contemporaries. The school mistress and husband who most likely inflicted the beating on this child were considered "genteel," and yet the treatment of a child whose skin color was different from her own did not merit compassion. Instead, it merited violence. Angelina understood that this was racism. If we were to determine the stage at which Angelina and Sarah were on the **Helm's White Racial Identity Development Model** (1995) (Appendix B), we see that they eventually demonstrated "determination to abandon White entitlement" and that, from an early age, they were "knowledgeable about the racial ... differences." In this case, we can conclude that the Grimké sisters understood the inferior status ascribed to "racial difference" and recognized the use of physical force that members of their community would use to sustain this differentiated status structures.

Colonel Shaw's story is testament to the power of transformation. His parents championed the cause of abolition; but, up until serving as colonel of the 54th Regiment, Shaw's view of racism and the various elements of its forces were at an intellectual distance. His parents bemoaned his detachment, which caused him to defend himself to his mother, "Because I don't talk and think Slavery all the time, and because I get tired ... of hearing nothing else, you say I don't feel with you, when I do" (Duncan, p. 13). Without a personal connection to the people whose cause he eventually championed, he could afford detachment, but he was called on it by his mother, Sarah.

Referring back to the Helm's Model of White Racial Identity Development, and following the Colonel's evolvement, we can easily determine that he was above the Contact Stage because he was not oblivious to the fact that racism existed. His parents attempted to expose their son to the inequities that existed in the United States and to use his privilege to serve those living under oppressive realities. Once he accepted the post of serving as the colonel of an all black regiment, he was forced to respond to the inequities directed at his men. Racism's aggression on the men of the 54th not only made the cause of his parents his own, the cause became *personal*. Prejudices he had formed about people of color changed once he had the opportunity to know and develop relationships with the men of the 54th. Additionally, he witnessed, firsthand, the inequities his men suffered because of the arbitrary negative association accorded the color of their skin. This experiential encounter may have served as the "painful or insightful encounter or event," as discussed in the Pseudo-Independence stage, which "jars" the individual from the previous stage of Reintegration.

The Colonel awakened to the first premise of racism, which is the negative association of skin color. He recognized the prevalent and unfounded perception that the men of his regiment lacked the valor to fight. The Colonel knew he had to provide the opportunity for his men to supplant this prejudice. Additionally, he had to contend with the inequities unleashed by the very government that enlisted these men and who purported to be in alignment with abolitionists. The false premise of appearing to provide "opportunity" and yet not providing equal means to succeed in their mission falls under the anti-dialogical force of **Manipulation** (Freire, 1998).

During the time when his men were in training, it came to the attention of the Colonel that his men would be paid $10 a month for their service to the Union army, while white men would earn $13. The justification for the difference in pay was that $3 would be deducted for clothing. Additionally, the men of the 54th Regiment would not be provided the same weapons as white men. They were expected to fight with pikes, a weapon used by foot soldiers and consisting of a long pole with a pointed, metal head. This weapon would have been useless against the muskets of the Confederates and would have resulted in greater mortality of the men in the 54th. The difference in pay and the inadequate armament are structural elements of racism.

On July 2, 1863, the Colonel responded to the inequities and appealed, on behalf of his men, to the governor of Massachusetts:

> You have probably seen the order from Washington which cuts down the pay of colored troops from $13 to $10. Of course if this affects Massachusetts regiments, it will be a great piece of injustice to them, as they were enlisted on the express understanding that they were to be on precisely the same footing as all other Massachusetts troops. In my opinion they should be mustered out of the service or receive the full pay which was promised them.... Another change that has been spoken of was the arming of Negro troops with pikes instead of firearms. Whoever proposed it must have been looking for a means of annihilating Negro troops altogether ... or have never been under a heavy musketry fire, not observed its effects (Emilio, p. 47–48).

The Colonel intervened. He knew that the only way his men could prove equal capacity to white men was through fighting alongside them on the battlefield. This required equal armament, and it merited equal pay. Subsequently, the Colonel not only had to train and outfit his men in the effort to make them soldiers, but he was thrust into the role of advocate to fight the structural forces of racism. Colonels leading white troops did not encounter these challenges on behalf of their men.

The unequal playing field accorded to racism is evident in the life of Dr. Rock. Despite being denied access to medical school, he still became a practicing dentist and medical doctor; but he arrived at these professions through a steeper climb of apprenticeships and access provided by allies to their personal libraries. His intellectual brilliance flourished, but only because of his persistence and the goodwill of people who made concerted attempts to level the playing field. These people speak to the value of intervention and believing that one has the capacity to positively affect the life of another.

The men of the 54th had to prove themselves on a different field, the battlefield. Colonel Shaw had to, once again, advocate when he became aware that white troops of other regiments were sent to an operation where combat was inevitable. His regiment was left behind. In his expression of his disappointment to General Strong, it is important to note his attempt to convince the general of not only his men's capacity to fight but also of the sociological significance in his men's need to prove themselves on the battlefield,

> "... I had been given to understand that we were to have our share in the work in this department. I feel convinced too that my men are capable of better service than mere guerilla warfare, and I hope to remain permanently under your command. It seems to me quite important that the colored soldiers should be associated as much as possible with the white troops, in order that they may have other witnesses besides their own officers to what they are capable of doing. I trust that the present arrangement is not permanent..." (Emilio, p. 49).

The Colonel's appraisal of his men was based on his day-to-day interactions with them. He recognized their worth, but he was also aware that they would be judged much more harshly as a result of the prevalent assumptions that his men were less capable and, more so, uncourageous. The Colonel knew otherwise. The men met the expectations of the abolitionists who contested that the battlefield would be the stage on which black men would prove their equality to white men. The battle at Fort Wagner exacted a high price by the number of lives lost. Having demonstrated their capacity in such a public venue, the men dislodged the negative association accorded to skin color. After the battle, one white soldier was recorded as saying, "We don't know any black men here, they're all soldiers."

Strength of a Mother

The Colonel's mother, Sarah, was a dominant force in her son's moral development. She and her husband laid the foundation for his eventual transformation. What we can further examine from the archives of historical records is how Sarah, herself, viewed racism and prejudice.

Not much is known about Sarah's early education, other than a fondness for art, music, and English literature. It is known that "from youth she devoted her efforts to the cause of Negro emancipation, continuing during the period of reconstruction to support schemes for Negro education and enlightenment" (Weinberg, 1967, p. 49). The status of women, during this era, was generally accorded unequal to that of men. Examples of the higher value accorded to men can be found in several sources that chronicle Sarah's life; even in an obituary published in *The New York Times* at her death, she is referred to as "the daughter of a Boston merchant, Nathaniel Russell Sturgis" (Weinberg, p. 49; New York Times). No mention of her mother is made. It is as though a woman of her era was only accorded acknowledgement or credibility through the standing of her male associations.

After her son's death, Sarah compiled the letters written by her son during the Civil War and published them for family members and close friends. Prior to their publication, Sarah made changes to the letters. Some deletions in her son's letters were intended to protect mentioned individuals from embarrassment or becoming angry, while other deletions extracted evidence of her son's early prejudices (Duncan, 1992). While we know that his attitudes changed, Sarah, a lifelong abolitionist and proponent for the educational advancement of people of color, recognized that his writings reflected poorly on her son and would taint his legacy if the vestiges of prejudice were not eliminated. Of value for us today is the model of a man who, by the time he died alongside men whose skin color was different from his own, had *changed his habituated thoughts.*

Racism Interrupted

This capacity for change is evident in another well-known historical figure, Benjamin Franklin. In his early years, Franklin bought, owned, and sold people as slaves. Later in life, he led the Pennsylvania Society for Promoting the Abolition of Slavery. It is vital to understand what prompted his transformation. In review of what our subjects understood about the structural elements of racism, we know that the Colonel had to advocate for equal access to the same weaponry as white men so his men could fight equally on the battlefield. Dr. John Rock attributed the relative inferior state of people of color in this country to the lack of "more favorable circumstances." In this regard, Dr. Rock spoke to a wider range of forces that maintained the inequities; first of all, laws were capriciously designed to maintain stricter control over people who were enslaved while providing absolute impunity to those mistreating them. Frederick Douglass provides a few examples of the state of affairs during his lifetime:

> In the single state of Virginia there are seventy-one crimes for which a colored man may be executed; while there are only three of these crimes, which, when committed by a white man, will subject him to that punishment.... If a colored woman, in the defense of her own virtue, in defense of her own person, should shield herself from the brutal attacks of her tyrannical master, or make the slightest resistance, she may be killed on the spot. No law whatever will bring the guilty man to justice for the crime (Douglass, pp. 405–406).

The second structural force by which to maintain the inequities relates to another powerful weapon, education. When a person is educated, she has the capacity to communicate and express herself verbally and through the written word. Education can promote a person's capacity to think critically and be in the world as a subject of her life. It is so powerful that it is threatening. Without equal access to an education, a subservient class of people remains marginalized. Jenny Proctor, born in 1850, speaks to the experience of the intentional effort made to withhold education from her and the expressed fear that stood behind the reasoning. Her testimony, recorded in 1937, speaks to the risks taken by people who were enslaved as they attempted to teach themselves how to read:

> None of us was 'lowed to see a book or try to learn. They say we git smarter than they was if we learn anything, but we slips around and gits hold of that Webster's old blue-back speller and we hides it till 'way in the night and then we lights a little pine torch, and studies that spelling book. We learn it too. I can read some now and write a little too (Botkin, p. 91).

For this reason, a structural component of racism made the education of blacks illegal. The Statute Book of South Carolina stated:

> AN ACT FOR THE BETTER ORDERING AND GOVERNING OF NEGROES AND SLAVES ... 1740. SECT. 45. And whereas, the having slaves taught to write, or suffering them to be employed in writing, may be attended with great inconveniences ... that any person who shall teach any slave to write or to employ any slave as a scribe in writing, shall forfeit 100 pounds (Lerner, p. 19).

These were the laws enacted to maintain a racialized hierarchy, which made Sarah Grimké's act of defiance in teaching her "waiting maid" to read all the more revolutionary. Though a child, she understood physical bondage to represent one form of aggression. Intellectual bondage, and the laws that prohibited access to a formal education, was an act of aggression of a different nature, yet one that she and her sister, Angelina, as women, knew all too well.

A hundred years later, after the creation of the aforementioned law, the Colonel had to ensure that his men were provided the weapons so they could have the opportunity to prove their equal worth on the battlefield. Anthony Benezet, a Philadelphian Quaker who lived during the mid-1700s, understood that free blacks would never be on equal footing with white people unless they were educated. Benezet sought to prove the intellectual capacity of people whose skin color was not white by tutoring them. Furthermore, he went on to teach his students that "it was slavery rather than any inherent racial differences that bred ignorance and degradation among African Americans" (Bordewich, p. 55).

Benezet understood that years of withholding education had entrenched a byproduct of racist ideology: **"internalized racism"** in which the people who are objectified come to believe in their own inferiority. This far-reaching and insidious arm of racism not only dehumanizes those who espouse a mechanized and compassionless view of others, but it also becomes ingrained in the hearts and minds of the oppressed. The resulting "self-depreciation" for their own worth gives rise to **"horizontal violence"** in which the oppressed retaliate at one another. Evidence of this behavior can be seen today in our society in which violence and crime are most committed not across racial lines, but are perpetrated within one's racial group.

Once rooted in a society's culture, racism activates an elevated element of "negative association" by affixing negative meaning to all things associated to the oppressed. This form of aggression is what Freire (1998) refers to as **Cultural Invasion**. The oppressors assert their dominance by attempts to displace and erase any vestiges of the targeted culture. This act of proclaimed cultural superiority serves as another weapon to sustain marginality.

> For cultural invasion to succeed, it is essential that those invaded become convinced of their intrinsic inferiority. Since everything has its opposite, if those who are invaded consider themselves inferior, they must necessarily recognize the superiority of the invaders. The values of the latter thereby become the pattern for the former. The more invasion is accentuated and those invaded are alienated from the spirit of their own culture and from themselves, the more the latter want to be like the invaders: to walk like them, dress like them, talk like them (p. 134).

Once this level of racism takes root in the hearts and minds of those who are oppressed, reversing it means not just the transformation of those who enact racism, but also of those who have been subjected to it. The Colonel had to ensure that his men had the same weapons as white men in order to fight equally on the battlefield. Benezet, on the other hand, provided education through schools he helped establish for free black and slave children. During his career, Benezet converted Benjamin Franklin to abolitionism by "demonstrating that his students were capable of the same level of achievement as whites, thus undermining popular assumptions about black intellectual inferiority" (Bordewich, p. 55). Franklin had a change of heart preceded by a change in his habituated thoughts.

"Policy" as a Weapon of Conquest

The question of who has the "power of the pen" will eventually lead to who controls the content of education. With a growing number of European immigrants arriving on Eastern shores, the need to accommodate the newly arrived immigrants prompted expansionistic policy that resulted in direct conflict with Mexico and with the First Nations already living here. The historic portrayal of U.S. policy as "divinely inspired" is inherent in the proclaimed entitlement of **Manifest Destiny.** This proclamation laid the foundation for acts of aggression that led to the illegal war against Mexico, the removal and genocide of Native Americans, and then the concerted effort to wipe out the culture, language, customs, and religions that stood in the way of United States imperialistic efforts to gain control of land from the Atlantic to the Pacific Oceans.

After fighting and winning independence from Spain, Mexican territory included parts of the larger Southwest and Western territories now held by the United States. The Mexican government welcomed a large number of colonists from the United States to settle one of their territories, known as Texas. Those who settled agreed to abide by conditions of occupancy set by the Mexican government; they agreed to become Catholics, to take an oath of allegiance to Mexico, and to abide by its laws. Mexico had gained its own independence from Spain early in the 1800s, and on September 15, 1829, Mexico not only abolished slavery on Mexican land, but it also attempted to eliminate the racialized caste system left in the wake of Spanish colonization and conquest.

Slaveholding Texans quickly determined a way not to lose the competitive, capitalistic edge they had by the use of enslaved labor. Their way of abiding by Mexican law was to free the people whom they had enslaved, only to turn around and sign them into lifelong contracts as indentured servants. This was in direct violation of Mexican law, which was, in turn, viewed by slave owners as an infringement of their personal liberties (Acuña, 2000).

Open defiance of Texans to Mexican laws, a series of skirmishes between Texan colonists and Mexican troops, and failed diplomatic sessions between opposing parties served as a prelude to the United States' declaration of war on Mexico in 1846. It took only two years for the United States to win the war and to take hold of the greatest amount of the northern territories of Mexico, which included California, Arizona, New Mexico, Texas, Nevada, Utah, parts of Colorado, small sections of Oklahoma, Kansas, and Wyoming. The **Treaty of Hidalgo**, executed on February 2, 1848, ended the war between Mexico and the United States but stipulated in Articles VIII and IX that all Mexicans would be granted U.S. citizenship. It took less than a year for the United States to renege on the agreements outlined in the Treaty:

> When the United States took over the new territories, it nullified Mexico's liberal racial legislation and began the process of racializing the Mexican population. Much as Spain had done, the United States gave full citizenship to Mexicans who were considered White and ascribed inferior legal status to people of color on the basis of race. At the time of the ratification of the treaty, the United States conferred full political rights only upon free Whites, while Blacks and Indians could be enslaved and indentured in most states. People of mixed European and Indian ancestry could not be enslaved, but they could be barred from voting, practicing law, becoming naturalized citizens, and, in many states, marrying Anglo Americans (Menchaca, p. 19, 1999).

The manipulation of policy and, in this case, the dishonoring of the treaty between two nations cast a people who were, by virtue of their "difference," relegated to an inferior status. The people who lived in what were previously Mexican territories and who were now incorporated into the United States were subjected to racialized U.S. policy that enacted differentiated opportunity structures for people of color. These people, and their descendents, were relegated to the status of "noncitizens," were not allowed to participate in the government that now held dominance on their homeland, and were further subjected to anti-miscegenation policy that prohibited cross-racial marriage. This is a powerful tool of **Divide and Rule** (Freire, 1998) intended to maintain clear demarcation between races so that domination of one group over the other can be enforced. The legacy of historical conflict and subjugation that second-generation Mexican immigrants experience as they are raised in the United States is the reason why Ogbu and Simmons (1998) place second-generation Mexican immigrants into an Involuntary Immigrant status.

Substandard pay, work and living conditions as well as lack of access to quality education have plagued oppressed populations over the decades forcing their collective response. In the early 1900's the united efforts of 12,000 Colorado miners of different national groups led by Mother Jones led to a strike. Subsequently, the miners and their families were "evicted from their company-owned hovels and forced to live in tents set up by the union" (Martinez, 1991). Other organized efforts of people to improve their lives in the early 1900's after the United States conquest of the Southwest include the 1938 strike of workers at 130 pecan industry plants. Emma

Tenayucca served as a prominent leader for the picketers; many who sustained being tear-gassed, beaten and jailed for their unified advocacy. Aggression as a tool to maintain oppressive conditions for people who are "othered" is a constant theme. Yet, the caste-like treatment of a conquered or colonized people does not change until people understand the rooted nature of how the habituated thoughts became rooted in our culture.

Humanists' Response To U.S. Policy

The precept for war, expansion of slave territories, did not go unnoticed by abolitionists. Many of the United States' intellectual community recognized that Mexico was still reeling after having fought and won its independence from Spain after 400 years of rule. William Lloyd Garrison, in his paper, *The Liberator*, openly stated his support for the Mexican people: "Every lover of Freedom and humanity throughout the world must wish them the most triumphant success." Abraham Lincoln, who at the time, was a freshman congressman, called the war immoral and proslavery. He demanded of U.S. President James K. Polk, who stood on an imperialistic platform, that he "identify the spot where Mexicans had shed American blood on American soil." For his position, Lincoln was branded a traitor and was denied re-nomination by his own party. People protested, and yet, the war went on.

© Lefteris Papaulakis, 2013. Used under license from Shutterstock, Inc.

Humanist resistance against this war took many forms. Brutality by United States troops against the people of Mexico was publicized in the United States. This decreased the base of support for the war, even while it was in progress (Digital History). One form of resistance was enacted by Henry David Thoreau who, out of defiance against U.S. policy that permitted the existence of slavery as well as supported the aggression against Mexico, refused to pay his poll taxes. His position was that he would not contribute funds that would, in turn, be used to raise arms that enacted U.S. expansionist policy and increase slave-holding territories. For six years, he did not pay his poll taxes and was subsequently jailed.

Thoreau's response to the United States' government resulted in his writing to the notion of passive resistance. In his written document known as "Civil Disobedience," he states, "When a sixth of the population of a nation which has undertaken to be the refuge of liberty are slaves, and a whole country is unjustly overrun and conquered by a foreign army, and subjected to military law, I think that it is not too soon for honest men to rebel and revolutionize" (Canby, 1939, p. 232). From a platform of nonviolence, Thoreau struck out against U.S. policy of aggression, not by attacking those who espoused violence but by attacking in another form; by not feeding U.S. coiffures that financed the war against Mexico. Thoreau's declaration of resistance to the U.S. government was clearly stated: "I do not care to trace the course of my dollar, if I could, till it buys a man, or a musket to shoot one with, — the dollar is innocent, —but I am concerned to trace the effects of my allegiance. In fact, I quietly declare war with the State..." (Glick, 1973, p. 84).

Modeled by John Brown was one humanist's response to U.S. policy that condoned aggression between people and between nations. His forceful but ill-fated attempt to undo the institution of slavery gained immediate attention and response. Thoreau's method was not so heralded nor well known at the time. He spent one night in jail, and his Aunt Maria, upon being apprised of his incarceration, paid the $1.50 Thoreau owed, and he was set free. Quietly, Thoreau went about his business, and his essay **"Civil Disobedience,"** which also was source of many of his lectures, did not take on a more powerful form until adopted by Gandhi in his campaign for civil resistance during the first half of the 1900s in India; later, it was adopted by Dr. Martin Luther King Jr. during the **Civil Rights Movement** of the 1960s in the United States. Simple acts of nonconformity have sparked large-scale movements. Humanists calling "it" what "it" is and responding individually and collectively has made a difference in the quality of life for all people in this country, if we consider the United States a work in progress. Thoreau's individual act of resistance earned him arrest and a quiet night sitting in a Massachusetts jail cell. We can draw comparisons between Thoreau's seemingly innocuous act of defiance of refusing to pay taxes that supported an illegal war to Rosa Parks' landmark refusal in 1955 to give up her seat in the front of the bus in defiance of racist segregationist policies.

© StampGirl, 2013. Used under license from Shutterstock, Inc.

© catwalker, 2013. Used under license from Shutterstock, Inc.

Another form of humanist resistance to the U.S. declaration of war on Mexico and the subsequent atrocities must be noted. The defection of U.S. soldiers of mostly Irish but also of German and Scottish descent to the Mexican Army was fueled by a growing disdain caused by the mistreatment from U.S. officers, and by their observations of how U.S. troops treated the Mexican people who, like them, were mostly Catholic. The Irish men who changed sides became known as the San Patricio Batallion. Many of these men, when captured, faced stiff punishment for deserting the U.S. army and received lashes, branding, and, in many cases, were executed. While these men are branded as deserters and traitors in U.S. history, they are revered, to this day, in Mexico for their bravery in battle and the courage it took to risk their lives and fight on the side they felt was just (Acuña, 2000).

© catwalker, 2013. Used under license from Shutterstock, Inc.

Education as a Weapon of Cultural Invasion

The United States won the war and seized half of Mexico's land but then grappled with what to do with those taken underfoot. Conquered Native Americans could be placed on reservations; however, there were many times when even reservation land was *desirable*. Then there was the question of what to do with the colonized Mexicans who also were different racially and culturally, and held different customs and spoke a different language. United States policy now turned to the ***assimilation*** of these people so as to Americanize them and force compliance to U.S. doctrine.

Schools became the weapon by which to wash out the "difference" of these people. Boarding schools and curriculum that instilled the superiority of Anglo-American revisionist history became the force of weapon to enact this arm of conquest,

> Commission of Indian Affairs John Oberly believed that the Indian student should be taught the "exalting egotism of American civilization, so that he will say 'I' instead of 'We,' and 'This is mine' instead of 'This is ours.' Thus did educators seek to create in the Indian students' mind the mental and moral concept of possessive individualism... (Adams, p. 158).

Clearly, the intention was to annihilate the value of collectivism inherent with indigenous communities and, in its place, to instill the ideal of individualism. Standard curriculum taught to Native American children who were removed, by force, from their parents and placed in boarding schools taught the value of "capitalism" and "self-determination." Further stripping of Native American cultural elements did not end here:

> Reformers invariably dismissed the Indian's native religion as a hodgepodge of barbaric rites and ceremonies totally devoid of any moral content. Beyond this, native beliefs were condemned for encouraging in Indians a naïve and childish tendency to seek spiritual meanings and truth in the natural world, for their failure to acknowledge any association between religious activity and material advancement... What reformers were objecting to was the fact that Native American religions reinforced and reflected the values and cultural patterns of Indian life, something they were committed to erasing (Adams, p. 159).

While many came from across the Atlantic Ocean to escape religious persecution, those who were already here were now forcibly prohibited from practicing their own faith system. Religion, another arm of conquest, would take volumes to properly address; however, its precept as a cause for war is well documented in European international conflict. This precept for conquest had now become a weapon of dominance in the United States. Similarly, as we examine the rooted manifestations of power, we can uncover, in modern times, how these weapons shape the realities of those intended to be dominated and those expected to carry out the acts of oppression.

White Humanist Resistance to Education as a Weapon

In the 1970s, Anna Bunker was fresh out of a teaching credential program from California State University, Sacramento. She applied for a teaching position through the Bureau of Indian Affairs (BIA) that would place her on the Diné (also known as the Navajo) reservation in Tuba City, Arizona. Upon reflection about her decision to apply for this position, Anna recounts how she was young, idealistic, and saw it not just as a possibility to teach but also as an opportunity to learn from immersion in a completely different culture from her own. She states that she was naive in expecting the assignment to be "an exciting experience"; by the third week into her new job, she felt something was really wrong. The principal explicitly told her not to let the children speak Diné. It was the policy. The training she received in her credential program did not provide any preparation on cross-cultural teaching, so she did not have any context by which to respond to her superior's directive to eliminate the home language of the children she was hired to teach.

Two major incidents stayed with Anna because they taught her the full tragedy that occurs when a place of learning is used as an arm of destruction and oppression. The first incident relates to when Anna was told by the principal that the class that she was assigned to was "uncontrollable and it was her job to control them." This was a boarding school, so the children had been displaced from their families, and Anna was expected to assert herself as "the boss." She was directed to be present when the children woke up in the morning and to be the last person they saw before they went to sleep at night. In response to this directive, Anna explained to the principal that school was not a jail. He, in turn, communicated that if she did not keep the students under her "watch" from morning until night, she would be terminated in two weeks, unless she found another way to control them. Anna turned for assistance to her teaching supervisor who, in turn, communicated that unless Anna learned to be authoritarian, she would be driven out and she would fail. Compliance with the policies and the authoritarian culture was expected.

Anna searched for ways to teach the children, but discovered that the principal had taken the children's books away. When Anna asked why they didn't have books, she was told, "They don't deserve books because they are so bad." The message underlying his statement was that the students didn't deserve to learn. Anna was horrified, and his response stuck with her. The fear she had of being fired was tempered by the acknowledgement that the children were destined to fail by design. Determined to engage her students through creative approaches, she discovered that the children enjoyed drawing and poetry so she brought in materials to encourage their development and expression. Her progress, however, ended abruptly when Anna was removed from her assignment with this class. She was replaced by a more experienced teacher who had more seniority within the BIA .

Anna was relegated to being a permanent substitute for the school. Since she was roving as a substitute, no one knew what she did once she entered a classroom. She took the liberty of allowing the children to speak their own language. Anna had a moment of conscientização when she was preparing to substitute a class for a permanent teacher. This situation led to the second incident that remains with her today and that still brings tears to her eyes in recollecting what transpired.

While Anna and the permanent teacher were both in front of the classroom, a little boy was sitting on the floor. With ugliness in her voice, the permanent teacher said to the child, "When are you going to learn to tell time? Are you going to be a dumb Indian all your life?" Prior to that moment, he was a happy little boy, but now Anna watched him shrink. Anna observed the force of the words permeate the child's being, and she can still recall how the boy's vitality left him. He went inside himself and vanished. His face became a mask. Anna remembers feeling horrified as she observed the impact of this incident. It was clear to Anna that the teachers and administrators wanted the children to be white, act white, and talk white. Subversively, Anna continued to work with children in creative ways, always closing the door so she could let them speak their home language, Diné, without fear of punishment.

Anna Bunker is now Dr. Anna Kato, and for 23 years she served as an educator and taught future teachers at the University of California, Davis. When she thinks about how her experience in Arizona has shaped her views of public education, she acknowledges that it incited her resolve to confront oppression in schools. In reflection, she recognizes how closely aligned sense of self and language are connected to one's identity. She is thankful to the Diné children who, as her teachers, gave her this important lesson. Her exposure to dominance provided lessons on two different but parallel levels. Foremost, the children were being subjected to an oppression that was not only soul killing but was also attempting to murder their identity.

The second lesson, which took Anna 25 years to realize, was that the color of her skin, white, was cause for the children's fear. This fear caused acting out behaviors that resulted in more punishment. The school, a place where children are supposed to learn, to value one another, and discover the joys of learning, only enacted a cycle of repression. The children had been taken from their families and forced to stay at this place where they were not allowed to be who they were. One child that Anna recalls was only five years old and sat with his head on the desk, not talking, not engaging, not expressing joy. The trust was not there and this, Anna came to understand, was the construct of oppression in which they existed.

Personal reasons led Anna away from this early career post, but she still recalls a conversation with another white teacher who was also new at this boarding school. They felt that if they stayed, they would, unwittingly, be sucked into buying into the oppressor's behavior because the norms of the oppressor's world reinforced and rewarded the behaviors the oppressor wanted to see. This is not what Anna wanted to become, and she decided that she would not engage in oppressive behaviors or express beliefs expected of her just because she had white skin. Like the San Patricios, she resisted and, to this day, teaches the value of multiculturalism and the beauty of diversity (Interview, February 9, 2011).

Omission and humiliation by design

After the Mexican-U.S. War, the United States reinvented ways to enact the forces of **Cultural Invasion.** The Mexican people left on the north side of the new Mexican-U.S. border and, after the signing of the Treaty of Guadalupe Hidalgo, were subjected to drastic changes in the curriculum taught in their schools. Similar to Native Americans, the intention was the same:

> The Mexican American presence in the Southwest was now interpreted through the eyes of the dominant Anglo group—an interpretation that generally tended to omit the contributions of Mexican Americans and to provide a distorted, stereotypical view of them and their cultural heritage.... History books, which began to appear a decade after the Mexican American War ended in 1848, contained only disparaging comments about the Mexican presence in the Southwest. These books consistently denounced the character of the Mexican people, and stressed the nobility of the Anglos" (San Miguel, p. 44, 1999).

Even today, the war against "difference" continues across the United States. Bigotry through policy and curriculum continues to subjugate conquered people while denigrating their culture and their history. These matters are continually at the forefront of school board and state government agendas that are attempting to "sanitize" their territories and erase the grounded presence of non-Anglo ethnic groups.

In studying the experience of U.S. education for second-generation young women of Mexican descent, the sanitization of U.S. history has far-reaching implications for Mexican American children even today. The evidence generated from the young women who participated in my dissertation study revealed their disappointment in the "American-centric" school curriculum. One study participant, Elizabeth Cruz, reflected on the impact that the one-sided rendition of U.S. history had on her:

> It's sad. Because it's going to be really hard to reach all those people and say, 'Hey, this is what really happened. What they taught you in eighth grade was bull. It was nothing.' But, in a way, it can't affect me because I know what really happened. It would have been really sad if here I am, a Mexican girl sitting in a history class learning about what they're teaching me and believing it! Oh, that would have been sad! I could have said that I would have been humiliated! (Borunda, p. 134, 2002)

Elizabeth expressed the personal toll on children of Mexican descent who are taught historical renditions that denigrate them. There is an element of disassociation with second-generation Involuntary Immigrants when exposed to curriculum that creates a psychological dissonance in the classroom. She also expressed the cost of the repeated lies upon generations of children who never come to know the truth. Elizabeth went on to elaborate on the divisive consequences that this one-sided rendition of history had on her relationships with Euro-American classmates who were exposed to the same curriculum.

> Frustration. Anger. Anger with the teacher of why are you teaching that? Why are you doing that? Why are you showing that? Why are you treating *me* like that? Them being an adult you would think they would know better. Kids go to school and they take a test on it. They have to know it. They're going to carry it on for the rest of their lives. They're being taught lies. They're being taught the wrong thing. At least about us. For me to say, 'What you learned in history class today was total crap.' It's frustrating because they look at you like, 'What are you talking about? You didn't get the degree. How would you know?' Then they act on it. It's sad because there goes another kid who could have had that friendship with me but they took it away (Borunda p. 134, 2002).

The lies perpetuate interracial discord. They unconsciously instill a sense of false superiority with white children and undermine the potential for cross-racial relationship building. Without discourse about history that reveals truths from a wide range of perspectives, our children, who are to become our nation's future leaders, lack the critical thinking to approach the issues of today by learning about lessons from our past. Instead, our children walk out of classrooms in silence and without the insightful understanding of dominance, in its many forms.

Elizabeth Cruz, though only 13 years of age at the time she made the cited statements, was simply stating the impact of "it." The ideological forces of Manifest Destiny, along with its closely aligned descendants of Manipulation, Divide and Rule, Conquest, and Cultural Invasion (Freire, 1998) did not go unnoticed by the humanists from the early development of the United States. And, as we can see from the life of Helen Hunt Jackson, calling "it" what it was had become her mission.

Blowing The Whistle on Manifest Destiny

The model of another humanist, Helen Hunt Jackson, provides further lessons in transformation. Hunt had a gift for writing, but hostile attitudes toward women writers during her era discouraged women's expression to write about meaningful subjects. Such was the case of Lydia Maria Child, who was the first person to research and document the history of slavery and the condition of African Americans. Her scholarly publication in 1833, *An Appeal in Favor of That Class of Americans Called Africans*, "devastated Child's literary popularity, reduced her income, and cost her many friends" (Foote, 2003, p. 36).

Child had stepped "out of place" when she took an unpopular position over a contentious cause. This was not considered the purview of women in an era that leaned toward the position that "the duties of women at all times consisted of making themselves useful and agreeable to men ..."(Odell, p. 64). Subsequently, Hunt's first attempts at writing were under the pseudonym of "Marah." She continued to use various aliases until she was awakened to the injustices inflicted upon Native Americans. Once she embraced this cause, she went on to write *A Century of Dishonor* and *Ramona*, literary endeavors similar to Child's, using her own name.

The evidence of Hunt's transformation begins at a time in which she not only espoused negative views of blacks and Indians, but also resisted the concept that "others" were her equals. We will explore what may have precipitated her transformation. Hunt lost her first two children to illness. Her first husband died in an accident. Still, in the wake of these personal losses, she continued to produce poetry and short stories. Her communications with friends and associates, however, revealed mental depression. Hunt had not taken any interest in temperance, women's suffrage, or abolitionism. In her earlier days, she had used terms such as "loathsome," "abject," and "hideous" in her writings about Native Americans. Her stage of development, according to the Helm's White Racial Identity Development Model (1995), reflects elements of the Reintegration stage in which she exhibits intolerance of other minority groups and espouses a conscious belief in white racial superiority. She had no context, initially, to understand that oppressive circumstances led to the oppressive conditions in which she may have initially observed First Nations people. As a result, she saw their conditions as a "fixed reality" without critical thought to the complicity of the United States government and its people. She did not make the connection until she attended a gathering in Boston, where she met the leader of the Ponca Tribe, Standing Bear.

What awakened Hunt to the suffering around her may be revealed in her "Author's Note" found in the opening of a *Century of Dishonor*. While she states that this publication is a "sketch" and not a "full history of any of these Indian communities, of its forced migrations, wars, and miseries, (which) would fill a volume by itself" she was, somehow, moved to change the focus of her literary gifts from poetry and short stories to making known the plight of Native Americans. One key event moved her to what would be considered the Pseudo-Independence phase of the Helm's White Racial Identity Development Model and sparked a sense of outrage that changed the trajectory of her life.

Chief Standing Bear was on a speaking tour of Eastern states at the time Hunt first heard him. His objective was to communicate a trail of injustices committed against the people of his tribe, who were known to sustain themselves primarily through agriculture. They lived in what is now known as the South Dakota-Nebraska boundary and had given up a strip of their land when they signed a treaty with the U.S. government in 1858. This opened up the best of their lands to white settlers. They continued in peace despite the U.S. government failing to protect them, as it had promised, from their ancient tribal enemies, the Sioux.

Ten years later, without explanation, the U.S. government gave all remaining Ponca land to the Sioux. The discovery of gold in the Black Hills, now Sioux territory, incited a rush of white settlers, which forced violent altercations with the Sioux. Even though the Poncas did not participate in battles with the white settlers, the U.S. government's strategy to resolve the conflict was to move all First Nations to "Indian Territory." This was the beginning of a series of forced removals and concerted attempts to dislocate the Poncas and other First Nations from their ancestral homelands without regard for their welfare. Hunt, touched by the chief's story, was moved to the Immersion/Emersion stage of the Helm's White Identity Development Model as she took an active role in making known the plight of the Ponca tribe. In her heart, Hunt believed that the American public would correct these injustices if people knew what was transpiring.

The subsequent trail of broken promises with not just the Poncas but with the Utes, the Cheyennes, and all the Northern tribes affected by the U.S. government's policy of removal became the focus of Hunt's newspaper publications. Her objective, as stated in her author's note, was to "show our causes for national shame in the matter of our treatment of the Indians. It is a shame which the American nation ought not to lie under, for the American people, as a people, *are not at heart unjust*" (Jackson, p. 7). Hunt trusted that her fellow citizens believed in "fair play" and that Native Americans had been denied such at the hands of the U.S. government. She put into effect an inspired effort to stop the violence enacted, by force of policy and troops, by the U.S. government on Native American people. This was racist policy resulting from the anti-dialogical force of **Conquest** (Freire, 1998).

Chief Standing Bear's oldest son was among one-third of the entire tribe who died of starvation, malaria, or related causes after removal to the Reservation. Having promised his son he would bury him in their homeland, Chief Standing Bear set out for Nebraska with 65 followers. Upon arrival, he was arrested for leaving the Reservation without permission. In his trial, Chief Standing Bear raised his right hand and stated, "That hand is not the color of yours, but if I prick it, the blood will flow, and I shall feel pain … The blood is of the same color as yours. God made me, and I am a man" (The Indian Journal). Chief Standing Bear speaks to an oppressive reality for people of color that becomes a prevalent theme in United States' culture. His statement contains the same sentiment as expressed 140 years later by the African American woman quoted in Paxton's dissertation, in which her "difference" subjects her to "unfair" and violent treatment.

While the subsequent ruling by the presiding judge, Elmer S. Dundy, on May 12, 1879, declared that "an Indian is a person," it failed to change the pattern of behaviors in which the U.S. government conducted itself with regard to relationships with First Nations. An excerpt from Hunt's *Century of Dishonor* reveals this pattern of "habituated behavior" adopted by the U.S. government and grounded in racist ideology.

> ... the Indian's "right of occupancy" in his lands was a right recognized by all the Great Powers discovering this continent, and accepted ... as a right necessary to be extinguished either by purchase or conquest,... the United States ... has... recognized, accepted, and acted upon this theory, it is next ... to inquire whether the United States has dealt honorably or dishonorably by the Indians in this matter ... there is rarely much room for discussion whether they be honorable or dishonorable, the standard of honor in men's conduct being, among the civilized, uniform, well understood, and undisputed. Stealing, for instance, is everywhere held to be dishonorable ... lying ... breaking of promise and betrayals of trust are scorned even among the most ignorant people. But when it comes to the discussion of the acts of nations, there seems to be less clearness of conception, less uniformity of standard of right and wrong, honor and dishonor. It is necessary, therefore, in charging a government or nation with dishonorable conduct, to show that its moral standard ought in nowise to differ from the moral standard of an individual: that which is cowardly, cruel, base in a man, is cowardly, cruel, base in a government or nation" (Jackson, pp. 17–18).

Standing Bear's speech asserted his equality with the white man who, through governmental policy and acts of force, had enacted the anti-dialogical force of Conquest (Freire, 1998). The specific tools to enact Conquest were through broken treaties, deceit, and forced removal of Native Americans, who were then forced to "adapt" to the oppressor's fixed reality. Hunt did not approve of this reality and she did not perceive the actions of the United States as "fair play." In truth, Native Americans were relegated to the status of objects that stood in the way of Manifest Destiny. The terms of disposal and removal of the Poncas was an extension of the initial encounters with Columbus as cognitive dissonance repeated itself over and over again. The recurrence of manipulating "policy" that enacts the purpose of Conquest is a theme that continues today.

Same Tired Song, Different Era

Courtenay Tessler, a modern-day humanist, relates an incident in which she witnessed, at the age of seven, the attempt to "enact policy" for racist purposes. Her father responded to a knock on the door of their home and, upon opening the door, her father came face to face with a man holding a petition. The interaction between the two was terse. Afterward, Tessler's father closed the door and Tessler, perplexed by what had transpired, asked her father what had just occurred. He communicated to her that the man said a black family was trying to buy a house in their neighborhood and that members of the neighborhood were trying to stop them from moving in. That is why he, a white man, was being asked to sign the petition. Tessler's father made clear to the man that he was not signing any such petition and that, furthermore, if a black family wanted to live in their neighborhood, they could buy any house they wanted. Her father, providing modeling that Tessler would carry with her for life, then told his young daughter, "Some people think they have the right to exclude other people and we don't believe that" (Tessler Taped Classroom Presentation, March 7, 2007).

As noted in Chapter 1, some Europeans escaped the harshness of colonial life and voluntarily choose to live with Native Americans. In these instances, which were many, we can determine that "the differences" were of no accord. Similarly, Zinn reveals that "in spite of subordination of blacks in the Americas in the seventeenth century, there is evidence that where whites and blacks found themselves with common problems, common work, common enemy in their master, they behaved toward one another as equals" (p. 31). This evidence attests to the capacity of humanity to note difference but not accord it a negative value.

Oppressors were so threatened by the unity of people across racial lines that all the slave states and three of the "free" states (Indiana, Illinois, and Michigan) passed **Anti-Miscegenation Laws.** These laws prohibited cross racial marriage. Even after the **Emancipation Proclamation**, a litany of laws now known as the **Black Codes** were created to maintain the oppression that was outlawed under the Emancipation Proclamation. Examples of further restrictions enacted to restrict those who had just been recently emancipated included denial of being able to testify against whites, and not being able to vote, serve on juries, or serve in the militia. In some cases, a judge could assign one's children to work for a former "owner," and the parents had no say in the matter.

This was followed by Jim Crow laws. Here we see, once again, the force of the anti-dialogical tool of Manipulation at its worse. People whose ancestors were brought in chains were given "separate but equal" status. In reality, this ruling systematized continued inferior economic, education, and social access. What resulted were separate schools, separate drinking fountains, and separate restrooms, as just a few examples of a culture perpetuating the ingrained legacy of racism. These are the laws that Rosa Parks resisted when she made a statement by refusing the order to give up her seat in the front of the bus to a white passenger. With the success of Jim Crow laws, it is no wonder that Tessler's father had to contend with a man attempting to secure signatures to keep their neighborhood white. These efforts had worked before. Subsequently, white humanists in this era, like Tessler's father, continue to confront and challenge the ways in racism manifests itself.

Eyes Open to Racism

As we have seen, the right to exclusion based on someone's ascribed "difference" is rooted in the habituated thoughts contained in racist ideology. It is enforced through overt physical violence and through violence of other means such as withholding of education, and oppressive policies. Previously discussed are the examples of racism that William Lloyd Garrison and John Brown witnessed in their lives. In the case of Garrison, it was the testimony of Benjamin Lundy that set him on fire. Garrison regularly posted in one of the earlier publications he worked for, the *Genius*, what he called the "The Black List," a column devoted to printing short reports of "the barbarities of slavery—kidnappings, whippings, murders." He did not directly bear witness to the barbarities, but he knew enough about atrocities committed against humanity that he used the power of the written word to expose "it."

Similarly, John Brown witnessed the mistreatment of another child and did not understand the rationale for the behavior. He was raised to believe in the equality of all humanity. He also understood that the child was not to blame for his condition. Rather, it was the misguided beliefs and actions of others that needed to be acted upon. Humanists intuitively understand that racism is a tool that is employed by elite whites to divide and rule others. The capacity to understand the insidious dimensions of racism is critical to the humanists' conceptualization of "it." With early and lifelong exposure to racism, humanists recognize it when they see it, and they call it what it is—it is racism.

The next theme, *relationship* with people of color, provides a lens to the antidote to the development and harboring of racist thoughts and beliefs. From the narratives of these white humanists, we learn that when white people have *bonds* with people of color, these bonds serve as an inoculation against the poisonous habits of thought embedded in racist ideology. Just as Tessler's father and other members of her family passed down a legacy of acceptance and appreciation for diversity (difference), the large body of evidence from the lives of white humanists speaks to how the bonds of cross-racial relationships sustained them in the face of hatred and ignorance that permeates the culture of our society.

QUESTIONS FOR DISCUSSION OR SELF REFLECTION

SELF-AWARENESS

1. In review of the Identity Development Models (Appendices B & C), at what stage of development do you believe you are at this time?

2. What factors have shaped your career goals? Are you on the path you truly desire want to take?

CLIENT WORLDVIEW

3. What was the Chinese Exclusion Act? Why was it created? Who did it negatively impact and who did it benefit?

4. What happened to Japanese Americans during World War II?

5. What U.S. policies or laws have had to be challenged over time so that we can move closer to the ideal of "equality for all?"

6. European immigrants were the first to be subjected to the process known as "Americanization," a process by which people lose their uniqueness and become solely English speaking. What are some of the experiences Europeans faced to become Americanized? What was the cost?

7. Critically examine the demographics of your community and/or where you grew up. Are there demographic patterns of segregated housing created by historical "red lining" policies? If you don't know what "red lining" is... conduct your own research and find communities in which this has taken place and what the impact was on people living in these communities.

COUNSELING RELATIONSHIP

8. The Multicultural and Social Justice Counseling Competencies (Butler, S.K. et al, 2015) provide four quadrants that inform the counseling relationship,

   Quadrant I: Privileged Counselor - Marginalized Client

   Quadrant II: Privileged Counselor - Privileged Client

Quadrant III: Marginalized Counselor - Privileged Client

Quadrant IV: Marginalized Counselor - Marginalized Client

9. Identity situations in which you interacted with an individual that fits the aforementioned Quadrants. Discuss what came up for you at the time of the interaction and how you would handle the situation now should this had occurred within the context of a counselor/client relationship?

10. With a classmate or friend, discuss the "isms" that are evident in your day to day reality; it could be from any one of the constructs of power and privilege which include not only racism but also heterosexism, ableism, classism, ageism, sexism, faithism.

11. Interview an individual who has a different background than your own and ask them about their family's struggles, values, and motivations.

COUNSELING AND ADVOCACY INTERVENTIONS

12. What are prevalent, persistent, and structural forces that maintain oppression related to race, gender, class, ability, faith? How can you respond to these forces from a policy perspective?

13. Expand your knowledge of Mother Jones and Emma Tenayucca. What did they do to advocate for others?

NEW CONCEPTS AND VOCABULARY TO REVIEW

Racism:

Habits of Thought:

Habituated Behavior:

Chinese Exclusion Act:

Japanese Internment Camps:

Anti-dialogical Forces: Conquest, Divide and Rule, Manipulation and Cultural Invasion:

Helm's White Racial Identity Development Model:

Manipulation:

Internalized Racism:

Horizontal Violence:

Cultural Invasion:

Manifest Destiny:

Treaty of Hidalgo:

Divide and Rule:

Civil Disobedience:

Civil Rights Movement:

Assimilation:

Anti-Miscegenation Laws:

Emancipation Proclamation:

Black Codes:

Activity

Assign small groups: 1. Native/American Indians, 2. Asian Americans, 3. Chican@/Latin@ Americans, 4. African Americans, 5. European Americans, & 6. Other Communities: People with Disabilities, Gay/Lesbian, Gerontology, Gender, Religion/Spirituality and discuss what historical processes, policies and laws that have impacted this group over time.

Begin to identify intragroup differences, anti-dialogical forces, acculturation vs. assimilation, and what cultural forces maintain uniqueness and identity?

References

Acuña, R. (2000). *Occupied America: a history of chicanos.* New York, NY. Addison Wesley Longman, Inc.

Anti-Slavery Convention Report; Report of a Delegate to the Anti-Slavery Convention of American Women, Held in Philadelphia, May 1838, (p. 14).

Bateson, G. (1972). *Steps to an ecology of mind.* New York: NY: Ballantine.

Bordewich, F. (2005). *Bound for Canaan.* New York, NY: HarperCollins Publishers, Inc.

Borunda, R. (2002). *Voices from the second generation. Young women of Mexican descent in American schools: defining and preserving self/sustaining hope.* Doctoral Dissertation. Ann Arbor, MI: University of San Francisco.

Botkin, B. A. (1945). *Lay my burden down.* Chicago, Ill; University of Chicago Press.

Canby, H. S. (1939). *Thoreau.* Boston, MA: Houghton Mifflin Company.

Douglass, F. (1994). *Douglass autobiographies.* New York, NY: Penguin Books.

Duncan, R. (1992). *Blue eyed child of fortune.* Georgia: University of Georgia Press.

Emilio, L. F. (1891). *History of the fifty-fourth regiment of Massachusetts volunteer infantry, 1863–1865.* Boston, MA: The Boston Book Company.

Foote, L. (2003). *Seeking the one great remedy.* Athens, OH. Ohio University Press.

Freire, P. (1998). *Pedagogy of the oppressed.* New York, NY: The Continuum Publishing Company.

Glick, W. (1973). *The writings of Henry D. Thoreau, reform papers.* Princeton, NJ: Princeton University Press.

Jackson, H. H. (2003). *A century of dishonor.* New York, NY: Dover Publications, Inc.

Lerner, G. (1998). *The Grimké sisters from South Carolina, pioneer for women's rights and abolition.* NY: Oxford University Press.

Martinez, E. (1991). 500 years of chicano history in pictures. Albuquerque, NM. Southwest Organizing Project.

Memmi, A. (2005). *Racism.* Minneapolis, MN: University of Minnesota Press.

Menchaca, M. (1999). *The treaty of Guadalupe Hidalgo and the racialization of the Mexican population.* In The Elusive Quest for Equality by José F. Moreno. Cambridge, MA. Harvard College.

Paxton, D. (2002). *Facilitating transformation of white consciousnes among Euro-American people: A case study of a cooperative inquiry. Unpublished doctoral dissertation,* California Institute of Integral Studies, San Francisco, CA.

Reynolds, D. (2005). *John Brown abolitionist.* New York, NY: Random House, Inc.

San Miguel, Jr., G. (1999). *The schooling of Mexicanos in the southwest, 1848–1891.* In The Elusive Quest for Equality by José F. Moreno. Cambridge, MA. Harvard College.

Standing Bear's Speech. Retrieved November 7, 2010 from http://www.imsmessenger.org/index2.php?option=com_content&do_pdf=1&id=92

Weinberg, A. (1967). *John Elliot Cairnes and the American Civil War.* London: The Kingswood Press.

Zinn, H. (1999). *A people's history of the United States.* New York, NY: HarperCollins Publishers, Inc.

Who is in *Your* Circle?

(Colonel) Shaw became attached to his men and defended them strongly against outside abuse. He had been forced by their actions to question, then conquer, his own misconceptions. They provided their intelligence, commitment to order, pluck, and adaptability to military life. As Shaw changed, he won the respect of his men. Recruiter William Wells Brown, a black man, and Corporal Gooding both wrote of the love the men held for their colonel. Shaw still wondered what they might do when they reached the battlefield, but he finally stopped calling them niggers (Duncan, 2005, p. 35).

A lesson I learned in my doctoral program is the concept of **"making the familiar strange."** This means that you look at everything around you as though you were seeing it for the first time. You assume the role of objective spectator, removed as a member of the community, and observe the currents of interaction, the unwritten rules of conduct that people follow, and the mores that govern ways of being with one another. With this set of eyes, I note what transpires in my classroom where I attempt to create a place and space for community and engagement to occur.

Each semester, I observe the same behavioral patterns in my classes. It doesn't surprise me that my students don't see it. They are blind to the patterns that are normal to their everyday reality. Many come from communities where they only see people who look like them. All have been shaped by a culture not of their making. Unconscious of their "Habits of Thoughts," these thoughts are, nonetheless, revealed in their "Habits of Behavior." Then, they come to a campus where there is a wealth of diversity. I will clarify what I mean by taking you through the patterns that generally transpire on the first day of class.

Prior to class starting, my teaching assistant(s) and I prepare the classroom so that everyone is seated in a circle, facing the center. Visual and physical proximity ensures that everyone is *in relation* to every other person, me included, in the classroom. The students arrive, one by one, and often stop in their tracks at the doorway, unsure of what to make of this arrangement. There are no desks to hide behind, no recesses of the classroom's corner to wedge into, and no "back of the classroom" to disappear into visual obscurity. Some welcome the unique layout with glee and boldly jump into the wave of this new arrangement, while others enter cautiously with stiff shoulders and tight jaws.

My teaching assistant(s) and I greet students as they enter or soon after arrival. Sometimes, it is difficult to secure their attention when attempting to shake their hand, even as I stand in front of them. It's as if they are overcome with so much confusion over the arrangement of the room that they suffer vertigo and are unable to "right" themselves. The spaces in the circle start to fill. My teaching assistant(s) and I generally have enough seats for everyone who is pre-registered. There are, invariably, a number of students wanting to add the class and a higher number caught in the traffic jams seasonal to opening of semester.

The winded late arrivals and hopeful "adds" congest at the classroom door. This means that despite our best calculations, we still don't have enough chairs. The people accumulating at the door eye the circle for a place to sit. Most of the chairs are occupied, but some are taken with the belongings of people who have staked out personal space, who make no attempt to accommodate the ones standing.

We ascertain who is already enrolled in the class and who would like to be in the class. This generally leads to adding more chairs to the circle and having to free up the chairs that have been "claimed" for holding personal belongings. Occasionally, a few students will extend themselves. They may already have a chair, but they are generally the first ones to get up and ensure that everyone has a place in the circle. My teaching assistant(s) and I are grateful to have these individuals in the class. They demonstrate genuine value of and care for their classmates. This genuineness easily carries over to their relationships with their clients in the near future, and their clients will know that the care is *real*.

Everyone eventually settles in the circle. In the case of some of my larger classes, where making a circle is not possible, we attempt to create a configuration that allows students to at least see one another. I then facilitate a discussion on what they have observed about the arrangement of the class. Eyes scan the circle and look at one another as though this was the first time they have encountered their classmates. Some state that they have previously been in classes with one another, but this is the first time they have interacted. This fostered isolationism and discouragement of interpersonal connection is a by-product of the banking method.

Many indicate that they haven't sat in a circle since kindergarten. Some express that it feels awkward. They feel exposed and uncomfortable. They also talk about everyone being "equal" in the circle, the feeling of vulnerability from the open arrangement, the heightening of the senses from being able to see and hear everyone, and the awareness of how closer proximity encourages everyone, and not just a few, to participate. I tell them that this is the standard arrangement of the class. They will be sitting in a circle for the rest of the semester with cell phones off and laptops stored away. They are being asked to Be where they Are.

Practicing Bridge Building

We talk about the importance of "inclusion" and the many ways to create connection and relatedness to one another by creating opportunities that enhance interaction. This is, of course, an important lesson learned not by "talking about" the value of relatedness but by participating *in relation.* From this vantage, I emphasize the point of **"Getting Comfortable with the Uncomfortable."** By virtue of this arrangement, those in the circle have no other choice but to engage with their classmates in ways that sitting in rows does not promote. This physical proximity forces us to *see* and *relate* to one another. The potential to liberate ourselves from the state of submersion and humanizing one another in the process is evident as the semester progresses.

In the circle, we cannot avert our eyes, turn away, and close ourselves off without it being extraordinarily apparent. My students have committed to a course of training to prepare for professions that require high engagement and *being* across from people who come from all walks of life and with whom they may have little or no experience interacting. Our region is one of the most diverse in the United States, and many of my students will be employed in agencies, schools, universities and government positions in which they will be serving people whose histories, culture, and backgrounds will be dissimilar from their own. In their profession, "Getting Comfortable with the Uncomfortable" will take on a level of relevance beyond the scope of their known realities.

For this reason, I make it my duty to provide a learning environment in which my students can practice reaching across the racial reality gap and forge meaningful interaction and, in some cases, relationships with the "other." While I have no control over their personal lives, my intention is that during the course of the semester, their habituated thoughts will be informed by meaningful and rich interactions with their own classmates. I tell them that if I have not made them uncomfortable at any point in the semester and expanded their comfort zone, then I haven't done my job.

In the following weeks, it is not uncommon to observe the occasional student who pulls a chair apart from the circle and sits at a far reach of a classroom corner. Or, there is, at times, another student who rather than engage with classmates in vigorous discussions about the topic at hand, chooses, instead, to hide behind the screen of a laptop. I have had to address this through statements in my syllabi to discourage students from being more engrossed and engaged with their computer (or cell phone) than using the moment to engage with and build relationships with their classmates who are in their presence. Then, there will be the individual who, despite seeing a late-arriving student standing at the door, will still use the seat next to her to hold her personal items;unresponsive to the needs of others.

Developing and heightening my students' relational capacity and fostering their intrinsic motivation to engage in their learning has its challenges. They have learned to succeed in a society where individualism, banking method teaching, and extrinsic motivation for learning is strongly rooted. Years of conditioning and subjection to prescriptive education underlies the students' expectation that I "lecture at them" and that I give them "the right answer" rather than trusting themselves to engage with and discover the world around them. And, while some may exhibit high aptitude for being "critical" of the world, the conditioning has disabled their capacity to be critical thinkers.

Nonetheless, small steps toward collective inclusivity are evident as the semester progresses and are well worth the effort to provide the students with the environment that fosters critical thinking skills, discovery of the world, and greater interaction with the diverse representation of classmates in the circle. The few students most discomfited by the problem-posing method may continue to resist. They crave what they are familiar with, the comfort of the banking method system, but I, in turn, resist the urge to be merely a "depositor" of information. The critical evaluations by these students are worth it; my colleagues and I recognize that liberation does not happen overnight, so the circle remains as my own act of resistance to the status quo.

If students arrive to the class before my teaching assistant(s) and I do, we sometimes find them sitting silently, miles apart from one another. We ask if they can help us put together the circle. With our prompting, some help cheerfully, others less so. On occasion, students set up the room before every one else arrives. They "get it" and are invested in the ideal of creating a community from the many. These individuals already seem to *know* how to *be* in relation and have now been given permission to do so in a public sphere. They seem to be at home with the classroom arrangement. The habituated thoughts that are evident in their behavior will carry to their work in the near future.

In the beginning of the semester, it is not unusual to see students sit with and interact more with students who look like themselves. I see them arrive together and leave together. I generally have assignments that require group work. This is intentional, and I tell them so. It is another effort to "Get Comfortable with the Uncomfortable." From the process of this assignment, it is my intention to replace the habituated thought of "difference is negative" with "difference adds value." At times, this intention is lost on a few who express their discontentment with the process of this assignment and write on my end of semester evaluations, "I would have preferred to have done the project on my own. It would have been easier." I agree with their statement. There are many times that working alone can be "easier," but working alone does not lend itself to transformative experiences. It doesn't provide the experience of exposure to, appreciation of, and integration of diverse perspectives. The circle remains.

Oneness From "Ones"

I don't fault my students. They are by-products of a culture that espouses individualism, separateness, and "otherness." Hundreds of years of brutal laws and normalized violence birthed a culture rooted in the anti-dialogical force of "Divide and Rule" doctrine (Freire, 1998). We have inherited the collective aftermath and, subsequently, live in what is termed ***de facto segregation***. This is not a segregation enforced by law. It is separateness evidenced in segregated school enrollment or housing patterns where economic challenges suppress upward mobility. These patterns of separateness have been so persistent and lasting that they appear *normal* and are accepted as fixed reality.

In our day-to-day interactions, the forces that dictate and shape our behaviors can be so discrete that we are not even aware of their influence. Paxton's study revealed the implications of **"White Supremacy Consciousness"** in the way we engage with one another (or not). Generally, people of color have had to adapt through assimilation or acculturation to Euro-American culture, while Euro-Americans are conditioned to view people of color as the "other." The tragic consequence is that this isolates white people, not just from people of color but also from one another. A group member participating in Paxton's inquiry on "Whiteness" states:

We aren't connected to anything: that is what it is to be White. When we come here we get connected. That's why it starts to get healthy when we're together, that connection (Kyle, December 8, 1999, Tape Sessions).

Let's explore this further.

My students are not bad people. In fact, they are generally good-hearted people. They have sacrificed time, money, and relationships with friends and family to earn higher degrees so they can "make a difference" in the lives of others. Some students readily or eventually embrace and integrate the concept of "in relation" as a core value (if they hadn't already). These individuals can be observed actively engaging with others and reaching across the racial and cultural divide. They offer their perspective and views in the circle and actually look at and see others (and not just at me or my teaching assistant(s)). During our breaks, they are observed talking with other students who they had not interacted with before then. Their transformation is evident. They see the humanity in others who they may have previously "objectified" in their habituated thoughts. In their transformation, they, too, become humanized. These students evolve over the semester and come to not just acknowledge "difference" but to *value* it.

For a few, the lesson is lost. It is not that they are openly hostile to "others." Instead, their behaviors demonstrate passive avoidance or intellectualized participation, as though their time in the class is a visit to a foreign country and they are tourists. They come to class and do what the professor expects to get a good grade, but they internally struggle with habituated thoughts that undermine the possibility for long-term change in their behaviors. Again, I don't fault these individuals. Centuries of conditioning have created this situation, and I cannot expect to change this positionality in one semester. My fear lies in the lost potential of the students who, because of their incredible intellectual capacity, will find positions of power where they could strategically enact change that would positively impact the lives of many. Yet, if these same students go through the motions to "earn the grade," or "get the degree" but fail to be moved at a heartfelt level to the inequities that exist in their reality, then they will only perpetuate the inequities. Their minds may be able to gain them highly desirable posts, but unchanged and uncompassionate hearts render blindness to the needs of others. Paxton's group inquiry speaks to the nature of this disconnection in a theme that emanated from the examination of "White Identity" that they called "Redefining Self through Connection." One group member revealed the patterns of behavior that maintain "separateness."

> I've been noticing how often White people put things in-between themselves and the person they are talking to so that they never really have to connect, to allow themselves to become ATTACHED and DEPENDENT. We are such loners here in this White-normed system. It makes me so sad, because I know that I do it too (Baela, March 26, 2000, Online Posting).

Two terms provide an explain to the phenomenon of how "good people" can be aversive to "difference," even when they know that by "getting comfortable with the uncomfortable" that they will be more effective in their chosen field. The first term, **Cultural Encapsulation,** encompasses an ***ethnocentric worldview***. In other words, one only sees the world through one's eyes and believes that this is the *only* way to be in the world. If a person has not been immersed in diverse communities or raised to appreciate differences in worldviews, then this individual may develop not just a monocultural view of the world but more detrimentally, a sense of arrogance that one's view is the *only* way to perceive the world. This does not lend itself to developing or desiring relationships with others on equal terms.

The second term, **Social Distance** (Burgess and Park, 1921), refers to the tendency of individuals to approach or withdraw from a particular racial group. The unwritten rules that govern thought define who the "us" and the "them" are. Subsequently, when "us" are now placed in a classroom setting with "them," and, furthermore, obligated to comply with the egalitarian structure of the circle, it feels strange and uncomfortable. Segregated communities, schools, places of worship, and family systems do not encourage escape from the walls of Cultural Encapsulation. Though parents may impart to their children the lessons of "The Golden Rule" and model humanism in their own lives, we can see from the life of Colonel Shaw that there are sufficient messages from outside the home that teach otherwise.

The good news is that, just like the Colonel and Hunt, the forces of Cultural Encapsulation and Normative Social Distance can be mitigated. There is the possibility for change. As we shall see from the humanists' lives, the prevalent theme of "Meaningful Relationships with People across the racial divide" provides an inoculation against racism. In their *relationships*, we see models of hope of what *could be normal* if we are availed the opportunity to *change* the way we think about one another which may very well lead to changes in the way we treat one another as well.

The Circle of Relationship

Imagine a household in which people are seated around the dining table sharing a meal. Each individual at the table is formally introduced, by the host, to arriving guests with equal accord. The host, a white man, serves everyone at the table, who all are treated with respect not commonly found outside this community. The people at the table are black and white. This scene was common in the community of North Elba, a region in the Adirondacks where free blacks and fugitive slaves found sanctuary. Brown attempted to create a community that would maintain itself on farming. In doing so, he lived among people who would not be allowed to live otherwise, peacefully or freely, close to larger cities.

John Brown lived comfortably *in relation* to people who were despised by others. For Brown, this proximity was not different from his childhood when he lived *in relation* with Native Americans. In North Elba, he worked, side by side, with black men. They socialized and entered one another's homes. Often, his children would accompany him on visits with his neighbors. There was nothing unusual to John Brown about this practice. What he perceived as normal patterns of behavior were deeply rooted in his belief that all people deserved equal and humane treatment (Reynolds, 2005).

Brown was raised by a father who denounced racism and modeled living *in relation* with humanity; all of humanity, not just those who looked most like him. Brown did not consider himself better than people whose skin color was darker than his own but he knew that his position in society accorded him the privilege to advocate for them. Brown used his privilege to coalesce people across the racial divide to support his efforts. Similarly, Mary Ellen Pleasant utilized the privilege accorded by her wealth to support the same cause. They shared the same circle.

On a recent walking ghost tour of San Francisco that I took with my son, Michael, the tour guide spoke about Mary Ellen Pleasant, one of the wealthiest women in San Francisco during the 1800's. The guide mentioned that at the time Brown was captured at Harpers Ferry that he had, in his possession, a bank deposit receipt with the initials M.E.P. I was intrigued by this connection between Mary Ellen Pleasant, a woman of African American descent, who was living in San Francisco at the time that John Brown was leading an insurrection against the establishment of slavery. I did further research and uncovered that Pleasant was born in segregated Philadelphia. There is speculation that her mother had been formerly enslaved in Louisiana and her father may have been white, or Cherokee, or Kanaka. She married a wealthy man, James Henry Smith, who was also of African descent and who upon dying left her a fortune which she, in turn, invested and amassed greater wealth. It is what Pleasant did with her wealth that connects her to Brown. She and her husband had been actively involved in efforts to abolish slavery while they supported the Underground Railroad.

> This shrewd businesswoman could have been one of the wealthiest people in California if she had been interested in making money; for her, though, money was but a means to an end. She gave it away almost as soon as she got it, for the most part using it to bring freedmen and fugitive slaves to California and to help them get on their feet once there. Her philanthropy was extensive, and she exercised considerable political clout as well. It was probably due to Mary Ellen Pleasant's support that a California law forbidding black testimony in a court of law was repealed. (Turner, 1999, p. 15).

Sarah Shaw provides a different model of being *in relation* that converts to the will of advocacy. Like Pleasant, she and her husband went to great lengths to use their wealth for greater good. She ensured that while exposing her children to the world through travel and education that they did not adopt capitalistic and materially oriented values. In attending functions at Brook Farm, a communal experiment created close to their home, she and her husband were observed interacting with residents of the commune who did not have the same financial means and who were not white. While we can recall Angelina's calling out members of the Anti-Slavery Society at a meeting in Philadelphia for not providing a chair for a black woman who had to, then, stand for the duration of the meeting, the Shaws would sit on the floor rather than expect "differential" treatment because of their white skin and class standing (Foote, 2003).

As the social forces of this nation have fomented the racial divide, it has taken intentional defiance over the generations to hold hope for a circle of connection in which humanity, in all its diverse beauty, is valued. Imagine the scene in the early 1800 encountered by the Grimké Sisters in their relentless attempts to find a place of worship in which skin color had no bearing.

Upon her becoming a member of the "Friends' meeting" in Philadelphia, what was her amazement to find that the Religious Society of Friends, whose moral courage in rebuke of slavery had put to shame all other churches,- that they had installed the "negro pew" as a permanent fixture in their house of worship! Thenceforward the two sisters made that "negro pew" their permanent seat, thus recording their public protest against that unchristian abomination. This was ever after their invariable rule. Wherever, in city or country, they entered a church having a negro seat (then they all had), they found their way to it, and shared with the occupants that spurning thus meted out to them (Weld, 1880, p. 41).

The Grimké Sisters choose to be within circles that reflected the value of acceptance and love, but as we know, living from the heart has many challenges.

Sarah's transformation moved her abolitionism from an intellectualized motivation to a force from her heart. Similar to Helen Hunt Jackson's heart awakening experience in attending a lecture by Chief Standing Bear, Sarah's awakening can be traced to the arrest of George Latimer, a man who was captured in Massachusetts after attempting to escape slavery. Even though Massachusetts was a "free state," the courts denied him a jury. Witness to this injustice, Sarah stuck to her principles of love for all people. She was incensed by the inaction of those who professed "Christian principles" but who did not extend their principles to people who did not look like they did.

Sarah was in charge of the home domain, more so than her husband, and the care of five children. This allowed her to use her home as sanctuary, but this did not stop prejudices, prevalent in the North, from crossing over Sarah's doorstep. During one of her stays in Boston, she and her husband assisted a young black man by opening their home to him while he found work. With the Shaws' inherited wealth, they employed at the time five white servants. Two of these servants were so upset with having a black man in the home that they threatened to resign (Foote, 2003). While the situation was eventually resolved, this outward expression of prejudice in her home demonstrates two important points: 1) Sarah's comfort with proximity to people who were "different" from her, which was founded on her perception of true equality of all people, and 2) Her willingness to side with and defend people of color against the irrational "habituated thoughts" of people from her own race. She defied racial cohesion. Once Sarah witnessed the mistreatment of people for ill-founded reasons, she expanded her sphere of influence by refusing to contribute funds to state-sponsored events as her way of protesting Massachusetts' support of the Fugitive Slave Act.

This theme of being "in relation" to people across the racial divide is constant with humanists in this manuscript. We know that the Grimké sisters flouted laws that maintained oppression, spoke out against their family members, and then spoke and wrote publicly about the cause. The nature of their relations with "others" became even more personalized with a revelation made by Angelina when she was already in her sixties and Sarah in her seventies. She read a notice in the *Anti-Slavery Standard* about a meeting at Lincoln University, Pennsylvania. The notice mentioned a student at this campus, an institution for black men, who had spoken at the meeting. His first name was Archibald. His last name was Grimké. This piqued Angelina's curiosity, so she wrote to this young man and asked the origins of his surname. Archibald responded, and this is when Angelina learned that she had three nephews fathered by one of her brothers, Henry.

The mother of these three young men was Nancy Weston, a woman held in bondage by Henry and who was the nursemaid for Henry's three children by his white wife.

The newly discovered nephew divulged the horrendous experiences that he and his two brothers were subjected to as the property of Angelina and Sarah's older brother, Henry, the man who was also their biological father. When Henry's wife passed away, he took in Nancy Weston, a woman he owned and the nurse to his three children. Ms. Weston had three children by Henry; Archibald, Francis and John. Upon Henry's death, he had left instructions with his son, Montague, to take in Nancy and her three sons as members of the family. This did not happen. Instead, Montague took all three brothers, his half brothers, as his servants. When Nancy protested, she was jailed. With emancipation came liberation for the three brothers. Two of the three sons made their way to institutions of higher learning. The youngest choose to live and work in Florida.

Angelina and Sarah, upon learning of the existence of these three nephews, did not abandon them or deny that they existed. Instead, they embraced their newfound relatives, and contributed to their tuition at Lincoln University, Princeton Theological Seminary, and Harvard Law School. Angelina attended Archibald's graduation from Lincoln University and provided constant guidance in her nephews' development. These young men were guests at their home. This fostering of relationship and ongoing mentorship was noted by Archibald and his brother, Francis, who carried on the work of their famous aunts (Lerner, 1998).

The modeling of Brown and the Grimké sisters demonstrate what life can look like when interracial social distance is nonexistent. Though laws existed that attempted to maintain separation and instill superiority of one group over the other, Brown and the Grimké sisters did not ascribe to the mores of their culture. They resisted racial cohesion. Rather, they sought to create communities of relationship with the very people who they were expected to dominate. Evident in their "habituated behaviors" was the benefit of "habituated thoughts" formed from being in relationship with people of color, as though these relationships inoculated them from the racism of their era.

Sarah Shaw, in her orientation and "habituated thoughts," always held a disdain for slavery and sought circles of relationship in which she engaged with people who did not have the privileges accorded to a woman of her status. She resisted cultural encapsulation. Her son, on the other hand, is transformed by being "in relation." The following excerpts from letters written by the Colonel speak to the transformative process. They can be read in their entirety in Duncan's (1999) *Blue Eyed Child of Fortune* as they provide testament to how the fostering of cross-racial relationship, and, in the Colonel's case, his relationship with the men of the 54th Regiment, transformed the Colonel's views and perceptions. Note the Colonel's language as time goes on and he has had sustained contact with the men of his regiment.

In a letter to his mother, Sarah, dated February 20, 1863, the Colonel made references to men of color who were assisting in the recruitment of black troops to serve in Union regiments. He writes, "Some of the influential coloured men I have met please me very much. They are really so gentlemanlike and dignified" (p. 290). This reveals his initial estimation of the capacity of black men being equal, but not quite equal because he states that they were "gentlemanlike" (like a gentleman). This is the intellectualized reaction of a tourist having a first encounter with a culture or a people unlike himself, so his words reflect comparisons to what he knows from a narrow and encapsulated worldview.

Moving forward to March 14, 1863, also in a letter to his mother, Shaw comments on the character and habits of recruits, "The company from New Bedford are a very fine body of men, and out of forty, only two cannot read and write. Their barracks are in better order, and more cleanly, than the quarters of any volunteer regiment I have seen in this country" (p. 308). He compares his men to other regiments because he has had no other context in his life to experience life with people other than those from his own privileged background. He is beginning to expand his frame of reference.

Soon after, the "social experiment" in which the Colonel participates receives favorable reviews by Union officers inspecting his troops. He writes to his mother on March 17, 1863, "... we had several officers ... take a look at the men; they all went away very much pleased. Some were very skeptical about it before, but say, now, that they shall have no more doubts of negroes making good soldiers" (p. 309). Shaw's "habituated thoughts" begin to evolve with daily contact that included military drills, marches at all hours of day and night, and living in open camp life. The ongoing contact and relationships formed from this contact mitigated the social distance that had previously contributed to the development of Shaw's prejudices.

By March 25, 1863, he again writes to his mother with additional observations, "Everything goes on prosperously. The intelligence of the men is a great surprise to me. They learn all the details of guard duty and Camp service more readily than the Irish I have had under my command" (p. 313). Two elements of this last statement should be addressed. First, Shaw's emergence from his state of submersion in a culturally encapsulated world reveals *his* awareness of his men's intellectual abilities. The experience of **cultural immersion** quickly challenged and shifted his habituated thoughts.

The second matter relates to the element of "**horizontal violence.**" Recall that the vast majority of European immigrants sought sanctuary in the United States for a range of reasons. The Civil War took place right after the decimating Irish Potato Famine. The United States was one major destination for the Irish who were escaping famine and poverty. In some major Eastern cities, this population became the underclass and competed with freed blacks for limited industrial jobs in the North. Additionally, resentment of being conscripted to serve as Union soldiers in a war in which they had no investment in either Southern or Northern interests further fueled Irish resentment toward blacks. The presence of the Irish in a nation struggling with what to do with free and fugitive blacks added to the tension between these two groups. The Irish men were not invested in this war and their disinterest, as reflected in the Colonel's statement, was observable.

In a letter to his father, Frances, on March 30, 1863, the Colonel cites the derogatory references to his men not as *his* words, but as theirs, "The mustering-officer '... is a Virginian, and has always thought it was a great joke to try to make soldiers of "niggers": but he told me to-day, that he had never mustered in so fine a set of men, though about twenty thousand had passed through his hands since September last. The skeptics need only come out here now, to be converted" (p. 316). Shaw's belief in his men is even firmer than before. In a short span of time, his habituated thoughts shifted. While taking on the post of colonelcy to oversee this social experiment of black men fighting as equals in a war, the Colonel was oblivious to the secondary outcome of the experiment in that he would become the greatest convert.

After his Regiment completed training they marched through the streets of Boston in a parade held in their honor on May 28, 1863. Shaw's reflection of this event in a letter to his wife, Annie, on June 1 attests to the fact that he now owned the cause of the men he was leading. Furthermore, he understood, from a personalized perspective, the cause that his parents had already championed. His behaviors were no longer governed by a compassionless intellectualized orientation, but were moved by a heart meaningfully connected to his men as he embraced their cause as his own.

> ... The more I think of the passage of the Fifty-fourth through Boston, the more wonderful it seems to me. Just remember our own doubts and fears, and other people's sneering and pitying remarks, when we began last winter, and then look at the perfect triumph of last Thursday. We have gone quietly along, forming the regiment, and at last left Boston amidst a greater enthusiasm than has been seen since the first three-months troops left for the war. Every one I saw, from the Governor's staff (who have always given us rather the cold shoulder) down, had nothing but words of praise for us. Truly, I ought to be thankful for all my happiness, and my success in life so far; and if the raising of coloured troops prove such a benefit to the country, and to the blacks as many people think it will, I shall thank God a thousand times that I was led to take my share in it (p. 335).

Persistent contact and being *in relation* with the men of the 54th served as an inoculation against the prejudices of others. While Shaw had espoused prejudice, immersion quickly eliminated them. By the time he and his men participated in extending Union capture of Southern territory, he saw, first hand, the conditions of recently liberated slaves. He did not fault them for their conditions, but directly attributed the broken families, lack of literacy and other symptoms of oppression to those who enacted the violence that maintained the institution of slavery. His letter of June 26, again written to his wife, reveals his understanding of racism and his newfound humanistic orientation:

> The only persons responsible for the depravity of the Negroes are their scoundrelly owners, who are, nevertheless, not ashamed to talk of the Christianizing influence of slavery. Whatever the condition of the slaves may be, it does not degrade them, as a bad life does most people, for their faces are generally good (pp. 359–360).

Slave owners justified human bondage by drawing from the premise of Manipulation; their slaves were better in bondage because they were exposed to Christianity. This contrived rationalization did not permeate the Colonel's emerging worldview. He understood that Christianity was being misused as a veil for an insidious purpose. Those espousing this position had adopted Cognitive Dissonance to normalize their behavior and then employed Manipulation to justify their reality. The Colonel knew better. In their self deceit, they were practicing racism rooted in green hearts.

Being in relationship with others expands our worldview. Reading a book about others or watching them from afar is a poor substitute for direct experience. Helen Hunt Jackson understood this when she was moved to action. After meeting Chief Standing Bear she didn't just study the chronicles of injustices committed against Native Americans; she headed west and spoke with members of various tribes. Many were suspicious of her, besides, how many had seen a white woman demonstrate interest and care in the plight of their tribe? This did not daunt Hunt who, in a very public sphere, engaged Native Americans and heard, directly from them, the abuses to which they were subjected. This fueled her righteous anger and drove her passion to research, first hand, the conditions of the people for whom she was advocating.

Garrison's mother relished the intimacy of relationship with people of color. Her communication of gratitude for the kindness with which she was treated during her convalescence must have fostered Garrison's gratitude, since he was living hundreds of miles away serving an apprenticeship. She wrote to him:

> I am well taken care of, for both Black and White are all attention to me, and I have every thing done that is necessary. The ladies are all kind to me, and I have a Coloured woman that waits on me, that is so kind no one can tell how kind she is, and although a Slave to Man, yet a free born soul, by the grace of God. Her name is Henny, and should I never see you again, and you should ever come where she is, remember her for your poor mother's sake (Garrison, 1885, p. 38).

The message imparted to Garrison by his mother was one of kindness and acceptance of all people, regardless of the value accorded them by others due to some arbitrary negative association of their *differences*. The appreciation that the ailing Mrs. Garrison had for Henny prompted her to request of her son that he consider reciprocity of good will for the woman that Mrs. Garrison held in such positive regard. The seeds of gratitude for relationships that transcend racial borders come to bear fruit when Frederick Douglass, only six months into his gained freedom, was handed a copy of Garrison's anti-slavery newspaper, *The Liberator*. Douglass valued the paper so much that he placed it next to his Bible.

The words in the paper provided an introduction for Douglass to Garrison because, once he read *The Liberator*, he stated:

> *The Liberator* was a paper after my own heart. It detested slavery—exposed hypocrisy and wickedness in high places—made no truce with the traffickers in the bodies and souls of men; it preached human brotherhood, denounced oppression, and, with all the solemnity of God's word, demanded the complete emancipation of my race. I not only liked—I *loved* this paper, and its editor. He seemed a match for all the opponents of emancipation, whether they spoke in the name of the law, or the gospel. His words were few, full of holy fire, and straight to the point. Learning to love him, through his paper, I was prepared to be pleased with his presence. Something of a hero worshiper, by nature, here was one, on first sight, to incite my love and reverence (Douglass, p. 362).

It was three years after escaping slavery that Douglass met Garrison at an Anti-Slavery gathering in Nantucket where Douglass was urged to provide a firsthand account of his experiences of being held in bondage. His rousing oratory skills eventually led Douglass to become a highly sought-after speaker, but on this occasion, he was invited by Garrison to join the anti-slavery movement as an agent. From this point, Douglass went on to become, as he claimed, Garrison's "faithful disciple." The two, joined by the cause of abolitionism, went on to travel and present at a wide range of venues throughout the Northern states of the United States. Garrison witnessed the verbal and physical assaults on his friend, Douglass, as he saw prejudice enacted even in the "free" states. Garrison called this behavior "American democratic Christian colorphobia" (Garrison, v. 3, p. 200).

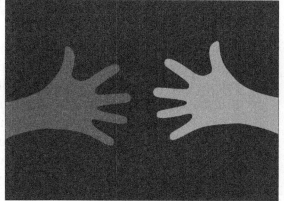

The Grimké sisters had the privilege to experience a personalized circle of intimacy. This circle strengthened human bonds that humanized them and further provided the inoculation from the racism of their culture and community. The proverbial circle when created, whether in the personal or public sphere, transcends prejudice and establishes communities like that of John Brown's North Elba.

Modern Humanists in Relationship

Elizabeth Johnson relates the value of having had the same African American teacher for two straight years during her elementary school years. She recalls being read to by her and learning black history before there was a Black History Month. This teacher was centrist in teaching history to her students. The love that Johnson developed for her teacher helped her come to her own conclusions when her teacher was challenged by parents for teaching black history to a class of white children.

Johnson came to not only accept and side with her teacher, but, in reflection of what had transpired during her childhood, she came to understand the insidiousness of racism. The relationship with her teacher, a relationship that was in the public sphere, served as the protective factor that shaped Johnson's humanist orientation.

Tessler's parents demonstrated the value of diversity. Their friends and family reflected a rich circle that not only normalized but valued difference. The value was so strong that when Tessler's high school principal called her parents to notify them that he had heard that Tessler was attending the senior prom with a black student, her mother responded, "Oh no, it's Joe! We love him and it's fine." Tessler's family had already turned away a white man who wanted their signature on a petition to maintain social distance and prohibit blacks from moving into the neighborhood. The principal could not, however, enforce cultural encapsulation on a family that already espoused and valued relationship with "others" in their circle. This family was already inoculated by the strength of meaningful relationships with people of color.

Being in and maintaining relationships across the racial divide can often bring challenges even from one's own family in which values may differ from one generation to the next or even from one region to another. Miah McNeal, a student in one of my courses, shared the following experience that demonstrates the value of bonds that transcend a world and history imbedded in divisiveness. Having known Ms. McNeal to be a compassionate and caring person I was saddened that she had to experience this but the story presents possibilities for an evolved reality in our future,

> As an African American young woman there are many challenges to face. A lot of opportunities I've had to work super hard for because of the color of my skin. We assume that racial profiling is no longer alive, however, there are still a lot of people in this world that are stuck in the past events of life.
>
> When I look at people I don't see a difference. Our determination and uniqueness is what makes each of us who we are and I'm so openly grateful that this is so. I totally love that each individual is different and diverse in their own way which allows us to learn new things from each other every day. Those differences are what makes us who we are as people and allows us the chance to connect with others and grow bonds and start everlasting friendships.

At this point we clearly see that McNeal values "difference" and that she sees the uniqueness of people, beyond skin color. It is evident that when she sees others that she perceives them from a place of heart when she states, "I don't see a difference." Her experience, however, conveys a racialized existence that she understands, cognitively, and she acknowledges that others perceive the world from this existence. She goes on to share the added value of her own reality,

> Growing up I had many friends from all different nationalities and racial backgrounds that I had fun with and learned a lot from. One of my best friends, Sandra (pseudonym), and I were friends from elementary school to high school. We used to see each other at school every day and talked on the phone for hours as if we weren't ever going to see each other again but that's what fourteen year olds do. On Christmas Eve I was invited over for a Christmas/Welcoming dinner when her Grandmother came into town from Idaho to Crockett. I couldn't wait to meet Grandma. I had heard lots of nice things about her and even talked to her a few times over the phone. I was so excited. Sandra and I had coordinated our outfits and how we would wear our hair. We were super excited that we were going to be spending a couple of hours together on Christmas Eve.

McNeal relates that she had met the rest of Sandra's family prior to this special event. Her impression of the aunts and uncles were that they were all "funny and cool." The interactions she had had with Sandra's Grandma, up until this point had all been by phone. Grandma knew that McNeal and Sandra were best friends and, she too, expressed excitement about the opportunity to finally meet in person and that when they did that she would show her how to make her famous triple chocolate raspberry cake and then lick the spoons!

McNeal goes on to convey the events leading to this face to face encounter,

> My mom agreed to let me go. She was funny about me visiting other people's houses but she knew that Sandra and I were inseparable. She had met Sandra's mom so she was sure I was in good hands. I made sure I was there on time because I didn't want to miss anything so I kissed my mom goodbye and walked to the door. Sandra greeted me. We hugged each other and we had the biggest smiles. She took my

coat and said, "Let's go meet Grandma!" I was excited and said, "Let's Go!" Sandra yelled, "Grandma, someone's here to meet you!" to which Grandma responded, "I wonder who?" I walked into the living room, smiling with open arms ready to give Grandma the biggest hug ever and as soon as I saw Grandma's face, I stopped. Apparently, someone forgot to tell Grandma I was black because when I walked up to her and she saw my face her whole face turned red... She looked directly in my face and said, "I think you have the wrong house little girl." I said, "No, Grandma, it's Miah, Sandra's friend. Remember, we talked on the phone?"

It is apparent that McNeal attempts to give Sandra's Grandmother the benefit of the doubt. Having just encountered an adverse verbal and physical response, McNeal's interactions with Sandra's family and even with the Grandmother had been only positive to this point. She had no reason to believe anything but the best from the rest of Sandra's family. She thought that perhaps because Grandma was a bit older that she had forgotten about their previous interactions. What follows, however, confirmed the worst.

She looked directly at me and said, "You're black, and blacks and whites don't mix. You need to go home and never come to this house again. You hear me?" and she demanded them to make me leave or she was leaving and never dealing with them again. I decided to be the bigger person, especially since it was a family event. I didn't mean to ruin it for everyone and I truly didn't even understand what just happened, so I decided to leave and allow her to have her moment.

With the benefit of objectivity, we can acknowledge that it was not McNeal who ruined the event. Yet, the micro-aggression had transpired and now the strength of the relationship between McNeal and Sandra was tested. Sandra and her family stepped up to the challenge and worked to maintain the circle of evolved relationships despite the incident that occurred.

Sandra and I sat and cried together on her front porch for forty-five minutes until my mom came. We hugged and cried because we didn't understand why she couldn't get over me being black. It was just a color of skin. Sandra and I got along so well and color didn't matter to us at all but even being fourteen we understood that some people were still stuck in the past. Her family sat me down and apologized for Grandma's behavior. I told them I understood everyone's thinking is different, however, it hurt my feelings because I was truly ecstatic to meet her and help make cake. Sandra's mom hugged me and said, "Sweetie, I'm so sorry for my mother's ignorant ways and she's wrong. You're very welcome to stay. You are a guest and a part of this family. In no way do we want you to feel uncomfortable. You are welcome anytime and I will speak with my mother about her rude, unreasonable and gross behavior."

Sandra's mother did not attempt to make excuses nor diminish the incident. Instead, she called "it" what it was; rude, unreasonable and gross. While Sandra's family did not relent to Grandma's wishes that they expel McNeal from the gathering it was McNeal who decided it best to leave. In reflection, McNeal stated that their offer to have her stay as "sweet." The bond that McNeal and Sandra had was not broken by Grandma and Sandra's mother, in her open refutation of the behavior, ensured that McNeal felt safe and welcomed at their home. McNeal goes on to state that the friendship did not change as a result and that their visits with one another became more frequent, though McNeal never visited Sandra's home when Grandma was visiting. The relationship survived despite the attempt to divide and lasted until Sandra moved out of state in the eleventh grade.

In reflection of the incident, McNeal recalls,

> The feelings that came over me experiencing this situation was crazy, unthinkable, gut wrenching and awful. I never wanted to feel that way ever again. It was sad that someone so old could be so set in their ways that they would hurt the feelings of a fourteen year old child and not even care. If I had been a kid that didn't have love, family or self-respect and cared about other's perceptions of me this event could have killed my confidence, courage, as well as friendship but I became more powerful by not letting her negative ways affect me and pushing through to continue my friendship with my BFF (Best Friend Forever), Sandra.... Over the years we lost contact, but the memories of growing up together will never fade. People don't realize the affect we have on children's lives. Just a comment can deter a child's thoughts and change the way the perceive themselves.

The value of bridge building as demonstrated by Sandra's family as well as the strong sense of self that McNeal's family had instilled in her helped her overcome the negativity inflicted by Sandra's grandmother. McNeal gives us one last word of warning as to the potential damage that can occur by those attempting to undermine the strength of the circle,

> Be careful of the stigma we give children and know that the things you speak can make or break a child's life. Positive communication is far more valuable than a negative word (McNeal, Journal Entry, Fall of 2012).

Engagement with others to build a circle of relationship requires positive communication which can also serve as a buffer against the habituated thoughts grounded in negative worldviews. In McNeal's case, the response by Sandra's mother to the grandmother's negativity ensured that McNeal would not develop a projected disdain for people who were unlike her. She retained a broad worldview and appreciation for people who are different from her.

The expanded worldview that Tessler and Johnson benefited from did not end within them. Rather, they, and the historical humanists, were compelled to act from their hearts in ways that dictated their behavior. While many people may state that they "care" for others, it is the activation of this care that touches the hearts of others and contributes to the relational evolvement of our families, cultures, and society. We will further explore what transpires when humanists activate their care, liberate the hearts of others, and contribute to the evolution of this racialized nation's origins.

QUESTIONS FOR DISCUSSION OR SELF REFLECTION

SELF-AWARENESS

1. As you examine you own community of origin, were there any groups of people with whom you had less experience as a result of cultural encapsulation? If so, what is the quality of your relationship with members of this group?

2. As you reflect on who you interact with throughout the day and week, are there days of the week in which you engage more with people who are dissimilar from you? What is the nature of this engagement and does it alter your perception in any way?

3. What are the messages you received from family, friends, community, society, about people who are different from you? How have these messages shaped your perceptions?

CLIENT WORLDVIEW

4. Are there marginalized groups of people in your community? What is their day to day realities? What sort of experiences and micro-aggressions are they subjected to?

COUNSELING RELATIONSHIP

5. In tracing the Colonel's transformation prior to and then during his experience of being in relationship with the men of the 54th Regiment, what stages in the Helm's White Racial Identity Development Model do you see him go through?

COUNSELING AND ADVOCACY INTERVENTIONS

6. The Grimké Sisters confronted their own family just as Sandra's family had to confront "Grandma" about her bigotry. What experiences have you had in attempting to forge a relationship with someone in spite of negative sentiments from those close to you? Discuss this experience with a classmate.

7. Role play these scenarios in front of the class so as to develop your capacity to engage in difficult interactions about "isms." Discuss what responses promote greater understanding and engagement.

NEW CONCEPTS AND VOCABULARY TO REVIEW

Making the Familiar Strange:

Being *in* Relation:

Getting Comfortable with the Uncomfortable:

de facto segregation:

White Supremacy Consciousness:

Cultural Encapsulation:

Ethnocentric Worldview:

Social Distance:

Cultural Immersion:

Horizontal Violence:

Activity

1. Go out for coffee or lunch with someone of a different background from your own.

2. When you enter a classroom (if you are a student) make conscious effort to sit next to someone different every time; engage with the people around you.

3. Put away your electronic devices in a classroom, restaurant, etc... without being told and engage the people around you.

4. When you get in an elevator, before pressing the button to shut the doors, look to see if anyone is coming and hold the doors for them.

5. Organize a pot luck with your neighbors.

6. Include/invite someone of a different background to one of your religious holiday events.

7. If you attend services for a religious faith, attend the services of your faith in a different community.

8. Research and uncover the work of Francis James Grimke (August 17, 1849–February 25, 1930) and Archibald Henry Grimke (November 4, 1851–October 11, 1937).

References

Burgess, E. W. and Park, R. E. (1928). *Introduction to the Science of Sociology*. Chicago, IL: University of Chicago Press.

Douglass, F. (1994). *Douglass autobiographies*. New York, NY: Penguin Books.

Foote, L. (2003). *Seeking the one great remedy*. Athens, OH. Ohio University Press.

Garrison, F. & Garrison, W. (1885). *William Lloyd Garrison, 1805–1879*, Volume 1. New York, NY: The Century Co.

Garrison, F. & Garrison, W. (1885). *William Lloyd Garrison, 1805–1879*, Volume III. New York, NY: The Century Co.

Lerner, G. (1998). *The Grimké sisters from South Carolina, pioneer for women's rights and abolition*. NY: Oxford University Press.

Paxton, D. (2002). *Facilitating transformation of white consciousness among Euro-American people: A case study of a cooperative inquiry*. Unpublished doctoral dissertation, California Institute of Integral Studies, San Francisco, CA.

Reynolds, D. (2005). *John Brown abolitionist*. New York, NY: Random House, Inc.

Turner, E. (1999). More than petticoats. Guilford, CT. The Globe Pequot Press.

Weld, T. (1880). In memory, Mrs. Angelina Emily Grimké Weld. Boston, MA. Press of George H. Ellis.

Actions Speak (and Heal) Louder Than Words

I am here concealing my whereabouts for good reasons (as I think) not however from any anxiety about my personal safety. I have been told that you are both a true man; & a true abolitionist "& I partly believe," the whole story. Last fall I undertook to raise from $500 to $1000 for secret service and succeeded in getting $500. I now want to get for the perfecting of **by far** the most important undertaking of my whole life. John Brown. Letter written to J. W. Higginson. Dated February 2, 1858.

This quote is an excerpt from a letter written by John Brown to Thomas Wentworth Higginson, a wealthy Northerner known for his progressive ideals, including women's rights and abolitionism. He was Helen Hunt Jackson's mentor and was also one of six wealthy men known collectively at that time as the "Secret Six." We have already discussed how Mary Ellen Pleasant was connected to Brown by contributing funds to his undertaking. The six men who, in addition to Higginson, funded Brown's "secret service" and "most important undertaking of his whole life" were George Luther Stearns, Gerrit Smith, Samuel Gridley Howe, Theodore Parker, and Franklin B. Sanborn (Reynolds, 2005). The words used by Brown in this letter were code words to conceal the steps in preparation for his all-out assault on the institution of slavery. In essence, he was about to proclaim war on slaveholders in the South.

I wasn't holding a reproduction of this letter. It was the actual letter penned by Brown himself. It was weathered, faded, and brittle, but still readable despite the 150 years since Brown wrote it. Accessing a rare document like this is not easy. First, you have to get to Boston, and then, make your way to the Rare Books and Manuscripts Department of the Boston Public Library. Once there, guidelines establish who can access these materials. A special pre-registration form should precede your visit.

The items maintained in this particular wing of the library are of historical significance. All are unique and irreplaceable. A person conducting research in this special branch must present proper credentials: valid picture identification, and possibly additional identification or a letter of introduction from a university or research library. In other words, accessing these materials requires credentials and a reason worth the threat of damage to these fragile and historic items.

A project deemed worthy must be worth the risk of exposure. The hope is that access to these materials might lead to publication; therefore, the privilege of access is not to be taken lightly and as I held and read this letter, I understood why. It represented our collective heritage yet is a story and perspective less known.

To get to the point of holding a letter penned by John Brown required prior clearance for access and then, upon arrival, checking in my personal items before entering the viewing room. Pens, food, or drink are absolutely not allowed. Once library personnel ensured that I had nothing but my laptop, loose paper, and pencils on my person, I was then allowed entry to the viewing room where it was explained to me that I could review only one item at a time. After I identified an item of interest I would complete a call slip so that a very helpful librarian could then retreat to the inner sanctions of the library and retrieve each item. Finding such items meant scanning thousands of index cards organized by category under the name of the individual I was researching. Finding useful information without getting sidetracked by related material was a challenge.

After hours of perusing a range of material, I located Brown's letter. I was almost in disbelief. I quickly recorded into my laptop the content of the letter as close to the original as possible. Even though I couldn't replicate the handwriting, I attempted to capture the misspellings, underscores, and bolded words. Knowing what I know now about John Brown, the substance of this letter takes on greater meaning for me because at the time I was holding the letter in my hand, I could only read, at face value, what was evident. With further study and learning about the polarized intragroup racial relationships of his era, I was able to read deeper meaning imbedded between the lines.

Careful inspection of this letter conveys two men, both white, who share a common set of principles that would categorize them as abolitionists. White people of this era had a wide range of beliefs and perspectives about slavery. There were those who profited from slavery and would die defending it. At the other extreme, there were those like Brown who were willing to die in an effort to end it. Many, like the anti-slavery newspaper editor, Elijah Lovejoy, already had died. Lovejoy was killed by a pro slavery mob that was attempting to destroy his printing press. In an exchange of gunfire as he and others were protecting it, he became a martyr but was buried in an unmarked grave to avoid its desecration (Weld, 1880). In between these two ends of the spectrum were a range of positions on the matter.

While a significant number of white people believed slavery was morally wrong, there were various reasons that a vast majority were hesitant to actively participate in abolitionist activities. Two main reasons for people's inaction were rooted in the fact that 1) Many people indirectly profited from the slave trade so stood to lose sources of income should the establishment of slavery end, and 2) Others feared the risk of danger if they became involved because they knew that those invested in maintaining slavery were not adverse to resorting to violence to ensure that their livelihood was not adversely impacted by abolitionist rhetoric or activities. These value orientations were constantly challenged by the most committed humanists, such as Garrison and the Grimké sisters, who had no tolerance for people who proclaimed to be Christians but who were selective in applying their principles when it negatively impacted their pocketbook. The Grimké Sisters (Weld, 1880) disassociated themselves from the religion of their family and searched for a place of worship where Christian principles were embraced and actively lived by everyone. In one interaction with her reverend in which he expressed support for Angelina's sentiments he indicated that "slavery was *in itself* a great evil, that the system was wrong, but to uproot it would deluge the city with evils vastly greater. All we could do is pray and wait." Angelina retorted with "pray and work" (p. 37). For Angelina, the suffering needed to end and prayer, alone, would not put an end to it.

Brown had no tolerance for cowards. His admiration for Harriet Tubman, a woman who had, herself, escaped slavery was an advisor for his mission and recruiter for his army. Brown's esteem for Tubman who had made thirteen missions into slave-holding states to safely escort seventy people to freedom, wrote of Tubman in masculine terms as a sign of respect, "He Hariet is the most of a man naturally; that I ever met with (Horwitz, 2011, p. 82). His letter to Higginson calls to question and measures Higginson's commitment to the cause. Furthermore, the letter reveals that Brown is taking critical steps leading to one of the most monumental turning points of U.S. history: his attempt to overtake the federal arsenal at Harpers Ferry, a trigger to the Civil War. Additionally, we can deduce from this letter that: 1) Brown needed financing to arm his small army of men; 2) He believed that the wealthy Northerner, Higginson, might not only have the capacity to provide needed funding but also be willing to *support* Brown's violent methods; 3) The nature of Brown's endeavor is such that he had to "conceal" his location; 4) The use of vague language in calling his purpose, "Secret Service," acknowledges the controversial and dangerous nature of his undertaking; 5) Brown declares this is the most important event of his life. And, to emphasize the central theme of this chapter is the evidence from this letter when 6) Brown calls Higginson to task when stating that he has been told by others that Higginson is a *"true" man* and a *"true abolitionist"* but holds judgment of whether Higginson is "true" by stating, "and I partly believe."

Harriet Tubman (1823 – 1913)
nurse, spy and scout

Brown, like Tubman, was a man of action. He detested people who claimed to be abolitionists, spoke eloquently in public, or ascribed to religious belief systems but did not *act* according to their principles. This is a theme in the lives of our humanists in that they not only "care" about others, but their care is evident in what they *do*. What we will now examine is the theme of active engagement in deconstructing racism and the evidence of two outcomes from the lived principles of humanists: 1) racial bridges are formed when humanists act, in alliance, across the racial divide, which subsequently leads to 2) humanists' actions minimize the prejudices that people of color hold for white people.

In the previous chapter, the value of meaningful cross-racial relationships was discussed. That discussion demonstrated how authentic relationship promotes transformation and evolvement. The degree of intimacy within the relationship ranged for each humanist and the point in the lives of humanists in which these relationships were formed differed. What separates these historical and modern-day humanists from passive humanists is their active engagement in social justice activity. Their actions place them on the front line, face to face, with varied forms of violence and opposition. They openly serve to mitigate the division left by this nation's racialized origins. They are observed working in concert across the racial divide to heal the deep racial wounds, to change cross-racial perceptions, and to provide a model of humanism that speaks through their actions, not just their words.

Also in the previous chapter, we addressed a further benefit of being *in relationship* in that authentic cross-racial relationships cement bonds that can create harmonious and pluralistic communities. This is evident in the power of relationship between McNeal and her friend Sandra that withstood the racist attack by Sandra's grandmother. Visible advocacy takes our relationships to another level. It stimulates the evolvement of our society by modeling a new pattern of behaviors rooted in principles of cross-racial equality and respect. Open advocacy promotes a value for differences and provides a more desirable alternative path than the trajectory of our racialized origins.

Let us explore this further. A society cloaked in a Culture of Silence (Freire, 1998) discourages questioning or challenging the status quo. Threats to the deeply rooted patterns of domination and oppression activate a range of responses from oppressors. The fear of oppressor's responses can immobilize even those with the best intentions because the range of responses can be as innocuous as a cautionary raised eyebrow or can be as virulent as cowardly acts of physical violence.

Activated Hearts

When humanists stand, eye to eye, with racists, they are confronting not only ignorance and greed but also the oppressor's fear. Memmi (2005) explains this phenomenon:

> Racists are people who are afraid; they feel fear because they attack, and they attack because they feel fear. They are afraid of being attacked, or they are afraid because they believe themselves attacked and attack to rid themselves of this fear. But why is there a fear of being attacked? Generally, it is because one wishes to obtain or defend something of value (p. 97).

Humanists who engage and confront the various manifestations of racism threaten something of value that can range from material wealth to a false sense of superiority. Those who seek to maintain what they have inherited or gained, though at the expense of others, will go to extreme measures to protect what they believe to be their right to hold on to it. This dimension of humanist realities is the price humanists pay to engage in the battlefield and will be addressed in the next chapter.

The humanists' lives we are examining teach us that actively challenging the status quo means coming face to face with the potential for all forms of violence. We also learn that their actions alter the ways people of color perceive white people. We have discussed ways in which racism manifests itself in the hearts of our white citizenry. We have also touched upon the possibilities for transformation when white people are in relationship with people of color. Let us examine, next, the perspective of race from people of color.

After years of being subjected to persistent and prevalent denigration and oppression, people of color would understandably hold a degree of *distrust* for white people. The **People of Color Racial Identity Development Model** (Helms, 1994) offers stages that people of color often have to work through in their own disassociation with dominant culture and distrust of white Americans. This distrust has been generationally transmitted after years of systemic and overt acts of violence. The testimony of Dr. Anna (Bunker) Kato speaks to the dictates of the principal of her school, who expected her to use her white skin as a symbol of dominance over the Navajo children who she was hired to teach. She refused to comply and, instead, proceeded to teach the children in what was considered an act of defiance. Others did comply, and the destruction enacted upon the hearts and souls of the children through violence against their culture leaves wounds measured by self-destructive patterns of suicide, alcoholism, drug abuse, and a larger host of maladies. The constant denigration is an ongoing barrage related to **negative social mirroring** (Suarez-Orozco, 2000), which is a result of Cultural Invasion (Freire, 1998) in which everything pertaining to people of color; language, skin color, culture, history, and family structure, is regarded and conveyed by the dominant culture as inferior.

Maintaining one's sense of personhood in the face of negating messages can be exhausting. Constant denigrations force people of color to consciously and unconsciously resist the attacks on their sense of self in order to maintain their identity. Some people of color are unable to resist the current of denigrations and choose to **assimilate**, losing the value of their uniqueness and the strength of their respective culture. Those who maintain strong affirmation of their uniqueness are able to derive the strength of their own culture and walk confidently in multiple cultures through a process known as **selective acculturation**. We can see the strength derived from being grounded in one's own culture and knowing historical truths as demonstrated by the testimony of Elizabeth Cruz who was grateful to know what really happened in the Mexico vs. United States War rather than believe what was taught in her history classes.

Regardless of the orientation or strategies employed by people of color to navigate a racialized existence, the historical distrust sits like a smog, and its density does not dissipate merely by being in relation with one white person. It is how white people respond (or don't) when acts of racism occur that clears the smog. This means that a white person who witnesses racism and remains silent unwittingly conforms to the dictates of his or her own racial group. People of color perceive the silence as condoning the act of violence and as an act of **racial group cohesion**. This also holds true for the perception of silence across all constructs of power and privilege; when men remain silent when sexist comments are made; when heterosexuals choose not to speak or act in the face of homophobia, etc. The silence is perceived as an act of allegiance with oppressive ideologies.

For example, we learned that Elizabeth Johnson had, early in life, formulated her thoughts and feelings about people of color from an established relationship with her elementary school teacher. Racist ideology, subsequently, would not permeate her perception of people who were supposed to be "othered," subjugated, and exploited. She knew, in her heart, that the precepts of racism were violent and inhumane and these were not values or intentions she espoused. Johnson could live her life with stated "care" for "all" people and live, harmoniously and peacefully, in a pluralistic community. However, if people of color in her community are attacked and she does not speak up on their behalf, then the authenticity of the harmony and peace of the community is threatened. Her silence would be perceived as complicit in the acts of violence. She would no longer be fully trusted and the potential for authentic cross racial relationship is compromised. She would be, instead, regarded with suspicion through the dense smog of historical distrust.

How, then, would people of color, who have been subjected to a racist society know that Elizabeth or any other white person's relationship is authentic unless their heart is revealed? This is not a topic of casual conversation in our society and is certainly not known upon first encounters. Our humanists model that action from humanist principles speak louder than words. This is how people of color come to know one's heart. On the flip side, when white people respond to injustices committed against people of color with silence, the silence conveys alliance with the perpetrators; it condones the injustice and it sustains the racial divide. The dissonance of a racialized society persists. In the minds of people of color, the silence becomes generalized so that it confirms that whites are "all in it together." This is why, if we are to create harmonious communities, concerted action must take place in order to transcend even the habituated thoughts that people of color have about white people.

John Brown was willing to lose his life as well as risk the lives of his sons and other men to activate his humanist principles. Prior to waging war on slavery, he was active in the Underground Railroad. He solicited funds from wealthy white and black allies to finance his mission, lived side by side with blacks as his equals in North Elba, and included white and black men in his hand-picked army. The decision to have blacks participate in their own liberation was, in part, Brown's vision to create a separate nation governed and led by free blacks, including women. In this regard, we cannot only consider Brown a humanist but he was also a **feminist**.

Not all humanists, however, resort to physical violence when they challenge racism. There is a variance of weaponry utilized when they step onto the battleground. Sarah Shaw and her husband, Francis, used their privilege as a weapon to alter the course of the Civil War by participating in the Underground Railroad, advocating with others for the cause to raise black troops in the goal of emancipation, and worked to create educational institutions to ensure that free blacks could gain equal status as citizens. They were considered two of the most prominent abolitionists from the beginning of the movement.

William Lloyd Garrison's weapon was his continuous printing of the longest running anti-slavery newspaper, *The Liberator*, from 1831 to 1865. His opposition to slavery led to the public burning, at a 4th of July picnic in 1854, of a copy of the Fugitive Slave Law as well as a copy of the U.S. Constitution which he called "a covenant with death, and an agreement with hell" (Horwitz, p. 40). This took place after federal forces forced the removal of Anthony Burns, a man who had escaped slavery, only to be captured and jailed in Boston. In an attempt to free Burns "the hot headed Higginson and other whites joined furious blacks in a planned assault on the courthouse that was repulsed by club-wielding deputies, one of whom was fatally shot by an unknown assailant during the melee. Garrison candidly condemned the violence; if he bore no arms, he said, it was not because he was false to his principles but true to them" (Mayer, 1998, p. 441).

Two major and opposing camps of abolitionists purported different views. One camp believed that freed blacks would never be equal to whites and supported a position of gradual emancipation in which freed blacks would be shipped back to Africa. This was the major thrust behind the Colonization Society. Grimké referred to their principles as "a suspicious kind of benevolence... which induces some southern professors to keep their brethren in bonds for their benefit" (Grimké, p. 36). As we know, Grimké was in relationship with people in bondage so the idea of sending away people that she loved as a solution was out of the question. She attributed the Colonization Society's position to prejudice. She called it what it was. Garrison and the Grimké's beliefs were different from many their contemporaries and so they were, subsequently, considered radical.

They believed that blacks could be equal to the nation's white citizens if provided with the means to do so. Garrison's newspaper articles were blamed for inciting slave revolts, including the Nat Turner revolt. Garrison, knowing that most slaves could not read found the accusations absurd, but relished the fear that his written word stirred in the hearts of slave owners.

Helen Hunt Jackson also used the written word as a weapon. Her efforts included exposing the government's mistreatment in her writings, circulating petitions, raising money for lawsuits, writing letters to newspaper editors, and arousing public opinion on behalf of First Nation people. Her outspokenness and unwillingness to back down to people or acts that she found despicable made her unpopular to many. Her activated humanist principles challenged a Presbyterian minister for whipping a child to condemning the U.S. government for its abuses of Native Americans.

Jackson's well-researched book, *A Century of Dishonor* (2003), chronicled and exposed the U.S. government's deceit, robbery, and cruelty committed against seven tribes: the Delawares, the Cheyennes, the Nez Percés, the Sioux, the Poncas, the Winnebagoes, and the Cherokees. She also dedicated one chapter to the massacres of members of three tribes: the Conestogas, the Guadenhüttens, and the Apaches. With her own funds, she printed a copy of the book and sent it to every member of Congress. The introductory section of this book speaks boldly. She not only confronts the lack of moral character of Congress, but urges representatives to enact policies that differed from the U.S. record with Native Americans:

> Suppose that a man had had the misfortune to be born into a family whose name had been blackened by generations of criminals; that his father, his grandfather, and his great-grandfather before them had lived in prisons, and died on scaffolds, should that man say in his soul, "Go to! What is the use? I also will commit robbery and murder, and get the same gain by it which my family must have done?" Or shall he say in his soul, "God help me! I will do what may be within the power of one man, and the compass of one generation, to atone for the wickedness, and to make clean the name of my dishonored house!
>
> What an opportunity for the Congress of 1880 to cover itself with a luster of glory, as the first to cut short our nation's record of cruelties and perjuries! The first to attempt to redeem the name of the United States from the stain of a century of dishonor! (Jackson, pp. 30–31)

Printed on the cover of each copy read, "Look upon your hands; they are stained from the blood of your relations." These powerful men were not accustomed to being called to task by a woman and certainly not on behalf of a people who were explicitly targeted for removal and genocide. Jackson's book, *A Century of Dishonor*, unfortunately did little to change governmental response to the way government treated Native Americans. Not one to wallow in disappointment, Jackson went on to draw from her experience as a romance novelist. Her friend, Harriet Beecher Stowe, wrote a successful book, *Uncle Tom's Cabin*, that was intended to reach the hearts of people in the United States by exposing them, through narrative, to the cruelties of slavery. This approach inspired Jackson to publish her own romantic novel, entitled *Ramona*, which was based, in part, on Jackson's firsthand communication with members of Native American tribes in Southern California. Unfortunately, Jackson, at the time, had a very narrow lens by which to examine the circumstances leading to the plight of California Indians. Lorimer (2013) states,

Although Jackson intended *Ramona* to shed light on the deplorable conditions of Indian affairs in the United States, as Uncle Tom's Cabin had done for African American slaves in the late 1850s, the picturesque landscape and idyllic atmosphere of California's fading Spanish era painted by Jackson drew the bulk of readers attention... Jackson spent a great deal of time in California investigating the contemporary condition of Mission Indians. Following deceitful negotiations, the United States government forced many California Indians onto secluded reservations where they struggled to survive. The government frequently failed to provide adequate supplies and food and greedy Indian agents stole from reservation stores as well...Jackson viewed the missions as a protective force in the lives of Native people. She did not look further back to the beginning of Spanish colonization and the establishment of the mission system as the origins of the devastation she previously described. Rather, Jackson viewed the Franciscan priests with great revere. (p. 58-59)

Jackson failed to recognize that the chain of events that turned the world upside down for California Indians started with the Spanish Era under the California Mission system. Even to this day, the destruction brought by the mission system to California Indians is rarely portrayed. Inadvertently, *Ramona's* inaccurate representation only obfuscated the true role and impact of the missions.

Jackson, afflicted with cancer and on her deathbed, found the strength and motivation to write one last note to President Grover Cleveland. It contained the following message: "I ask you to read my *Century of Dishonor*. I am dying happier for the belief I have that it is your hand that is destined to strike the first steady blow toward lifting this burden of infamy from our country and righting the wrongs of the Indian race (Odell, 1939, p. 219). Dated August 8, 1885, this letter was written right before morphine was administered to quell her pain. She died four days later.

Speaking truth was the weapon employed by Angelina Grimké. When humanists speak truth, it threatens oppressors who thrive in the Culture of Silence (Freire, 1998). Evidence of how threatening the truth can be can be found in the following account in which Grimké was scheduled to speak at the Convention of Anti-Slavery Women in Pennsylvania Hall, Philadelphia, on May 16, 1838. Threats of violence had already been made. Grimké's courage provided the strength to hold her ground in the face of a riotous mob that numbered in the thousands. The hall was so packed that the crowd spilled outside, and the uproar of those beyond the walls of the hall could be heard inside. Maria Chapman, another notable abolitionist, had already attempted to introduce Angelina but could not be heard over the roar of the crowd.

Undaunted, Angelina rose to her feet and said, "As a Southerner I feel that it is my duty to stand up here tonight and bear testimony against slavery. I have seen it—I have seen it. I know that it has horrors that can never be described." Stones thrown from outside came crashing through the windows. The tension was palpable, and the anger mounted. Yet, she continued: "What is a mob? What would the leveling of this hall be? Any evidence that we are wrong? Or that slavery is a good and wholesome institution?" Another distraction from a loud crash and still she proceeded: "I thank the Lord that there is yet life enough to feel the truth, even though it rages at it—that conscience is not so completely seared as to be unmoved by the truth of the living God" (Wilbanks, xi). The "truth" that Angelina shared that evening, however, infuriated many. She delivered this speech the evening after her marriage. The next day, "the Pennsylvania Hall...dedicated to liberty...was burned by a mob. They first tore up the seats and platform, chopped into pieces its costly furniture, piled the whole upon the floor, and made a bonfire of it, while the flaming hall rang with frantic yells of the mob, as they cursed the abolitionists" (Weld, p. 44). Despite the level of violence, Grimké continued her work as she found other means by which to activate her humanist principles.

Grimké's journals speak of her torment from regularly witnessing violence inflicted upon human beings. Despite the fact that she stood to materialistically profit from slavery, she envisioned that someday slavery would end. For her, living in a culture steeped in violence against humanity was more frightening than the raging mob that stood before her. Her budding stalwart courage can be measured from her journal entries, where she pours out the anguish from her earlier state of helplessness of not being able to intercede in the brutality committed against human beings. On May 12, 1834, her journal entry stated, "Five months had elapsed since I wrote in this diary since which time I had become deeply interested in the subject of Abolition." To this point, she had already confronted immediate family members with their mistreatment of the people they owned as slaves and, with little success, attempted to persuade them toward abolitionism. She goes on to write:

> I had long regarded this cause as utterly hopeless but since I had examined Anti-Slavery principles I find them so full of the power of Truth that I am confident not many years will roll over before the horrible traffic in human beings will be destroyed in this land of gospel privileges. My soul has measurably stood in the stead of the poor slaves and my earnest prayers have been poured out that the Lord would be pleased to [be] instrumental of good to those degraded, oppressed and suffering fellow creatures. Truly I often feel as if I were ready to go to prison and to death in this cause of justice, mercy & love, ... (Wilbanks, p. 209).

Angelina's torment turned to activism. Her writing turned from private to public. She wrote a letter to William Lloyd Garrison in support of abolitionists, which he printed in his highly controversial publication, *The Liberator*. It should not be surprising that when she was urged to direct Garrison to retract her letter, she refused. Her journal reveals her desire to be an "Instrument of good" and now she had an outlet for the torment she had internalized.

Angelina understood her unique position in that she was, herself, a member of the elite plantation and slave-holding society. She used her position to speak directly to her peers by writing a published letter entitled "An Appeal to the Christian Women of the South" where she movingly and explicitly called upon other slave-owning Southern women to set their slaves free. Grimké recognized that, in most cases, women would have to persuade their male relations in this matter. She also suggested that if people, once liberated, chose to stay that way, they should be paid for their labor and that Southern women should ensure that newly liberated people received an education. For enslaved people who were out of the sphere of a woman's influence, Angelina urged her white peers to ensure that they were treated humanely and that cruelty was eliminated. Freedom, pay for one's wages, and access to an education sounds so basic now that many, today, forget that these are rights that had to be acquired through social activism.

Angelina's will to speak and write about the "truth" provides visible testament to her active involvement in deconstructing racism. She stood firm against threats of violence and did not succumb to the insults of men who took offense to a woman speaking in public. Instead, the heightened level of sexism leveled at her motivated Angelina to expand the use of her voice and position to include women's rights. Grimké's use of her power and privilege laid the foundation to challenge racism and sexism. She modeled activated humanism.

Times Have Changed?

We can delude ourselves and say that, today, times have changed. Lynchings, slavery, forced relocation, burning people alive, genocide, "separate but equal," and all the inequities of the past have been redressed through laws and policy. "Times have changed" is what I hear. Others would say that the habituated thoughts that gave rise to these laws still exist, but they have transformed and are veiled.

Recall the influence Elizabeth Johnson's elementary school teacher had on her. This African American woman exuded love and care that the children reciprocated. It was a relationship that opened Elizabeth's worldview and served her years later, when taking a position as general manager of a rice-drying facility. Invited to take the post for a company headed toward bankruptcy, Elizabeth recognized what the owners of the company could not see, and their blindness was contributing to their own demise: years of racialized employment practices in which white men, whether most qualified or not, operated the machinery and enjoyed the largesse of privileges accorded by the company. Mexicans were relegated to the work requiring the most intensive labor and their most basic needs disregarded. Johnson concluded that these very practices undermined employee morale as well as the company's productivity.

Johnson's goal was to turn the company around. This meant increasing its capacity to make money and gain the most productivity from the employees themselves. The principles that framed her strategies were to make more money for her employer without exploiting the employees. Freire (1998) speaks to engaging pedagogy *with*, not for, the oppressed, and with this orientation, Johnson dialogued with the workers of the rice-drying plant to solicit strategies that would improve the workplace. She valued the input of all employees and enacted policies that provided fair practices for everyone. This democratic process instituted by Johnson as the general manager had not been previously utilized.

Visible changes would be evident. The practice of Mexican workers eating in a separate, unheated, and dimly lit area where the dirt floor was riddled with evidence of rats and spiders ended. They were allowed to eat in the clean break-room that had a restroom and was cleaned by a contracted janitorial service. The pay schedule was redrawn to reflect new job descriptions, and employees worked in teams determined by skill and job requirements, not by race or culture. Johnson discontinued the family practice of "borrowing a Mexican" to do labor at the home of the owners. These men had work to do at the plant.

Improved conditions, equal wages for Mexicans and whites, and engaged participation of workers in plant operations contributed to a more productive business. Racial equality served not only the Mexican workers, it served everyone. Johnson challenged and deconstructed the entrenched structural racism of her company and in doing so, met the needs of the company, which was to turn a profit. In valuing and humanizing the employees, morale improved and oppression was eliminated.

Courtenay Tessler, in her early life, was regularly in relationship with people of color. This inoculation against racism provided the confidence to act in accordance with her family's humanist principles in her career as a counselor. When the opportunity arose for her to serve as an advisor for a newly created multi-racial group called Youth In Focus, she stepped up. The group's purpose was to conduct participatory research in its community, uncover themes from its realities, and enact strategies to improve its community. The group endeavored to explore racial perceptions on her high school campus and to present their findings at a public forum.

Tessler stood by group organizer, Dr. Jann Murray-Garcia, an African American pediatrician, and participated with students in small group discussions where they came to know one another as team members while also uncovering and then challenging their own internalized oppression and prejudices. The students' transformation not only eliminated their own prejudices but also led to lifelong friendships that would not have occurred had they not been brought together in a manner that broke down the walls of each individual's cultural encapsulation. The authentic relationships provided a more solid foundation to enact school-wide small group discussions with their peers on the topic of racial perceptions on campus.

The forum in which the results were presented was scheduled for the 50-year anniversary of *Brown vs. the Board of Education*, a landmark decision that reversed "separate but equal" schools, which were, in fact, separate but not equal. Youth In Focus students presented their findings to an audience of faculty, administrators, parents, and peers. The disparities at their high school were revealed to a community priding itself on its students' reputation for academic achievement. The results of the research revealed, however, that while the district enjoyed stellar academic programs and outcomes, students of color, as a whole, were not faring well in the current environment. This collaborative effort of students, faculty, and community members set off examining what was creating the disparities so that strategies could be enacted to produce equitable outcomes.

During this self examination many of the students of color shared their painful experiences of hearing racist jokes or comments on a daily basis. Tessler's visible activism thrust her into the center of a movement that sought to change the factors creating a toxic culture for students of color. Tessler continued to model being in relation to those committed to a painful yet revealing process. Additionally, the research conducted by Youth In Focus uncovered the perception that some teachers held lowered expectations for students of color and that when being disciplined for the same offenses as their white classmates, students of color received harsher treatment. This is the legacy of racism in which our modern-day humanists engage in deconstruction. While Tessler's endeavor related to Youth In Focus focused on attitudinal perceptions, Johnson looked to improve employee morale by deconstructing structural inequalities based on racist ideology.

By-Product of Activated Humanism

The activism of humanists does not go unnoticed by people of color. John Brown was hailed by the African American community. Colonel Shaw not only earned the respect of the men of the 54th, but they were also grateful for the opportunity to free their brethren still in chains. The actions of humanists cut through the veil of historical distrust through which people of color have been conditioned to perceive their white counterparts. This humanizes people of color and has the potential for moving people of color past the Immersion/Emersion status of their respective identity development model (Helms, 1994). Johnson recalled in a classroom presentation (March 12, 2007) the observable and marked physical difference in how the employees of the rice-drying company carried themselves when the owners of the plant came on the premises, "hunching of the shoulders, the eyes looking down, the differential demeanor that the Mexican workers would adopt ... versus the shoulders back, eyes forward and up ... and more of a confident ... different body postures ... part of a societal component ... because of race." Once treated like equals, people who have internalized oppression *change*.

The men both black and white, who fought side by side with John Brown, as well as the men of the 54th Regiment, were entrusted as *men*. Perhaps John Brown would say they were *true men*. They stood tall when the yoke of oppression was removed and they were given the opportunity to prove their capacity.

Students in my class entitled, "Power, Privilege and Self Identity" complete an assignment in which they research their family heritage. It is always an incredible discovery for students in my class to learn about and uncover the challenges overcome by those who came before them. In an effort to learn about her ancestry Latasha Strawder discovered her connection to Colonel Shaw. She shared the sentiments in a letter that was eventually shared with Bob Shaw, a descendent of the famous Shaw family who has served as a resource for this book.

> When researching my family genealogy, I was caught off guard when discovering the intimate details associated with freedom in the United States. The astounding connection between Colonel Shaw, my great, great, great Uncle Aristide and Grandfather Octave put me in an emotional state.
>
> In 1837, Octave Monde Johnson was born in Orleans, Louisiana to Nina Honore and Pierre Sauvinet Monde. Octave was of French and African descent. Nina and Octave were eventually separated due to being sold to different plantations; Octave was sold for $2400. As a young adult, Octave grew weary of being beaten by his owner, S. Contrell, and concocted a plan along with other slaves to run away from the St. James Parish. They broke free and hid in Bayou Faupron while bloodhounds searched for them. There was an incident where Octave and the other slaves escaped from alligators by throwing in the dogs instead. Finally making their way to Camp Parapet through the adverse journey, Octave and the slaves found a place of safety. Octave became employed in the Commissary's office. Later he became a servant to Colonel Hanks and eventually joined his regiment. Corporal in the 15th Regiment, Corps d'Afrique, which later became the 99th Regiment; Octave served in the Civil War fighting with the Union against the Confederates. Octave Monde Johnson told his story and was interviewed by the American Freedmen's Inquiry Commission in 1864. Octave was not the only kin who fought for the greater good of African American freedom. Octave's brother, Aristide Monde, fought in the 54th Regiment in Boston, Massachusetts under Colonel Robert Gould Shaw. The movie 'Glory' tells the story of this heroic tale between an all black regiment, leading the U.S. Civil War to fight prejudices and racism despite a nation experiencing a cultural divide.

The demonstration of selflessness is evident with many people who, despite escaping oppressive conditions, put themselves at great risk in order to rescue others from those same conditions. That a person would commit their lives to ensure that others have a chance at freedom while facing the perilous conditions of war demonstrates courage. These are actions by those whose names rarely grace historical books yet whose decision to jeopardize their lives deserves recognition. Strawder goes on to reveal the impact of learning about the contributions of her ancestors that contributed to the evolvement of our nation.

> I felt admiration because the freedom fighters that I have read about throughout my life, are associated with the existence of being able to run, jump, smile, embrace the beautiful skies, and are the reason that I am able to live and pursue my dreams. It is one thing to read about the courageous, fearless, lion-hearted individuals that expressed selflessness in the eyes of death in such a hateful time; but to know that I come from resolute, valiant slaves that decided to risk their lives for freedom... truly overwhelms me. Slaves no more, victimless spirits have arose for the occasion. This is coming from a person that had no interest in history, who almost missed out on the happy ending which made it okay to live without anger, hate, and to have pride in the history of this country. Now, when I study history, I embrace the faults of man, my victimized ancestors, painful tears, and the heartbreaking struggle; because now I am able to recognize deliverance in increments over the years. I have learned that my ancestors were not tolerant of crude behaviors and treatment caused by slavery and decided to have courage in a time where they could have been killed. To read about the color barriers being destroyed in hopes of discontinuing the discombobulated views of Conservatives, gives me great joy. What a beautiful journey it has been. I pray that I am able to pick up the baton where they left off. (Strawder, Self Identity Paper, Fall of 2011)

While the men at the rice-drying company were living in a different time and under different circumstances, the capacity to walk tall and to be subjects of their lives rather than objects to be exploited was liberating.

When humanists engage in active deconstruction of racism, not only does racial bridging occur in the effort, but the prejudices projected to white people by people of color are mitigated. Further testament to the healing of prejudice is provided by Frederick Douglass who, despite being subjected to bondage for the first 20 years of his life, was humanized by his experiences with white people once he gained his freedom in the Northern states. "Much of my early dislike of white persons was removed, and their manners, habits, and customs, so entirely unlike what I had been used to in the kitchen-quarters on the plantations of the south, fairly charmed me, and gave me a strong disrelish for the coarse and degrading customs of my former condition" (Douglass, p. 416, 1994).

Douglass came to know white people who held no malice toward him as a human being, who saw and treated him as an equal, who valued his strengths, and who strongly supported his efforts to recognize that the "limit-situation" imposed upon people was not an ascription to all white people but to a culture enmeshed in exploitive capitalistic roots.

It is possible to arrive at this same level of awareness even now as a result of people learning about those who lived by and activated their humanist principles. Another student, Beverly Williams, in the "Power, Privilege, and Self Identity" Class expressed the following sentiments after learning about the people who worked to obliterate the institution of slavery which had held her ancestors in bondage, "Never judge anyone, all European Americans are not alike. Many of them truly care about the mistreatment of minorities. A long time ago I was not convinced of that but the Secret Six totally changed my thought process" (Journal, September 9, 2011).

Evidence of social justice advocacy abounds in the lives of our historical and modern-day white humanists. Commitment to this form of advocacy requires a level of courage that can be difficult, for many, to muster. For Angelina Grimké, getting to the place where she could use the power of her word and her pen required years of prayer and journaling. Her advocacy effort began with immediate family members. She would eventually fight slavery in the public sphere, and she fully knew that she would be challenged and, very possibly, evoke violence. John Brown knew slave owners would not give up their way of life without resorting to violence. This is why he solicited funds from Higginson: to purchase weapons. It was not long after that Colonel Shaw and the men of the 54th would fight, side by side, with weapons to deconstruct not just the institution of slavery but also the attitudes that were birthed by the habituated thoughts that justified slavery. Garrison, the Grimkés, Jackson, Tessler, and Johnson employed other means to deconstruct racism, and each made a difference from the activation of their principles.

The hope for communities where diversity is valued and all people are treated equally has already been modeled. In communities such as North Elba, where, truly, color did not matter, the context of relationships takes on new dimensions. For example, after Brown's failed expedition in the South, African American people in the North were known to have rallied around Brown's remaining family. And, in the bloodline of the Grimkés, a generation after Angelina, one of her nephews, Archibald, who was fathered by Angelina's brother Henry with his slave Nancy Weston, named his daughter after the famous aunt. The great-niece was Angelina Weld Grimké, who became a published poet, playwright, essayist, and short fiction writer, bringing voice to the continued racial injustices that were being committed during her lifetime. Like her famous great-aunt, Angelina Weld employed the power of the pen to evoke change and continue the battle.

The legacy of the Grimké Sisters did not end with them. Cross racial bonds have continued to defy racism. The Forten Family, a wealthy, elite black family in Philadelphia were actively engaged in the Underground Railroad. As early as 1800, James Forten and other free blacks petitioned to end the African Slave trade and to weaken the Fugitive Slave Act of 1793. At that time, U.S. Congress voted 85 to 1 against it. His daughter, Charlotte Forten, went on to marry one of the Grimké Sisters nephews who was conceived by Nancy Weston, former nursemaid to the children of her "owner," Henry Grimké. Prior to her marriage but having already the privilege of education, Charlotte Forten was one of the first black teachers to go the South at the end of the Civil War and educate those who were recently emancipated (Stevenson, 1980).

We will return to Memmi's definition of racism and discuss the real and sobering element of the force employed by racists to sustain it. What comes from this force is addressed as the theme of our next chapter, the price that humanists pay for their activism. Humanists who confront the forces that maintain racism challenge values rooted in exploitation. The reaction to their challenge puts them at risk. The response by oppressors may be minor, and in other cases, the response is extreme and deadly. Regardless, there is a price to pay. And, for modern-day humanists who endeavor to infuse their principles into their life work, this becomes the challenge as we determine the ultimate impact we desire to have in our professions.

QUESTIONS FOR DISCUSSION OR SELF REFLECTION

SELF-AWARENESS

1. Have you been subjected to negative social mirroring? What happened? Discuss with a classmate.

CLIENT WORLDVIEW

2. In review of the People of Color Racial Identity Development Model (Helms, 1994), what attitudes and behaviors can you identity that reflect the various stages of development?

COUNSELING RELATIONSHIP

3. Violence committed in our communities as a result of Conquest and Colonization can have far reaching and generational impact that perpetuates historical distrust. What acts have been committed in your community that have not been acknowledged or reconciled? What would be the value of doing so?

COUNSELING AND ADVOCACY INTERVENTIONS

4. What were the various strategies used by humanists to deconstruct racism? How can these same approaches be employed today, in your community?

5. What are ways of fostering acculturative, as opposed to assimilative processes in your community?

6. As Transformational Leaders, (Appendix E), what strategies would you employ to instill meaning in the work of people who you supervise or with whom you work side by side?

7. As a Transformational Leader, what would you do in order to mitigate the factors contributing to negative social mirroring?

NEW CONCEPTS AND VOCABULARY TO REVIEW

People of Color Racial Identity Development Model:

Negative Social Mirroring:

Assimilation:

Selective Acculturation:

Racial Group Cohesion:

Feminism:

Activity

Consider ways to non-violently express your humanism:

1. Write a letter to the editor over an injustice you have witnessed.

2. Read the books listed in the References section and discuss the content with family, friends, co-workers, fellow parishioners.

3. Commit "Acts of Kindness" every day.

4. Start a blog about a topic that needs your support.

5. Write a letter to your elected officials and express your sentiments about topics that need your active support.

6. Encourage your local school board to adopt books and multi-media that reflect a more inclusive perspective of history.

7. Actively protest hate crimes committed in your community.

8. Actively seek out and support people who have been targeted by hate crimes.

References

Freire, P. (1998). *Pedagogy of the oppressed.* New York, NY: The Continuum Publishing Company.

Helms, J. E. (1994). *The conceptualization of racial identity and other "racial" constructions.*
In E. J. Trickett, R. J. Watts, & D. Birmen (Eds.), Human diversity: Perspectives on people in context (pp. 285–311). San Francisco, CA: Jossey-Bass.

Horwitz, T. (2011). Midnight Rising. New York, NY. Henry Holt and Company, LLC.

Jackson, H. H. (2003). *A century of dishonor.* New York, NY: Dover Publications, Inc.

Lorimer, M. (2013). Reconstructing the Past: Historical Interpretations and Native Experiences at Contemporary California Missions. Dissertation. U.C. Riverside Electronic Theses and Dissertations.

Mayer, H. (1998). All on fire. New York, N.Y. W.W. Norton and Company, Ltd.

Memmi, A. (2005). *Racism.* Minneapolis, MN: University of Minnesota Press.

Odell, R. (1939). *Helen Hunt Jackson.* New York: NY: D. Appleton-Century Company.

Reynolds, D. (2005). *John Brown abolitionist.* New York, NY: Random House, Inc.

Stevenson, B. (1988). The journals of Charlotte Forten Grimké. New York, N.Y. Oxford University Press.

Suarez-Orozco, C. (2000). *Identities under siege: immigration stress and social mirroring among the children of immigrants. In Cultures Under Siege. Collective violence and trauma.* New York, NY: Cambridge University Press.

Wilbanks, C. (2003). *Walking by faith, the diary of Angelina Grimké, 1828–1835.* Columbia, SC: University of South Carolina Press.

Not for the Meek of Heart

When we emerged into the open daylight there went up a roar of rage and contempt, which increased when they saw that we did not intend to separate, but walked in regular procession. They slowly gave way as we came out. As far as we could look either way the crowd extended—evidently of the so-called 'wealthy and respectable'; 'the moral worth,' the 'influence and standing.' We saw the faces of those we had, till now, thought friends; men whom we never before met without giving the hand in friendly salutation; men whom till now we should have called upon for condemnation of ruffianism, with confidence that the appeal would be answered; men who have repeatedly said they were 'as much anti-slavery as we were,' that 'our principles were righteous,' and that they only objected other rashness of upholding them.... With ready forethought, Mrs. Chapman whispered to her associates filing out, while she stood between them and the Mayor; "Two and two, to Francis Jackson's, Hollis Street, each with a colored friend," thus giving what protection a white skin could ensure a dark one.

Mrs. Mary Chapman, 1835, recollecting the attack by Bostonians on William Lloyd Garrison, Abolitionist, in an attempt to lynch him as the women of the Anti Slavery Society gathered at his office for a meeting (MS. Nov. 12, 1882).

Where do you stand with your own beliefs and principles? How far would you go to defend your principles if they were challenged? Do you have any principles for which you would be willing to die? Or, do you find that you back down at the slightest hint of opposition and later regret that you didn't hold your ground?

Fear is real. It can immobilize the kind-hearted and paralyze the courageous. It can grip your tongue and silence you when you know you should be speaking, and it can force you to avert your eyes and physically back down when you should be stepping forward. There may be times when you weigh the level of risk to determine if it is safe enough to speak up. When the risk seems too high, you hold your opinion close and tell yourself, "I'll say something next time."

The regret that you feel when you don't speak or act on your principles can haunt you for days, and sometimes longer. The incident spins, over and over, in your head. You ask yourself, "Why didn't I do this ... or why didn't I do that?" It is usually an incident or statement made at the expense of someone else. It discharges from any of the constructs of power and privilege in which someone with power felt safe to attack another with less power, through word or act, and it could be an act of racism, sexism, heterosexism, anti-Semitism, ablism, or classism.

In your heart, you didn't agree with what was said or done. In fact, when you heard it, you felt like you had been punched in the stomach and your heart suddenly felt heavy. In situations like this, there is a brief moment of tension in the air. You furtively look at others who are present to see if they felt the same jolt, and you hope that someone else speaks up, but nobody does. The moment is awkward. Some go along and comply, while others turn their eyes away and pretend the offense didn't happen. After all, no one likes to rock the boat and make enemies. And you? You feel fear and so say or do nothing. Then, you feel shame.

And what, in truth, is it that we fear? We fear the range of violence that we may bring upon ourselves from the oppressor's retaliation. This can take many forms, from a moment of discomfort in which the source of the attack responds or looks at you with anger, hurt, or disappointment for you not siding with him and for calling him on their behavior. It can also mean setting off the extreme reaction resulting in the loss of your life. Memmi (2005) explains the source of the oppressors' virulent behavior. They strike out because *they* fear losing something that they value. Subsequently, their offensive discharges assert their position of power. Their investment in maintaining the power structures counts on and thrives in a Culture of Silence (Freire, 1998) where their claimed power goes unchallenged and their acts of violence go unchecked. Our humanists engage the oppressor's fear with hearts grounded in principles so firm that they are able to stand up to and speak out, boldly, over the oppressor's fear. The example of this is provided in the previous chapter in which Angelina Grimké was addressing the Convention of Anti-Slavery in Philadelphia. Her words, they knew, would be threatening, so their reaction, before she even spoke a word, was one of hostility. Grimké (1838) stated, "I know that I never could express my views freely on the abominations of slavery, without exciting anger, even to professors of religion" (p. 98). She recognized that silence to the atrocities was what was expected of her. Yet, a Southern minister had expressed to her, "Don't give up Abolitionism – don't bow down to slavery. You have thousands at the South who are secretly praying for you." He further conveyed to her that freedom of speech and opposition to the institution of slavery was suppressed by what he referred to as the "Reign of Terror" (p. 67). This engagement is not for the meek of heart. Humanists pay a price for actively living their principles, and when doing so, they recognize that in confronting oppressors, they must also be prepared to face a potentially explosive and virulent response.

Divide and Rule

The events detailed in Mary Campbell's recounting of the mob attack on William Lloyd Garrison demonstrate the possibility of eminent violence when undertaking active social justice work. At face value, it all seems righteous and justified: a multi-racial group of women, gathered in

Boston for an Anti-Slavery meeting. Why would anyone want to disband their meeting, destroy the premises, and attempt to lynch their host, William Lloyd Garrison? The meeting took place in a state that did not practice slavery and was often the hotbed for anti-slavery rhetoric and activities. However, authentic support and belief in the principles of abolitionism ranged. Southern slave owners counted on this variability in Northerners' sentiments and used it to wedge the weapon of Divide and Rule (Freire, 1998). The threats made by Southern slave owners incited frenzy among the Northerners, people described as "wealthy and respectable," "the moral worth," the "influence and standing" who subsequently turned their rage against one of the most prominent figures of abolition, William Lloyd Garrison.

Garrison was closely connected to a fiery and prominent British abolitionist, George Thompson. This association almost resulted in "men of good standing's" lynching of Garrison. This incident was provoked when Thompson made a statement that was twisted, and when heard by slave owners in the South, it raised their ire. The rumor implied that Thompson supported enslaved people being taught to cut their masters' throats. This touched a sensitive nerve with Southerners who were familiar with insurrections and lived in constant fear that enslaved people would rise against them. This rumor incited so much anger that a price was placed on the heads of Garrison and Thompson.

Yet, it was not the death threats against Garrison and Thompson that angered Northerners. It was what the Southerners did next that drove Northerners to pursue Thompson at any venue in which it was believed that he would appear. They clearly stated their intentions of tarring and feathering him. The Southerners strategically enacted a Divide and Rule tactic on Northerners by threatening to boycott Northern products and to destroy any Northern establishments in the South that were known to support abolitionists. They didn't stop at this, though, as they counted on Northern businessmen to place greater value on their sources of income than their abolitionist principles. Southerners, invested in maintaining the establishment of slavery, seized upon this lack of unified principles and extended their force of violence by enacting tactics that would prompt Northerners to carry out their brutality. Southerners threatened to enforce a boycott on any Northern businessmen who did not openly oppose abolitionists, if they allowed abolitionists to hold meetings or to publish papers in the merchants' town. This placed all grounded humanists at risk and as targets of violence by their own neighbors.

The Southerners counted on Northern businessmen's fainthearted commitment to abolitionism, and it worked. Men abandoned their abolitionist leanings and set course for carrying out the Southerners' violence against the most prominent and radical abolitionists. These men tracked a rumor that Thompson was scheduled to make an appearance at Garrison's office where, in truth, the women of the Boston Female Anti-Slavery Society were gathered for an election of officers. The mob had no idea that Thompson was not on the premises, but their rage sought an outlet. They gathered outside the building where the women were already meeting and leveled their anger at the women, at the premises, and at Garrison.

The sentiments of the men in this furious mob were that the women had better things to do within the domestic sphere than to be stirring up problems between the North and the South. They proceeded to tear down and demolish a posted sign that read, "Anti-Slavery Rooms," made their way up two flights of floors where the women were conducting their meeting, and tore down the door to Garrison's office. The mayor of Boston, assisted by a police escort, persuaded the women to leave for their safety. Garrison found escape through a second-floor back window. He didn't get very far. He initially found refuge in a vacant room of a carpenter's shop where a young boy covered him with boards in an effort to hide him. He was found anyway.

Members of the enraged mob threw a rope around Garrison's body and were ready to throw him out the second-story window, lynching him in the process. They thought better and allowed him to climb down a ladder. Garrison was then dragged through the streets of Boston, the mob tearing his clothes off as they went. The crowd had been waiting for him, at the Boston Common Frog Pond, "a barrel of tar, a bag of feathers, a corrosive liquor, and a quantity of an indelible ink" (Garrison, Volume II, p. 21). The intention was to take Garrison and Thompson to the Boston Common, strip, tar, and feather them both and then dye their faces and hands black. The intervention of the mayor and the Boston police department saved Garrison from this fate. He was placed in the Leverett Street Jail for his own protection, and was eventually snuck out of the city; he stayed away for several weeks.

Unity Trumps Divide and Rule

Everything has its opposite. The presence of one extreme in the face of the other has the potential to overpower and eliminate the presence of its opposite. Think of a completely darkened room, devoid of any singular presence of light. Then, imagine a lit candle in the midst of this dark room. The presence of this one source of light illuminates everything around it. Viktor Frank speaks to the capacity of even one person's capacity to be that luminous force. In the Nazi concentration camps, he spoke to the power of one person, also a prisoner, acting with kindness and generosity in the midst of the most extreme manifestations of human cruelty. Witnessing these acts of humanism restores the humanity of those in its luminous presence.

The women's response to the mob attack provides critical lessons in how grounded humanists employ dialogical approaches to challenge violence. They had witnessed the men of their community bow to Southern slave owners will. The men in this mob fell to the anti-dialogical force of Divide and Rule. The women, on the other hand, modeled the powerful force inherent in the dialogical tool of **Unity** (Freire, 1998). Their reaction to the mob and subsequent behavior is worth further examination. As they exited the building, they faced the fury of a mob. Members of this mob had already penetrated the building, made their way up two flights of stairs, destroyed an office door, and were giving chase to Garrison. The women laid eyes on what many estimated to be a crowd in the hundreds, if not more. Rather than bend to the fear, the women enacted behaviors that demonstrated their unified principles even when the angry mob's fury escalated at their appearance. With linked arms, they walked out, together. They demonstrated strength in numbers and, more so, strength in unity. The mob left them alone. The women went on to another location and resumed their meeting.

One more dimension of this incident must be noted because it is key to understanding how the powerful dialogical forces of unity, cultural synthesis, cooperation, and organization can transcend and evolve our society beyond its racialized existence. The white women in this group knew they were in danger, but they understood that the black women in their group were at greater risk of harm. The white women understood that their black sisters were less valued and, subsequently, were more vulnerable to the rage of the mob that stood before them. Violence against African Americans was not only sanctioned and openly practiced, but also those who murdered and maimed did so with impunity. Knowing this, the white women did not desert their fellow group members and act in a way that just ensured only their own safety. Instead, the white women expanded their sphere of protec-

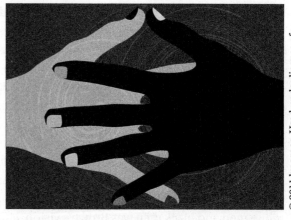

tion to their black sisters. The linking of arms was not only strategic, it was symbolic. The women, in their action, transcended the violence and modeled what an authentic community looks like. Their humanistic "habituated thoughts" translated into "habituated behaviors" that were employed at a moment of crisis and overt violence.

Consider the perspective of the black women in the Anti-Slavery Society as they experienced the mob attack and, more so, how they interpreted the actions of their white sisters. Like the candle in a dark room, their actions spoke volumes. These women knew too well the realities of violence committed against anyone whose skin was not white. Nonetheless, the white women put themselves at risk to protect their black sisters. This act of unity modeled hope. It strengthened the bonds of cross-racial trust because this act of unity also demonstrated that not all hearts are driven by self gain.

Mother Jones (Zinn, 1999), labor organizer for the United Mine Workers in the early 1900's, was "arrested, kept in a dungeonlike cell, and then forcibly expelled from the state" of Colorado (p. 354). The united efforts of eleven thousand miners which included foreign born men and their families from Greece, Italy, Serbia and Mexico led to an attack on the miner's make shift tent city by company and national guards. "Their leader, a Greek named Lou Tikas, was lured into the hills to discuss a truce, then shot to death by a company of national guardsmen. The women and children dug pits beneath the tents to escape the gunfire.... At dusk, the guard moved down from the hills with torches and set fire to the tents...thirteen people were killed by gunfire....the following day, a telephone linesman going through the ruins of the Ludlow tent colony lifted an iron cot covering a pit in one of the tents and found the charred, twisted bodies of eleven children and two women" (p. 355). This is known as the Ludlow Massacre. With Unity, change came but with a high price as people across racial lines worked together to improve work conditions, wages and a better future for their children.

Brown paid a dear price for his ill-fated attempt to overtake Harpers Ferry. He was charged with treason, murder, and insurrection. Of his army of 22 men, 10 men died during the raid. This included two of his sons, Oliver and Watson, who died at Brown's side of gunshot wounds. Five men managed to escape. A third son, Owen, who participated in the raid, was among this group and was never captured. One man drowned while attempting to escape. In the end, six of the captured men were later executed, as was Brown himself.

Brown's lifelong mission did not succeed despite the level of sacrifice he was willing to make. Like Angelina Grimké, Brown would not rest knowing that slavery persisted in his lifetime. The modeling of the price he was willing to pay heightened Northern abolitionists' resolve; they were further inspired by Brown's martyrdom. Abolitionists attempted to save Brown's life when he was on trial. They wanted him to plead insanity so that he might be given a lighter sentence. Brown denied any claims of insanity, stood firm in his position that he acted on his principles, and accepted the verdict of the jury, execution by hanging.

Brown's mission did escalate political tension between the North and the South, which eventually led to the Civil War. Abolitionists, fueled by Brown's sacrifice, seized the opportunity to carry out Brown's plan by convincing Abraham Lincoln to enlist free black men to fight on behalf of the North. The will to match slave owners' violence with the unified force of armed white men and black men was Brown's vision, and while Brown did not live to see his vision to its successful end, it was fully activated by Colonel Shaw and the men of the 54th Regiment.

Slave owners lived in fear that the people who they held in bondage would revolt, so they employed a range of strategies to ensure that enslaved people lacked access to the means by which to liberate themselves. For example, knowing the danger of an educated mind, slave owners forbade their slaves to learn how to read and write. Ellen Betts, a woman who had experienced enslavement in Louisiana, gave testimony of her experiences before emancipation. Born in 1853, she was interviewed when she was 84 years old and recalled serving as wet nurse to both black and white children. Though she, herself, was never struck by those who claimed to own her, she testified that if she or any other enslaved person had been caught with a paper in their hand, they would surely have been whipped. It was deemed that those who were enslaved were not desirable if they were "bright." If they were, they were quickly sold. She further recalled the slave owner saying, "Book larning don't raise no good sugar cane" (Botkin, p. 126, 1945).

Slave owners went to great lengths to ensure that the people they kept in physical bondage were also kept in mental bondage. More so, they abhorred the thought of a weapon in the hands of an enslaved person. Subsequently, the idea of a white man leading armed black troops went against the grain of their racially constructed way of thinking.

A considerable number of men from the 54th regiment died as they attempted to overtake a Confederate stronghold, Fort Wagner. Colonel Shaw died with his men, suffering a rifle shot to his upper chest as he crested the stronghold's fortification. There are codes of conduct by which "civilized warfare" is enacted. An officer whose body is retrieved by the enemy after death on the battlefield is supposed to be returned to the opposition for proper burial. The Colonel acted against expected racial allegiances by the fact that he was leading armed black troops. Because of this, he was not accorded this courtesy. Instead, his uniform was stripped from his body, and his watch and chain and other regalia were stolen by a Confederate private.

Confederate General Johnson Hagood knew the Colonel prior to the outbreak of war and held him in high regard. Hagood was also responsible for the contempt of protocol and subsequent disrespectful treatment of the Colonel's remains. This Confederate officer had indicated that had the Colonel been leading white troops, he would have given him a proper burial. Since Colonel Shaw was leading black troops, he then, out of insult, buried the Colonel in a manner intended to convey his disrespect and to give a message to all white men who did not act in accordance with racialized allegiances. He had the Colonel's body thrown into a trench and buried with the men of the 54th who died with him (Emilio, 1891).

People from the North, hearing of the disrespectful treatment of the Colonel's remains, were outraged. Word got back to the Shaw family of what had been done to their son. The response from the Shaws to the desecration of their son's body, however, was not what the Confederate officers expected. The Shaws' vision of a society in which racial unity was possible transcended the racialized worldview. In the end, the Confederates were, perhaps, even more affronted by the manner in which Shaw's parents, Francis and his wife Sarah, responded to the intended insult. The letter they sent to Confederate Brigadier-General Gillmore, Commanding Department, dated August 24, 1863, follows:

> Sir, I take the liberty to address you because I am informed that efforts are to be made to recover the body of my son, Colonel Shaw of the Fifty-fourth Massachu-setts Regiment, which was buried at Fort Wagner. My object in writing is to say that such efforts are not authorized by me or any of my family, and that they are not approved by us. We hold that a soldier's most appropriate burial-place is on the field where he has fallen. I shall therefore be much obliged, General, if in case the matter is brought to your cognizance, you will forbid the desecration of my son's grave, and prevent the disturbance of his remains or those buried with him. With most earnest wishes for your success, I am, sir, with respect and esteem,

> Your obedient servant,
> FRANCIS GEORGE SHAW
> (Emilio, pp. 102–103)

Despite the grief from suffering the loss of their only son, Francis and Sarah Shaw maintained and demonstrated a level of respect for the men who died alongside their son. The sanctioning of the breach of military protocol was reframed by the Shaws as a way to consecrate the bond of relationship between their son and the men of the 54th. The cross-racial burial was subsequently elevated to a symbol of unity, in death as in life. This was a perspective that the Confederate officers could not conceive of in their worldview. The humanist principles that the Shaws lived by transcended the intended insult, and even in the face of the intended desecration, they modeled a way of being that emanated from true love for all humanity.

The intended insult by the Southern general backfired and, instead, elevated the Colonel's status as he lay, side by side, with the remains of the men he came to respect and admire. The Colonel paid the price of his life for serving the cause of elevating the perception of African American men. He completed his mission, and even his burial served to represent a transcendent model of freedom from the racism that held so many, black and white, in physical, psychological and spiritual bondage.

Recall the women leaving William Lloyd Garrison's office in the midst of a furious mob, linked, arm in arm, white woman and black woman. They, too, rose above the racialized construction that reduced what were, otherwise, considered civil and good human beings to violent perpetrators. They had no idea whether the rage of the mob would be directed at them. They had just witnessed the fury of these men destroying the property in which they were holding their anti-slavery meeting, so they knew that the threat of violence was real; it was around them, and yet, they were willing to pay the price of protecting those who were at greater risk. Their unity and resolve carried them past the fury to safety.

Yet, safe passage is not always the outcome when humanists put themselves at risk. The last time Sarah Shaw saw her son was May 28, 1863. The 54th Regiment had completed their training, and the people of Boston threw a parade in their honor. Sarah had a feeling she might not see her son alive again, even as she proudly observed him at the head of the regiment from the vantage of a balcony. In fact, Sarah never saw her son again.

Letters written between Sarah and her son reveal her deep passion for the causes she supported. She implored her son to reconsider his decision when he did not accept the post of colonel of this particular regiment. The chain of events during the Civil War led to his regiment being chosen, after having proven their bravery at other battles, to lead the assault on Fort Wagner. Troops on the front line generally sustain high casualties. Once the colonel knew that his regiment was called to this perilous duty, he accepted the probability that he would not survive, and he didn't. The outcome is now history, and his mother, a strong influence in steering her son's career, was branded, similarly to John Brown, as a "fanatic." This was the price she paid. Already presented was the case of Elijah Lovejoy, an abolitionist, who died protecting his printing press. His grave was left unmarked for years because of the fear of desecration. Another price paid.

Angelina's Grimké's weapons were her truth, which she spoke fearlessly, and her pen, which she employed freely. Slave owners were taken aback by one of "their own" standing not just apart from them but against them and even against her own family. Angelina, encouraged by the publishing of her letter in Garrison's newspaper, *The Liberator*, went on to write the pamphlet entitled, "An Appeal to the Christian Women of the South." Her sister, Sarah, followed her younger sister's example and wrote, "An Epistle to the Clergy of the Southern States." Both these pamphlets were publicly burned by South Carolina officials as a symbol of their disdain for the sisters and the sisters' open abolitionist stance. The sisters were threatened by city officials of their hometown that should they ever return home, they would be arrested and imprisoned. Furthermore, there were threats of "personal violence at the hands of the mob" (Weld, p. 53) should the Sisters defy their orders. The sisters never did return to their home state of South Carolina. They remained in the North, where they died and are buried. This is the price they paid.

Paying the Price Today

Our modern-day humanists would tell us that times have changed in some ways, but not so, in others. Garrison was physically attacked by a mob in the "free" North and narrowly escaped being painted "black." The Colonel was buried with his men in a trench rather than accorded the burial entitled to an officer. Both these acts were intended as insults. The Shaws would tell us, however, that one's *perceptions* ultimately determine the meaning of such acts. A humanist is devoid of negative association to skin color or any other arbitrary characteristic that is targeted for differentiated treatment. Subsequently, insults such as those directed at the Colonel and Garrison do not hold the intended negative affect or impact. They miss their mark when hurled at humanists.

We have seen how threatening it can be to speak the truth. Angelina Grimké incited violent reactions when she spoke truth. When humanists break the Culture of Silence, it is like the lone candle illuminating darkness. The light reveals what is intended to be hidden in darkness. People invested in maintaining the darkness detest and are angered by the light because, in short, truth reveals what they would rather keep concealed.

Courtenay Tessler, one of our modern humanists, discussed in a classroom presentation the aftermath of the Youth In Focus (YIF) presentation to the community. Tessler shared that the YIF scholars had constructed a survey designed to uncover perceptions about race at their high school. In other words, they shared how students of color felt that teachers thought about them, how parents thought about them, their peers, etc. One of the questions, "How many times do you hear racial jokes on campus?" revealed that many of the students of color at her high school were exposed to negative social mirroring in their day-to-day reality.

Tessler recalled how the day after Youth In Focus students presented their findings on the 50-year anniversary of *Brown vs. the Board of Education*, she was confronted in the parking lot by a co-worker, who had arrived at work the same time. As Tessler got out of her car, her co-worker said, "Now you've done it. Now you have really done it." Tessler was in disbelief over her co-worker's behavior. She asked, "Done what?" to which her spurious co-worker responded, "You know exactly what that was about! *Brown vs. the Board of Education* and making us look bad. Getting it out there. You knew exactly. How dare you."

This was the first of a deluge of comments from disgruntled community members who were angered by being made to "look bad" by the Youth In Focus findings. Tessler tried to "stay cool about it" and took comfort in the support of others who voiced their support. She tried to avoid verbal entanglements, even when she was accused of "stirring and riling things up."

Before divulging to the reader the intended insult hurled at Tessler for her alliance and visibility with a multi-racial cooperative of students and community members, let us provide context. It has been almost 150 years since Colonel Shaw, even in death, was at the receiving end of an intended insult. The Confederate general who approved of the Colonel's burial justified his disregard for protocol due to the fact that the Colonel breached racial group loyalty. Racial construction requires allegiance to skin color. Tessler's commitment, as with the Colonel, to humanist principles rejects and transcends same-group racial loyalty. It also attracts attacks. For his reason, in addition to the many comments directed at her about breaking the Culture of Silence, Tessler was also called "Race Traitor" (Tessler Classroom Presentation, March 7, 2007).

"Difference" is inherent in everything. There are variances in abilities, appearance, gender, etc. The differences do not have to take on negative connotation unless we choose to make the differences negative. In the case of racism, if people choose to ascribe to the notion that a particular color of skin holds negative value, then the perception of anyone with that skin color is now clouded by a socially rather than a personally constructed meaning.

The mob who attacked Garrison in Boston intended to dye him black. This, we can acknowledge, was meant as an insult. Tessler, on the receiving end of a backlash to the Youth In Focus report, sidestepped intended insults, but the critics missed their mark because humanists do not possess the same worldview and negative associations as racists, sexists, ablists, etc. So, when Tessler was told, "Now you've done it! Now you're black!" she had a simple and easy comeback, "No, I'm Courtenay."

Tessler understands that the construction of racism depends on the negative association of skin color that is not white. Her non-racialized view, however, does not mean she discounts the racialized orientation of those around her. As stated in our previous chapter, "Call 'It' What 'It' Is", humanists understand how the constructions of power and privilege manifest themselves, and when they see it, they know how to respond. Tessler's explanation to a class of aspiring counselors elaborates on how her response casts confusion on those who live in a state of submersion:

> When we start defining people as black, white ... isn't that racist? ... We have to label people a color, and then when we get really mad at them what do we do? You say the thing that will be hurtful. Well, now you've turned black. Well, that didn't hurt me so why would you say something like that? Is that a bad thing? Are you calling me that because you think black is bad? And then people ... if you call them on that, then they get more confused. They don't know what to say (Tessler Interview, April 10, 2007).

Humanists can disarm oppressors with the transcendent force of their worldview and can dismantle the constructs of power and privilege. The alliances that Tessler maintains with colleagues and community members, of all backgrounds, are people with similar visions and goals committed to reducing the achievement gap. This is a work in progress but, nonetheless, Tessler's reputation for "riling things up" and not giving credence to being a "race traitor" places her at the crosshairs of those displeased with her worldview. It is a price she pays, but she does so willingly. Like Angelina Grimké, the weight of *not* acting from her principles would be worse because it would be incongruent with her humanist principles.

Johnson also experienced the price to be paid when endeavoring to live from her humanist principles. In a classroom presentation, Johnson openly shared her efforts to undermine the racialized structure and evident racist behaviors at the rice-drying company that she was hired to oversee. She instituted equitable pay structures, expanded health benefits created a pathway for employment mobility, and integrated employee facilities. Despite the monetary reward that the owners benefited from as a result of the improved morale and employee production, the family terminated Johnson. They buckled to the pressure of other members of the rice industry whose workers demanded the same work conditions as the company overseen by Johnson. The other companies were not willing to make the same adjustments. And, because, as was conveyed to Johnson, "the Mexican workers are acting up," the owners of the company that employed Johnson were told by their peers, "Get rid of her." Subsequently, Johnson was told she had "overstepped" her duties, was forced to leave the premises, and was then placed on administrative leave. They referred to the fact that, under Johnson's administration, a Mexican person was in a position of authority and could come into the office when he wanted to. This was not appreciated, and neither was the equitable distribution of bonuses and pay, which was seen as "wasting profits."

Johnson's position was terminated. This was, initially, the price she paid, but it didn't end there. What followed falls in the genre of cowardly acts inherent to racist ideology. Her life was threatened. At the time this occurred, Johnson lived alone in the middle of the country and started receiving threatening phone calls. She recalls the worst call was what she believed to be the voice of a man, but it was difficult to determine if it was because he disguised his voice. He said, "How does it feel to be the most hated woman in (Name Deleted) County?"

Perpetrators continued to harass Johnson with anonymous e-mails. People stalked her and knew when her children were home. Johnson admits it took her 10 years to recover from the terrorism she experienced during this period of her life during which she lived in constant fear of retaliation. The price that Johnson paid was much more than battle fatigue; she paid through the wounds inflicted from the threats of violence made on her and the danger that the aftermath created for her children. To heal the wound, she found herself seeking connection to people and subsequently pursued her Master of Science degree in counseling, where she was provided the opportunity to reflect on her experience and develop the tools to name what it was she had fought. She learned that she had come, face to face, with the forces of violence inherent with racism (Johnson, Classroom Presentation, March 12, 2007).

The price that humanists pay for engaging in the dismantling of social constructions is not for the meek of heart. The various examples of how our humanists overcame and transcended their fear emanates from deeply rooted beliefs and orientations. The theme that follows is another common trait found in our humanists. It's a spiritual identity orientation that rises above the superficialities of constructions founded on self interest and greed. It's an orientation from which they perceive a reality well above the oppressive forces of their lifetime.

Walking Into the Fire

The discussion about the potential for drawing violence upon oneself must be a sober one when humanists consider their activism. As we can see from the lives of our historical and modern-day humanists, they paid a price for their efforts and the range of responses resulted in everything from verbal insults and exile to death threats and execution. The degree by which a humanist, possibly you, the reader, can sustain the range of responses is why this particular chapter is entitled, "Not for the Meek of Heart." So, while we may acknowledge that many people have good hearts and care for others, the fear of acting on one's humanistic principles may immobilize even the well intended. Courage must at times be cultivated and fortified.

The means our historical and modern-day humanists employ to walk into the fire reveal various approaches by which to bolster their capacity to act upon the oppressive realities in their midst. Angelina Grimké's journal provides evidence of an intensification in her disdain for slavery, as well as a despair over her own efforts to address the issue with family members and the community. The journal seemed to provide a means by which to sustain her sanity as she bore witness to countless cruelties inflicted upon humanity. The journal also served as a source by which to express her vision for a just world. Regular prayer grounded Angelina. She prayed to a higher being, which affirmed her set of beliefs that were in direct opposition to the "habituated thoughts" and "habituated behaviors" of the slave-owning culture. The desire to find the companionship of like-hearted Christians moved her to circles of various faith systems in an effort to identify people who understood, as she did, the application of Christian principles as universal. She went from writing in a journal and praying to a higher being to writing letters and bearing verbal testimony in favor of abolitionism. Angelina's close relationship with her older sister, Sarah, who also shared the same disdain for slavery, allowed her to stand with her sister against the value system of their family. This alliance must have strengthened Angelina's resolve in her principles while reducing feelings of isolation. By all these means, Angelina fortified her capacity to walk through the fire to become actively involved in the abolition movement (Wilbanks, 2003). Her heart-felt commitment allowed her to step forward and speak openly with "serene indifference to the judgment of those about her" (Weld, p. 30).

John Brown, we know, maintained relationships with a small army of men who believed, as he did, that the establishment of slavery would only be eliminated if they and others were willing to put their lives at risk. Their shared vision fueled their courage though the mission failed. Similarly, as the Colonel charged upon Fort Wagner with the men of the 54th Regiment at his side, we can recognize that the persistent vision of his parents, Francis and Sarah Shaw, must have served as a source of strength. The Colonel's development of relationships with the men he came to serve and lead, coupled with the conditions of the people held in bondage that he saw, first hand, in the Union army's expeditions into the slave-holding South, moved the cause of his parents from what was previously an intellectualized orientation to a commitment that he embraced of his own accord.

The privilege of access to our modern-day humanists, Courtenay Tessler and Elizabeth Johnson, provided further perspective on how they perceive the risk of taking on racism. As a researcher who wanted to know more about how white humanists engaged the potential for violence, I set up a joint interview session with the two modern-day humanists to ask them about this experience, I prompted their thoughts with the following question: "In relation to the stories you have shared, which I equate to as "walking into the fire," what have you learned from those experiences?" Their responses provide a set of guidelines for humanists who may feel paralyzed when called upon to act.

> First of all, it depends what stage the fire is at; if it's just starting, if it's a huge blaze. If it's just smoldering. There are a lot of little fires you step into. Sometimes it's a little too hot like the firefighters go into "forts" and they're always putting fires out. And they can handle that but sometimes the blaze is so huge and it's so hot you just have to back off. You can't do it. So when you step into those fires you have to evaluate yourself, how much you personally can handle like, can you really stand up to it. How much energy do you have? Can you negotiate yourself around this? What skills do you have that you can bring in that will be useful in that situation. And, how much emotional energy are you willing to put into it. See, you are constantly reevaluating and at some points it just gets too hot and you've got to get out of there or you're going to get burned. You have got to get out of there and then you wait for the fires, the flames to go down again before you step back in. And, not everyone can do that. They don't have the knack or the ability how to do that. So, it's kind of difficult (Tessler, Joint Session, April 27, 2007).

Tessler readily identifies "emotional energy," which confirms the historical humanists' demonstration of their passion for the causes in which they engaged themselves. The other area of "skill" speaks to what humanists employ as tools to engage the presenting challenges. Readily, we can recognize the various skills employed by our historical humanists, such as their oratory skills that were put to use in public speaking; their ability to write, which resulted in newspapers, publications, and books that spoke to the issues at hand; their leadership skills in leading and working with others toward a common goal, as well as advocacy by way of using their status in the communities in which they lived to lobby for the causes they upheld.

Determining the best means by which to approach the fire is further elaborated during this joint session by Elizabeth Johnson:

> I think what I've learned from the fires that I have stepped into or have walked through … is that there is a price to pay. And, it brings me to places in my spirituality and my integrity. I think what I've learned the most is that I have an obligation to do something. If I see a fire and I no longer am able to walk around it. I see a fire and I have found myself in the middle of the fire that I need to do something and what that something requires that is appropriate. That might have the most successful outcome and have the most change. So, there is a kind of evaluation of what might affect the most change at this point and I think that is what I have learned that there are different ways and different things to do and different reasons why to do them. Sometimes, explaining *why* is as important as *what* is being done. That it becomes an educational piece. And I think that I've learned that I was indignant and that I was angry and that really doesn't affect a lot of change many times as much as maybe providing additional information and a different perspective in a different way to put the fire out or do something that will affect a change with that fire (Johnson, Joint Session, April 27, 2007).

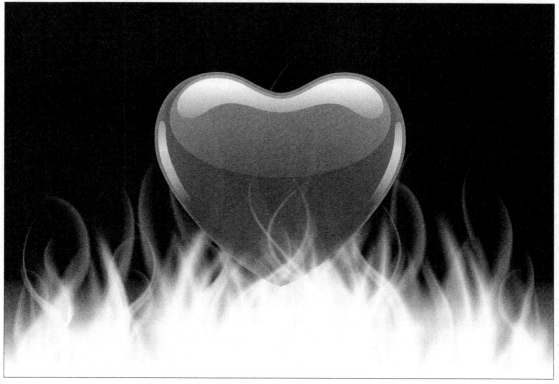

Johnson adds another valuable piece to humanist responses to "walking into the fire." She proposes selecting how one responds from a place not just informed and driven by one's emotions, which may not be as well received as coming from a place of education and logic. Understanding the irrational beliefs behind the constructs of power and privilege, a humanist can bring a set of truths as a force by which to address ill-founded and ill-conceived "habituated thoughts." The force of truth and using truth to educate was repeatedly drawn from by Angelina Grimké in her public appearances and writings, in Garrison's abolitionist newspaper *The Liberator*, and is what John Brown drew from when he was captured and tried in court for his attempt to demolish the institution of slavery.

The causes that call forth our advocacy still exist and take on different forms. As we look at all the constructs of power and privilege that maintain structures of oppression and predetermine marginalizing outcomes for those subjected to these structures, we can identify where our efforts are needed to enact change. Walking through the fire, as we have seen, can bring forth undesirable behaviors but can also create opportunities for evolvement in our world. The following contribution from Dr. Lisa Romero, a former high school principal, speaks to the value of acting from one's heart and taking on what others perceive as "normal." She relates not only the feelings she had when witnessing something that didn't feel right to her but also the reaction to her intervention,

> When the bell rings signaling the end of lunch, a ritualistic dance begins between administrators and high school students. Students, enjoying time with their peers, slooowly gather their backpacks and belongings, while the administrators spring into action. We move from table to table encouraging students to; get to class on time; do well in class; please remember to put their trash in the trash cans; stop texting and put their phones away... all before they enter the classroom door.
>
> After lunch, I would stay outside for another 10 or 15 minutes and help our sole day time custodian (at our school of over 3,500 students) clear tables and pick up some left behind paper and food wrappers. As the new Principal, I did this as a sign of respect for our overworked custodian, but it was also an opportunity to talk with him, ask him about his family, and establish rapport. That rapport gave me an opportunity to learn from a different perspective about my school, my staff, and the community. But that was not all I learned. Staying outside after lunch made visible things that I would not have seen sitting in the Principal's Office. *The familiar became strange.*
>
> When we hear the word curriculum, we usually think of the formal, written curriculum found in lesson plans, standards, and text books. But, there is another curriculum, the "*hidden curriculum*" that students learn every day. The hidden curriculum is unwritten, but powerful. It functions to reify and reproduce the existing social structure. It consists of rules, messages, norms of behavior, and learning expectations that are taught alongside the formal curriculum. Whether intended or unintended, the hidden curriculum is not neutral, nor evenly applied to all. The hidden curriculum conveys subtle, yet pervasive and inescapable messages about

race, ethnicity, class, gender, and ability. It is called hidden in part because it is unwritten, and also because it often goes unseen and unquestioned. The hidden curriculum hides in plain sight, in seemly unbiased decisions about class schedules, course content and learning activities. It is about "what gets taught and to whom" (Apple, 1982; Freire, 2002).

In reflection of Dr. Romero's opening statements, she provides us with insight to the elements of our day to day realities that, because they have become part of our regular and acceptable way of engagement, that we never question it's origins or impact. We continue to do what is done because it has always been done this way. The inherent message of doing what has always been done teaches implicit messages about who and what is of value. Dr. Romero provides a specific example to demonstrate this point,

> As I was outside, I noticed across the quad a small group of people going through the campus trash. Because the school was in a low income area, it was not unusual to find homeless people, or others struggling with poverty, collecting bottles and cans late in the day when the campus was largely deserted. But this was the middle of the school day. I walked toward the group. To my surprise, I realized that they were my students – my special education students. They were leaning over, reaching in, and picking through the trash cans, pulling out bottles and soda cans. I observed a bit more and was surprised to see their teachers were watching and encouraging this behavior.
>
> I remember being both shocked and disturbed, but it was a busy day and my actions were limited to casting a questioning and slightly disapproving look toward the teacher. Oddly enough, the teacher smiled at me and had her students wave a friendly hello to the Principal. I decided I would inquire about this later.

At this point, Dr. Romero has challenged an ongoing practice at her school site. Acting on her gut feelings of being "shocked and disturbed" it was the following day in which she approached the teacher. "Walking through the fire" means confronting the situation. Her initial feelings caused her to give a "questioning and slightly disapproving look" but this would not be sufficient to *change* the rooted practice. More would be required of Dr. Romero,

> I went inside, and although bothered, forgot about the incident until the next day, when— to my surprise, the same thing occurred. This time I approached the teacher to find out what was going on. The teacher quite happily, informed me that the students were recycling. Hoping to redirect the teacher's enthusiasm, I "wondered" if there might be a cleaner, healthier way to recycle (to my horror the students were not only digging in trash cans but also using their bare hands). I also made clear that our special education students, like everyone else on campus, should be engaged in learning and that I was not comfortable with asking them to go through trash.
>
> The teacher gave me a look that I can only describe as mix of astonished and annoyed and informed me that 1) the students usually wore disposable gloves but she had run out of gloves ("as you know" the budget is tight). 2) The activity was

part of a lesson about the importance of recycling. Although she was annoyed, I thought I had made my point and that would be the end of seeing special education students digging through trashcans. I should have known better.

When we talk about how we use our power and privilege it is to affirm that sometimes we have unearned privilege (skin color, gender, age, class, etc..) that can be employed to build bridges, enact a different reality, and to challenge power structures that undermine the potential for growth and opportunity for others who have not been born into the position of power and privilege. On the other hand, there is earned ascribed credibility from the credentials that one earns. In this case, Dr. Romero's position as the Principal allowed her to start a dialogue that would hopefully change the reality of students in the special education program,

> The next day could have been a scene from the movie Ground Hog Day. The only difference was that the students were each wearing a single disposable glove on one of their hands. I would talk to the teacher with her union representative later in the day. I called my Assistant Principal in charge of Special Education to discuss the situation. I asked her when the recycling lesson or unit would be finished, and told her I wanted it revised before it was taught again. To my surprise my Assistant Principal said, "Lesson? They do that every day after lunch." My assistant principal continued, "It bothered me when I first came here too, but "Linda" said that it had *always* been done this way, so I just accepted it. Besides, whenever you talk to Linda she always brings a union rep. And I think she's close with school board members."

Threats can come in multiple forms. At this point, Dr. Romero is expected to back down to the capital possessed by the special education teacher whose practice she is challenging. The fact that Dr. Romero is now hearing that this behavior is not just a "lesson" but rather an ongoing activity that the students do every day and they do so during instructional time magnifies the severity of the behavior.

> 'How we have always done it.' I had heard that expression a lot. It may have always been that way, but I was determined it wasn't going to continue, at least not while I was the principal. My special education students were not going to dig through basura (garbage), as if we were training them for life on the streets. Not while I was the principal.
>
> My Assistant Principal warned me that Linda would fight me and that she "needed" the recycling money for her program. 'Linda takes the cans and bottles to the recycling center and gets money that they use to take the kids out to lunch every Friday. They usually go to Chuckie Cheese or Pepitos. It really bothers me because the kids are always eating such fattening, unhealthy food. I wish they would go somewhere healthier or cook more healthy food in class. They make nachos and brownies or cake in class every week.' I felt like I had fallen down the rabbit hole.

The complexity of the matter worsens as Dr. Romero poses more questions for us to consider as to the positioning of the students in the Special Education program,

What lessons were our Special Education students being taught? And just as importantly, what was the lesson to all who observed them digging through trash cans? It was a lesson from the hidden curriculum; Special education students, as people with disabilities, are low social status individuals, not fully-valued (or valuable) members of society. We should set our expectations for them, in life and in learning, low. They are not capable of more. It was also a lesson about income, ethnicity, immigrant status and power. Students from more privileged backgrounds would not have been asked to dig through trash cans. High income families would have put an immediate stop to it. Only in a community, like the one my high school served, could this "way we have always done it" have existed for so long. My high school served a predominantly Latino community. Almost all of the parents and guardians made little money and few had the luxury of a college education. Many spoke little or no English. Many were undocumented. Who would complain, or even question, the practices of the school?

Dr. Romero recognizes that the population she is describing may not feel empowered to address the behaviors. As the people in the school system are often esteemed as being "the professionals" who are supposed to have the best interest of their children at heart, parents may not feel that they are in a position to challenge the practices of people trained to educate their children. With critical insight, a framework of social justice, and employing her leadership skills, Dr. Romero, proceeded,

I stood my ground. I was not going to have my special education students (or any other students), digging through trash cans. More importantly, I was not going to have trash picking skills taught at my school. If recycling was important, another way to recycle would have to be found. If money was an issue, we had plenty of money earmarked for special education. I encouraged my Assistant Principal to find another solution. She had an idea and I told her to run with it.

And, that's when the phone calls began. The first phone call I got was from the Union President. The second was from the district Special Education Coordinator. The third was from the Superintendent. Not long after, the President of the School Board paid a visit.

I politely but firmly handled the call from the union president. This was a curricular matter, not a contract matter. I would do what was in the best interest of students. The call from the Special Education Coordinator was initially contentious but ended with an ally once she heard the whole story. Before we talked, her understanding was that I was "anti-special education," and was destroying programs and cutting off funding.

The Superintendent, after questions from the union and some school board members, asked me why she was hearing that I was dismantling the special education recycling program. When I explained, her response was supportive, but cautionary. She explained that school board members had been getting phone calls and that I might get a visit.

The school board president, "Gloria," was known for "dropping by" schools where she had heard complaints. I expected her visit and planned for it. Gloria was formerly a special education teacher's aide at my high school. She was an advocate for special education students, but she was also an elected official and the special education teachers were her friends and among her strongest supporters. In spite of this, I was pretty sure I could win her over.

Dr. Romero held her ground. While she took up the position of a Transformational Leader (Appendix E) in which she not only served as a role model to others but guided the constituents of her school site towards individual and institutional success (Nevarez & Wood, 2010). Within her institution she encouraged the adoption of high expectations of and value of the students in the special education program. Additionally, she employed a high degree of "team" effort in that the solution to addressing this issue would come from behaviors that demonstrated a school wide value and inclusion of all children.

My Assistant Principal had come up with a fantastic alternative. She talked to the Advance Placement (AP) Environmental Science teacher. His AP students had an after school environmental club. They also recycled and used the money for club activities. Their club placed recycling boxes, some for paper and others for cans, around campus. My Assistant Principal proposed that the AP and special education students join forces in a cooperative recycling program. Both the Environmental Science teacher and his students all embraced this idea. It was brilliant—two groups of students whose paths rarely, if ever crossed, would work together to create and distribute more recycling boxes. The Special Education teacher though still not happy, agreed to try it.

When the School Board member visited, I quickly brought up the subject, asking her if she had heard about our wonderful new recycling program that paired special education and Advanced Placement students. I also "causally" mentioned that I won't want to read in the newspaper about special education students being required to pick through trash, or otherwise, be sued. She left campus satisfied with the change.

As a new principal, I learned some important lessons. First, it was worth it to stand up for the rights and the dignity of students – all students. Second, not everyone will agree with you. Expect that you will be challenged. Remember that almost all educational decisions are also political decisions, and must be viewed through and planned with that lens. Third, don't be afraid to uncover, question, and challenge the hidden curriculum. You will be a better educator for it. And don't think you are ever finished. This was only the first round in the fight over what special education students were being taught. But, for the second round, I was ready.

Final reflections from Johnson speak to the measured use of one's passion in "putting out the fire" that humanists can, at times, find themselves in the midst of:

I have to control my desire to do that (quell the fire all in one attempt). I have a really strong desire just to get the fire truck and shoot at it with water which I can now assess better how much water to put on it. (laughter). But the obligation is that there will be water. It's just how much and how forceful and what it is. I think it is something I've learned more through my experiences how to better assess that (Johnson, Joint Session, April 27, 2007).

Tessler went on to discuss how she tried to engage her school community in escalating tension surrounding the Black Student Union on her campus as the students were continually challenged for their attempts to hold activities on campus. Yet, those who she tried to engage remained passive while the group continued to be subjected to racism. Courtenay reflected on her response to the growing discord that she equated to an "active volcano" that eventually "exploded" and "spewed all over the place." On reflecting on her experience with the community's initial negative response to the Black Student Union, she stated, "You never sense that it's going to get out of control or out of hand and that's where people who are really good managers become really skillful at being able to have a second sense about all that is coming in and trying to listen … when you have to listen, when you have to back off, when you can do something, when you can't and try to get people in a different direction."

Using **Praxis** (Freire, 1998), which is the tool of action and reflection, allowed both these humanists to talk openly about their activism and to not only determine what works but also to share what they learned about themselves and how to be more effective when stepping into situations in the future. This process of reflecting upon their experiences provided insightful observations of how they handled racism and demonstrated their capacity to understand the positionality of people of color who are subjected to racism but feeling disempowered to respond. Johnson provides a thoughtful example of how she learned about herself from her past experiences in working at the rice-drying company and how she applied her growth to another incident in which she, as a white woman, was compelled to intervene:

Another piece that I learned through my first real experience at the rice dryer was that my initial method was very paternalistic and very taking care of those who are in need. What I have learned more over time is to be supportive for those who I am trying to empower or support those who are hurt.

Johnson provides us another powerful tool as a humanist, this being using one's power and privilege to empower those who are subjected to oppression. The value of this, as we know, not only strengthens cross-racial bonds such as seen through the work of Colonel Shaw and John Brown, but can also be employed through the speaking of truth. Frederick Douglass bears testament to the power of self efficacy developed when engaged by William Lloyd Garrison to speak to the truth of his experiences as a man who had been held in bondage.

After years of living in freedom and having written and spoken about the horrors of his experiences, Douglass wrote to his former "master," Thomas Auld. Douglass' letter states that perhaps the former master had heard of Garrison. This, we know, would hold true as many slaveholders were fearful of the uprisings that they thought would be incited by Garrison's activism, as well as the attack on the immorality of slavery. Douglass goes on to state in his letter that it was Garrison who "put it into my head that I might make myself serviceable to the cause of the slave, by devoting a portion of my time to telling my own sorrows, and those of other slaves.... This was the commencement of a higher state of existence than any to which I had ever aspired" (Douglass, p. 415, 1994). The power of the relationship between Brown and the black men he recruited to serve in his army, as well as the bond between Colonel Shaw and the men he trained from the 54th Regiment, provides the element of white humanists using their status to, as Johnson stated, "support" people in the effort to address the injustices.

The use of speaking truth had an empowering effect on Douglass. His letter reveals an acquired sense of worth as a man *equal to* the former master who he confronts for the mistreatment inflicted upon himself, his sisters, his mother, and his "dear old grandmother." Douglass inquires about his grandmother's wellbeing after accusing Auld of having "turned out like an old horse to die in the woods" after her many years of bondage. Despite this, we see from Douglass, given his newly contextualized relationships with white people like Garrison, that he holds no malice toward Auld and rather than speak as an oppressor in his newfound freedom, he, rather, speaks from a place of strength and grace.

> I intend to make use of you as a weapon with which to assail the system of slavery—as a means of concentrating public attention on the system, and deepening the horror of trafficking in the souls and bodies of men. I shall make use of you as a means of exposing the character of the American church and clergy—and as a means of bringing this guilty nation, with yourself, to repentance. In doing this, I entertain no malice toward you personally. There is no roof under which you would be more safe than mine, and there is nothing in my house which you might need for your comfort, which I would not readily grant. Indeed, I should esteem it a privilege to set you an example as to how mankind ought to treat each other (Douglass, p. 418, 1994).

Douglass signed this letter, "I am your fellow-man, but not your slave." For Douglass to get to this place of grace meant that a multitude of humanists worked in concert to promote and elevate his position in society as a man, as a "fellow-man." The various means by which to fight the fire gave Johnson an opportunity to recall another incident in which a Japanese American was the only person of color in a room full of white people, and that with a threatening protest brewing outside, "it is the white person's place to speak up about the concern. How might that Japanese American person feel because right now that person is not feeling safe to bring up anything about it? So recognizing the empowerment of the person and perhaps the person has too much fear to speak up about it and then it's my job to ask about it. 'Are you feeling safe?' and 'How is that affecting you?' because that person in that situation shared that she did not feel safe enough to talk about it. Yet, she was too afraid to go outside."

The supportive role discussed by Johnson is another tool employed by humanists. Being able to call "it" what "it" is and understand how it impacts those who are threatened by the violence is vital. As we move further on to discuss another major theme from our historical and modern-day humanists, we revisit what Johnson previously touched upon in the joint session, when she talks about how confronting the fire takes her to a place of her "spirituality and integrity."

QUESTIONS FOR DISCUSSION OR SELF REFLECTION

SELF-AWARENESS

1. What feelings come up for you when you hear hateful comments or witness hateful acts?

2. How have you handled these situations in the past? What would you do differently, if anything?

CLIENT WORLDVIEW

3. What is the cost, psychologically and physically, of being subjected to attacks?

COUNSELING RELATIONSHIP

4. Tessler talks about "emotional energy" and "skills needed to "walk into the fire." Discuss sources of your "emotional energy," and what you can do to strengthen this source of strength to minimize the feeling of being "meek of heart?" What are "skills" you possess, and what can you do to develop and/or strengthen them?

COUNSELING AND ADVOCACY INTERVENTIONS

5. The humanists in this book all encountered various levels of violence directed at them. What are ways to protect yourself from these attacks and/or minimize the likelihood of such attacks?

NEW CONCEPTS AND VOCABULARY TO REVIEW

Dialogical Force: Unity:

"Praxis": Hidden Curriculum

Activity

1. Discuss with a classmate, friend or family member the emotions that get in the way of your being authentic and true to your values.

2. Discuss what are your values and to what extent would you put yourself at risk?

3. What are sacrifices that you would make (or have made) to support a cause? What price would you be willing to pay?

References

Apple, M. W. (2004). *Ideology and Curriculum*. London: Routledge & Kegan Paul.

Botkin, B. A. (1945). *Lay my burden down*. Chicago, IL; University of Chicago Press.

Douglass, F. (1994). *Douglass autobiographies*. New York, NY: Penguin Books.

Emilio, L. F. (1891). *History of the fifty-fourth regiment of Massachusetts volunteer infantry, 1863–1865*. Boston, MA: The Boston Book Company.

Freire, P. (1998). *Pedagogy of the oppressed*. New York, NY: The Continuum Publishing Company.

Freire (2000). *Pedagogy of the Oppressed: 30th Anniversary Edition*. New York: Continuum.

Garrison, F. & Garrison, W. (1885). *William Lloyd Garrison, 1805–1879*, Volumes I & II. New York, NY: The Century Co.

Grimké, A. (1830). Letters to Catherine E. Beecher. Boston, MA. Printed by Isaac Knapp.

Memmi, A. (2005). *Racism*. Minneapolis, MN: University of Minnesota Press.

Reynolds, D. (2005). *John Brown abolitionist*. New York, NY: Random House, Inc.

Wilbanks, C. (2003). *Walking by faith, the diary of Angelina Grimké, 1828–1835*. Columbia, SC: University of South Carolina Press.

Zinn, H. (1999). A people's history of the United States. New York: NY. Harper Collins Publisher.

"You Are My Other Me"

"I see you willing to give your support to the cause of truth that is lying crushed and bleeding, I believe the time to be the fulfillment of the Prophecies, that we are beholding the Second Advent of Christ ... I do not fear the lions in your path."

Sarah Shaw, mother of Colonel Shaw, in a letter to her son as he consented, at her urging, to lead the first newly created black regiment in the Civil War (Duncan, 1992, p. 37).

For four years, I taught at California's only tribal college when its enrollment was thriving with the richness of indigenous people from many First Nations of the Americas. The students attending this college represented a fraction of the diversity of American indigenous nations from Peru to Washington state. Students and instructors were identified as Mayan, Choctaw, Pomo, Hualapai, Mexica, Wintun, MiWok, and Yakima, to name a few. As diverse as the tribes of origins were, our students all shared a common history: they were survivors of Conquest and Colonization (Freire, 1998).

During my four-year tenure at this college, I was exposed to a wide range of traditions and worldviews. The privilege of having different tribal affiliations represented in the classroom allowed students and faculty to share, cross tribally, our respective ceremonies and traditions. Many indigenously identified people, including myself, have lost the traditions and ceremonies of our respective tribes and nations. This is the outcome of Conquest and Cultural Invasion (Freire, 1998). We shared everything from tamales to fried bread, cleansing ceremonies to creation stories. We did not hold one tradition over another, but rather practiced **Cultural Synthesis** (Freire, 1998) in which we valued and respected the uniqueness and diversity of other tribal belief systems and felt blessed to recapture the essence of our shared heritage.

During my years teaching at the tribal college, I completed my doctorate degree at the University of San Francisco. I participated in the traditional graduation with my classmates in the campus chapel. The students at the tribal college hosted another ceremony in which my regalia was received and blessed by the community. The ceremony was not intended to celebrate my individual accomplishment; rather, it was meant to honor the completion of my doctorate as a reflection upon the community. It also symbolized the journey taken toward completion of the degree and, now, the responsibility I bore to serve others with the acquisition of my knowledge and credentials. This is collectivist thought in which the individual *is* only because the individual is *in relation* to one's community.

For the ceremony, the students formed a circle around me as I stood in the middle wearing my graduation regalia. My mentor, Dr. Olivia Gallardo, presented me with an indigenous patterned stole that she made from a blanket. A young man, a two-spirit who is affiliated with a Plains tribe, honored the completion of the degree by doing a grass dance as part of the blessing ceremony. It was summer time, in a non-air-conditioned room, but his rhythm and intensity were undaunted by the mounting heat as he circled around me in the midst of the community circle. I wear the stole every semester when I participate in graduation ceremonies. It affirms my indigenous roots, and reminds me of my obligation to the larger community and the sacrifice required to be *in relation with others*. This is one of the values re-learned and one of many culturally grounded lessons I received during my four years at the tribal college.

During this period while I was teaching, I felt as though I was mostly the student. The experience provided opportunities for immersion in cultural activities from sweats to rites of passage ceremonies. One lesson came from an interaction with one of the resident hall advisors, who was, himself, from a California tribe. This man shared with me the reason for the great pride he had for his young son. In anticipation for the son's upcoming birthday, the father had asked his son whether he would like a Game Boy or an eagle feather. The son chose the feather. The father stated that, in his tribe, material possessions of this world held no value; every year, he gave away the possessions he had accumulated over the year. By doing so, he would not grow attached to the material world and, subsequently, become possessed by his possessions. The values that he claimed and lived by were of a spiritual nature, which is why he was so pleased that his son retained the culturally grounded appreciation of the eagle feather over a material possession.

Leaving me with one more lesson to ponder, he made a statement that conveyed his worldview. He simply stated, "**You Are My Other Me**." (Personal Communication). These few words speak to an inherent belief system that says we are all spiritually connected so that a transgression against another human being is a transgression against the self. "Differences" in the variations of humanity, whether it be skin color, class affiliation, religious belief system, sexual orientation, or physical or mental ability levels, have no significance since this belief system purports that we are all from one source. But, in this lifetime, each person experiences a different reality as related to the body we each inhabit. In short, each person is, primarily, a spiritual being living a physical experience.

The profound nature of this simple statement made me consider similar statements from other belief systems that espouse treating others as you would have others treat you. Most faith systems espouse "brotherly" and "universal" love for all. The application of this principle seems to be, however, our greatest challenge. Human beings from all faiths are tested with choosing between material possessions of this world and principles grounded in their faith. The choices one makes each day, however, are what speak, regardless of the claimed faith and what others perceive to be the true nature of one's heart.

This chapter addresses another common theme in the lives of our humanists: their belief in a higher power and how this higher power serves as their source of strength. The nature of the belief system varies from one humanist to the next, but what is clearly evident from their actions and their words is that they draw courage and inspiration from their spiritually grounded principles and then use this orientation to overcome challenges, confrontations, and their own fear. Within

their belief system is a sense of connection with all humanity that transcends social constructions and materialism. In their words and in their actions, our humanists were driven by values far from the motivation of greed and material gain. Just as Angelina Grimké referred to people in bondage as "fellow creatures," our humanists did not see the people they were fighting for as less than themselves; they saw them as "My Other Me." We will consider the evidence from the lives of our humanists to see how their spiritual orientations manifested themselves in their time on earth.

"Game Boy or Eagle Feather?"

Angelina Grimké was born into her family's Episcopalian faith; but, at the age of thirteen, she refused to be confirmed into the ancestral church of her family. For this act of moral courage "the rector pronounced it an ominous symptom in one so young, which he feared might ripen into insanity" (Weld, 36). She converted to the Presbyterian faith "where she hoped to find a home for her spirit" but "found instead that it scouted the spirit of Christ, while clinging to his name" (Weld, 38). Not finding support for her abolitionist principles in this faith, she then adopted the Quaker traditions. Despite the fact that she did not receive the swift and decisive support for her principles even in this tradition, she found outlets for her beliefs. "The eager soul must work, not rest in testimony." Once she decided to self-exile to the North, "she made her own religion,—one of sacrifice and toil" (Weld, 30).

The fuel that inflamed her adherence to abolitionist principles can be directly correlated to the violence she witnessed every day. It maintained the institution of slavery, as well as contributed to the devolvement of humanity. Grimké repeatedly chronicled in her journal the multitude of observations in which her family members treated one another with disrespect and hostility. She pointed this out to them, particularly when they accused the servants of not behaving courteously. Her retort to her family's criticisms of the servants' behavior was asking how they could expect differently of the servants when the family members, themselves, behaved discourteously and rudely to one another. Their behaviors were the models.

Despite prevailing discontentment and divisive tension in the Grimké family, no efforts were made to free their slaves. The lifestyle was comfortable. It is what they knew. They enjoyed privileges that, from Angelina's estimation, were more obstructive to having true relationship with one another than adding value to their earthly existence. Her journal entry of August 12, 1829, emphasizes the strained relationships evident within other families in her community, as well as the emotional distance that the institution of slavery bore on her own family,

> It appears to me there is a real want of natural affection among many families in Carolina, & I have tho't that one great cause of it is the independence which the members of families here feel—instead of being taught to do for themselves & each other, they are brought up to be waited on by slaves, and then an unamicable, proud, selfish spirit is cherished. I have many times felt exceedingly tried when in the flowings of love towards Mother I have offered to do little things for her & she has refused to allow me by saying that it was Stephen, or Williams duty & she preferred their doing it; the other night of tea being refused in this way I said, being hurt by it, Mother it seems to me thou would at any time rather have a Servant to do little things for thee than me; she replied, it was their business. Well said I Mother, I do not think, it ever was designed that parents & children should be so independent of each other, our Heavenly Father intended that we should do for others and be dependent on each other, not on Servants (none of them were in the room). From time to time ability is granted for me to labour against Slavery. I may be mistaken, but I do not think it is any longer without sin in Mother, for I think she feels no way sensibly, now that it is not right, tho' she never will acknowledge it (Wilbanks, 2003, p. 117).

Angelina's sentiment reflects strong dissatisfaction in the lack of intimacy between her own family members. She also recognizes that this "lack of affection" is a current that runs through slave-holding families. She attributes this outcome to family members' lack of dependency on one another. Instead, they depended on human beings who were viewed as objects to serve them and do so out of the pure motivation of fear, not out of genuine affection. In their worldview, the Game Boy would have meant more than the eagle feather. The "selfish spirit," maintained by the by products of wetiko, violence and greed, holds greater value than what Angelina ascribes to her "Heavenly Father's intentions." The construction of a worldview grounded in "You Are My Other Me" means relationships of reciprocity in which the value of *you* is greater than the value of material possessions.

Angelina and her sister, Sarah, were unable to secure a caring and nurturing relationship with their family members, including their mother. They left behind a world of material possessions that included human beings as part of their inherited "capital" wealth. For the Grimké sisters, this wealth held no value, so they walked away from it. Later, when they had the opportunity to do so, they emancipated those who fell under their inheritance. They choose the feather.

The Golden Rule

John Brown was raised as a Calvinist. This belief system holds that human beings are depraved and that only a chosen few are selected for salvation. The existence of slavery, for him, confirmed the depraved state of humanity. Such an extreme form of mistreatment was indicative of humanity's sinful nature, whose very existence stained the soul and character of this nation. Brown considered it proper through his actions to atone for the sins of others.

After his capture at Harpers Ferry, Brown responded to one of his interrogators, who asked, "Who sent you here?" Brown replied, "No man sent me here; it was my own prompting and that of my Maker; or that of the devil, whichever you are pleased to ascribe to. I acknowledge no master in human form." When further questioned by Virginia Senator James Mason about the nature of Brown's mission, Brown replied, "We came to free the slaves, and only that." Mason further prodded Brown to justify his acts, to which Brown replied, "I think, my friend, you are guilty of a great wrong to God and against humanity-I say it without wishing to be offensive and I believe it would be perfectly right to interfere with you, so far as to free those you wickedly and willfully hold in bondage. I think I did right, and that others will do right who interfere with you at any time and at all times. The Golden Rule applies to all who would help others to gain their liberty" (Reynolds, 2005, p. 330).

A foundational principle of Christianity, "Do Unto Others As You Would Have Them Do Unto You" is not so dissimilar to "You Are My Other Me." Both of these principles speak to the foundational element that *all* deserve respect and love. Brown did not differentiate the worth of the individual due to any value accorded to the arbitrary difference of skin color. The orientation by which Brown derived the motivation to declare war on the institution of slavery can be found in his response to a bystander's question during his interrogation: "Do you consider this a religious movement?" Brown's response does not claim a religious affiliation, but instead demonstrates an impetus generated from his relationship with a higher power. His response to this question was, "The greatest service man can render to God." The activated principle of the Golden Rule is, again, evident when he provides justification for his actions. "I pity the poor in bondage that have none to help them." He said he was not here "to gratify my personal animosity, revenge or vindictive spirit. It is my sympathy with the oppressed and the wronged, that are as good as you and as precious in the sight of God" (Reynolds, p. 331). Brown's response clearly provides his perception that, while people in bondage were not held in value other than as a material possession, Brown perceived these same people "as good as" and "as precious" as anyone else. Skin color had no bearing in Brown's value of "the other."

The Holy War

Sarah Shaw perceived her son's work as a continuation of John Brown's effort. She referred to the Civil War as "The Holy War." In referencing her son's willingness to take up the post of Colonel for the 54th Regiment, she saw it as "God's mission." In other words, it was not just another military appointment, but was a duty discharged from a higher calling. After Brown's failed attempt to overthrow the institution of slavery, there was a common "truth" in abolitionists' perception that, when unified, worked to lobby resources, support, and public opinion which, collectively, led to the undoing of the institution of slavery. Sarah saw this effort as "the fulfillment of Prophecies." Acknowledging the elevated danger inherent with her white son leading black troops, she drew from her belief system to garner strength and shared this strength with her son as he committed to the cause of liberating human beings held in bondage. "I do not fear the lions in your path" (Duncan, p. 37). Sarah's views reflected a belief that life on earth was temporal; subsequently, one's deeds during a lifetime granted eternal life. For Sarah, her son's sacrifice in dying for the cause meant that his life, as well as her own, had meaning and purpose.

Ordinary Mortal?

This "cause" had an encapsulated meaning for the Civil War that elevated the war's purpose beyond the reasons that sparked it, reasons rooted in economic and social differences between the North and the South. The war provided the vehicle to further the abolitionists' cause, but the Colonel, initially rejecting the offer to lead the 54th Regiment, was left having to explain to his mother the reason for his decision. He indicated, "I would take it (the position), if I thought myself equal to the responsibility of such a position." He recognized the responsibility that came with the position and stated that he was just "an ordinary mortal" (Duncan, p. 24). His self assessment reveals that he was, initially, unable to call upon internal resources required to meet the needs of this higher cause. His disappointed mother instructed him to "pray" about his decision. He relented and accepted the post.

After months of training and battles that proved the worth of his men, the Colonel took his order on behalf of his regiment that they would be the first to engage the Confederacy in hand-to-hand combat and sustain heavy artillery fire as they attempted to approach the fort. This was a mission not for the faint of heart and, most certainly, would sustain heavy casualties for many and death for many more. The Colonel, prior to leading his troops into the fray of the battle, confided to Colonel Hallowell, "I trust God will give me strength to do my duty." The Colonel led his troops from the front, rather than the back, on this perilous attack. He completed his duty and lost his mortal life in the process, but was immortalized for his strength to serve the higher cause. He rose above his original self estimation of being "an ordinary mortal".

Baptism Through Immersion

Garrison, raised as an ardent Baptist, was never baptized. He considered immersion as the only form of baptism. Garrison knew the Bible well. He could repeat verses by heart and applied the full meaning and power of Biblical references once he took on the cause of emancipation. Upon the turning point in his life when he committed his life's work to abolitionism, he returned to the Bible and studied the book anew.

Garrison, unlike the Shaws, grew up amid familial and economic hardship. His father deserted the family when Garrison was still a child, and his mother was often dependent on others to provide care for her son while she found employment in other cities. Garrison's mother died before he committed to the cause of abolitionism, but prior to her passing, she lived in multicultural communities where she came to appreciate the comfort, love, and care of African Americans. The last letter Garrison received from his mother holds a strong tone that urges her son to pursue *meaning* in his life's work. While she expressed reservations about whether his chosen profession of writing could sustain him, she had further sentiments about what he chose to write about:

> you think your time was wisely spent while you were writing political pieces. I cannot join with you there, for had you been searching the scriptures for truth, and praying for direction of the holy spirit to lead your mind into the path of holiness, your time would have been more wisely spent, and your advance to the heavenly

world more rapid. But instead of that you have taken the Hydra by the head, and now beware of his mouth; but as it is done, I suppose you think you had better go on and seek the applause of mortals. But, my dear L., lose not the favour of God; have an eye single to his glory, and you will not lose your reward... (Garrison, 1885, p. 51).

Garrison's mother, Frances, clearly expresses her displeasure in Garrison's literary focus prior to his embarking upon a life committed to abolitionism. Her reference to "applause of mortals" refers to rewards of this world such as the game boy, rather than rewards that would be in the "favour of God which can also be represented by the feather." It was not until after her death that Garrison became more involved with the abolition movement. This is when he drew upon his strength as a writer, his knowledge of scripture, and fulfilled his mother's desire of using his "mind" for "holiness." "No American before Garrison had so dramatically challenged his government's failure to realize and protect its ideals; no citizen before Garrison had staked the survival of the nation upon the spiritual revelation accomplished by a minority liberated from conventional politics and armed only with a righteous conviction of truth" (Mayer, 1998, p. 445). Garrison, similar to the Grimké sisters, was not averse to recognizing the hypocrisy of people who claimed to be Christians yet did nothing to speak out against war or slavery.

Minister's Daughter

Helen Hunt Jackson was raised in a religious family, but, by time of her death, had gravitated toward spiritualism. She was not known to attend church, though she was the daughter of a minister. Her orientation to the world was such that she worshiped in "the great cathedral known as Cheyenne Canyon" (Odell, 1939, p. 134). A few days before her death, she wrote to her long-time mentor, Colonel Higginson, the following communication that not only reveals her belief in an afterlife, but also her regret for having committed to her cause on behalf of Native Americans so late in her life.

> I want you to know that I am looking with an almost eager interest into the "undiscovered country" and leaving this earth with no regret save that it was so late in the day when I began work in earnest. But I do not doubt that we shall keep on working- Any other conception of existence is to me monstrous. It seems to me almost impossible that we shall not be able to return to this earth and see our loved ones. Whether we can in any way communicate with them I doubt-but that we can see them I believe (Odell, 1939, p. 82).

Hunt conveys her belief in a spiritual realm that co-exists with the mortal world. Doubting whether communication is possible, she nonetheless believes in the ability to see those left behind. This theme of a "spiritual mission" while on earth is, once again, evident with our modern-day humanists. It is a grounded perception of one's reality that transcends the constructions of power and privilege while moving the mortal body to do the "work" required to improve the lived reality for others.

Modern Day Humanists

Similar to our historical humanists, our modern-day humanists possess roots grounded in religious orientations. Courtenay states that her principles are rooted to a religious family with great-great grandfathers from both sides of her family serving as Methodist ministers. With this said, she indicates that they were also very spiritual. Her father, heavily involved in the Presbyterian church, exposed her to the activities of the church community.

An interesting parallel can be found with this modern-day humanist and Helen Hunt Jackson, as related to their spiritual orientations. It is well known that Hunt's life was plagued with tremendous losses. Her mother died when Helen was 14, and her father passed away three years later. Her first husband died in a military accident after 11 years of marriage. Both children by this marriage died of natural causes. By the time Hunt was 35, she was widowed, childless, and depressed. The adopted cause on behalf of Native Americans provided purpose for her to move forward with her life. It also appeared to be a turning point in which she embraced a spiritual orientation (Odell, 1939).

Tessler, losing her own mother suddenly, distanced herself from the church in which she was raised. She periodically attends the church of her family but she also holds on to a more inclusive belief in God and a strong spiritual orientation. She embraces the notion that access to a higher power can take different forms for different people. In other words, there is more than one way in which to access this higher power, so she respects the diversity of belief systems.

To this day, Tessler, whose husband is Jewish, attends services from a range of faith systems. "I go to synagogues. I go to Catholic churches. I go to Presbyterian. I go to the temples. I go to the Gurdwara. I enjoy that fluid thing that I do and ... I gain from all of it. But I'm not defining myself as one thing but I'm clearly very spiritual in my belief system that we are here for a reason and that there is spiritual strength that comes from lots of different sources and I think it is very important in people's lives" (Tessler Interview, March 28, 2007).

This "reason" for being here as discussed by Tessler provides context for the challenge that Johnson discusses when she talks about the nature of relationship with others while on this earth. She discusses the modeling she tries to provide for her children of living a life in which they are open to others, living *in relationship* with others, and having "respect for every living thing. Respect for people. Respect for plants, animals, food, respect for the planet" (Johnson Interview, March 7, 2007).

In this reflection on Johnson's desire to raise children who do not acquiesce to the forces of the dominant culture, she emphasizes what all our humanists come to know when having to not only step away from dominant culture ideologies but to stand apart from beliefs that they do not embrace. Johnson tries to impart to her children what our historical humanists and Courtenay have all come to know, "that it's o.k. for people not to like you." With this comes a recognition that people from their own cultural group may not approve of some of their views and that, at some point, if they are to live lives grounded in humanist principles, they need to accept that their own views may differ from the dominant culture. Furthermore, they explain that they must not bend to the pressure and allow themselves to be belittled into adopting views incongruent with their hearts.

In my interview with Johnson, she stressed the importance of not seeking the approval of people whose approval she did not care for. In other words, there is no need to invest in relationships where the values are incongruent with one's own. Similar to Angelina Grimké, who demonstrated "serene indifference to the judgment of those about her" (Weld, 30), Johnson elaborates on the importance of not conceding one's values by giving into pressures that would make one live in ways that are not grounded in one's own principles. As an educator who has the privilege of being in the classroom with people who have committed their lives to serving others, I have heard many stories from my students of the challenges they face just to be in the position to heed the calling. One student, Serey Vann, relates his experience of how he finally arrived to being a graduate student in our Counselor Education program,

> I am Cambodian, heterosexual, male, Buddhist. My ethnicity and cultural background has helped shape my values of obedience, respect, collectivism, and determination. My gender has taught me to be tough; physically and mentally. Buddhism has taught me to have compassion for all beings; provided me with the belief in Karma, that I should do good things in this life so that the next life would be good also.

Vann recognizes the principles of his faith that inform his choice of action which subsequently direct his life. He acknowledges, however, that due to the many challenges that people face due to exposure to violence, immigration stress, and oppressive living conditions that others facing the same set of circumstances may have different outcomes,

> Being displaced from Cambodia, escaping from the Khmer Rouge, my parents and many other Cambodians came to the United States for better opportunities but instead, they were placed in the ghettos where there are a lot of gangs and liquor stores. A lot of Cambodians have lost their psychosocial connections; they lost their homeland which was meaningful to them. Therefore, a lot of Cambodians began drinking alcohol and got addicted to it.

While witnessing the negative outcomes of many of his peers, Vann followed a path that sent him down another direction. The options available to him were limited to the paths taken by family members who he held in high esteem. Nonetheless, he did not find fulfillment in pursuing the same course of study,

> My parents held very high expectations for me because all of my siblings are successful. Two of my oldest brothers are electrical engineers, my oldest sister is a pharmacist, another brother is a program director for a non-profit organization and yet another is a mechanic for BMW. Even my younger sister makes a lot of money working as a pharmacy clerk. I didn't want to let my parents down, therefore, I majored in Bio-Chemistry for them even though my heart wasn't in it.

Vann acknowledges the strength of having caring adults who hold high expectations and he appreciated the opportunity to pursue a post-secondary degree at a private institution. Yet, overcoming the odds of becoming addicted to drugs and alcohol or becoming involved with gang life,

Vann reveals that something was amiss and the symptoms of this incongruence between what he wanted to do and what he was expected to do became apparent,

> For four and a half years I went to classes, dragged my feet, dreaded lectures and lab experiments which I hated so much. I knew I didn't like the courses and my grades were beginning to reflect it. I felt like a robot just memorizing formulas and elements. The style of instruction was not for me. My heart was in Psychology, the mental processes, and compassion in helping others. But there I was, in a setting where every student was for themselves; competition was the norm. For a very long time, I knew the major wasn't for me but I didn't want to disrespect my parents and my family. I felt that if I told them I wanted to major in Psychology, which was what I really wanted to do coming out of high school, my family would be disappointed in me, feel sorry for me or look down on me because it is not as prestigious or pay as well as other medical fields.

At this point, Vann has conceded the point of conflict; pursuing what was in his heart or pursuing fields that he perceived to provide more lucrative salaries or prestigious titles. The opinions of his family are important to him as they have undergone tremendous challenges in their lives and, as refugees living in the United States, only wish the best for the next generation. This is where Vann attempts to reconcile the desire of his family along with heeding the call of serving others,

> Finally one day, I took action and told them of my intentions of dropping out of private school and changing majors to something I felt was in my heart, the right thing to do. It was very tough. My oldest sister, the pharmacist, was very disappointed in me. My parents were too but eventually they supported my decision. During those four and a half years, I went through so much pain, anguish, and depression that I couldn't even think about becoming successful. My self confidence took a hit because of it. It is where I got my faulty thinking, my self doubts, and my anxiety. Once I finally spoke up about my passion, I took action, my mind became clear and I knew which steps to take to get where I want to be.

Heeding the call to serve others can be difficult. Yet, as Vann further narrates, once the decision to follow this path was enacted and he gave himself permission to live congruently; his heart and his actions, the rewards from this life changing decision have provided great fulfillment as he has gone on to positively impact the lives of others. He provides an example of how following this calling has enabled him to achieve another form of success that goes beyond the size of a paycheck.

> One of the most influential helping relationships I ever experienced was when I was working at an after school program. Manuel Moralez (pseudonym), a Mexican-American young man who was a senior at the time, needed ten credits to graduate high school. He often acted out during class and got into fights. One day I spoke with Manuel, informing him about the YMCA after school program and how it offered many leadership and community service opportunities for high school

students. Realizing that students can earn credits by doing community service, I spoke with his counselor to see whether or not students could receive credit if they volunteered with the YMCA after school program. When I got the "ok" from the counselor, I then proceeded to convince Manuel to volunteer for th YMCA. Once he started to volunteer, I stressed to him the values of respect, honesty, caring, and responsibility, which are the four values of the YMCA. For the next five months of the school year, everyone could see how much Manuel changed. He went from cutting classes and cussing at people to studying often in the library and treating everyone with respect. He took advantage of volunteering for the YMCA by giving back to his community and at the same time earning credits so that he could graduate from high school. By the end of the school year, I was proud of Manuel as he walked across the stage to receive his diploma.

What is evident from Vann's intervention is that Vann becomes the caring adult in Manuel's life who provides high expectations and a way by which Manuel could also participate in making the world a better place for others by "giving back to his community." The reward and fulfillment derived from changing Manuel's life holds promise in Manuel's embracing the accomplishment and recognizing that he can now hold the same bar of hope and expectations for others, While Manuel acknowledges that meeting one's goals may not always be easy, success be attained by one's directed efforts. Vann vividly recalls Manuel's reaction to turning his life around,

> "Being the first one in my family to earn a high school diploma is a big relief off my shoulders ... it feels like I won the lottery because I worked so hard for it." Manuel beamed with a smile. Manuel was able o set a good example to his siblings as well as his fellow classmates by showing that with determination and focus one can achieve any goal in life. (Vann, journal entries, 2012)

Once Vann was in the position to serve others he found meaning to his life as he went on to make a difference in the lives of others. Vann took the risk of responding to his heart and is now living congruently with the values of his heart. Johnson shared her final thoughts about being in relationship with forces that pull us from our true selves: "Evaluate that if you are not receiving approval is it from someone whose values you respect? And if so, then you need to look at yourself and if not, then let it go." Angelina and Sarah Grimké walked away from the inherited wealth that included owning human beings in bondage. In a letter to one of William Lloyd Garrison's sons, Frank, that was dated October 20, 1872, well after the ending of the Civil War, Sarah Grimké expressed her distinctive worldview after having spent some time with the Garrison family at their home. She states, "I regretted not seeing you when I was at your dear home, but I did enjoy your father and mother very much. I hope to accept your mother's invitation to come again—the fact is my heart cleaves more and more to those blessed spirits who stood in the fore front of the battle against that surpassing sin of slavery that I cannot resist any opportunity to be with them." Their lives reflect an orientation grounded in the spiritual realm of relationship. Johnson would concur with this way of being that may necessitate walking away from relationships that do not allow us to live *in relation* to the other (Johnson Interview, March 7, 2007).

Our humanists exist(ed) above the motivations of self gain, despite tremendous influences that could have fostered materialistically centered values. Passing humanistic values to the next generation in light of exposure to major cultural and social influences can present many challenges. This is evident in Sarah Shaw's attempts to urge her son to rise above his self assessment of being "a mere mortal." In the same vein, Johnson urges her children not to bend to expectations that are not *in relation* and respectful of the world around them. These elements of an identity that perceives *the other* as himself, is one consciously exuded as these humanists attempt to live lives of nonconformity, *in relationship,* above the constructions of power and privilege, and devoid of material gain. The constant theme of "meaning and purpose for one's life" continues to ring true for those committed to leaving the world in a better place than how they found it. Mariel Fernandez, another graduate student who I have had the privilege of having in my classes, provides, similar to Vann, further evidence to the value of living in congruence, with one's heart,

> A meaningful life is when an individual can hold a mirror up to society, community, a friend, and themselves—to show its many follies, and to stop blaming each other and making excuses for our wrong behavior ... Sometimes I question why people's search for happiness is always associated with money. As long as a person looks at his or her happiness through the size of their wallet, finding it may be a destination never reached. I say never reached because it will be discovered that no matter how much money you earn if your heart is not in the right place, you can never really know what happiness and contentment is.

Fernandez points out a value system in which "happiness" is not necessarily determined by the amount of one's paycheck but asks us to search our hearts, for those committed to this path, to uncover one's true meaning in life and commit action to one's values. She goes on to elaborate on "a purposeful life."

> ... how can we be truly happy when our fellow man isn't, or when homelessness, calamity, disease, poverty, and the third world exist? Focusing on the things that truly matter and helping each other is what a purposeful life means to me. All of these factors are important to me and I do put such high value on it that I require it from my friends and my partner.

Fernandez speaks to "you are my other me" when she shares a story in which she had to "hold up the mirror" to others and ensure that another human being was treated with care and compassion.

> One busy day... I was working at an Optometry office in the mall. I had the pleasure of working with a man named Kevin (pseudonym). He came to the office politely inquiring if we took Medi-Cal. I said yes, handed him the paperwork, and took him in as a same day patient. Kevin could not make out what was written on the paper, he was squinting and my heart broke just a little. I asked him if he needed help filling the paperwork out and he stuttered to tell me that he cannot see the words. I told him that I could fill it out for him and all I needed was his Medi-Cal card and/ or any identification. He said his I.D. was missing and all he had was his Medi-Cal card. Despite my manager's objections, Kevin was seen the same day. She told

me that he was stinking up the office, and he was. I agreed with her but I told her we can't deny him services just because he smells. She started giving me attitude which we were all so afraid of. She had been known to bully the staff around and she got her way all the time.

Humanists may discern situations and determine when and where to step into a situation that requires their intervention. For Fernandez, when her peers do not protect themselves it can be one matter but for those who have no recourse and the most to lose by way of having their primary needs denied, this was where she drew the line in the sand,

I was fairly new to the office and I always just kept my mouth shut about the micro-aggressions she showed the staff but I have a heart for the underdog. I knew this was not one of those times I could look the other way. Kevin was seen that day and he was so happy. The whole staff was happy except for the manager. Kevin's eyesight is so bad that he is legally blind without his glasses. He can only see shadows and silhouettes. This was why he couldn't make out the patient form to begin with.

He was prescribed glasses which he would get in 3 to 4 weeks. He had no phone number so he would come by the office almost every day to check if they came in, his presence was despised by my then manager.

Fernandez goes on to elaborate on the reasons for and the length by which the manager responded to Kevin in such a dehumanizing manner,

Kevin is a homeless man who was always on the street in front of the mall. I recognized him from seeing him and his brother every day, just standing at a corner asking for food or money. I shared my meals with him many a times by giving him half of my lunches or dinners whenever I am in the area. The Optometry office is a pretty posh place. Imagine two homeless men with their carts in the lobby. I admit

it was not a pretty sight, but I could not turn them away. My manager called security from the back phone and tried to have them escorted out. In the end, security personnel kicked the brother out with their cart of belongings and he waited outside as Kevin finished his eye exam. At one point, Kevin remembered my name but as the months went by he would just call me his "angel from the doctor's office." (Fernandez, Class Journal, Fall of 2012).

Despite the challenges and oppositional opinions of others, "angels" choose the feather. You are my other me.

QUESTIONS FOR DISCUSSION OR SELF REFLECTION

SELF-AWARENESS

1. What do your belief systems encourage you to believe about others whose belief systems are different than yours? How do your beliefs conflict with societal norms about the way you are encouraged to view "difference"? How do you reconcile the conflict?

2. What messages would you want to impart to future generations about how they should live? What steps are you willing to take to crate and model this for future generations?

CLIENT WORLDVIEW

3. Historically, have there been instances in which people have used religion to harm others? How has this impacted people who have been subjected to the violence? How has this impacted people who belong to this religious faith but had nothing to do with inciting the violence?

COUNSELING RELATIONSHIP

4. How would you address tensions that arise from any one of the four Quadrants of Counselor-Client Relationship?

COUNSELING AND ADVOCACY INTERVENTIONS

5. Cultural Invasion is the polar opposite of Cultural Synthesis. What are ways in which you can affirm someone's values within the multiple levels of intrapersonal, interpersonal, institutional, community, public policy and international/global.

NEW CONCEPTS AND VOCABULARY TO REVIEW

Cultural Synthesis

You Are My Other Me:

Activity

1. Graduate student, Amita Khare, recommended expanding one's knowledge of those who lived by the principle of "You Are My Other Me" by learning about more Abolitionists than just those presented in this book. She provided the following link to an online video: http://www.pbs.org/wgbh/americanexperience/films/abolitions/

2. At an international level, you can read about the lives of people also living under the principle of "You Are My Other Me" and learn about ways to intervene, just as Vann and Fernandez did at a local level: Kristof, N. & Wudunn (2009) Half the sky. New York, NY; Knopf Publishers

References

Duncan, R. (1992). *Blue eyed child of fortune*. Georgia: University of Georgia Press.

Freire, P. (1998). *Pedagogy of the oppressed*. New York, NY: The Continuum Publishing Company.

Garrison, F. & Garrison, W. (1885). *William Lloyd Garrison, 1805–1879*, Volume I New York, NY: The Century Co.

Kristof, N. & Wudunn (2009). *Half the sky*. New York, NY; Knopf Publishers.

Mayer, H. (1998). *All on fire*. New York, N.Y; Norton and Company, Ltd.

Odell, R. (1939). *Helen Hunt Jackson*. New York: NY: D. Appleton-Century Company.

Reynolds, D. (2005). *John Brown abolitionist*. New York, NY: Random House, Inc.

Wilbanks, C. (2003). *Walking by faith, the diary of Angelina Grimké, 1828–1835*. Columbia, SC: University of South Carolina Press.

PART II
Activating Humanism— Bridging the Gap

What *is* the Color of Your Heart? Personalizing Humanism

Chapter Contribution by Dr. Rolla Lewis

It is difficult to generalize about anything, even ways of uprooting prejudices. How does one transform and embrace one's capacity toward being an active humanist and a compassionate advocate who has the courage to confront racism, hatred, and oppression? I will avoid making broad, sweeping statements about humanism and instead personalize humanism as a principle guiding my everyday life. The rough-and-tumble actions taken in everyday life are where our life narratives are shaped and defined. But first, before going deeper into this chapter, I feel compelled to offer an introduction about my humanistic way of being in the world.

Introduction to My Humanistic Way of Being in the World

Our lives are made up of varied events and actions; most are small everyday decisions that have to do with merely getting by in life, and few lead to monumental acts that change our lives forever. My humanistic way of being is found in the everyday and ordinary world we wake up into each morning. Our ordinary lives get taken up by cooking, eating, talking, working, and doing what is necessary to make it through the day with as much joy and vibrancy as possible. In describing our world, broad, sweeping statements lose their power when considering the everyday reality they purport to describe. So, we humans get by telling everyday stories about the world where we find ourselves. We all describe our "life world" using language, and we use language to shape the stories we tell about the world.

Humanism, a human construction, is made from a variety of narratives that are described, embraced, and criticized for many contradictory reasons. There is no single narrative or way of describing humanism because there is a range of humanisms. All humanisms, like all stories, come from a certain point of view—yours, mine, or our combined perspective about the world. The humanism described in this chapter comes from a certain perspective. When I talk about humanists or "they" in this chapter, I am really talking about my perspective of what defines humanism and makes it integral with my everyday life and actions. At the same time, I am not merely inventing my humanism moment to moment. My humanistic narrative is tied to the history of humanism and aligned with what others have said about humanism, beginning as far back the Sophist Protagoras of Abdera's (c. 490–c. 421 BCE) statement, "Man [sic] is the measure of all things." But, because I exist in a different time in history and with a different understanding of equality, I would change the statement to "men and women are the measure of all things in their environment."

Men and women describe all things via language that flows from our history, culture, social relationships, and personal experience of being in the world; we exist in certain environments and life contexts. In other words, the humanism that I talk about is not some wild idea popping out of my head, but one that emerges from human history, my own reading of that history, the time and environment where I have come into being, and my understanding of certain ideas shape humanism, from my point of view (Lewis, 2011). My humanism is shaped by the ideas of others, both in the conversations I have and in the opportunities to read the significant thought of other people, especially those who come from cultures other than my own (e.g., West, 1993, 2001, 2002). Listening to and reading about the experiences of others, especially the oppressed, opens your heart to seeing the world anew and challenges you to take the courageous stand that they have taken.

In my own description of the world, I embrace the language and stories available to me. I take responsibility for the first-person narrative undergirding what I am saying. I do not pretend that there is some "objective" place where the world is described from the outside; even when using the third person, I am speaking from inside my world, as much as my world has been created by the language I have been born into and the dialogues I have had with others in the course of my life. Ultimately, I am in what the Germans call my *Lebenswelt*, or my life world. We really do not have an English word that captures the notion.

This chapter is about your responsibility for developing a narrative about your world from your point of view. In understanding our own responsibility for constructing our own world narrative, it is necessary to also recognize that some narrative points of view might be more effective than other narratives. In other words, I want to be humble in my story claims, recognize that I could be wrong, and acknowledge that other possibilities for better and more vibrant narratives exist. For example, let's say I am going to select a doctor because I am ill. I would prefer to have the doctor who is operating on me to be working from the narrative offered by the best medical practice and not from a medieval healer's medical view. This is why I must be alert to the fact that some perspectives, stories, and practices are more effective and work better than others.

Coupled with the realization that some perspectives, stories, and practices are more effective than others is the fact that I cannot leap free from language because language is what we use to describe and define the world. At the same time, there are always gaps in language where things are not said, where stories are not told from all points of view, and where certain ways of narrating stories get embraced. Hence, I must take responsibility for my language and cultural perspective, limiting as they are. Such an understanding keeps me alert to the linguistic, cultural, and philosophic currents informing my personal or professional actions. In other words, understanding that we are born into language and a world that has already been narrated in a certain kind of way helps me to remain open, critical, and filled with wonder about how the world is described by others. This keeps my active humanism humble and always open to change, revision, and renewal. Such an active open stance keeps me more alive, and critical in a constantly evolving story.

Because I see the world differently, I use a different way of describing a humanist continuum, placing **collectivist ecohumanism** on one end and **individualistic solipsism** on the other. Solipsism is a way of being stuck alone in one's head and thoughts—somehow cut off from being influenced by others. Individualistic solipsism is a way of seeing oneself as different, separate, deserving of more even when others are suffering with less, and in addition, somehow separate from others and the ecological consequences of the choices one makes. Individualistic solipsism is a story about being special.

Collectivist ecohumanism would be defined as a perspective that recognizes people are always part of communities, both social and biological. We are all part of something—families, clubs, gangs, groups, fans, etc. We are even part of relational and ecological communities where pollution from one person can do harm to many others.

To be humanistic is to be part of diverse humanistic traditions that explore the meaning in life and actively create or appreciate human expression such as music, art, poetry, sport, novels, essays, research and other endeavors concerned with relationships, growth, and human potential; endeavors designed to make life's flow less solitary, brutish, and cruel.

There is no definitive set of beliefs defining a singular worldwide humanistic doctrine. Humanism is really about different people talking about and appreciating how they and others are in the world. For humanists emerging from Western Europe, there is a cultural flow that dates humanism back to the fourteenth century when scholars studied what they thought was an ideal of human life. Beyond that, there is also a human web where all people in this world wonder about and celebrate what their own diverse cultures consider beautiful and life fulfilling.

Humanism expanded from a provincial European understanding with taproots in Greek, Roman, and the Renaissance culture to a deeper appreciation for the human expression across all world cultures. Now tied to multicultural expression in the United States, humanism is linked to systems of thought that measure truth by what works. One of our deep assumptions in the United States is that we value "what works." This deep appreciation for multicultural diversity and value for pragmatic truth support current humanistic practice and action. For instance, humanistic counselors, teachers, and administrators become advocates when working with youth who are put at risk living in communities and attending schools that fail to appreciate and celebrate diversity, human potential, and the capacity to contribute to the human ability to live life fully.

Humanistic philosophy is often associated with secular humanism, but humanistic orientations range from people who believe in God and people who do not. God-talk abounds, but such talk is framed in human terms. Because we are aware of culture and language, humanists question any person who proposes to speak for God. They know it is a person speaking and not God speaking. There is no expectation that God will be interviewed on the Oprah and Larry King shows or in some other public venue. Theistic (or those believing in God) humanists simply do not claim a religious position that gives them the power to speak for God, but they **do** deeply embrace their spiritual orientations.

Nonetheless, all humanists recognize that humans are creatures who use language to foster relationships, create meanings, families, societies, and cultures. Humanistic counselors present their meaning-centered approach as encouraging language and narratives that promote multiculturalism, diversity, and the fulfillment of human potential. At the heart of humanism, narratives flow from our different languages and point toward diverse ways of living and being in the world. Simply put, different human languages and religions provide opportunities for humans to express diverse ways of being in the world.

That is the essence of humanism—the appreciation and celebration of the different ways people live in the world. Different human languages capture and describe the world in ways that another languages cannot. From those divergent ways of talking about the world, cultures and stories are created to describe ways of relating to and being in worlds from which they emerge. Differing narratives are possible; there is no singular or narrowly correct narrative for being in the world. The human challenge is to be at peace with different ways of being in the world. Humanistic counselors and educators move in a meaning-centered direction concerned with relationship, diversity, social justice, and the understanding that there is value in any approach that lessens the psychological suffering of others.

Deconstructing and Storying Rolla E. Lewis

So what? That is a lot of academic talk, a lot of broad, sweeping words. The real question is not explanatory; it is practical and about living. How do I go about uprooting prejudices, transforming, and embracing my capacity toward being or becoming an active humanist? I begin by looking at who I am and how I use language and judgment in that description. Such descriptions are frequently made in terms of age, religious affiliation, race and/or ethnicity, gender, and occupation. Because these terms are packed with unspoken meanings, it is important to deconstruct them and expand upon their meanings and the story being told. By deconstructing, we clarify and expand upon both the told and the untold story, as well as the possibilities for becoming an active humanist. An example of my deconstruction and story follows. For the purposes of this chapter, I will leave out occupation. Let's move into the broad description of who I am.

I am a 63 year-old, Radical Christian, white male who was born and raised in California. Spend some time with that image. Create an image in your head based on that description.

Image courtesy of Rolla Lewis.

Alexandra with her dad, Rolla

In fact, take some notes that might fill in your own prejudices about old white guys—geezers, so to speak. After you do that, let me deconstruct the descriptors: age, religion, race/ethnicity, and gender. Let me thicken those one-word descriptions into a story that will leave gaps but will provide a more complex narrative than what single words convey about who I am. That being said, my story has more narrative possibilities than what is said by me or any other person.

Age: I am 58. My hair is white. I have not been around as long as many folks I know, but I have been around long enough to see in my lifetime the introduction of personal computers, cell phones, and other technological innovations. I have also been around long enough to bear witness to the destruction of rainforests, grasslands, and the loss of numerous species of animals forever from existence in our world. To illustrate that I am connected to others in time, I have a wife from Switzerland who has been married to me over 35 years. We have two adult children; Alexandra became an ICU nurse after two years in the Peace Corps. Ryan is enrolled in a MS: Environmental Engineering Program. The four of us work to respect each other's choices and to support each other's dreams. As I age and notice myself thinking rigidly about anything, I ponder and reflect upon one of my favorite poems by A. R. Ammons (1996):

Old Geezer
The quickest
way
to change

the
world is
to

like it
the way it
is.

"Old Geezer", from BRINK ROAD by A.R. Ammons. Copyright © 1996 by A.R. Ammons. Used by permission of W.W. Norton & Company, Inc.

Religion: Radical Christian. The term Christian is so limiting because, just as there is a range of humanisms, there is a range of Christianities and possibilities for living the Christian life (West, 2002). Nominally, I am Christian because I grew up un-churched in a family that celebrated Christmas. Outside of attending Sunday school in the fourth grade where I learned core Bible stories, I have never attended or joined a church; but, there is no getting away from one's religion (Taylor, 2007). Because I grew up un-churched in a religiously diverse and spiritually open community in California, my religious perspective and beliefs have been influenced by conversations with Quakers, Protestants, Evangelicals, Catholics, Taoists, Jews, Buddhists, deep ecologists, atheists, and more. In high school, Transcendentalist ideas expressed by Thoreau and Muir informed me as I pondered the meaning of life.

Beginning in college, I was mentored by George Sessions and influenced by his deep ecological ideas that grew out of his philosophical conversations and climbing experiences with Arne Naess, the Norwegian philosopher who expanded the notion of self to include the environment in which we live and our being to existing as part of ecosystems and the ecosphere (Lewis, in press; Naess, 2002; Sessions, 1995). Later, the panentheistic expressions of Meister Eckhart, a twelfth century German mystic were a major influence upon my appreciation of more ecological creation-centered ideas perking out in the West (Fox, 1980).

Living in California, I have been significantly influenced by Taoism and practiced tai chi for over 20 years with a Taoist sifu (teacher); such practice is not merely ideas rattling around in the head but action embodied in movement, centering, and mindfulness—physical exercises directed at deepening one's experience of the moment. Many of my adult friends are Jewish, and I spend holiday celebrations with my Jewish brothers and sisters, where they talk about me as part of the tribe. Our dialogues have helped me to appreciate Jesus as a Jewish sage (Cupitt, 2009).

I currently make every effort to live what Cupitt (2010) calls a solar ethic, pouring out and passing away life like a fountain, saying yes to all of life, to love, and to the lived moment. In other words, my religion is thicker than a one-word description and filled with possibilities that transcend narrow dogmas, rules that oppress women, and hate dressed in biblical garb. The point is not to approve or disapprove of my philosophical or post-theistic theological position, or for me to convince you to take up my position or path. The point is to show some fragment of my path and position and to illustrate, once again, a thicker and deeper description exists than that what is contained in a single word, like Christian. More than Christian, I am hyphenated: Christian-Jew-Taoist-Deep-Ecologist- etc. But how am I going to talk about that? I must also note that simplistic constructions about beliefs can perpetuate misunderstandings, as well as promote fear and hatred.

Race: I am called white. In using the term white, Carl Anthony's chapter, "The Deconstruction of Whiteness," in *Ecopsychology* (1995) provides a way to address this term. An African American, Anthony shares the story about how the Irish indentured servants and black slaves worked together under similar circumstances in the early part of the nineteenth century in the United States. When both groups began to unify against their oppressors, the Irish were told they were white, hence better. White became a marker fixed in racism. I prefer to talk about myself as a Euro-American because it forces me to look at my history where for thousands of years Europeans fought and killed each other over land, religion, power, and other things. It also forces me to look at the colonializing quality in the European culture. Still, an important part of that story is that Europeans saw real differences in each other in terms of language, culture, religion, and disposition, and they killed each other in an attempt to assert some form of dominance or power because of those differences.

For myself coming from that history, besides being Euro-American, I was brought up to be keenly aware of my Welsh ancestry. The Welsh were the first people oppressed by the English, and my family always claimed a separate identity from being English. In grade school, when one of my geography teachers talked about England as the island off the coast of Europe, he left out Wales and Scotland from his generalization. My response was to assert that Wales was part of that island with its own language and traditions that were swallowed up by the English. I was treated like a smart aleck for giving voice to my peoples' history.

Having a Swiss partner and being from California, I find myself part of a multi-ethnic extended family. Our diverse extended family includes Mexican, Cambodian from Cambodia, Afro-Brazilian, Swiss-German, and Japanese. My European family and Welsh ethnic identities dissolve into a transnational identity talked about a century ago by Randolph Bourne, a New England radical who died much too young. Bourne asserted that the United States would be a greater country if we encouraged multiple identities, such as Italian-American, Mexican-American, Japanese-American, etc. His point was that our country would be more vibrant and better able to relate to the rest of the world if individuals did not give up part of themselves, their language, culture, and their history to become Americans. Appreciation and value for difference is vital.

In my diverse family and group of friends, we come together as families and friends do in a nation whose motto is ***e pluribus unum, out of many, one***. Two short stories will put this *e pluribus unum* notion into perspective. I remember dad telling me the story about my uncle on his dying bed saying, "Growing up I never could have imagined having a Black grandchild and loving him so much. Times have changed." More importantly, I remember another uncle, a hero and a survivor in World War II's Pacific campaign, where waves of marines died invading islands held by the Japanese. He hated the Japanese, but respected their thoughtfulness. In my youth, he showed me the Japanese rifle he brought back from the war and told me that they had designed it to use ammunition from the American M-1 but that their ammunition could not be used in the M-1. Smart people. Still, he was open in his racism and dislike of the Japanese.

When one of his two daughters married a Japanese-American man, my uncle learned to be respectful and to contain his racism. After marriage, and at the arrival of his daughter's and Japanese-American son-in-law's child, they told him they would use the Kuper last name rather than the Ozima last name for their son. This was because the Ozima family had another son whose child would be carrying on the Ozima name and they felt an obligation to keep the Kuper name alive. My uncle melted. He was so touched that he was transformed into a more loving and compassionate person the rest of his life.

I also recall my grand-nephew, whose father is Mexican-American and mother Euro-American, observing at a restaurant, "There sure are a lot of White people here." I had a similar experience when I moved to Oregon from California and was living outside of Portland in a predominately Euro-American community. One day as I was walking up and down the isles of the supermarket, I began to feel uncomfortable and started looking around at all the customers. All I could see were white faces. Then words came to me, "White people." I realized that I was no longer in the diverse Californian community where I had come from; I was in a different world.

One of my mentors told me the story of her father pointing to her skin and asking, "What color is your skin?" She told him, "White." He then replied, "Never use the color of your skin to your advantage or to put others down." Her story stays with me as if it were my own. Perhaps I love to share this story to assert that we must recognize and confront white privilege. There is no color blindness. I find it offensive when a Euro-American will tell me that they are American, just like all people who are citizens of the United States. There is a denial of power and white privilege in such statements. The "I am an American" discourse fails to recognize and appreciate the color and culture of numerous people who feel they do not look like the stereotypical Euro-American. The position also fails to encourage Euro-Americans from exploring and deepening their appreciation for their culture of origin and their responsibility in recognizing and living into what is best in their culture. There are more stories, but the point is that in California, for many of us, our families have become diverse, and there is a deep respect and appreciation for our differences, because in cases like mine, we really are all family.

Gender: I am male. I inherit a certain responsibility to address sexism and advocate for equity for woman and for gays, and anybody who is marginalized and abused. I have fostered an

Image courtesy of Rolla Lewis.

Rolla with his son, Ryan

adventurous spirit in my children, both female and male. Of course, I worried constantly about my daughter who was in the Peace Corps in Mozambique. When she was robbed at machete point, I told her to come home. She told me that her life was her own and that a couple of thugs did not define a country. Her expression of such power in her decision and the way she would live her life was humbling; she was living the lessons she learned at home.

My first name is frequently confused as being feminine, and I have always had to tell people that it is the name of a Welsh great grand-uncle. Ironically, when visiting Wales, upon introducing myself, I was frequently asked, "Where does that name come from?"

Cultural Contact

You must begin with yourself in uprooting prejudices, transforming and embracing your capacity to be an active humanist. There is no getting away from doing the work, the tenacity, the courage, and the pain of doing the work. I suggest writing your own deconstruction process like I did above as a beginning. Obviously, I could have written a chapter on each—age, religion, race/ethnicity, and gender. The point was to illustrate that we cannot be reduced to simple stories. Our stories are rich with possibilities for expansion and revision. Because we might have tolerated a racist statement in our past does not condemn us to being quiet or guilty; it calls us to action. To confront internalized racism and to learn tap our courage and capacity to change. We are walking stories that can be shaped and transformed as we live our lives. The next step involves stepping out of your comfort zone.

One area that deserves comment for those who are actively committed to this path is to thicken your cultural contact. Find opportunities to put yourself in a situation in which *you* are the minority. Visit a restaurant, go shopping, tutor through a community library, or otherwise put yourself into a situation where you can learn about "the other" by being the other. The first step is to cultivate **mindful wonderment** about other people and cultures (Lewis, Lenski, Mukhopadhyay, & Cartwright, 2010). Mindful wonderment is acting in a way to maintain open wonder and curiosity about possibilities for seeing, hearing, and even responding to others from a fresh perspective. Mindful wonderment is aligned with cultivating appreciative inquiry, concentration, and mindfulness in professional practice (Cooperrider & Whitney, 1999; Greason & Cashwell, 2009; Kabat-Zinn, 1994; Langer, 1989; Siegel, 2010). Mindful wonderment is an expansive term developed by researchers to take a stance and position with no preferred or monolithic position. Appreciative inquiry shapes mindful wonderment and illuminates work, relationships, and actions (Cooperrider & Whitney, 1999). By beginning with mindful wonderment, you are inviting those you engage with to talk about their strengths and passion for life.

This sounds fancy, but mindful wonderment is really about openness, curiosity, and being open to learning about something new. Let me provide an example. When I was a teenager, one of my Mexican-American friends invited me to spend the night. When we got up in the morning, he asked, "Do you want some chorizo and eggs?" Simple enough question. Only I did not know what chorizo was, so I replied, "What's that?" Soon, I could hear my friend as he went around the house telling each member that I had never had chorizo and eggs. When I brought up my downcast eyes, each person would look at me as if I had been abused or deprived of something special. When breakfast was served, everybody in the family took the time to show me how to use the homemade tortillas to eat the chorizo and eggs. It was a rite of passage. The Beltran family was thrilled to help this poor, deprived young man learn how to eat chorizo and eggs like a Mexican.

There are other stories that involve cultural contact and mentoring by a Mexican man I worked for when I was a flower delivery boy, but because this is a short book, I will have to hold back on the thicker part of my story. My point is to put yourself in contact with folks who are different. If nothing else, go to an ethnic restaurant owned and operated by folks of the group. If you like the food, frequent it and get to know the waiters and waitresses. Be curious and use mindful wonderment to open yourself up to experiencing something new and different. It might take time, but sooner or later you will usually be able to engage someone in conversation that is guided by mindful wonderment and respect.

When you do look deeply into yourself, improve and deepen your cultural contact, and begin to engage in mindful wonderment about that culture, you will begin to recognize your own moral obligation to stand with them against racism and oppression. You set yourself up to move beyond racism (Marsh, Mendoza-Denton, Smith, 2010). After all, we are all family.

Replacing White Guilt with Euro-American Responsibility

Exploring **white guilt** and understanding **white privilege** are crucial in recognizing **European-American responsibility** for confronting racism. White guilt gets played out in a variety of ways. Generally, white guilt results from a breakthrough in the consciousness of some European-Americans and their recognition that the historic oppression and colonization of others, especially people of color, is not only dreadful but also immoral. It is a feeling of sickness that results from a sense that "My people did this." This white guilt gets played out in many ways, but for the purposes of this chapter, I will highlight two extreme responses for the sake of argument. European-Americans respond to such a breakthrough in consciousness by recognizing the impact of colonization on people of color and influence of sexism on women. The two extreme responses range from denial to becoming a sniveling self-blamer. At the one extreme, there are those of European ancestry who shift and deny the destructive nature of European racism. They say, "I'm an American." At the other extreme, are those who become sniveling self-blamers condemning everything European—the "sorry I'm white" option.

On one hand, the deniers fail to embrace their culture, analyze its flaws, forget history, and abnegate their responsibility in being part of the current cultural and historical flow of history. Deniers fail to analyze and do not want to recognize their White privilege. Deniers say, "Oh, all that is in the past. Everybody has an equal chance. We're all Americans" and stuff like that. Deniers fail to take responsibility for looking at and being part of their larger communities and challenges in those communities; they do not see themselves as woven into society. Deniers fail to see addressing the achievement gap is their responsibility because advocating for change might cost them something. Giving poor kids of color more educational resources seems like some give-away to the undeserving that costs hardworking tax payers the fruits of their labor. The deniers' logic seems social Darwinist and plain selfish to me, but I'm a humanist who thinks we have a moral obligation to help all children live up to their greatest potential.

On the other hand, the snivelers recognize the history of colonization, frequently they deny sparkling moments in European culture and fail to appreciate Europeans who advocated for the dignity of others. They fail to fully understand, appreciate, or celebrate the lives of those who have struggled and died promoting greater equality and justice in European and U.S. history. Snivelers do recognize the brutality inherent in European and U.S. history and colonization. At the same time, they seem to lose sight of the art, ideas, and social movements usually arising from churches or labor organizations that fought to broaden human rights and political power in European and U.S. history.

The brutality in European and U.S. history is not to be denied, but the cultural evolution and struggle toward an expansion of human rights and political power should not be downplayed either. Yes, Giordano Bruno was burned at the stake in 1600 for heresy after asserting the universe was infinite and that the sun was one of many stars. He also had the courage not to recant what he believed and embodied a way of being that lives a personal truth regardless of consequences. Yes, Thomas Jefferson was a slaveholder and a racist, but he also gave us words that have helped to press our cultural evolution forward—that we are all entitled to "life, liberty, and the pursuit of happiness." It is important to reclaim those principles for all people. Be critical of Jefferson, but do not lose sight of what he gave us, including freedom of religion in Virginia when heresy was still a capital offense in that state.

It is too easy to split people up dualistically into good and bad, especially when we have to take the responsibility for sorting out the good and bad found in others in history and in ourselves if we look honestly. Jefferson was arguing for greater justice in his historic context. People like Jefferson are a mixed bag. Jefferson illustrates that contradiction better than any founding father. He wrote the Declaration of Independence and some of the United States' core principles are found in that document. He illustrates that people are products of history. We should call him out on his racism, but we should also note that we have to take the responsibility to claim "life, liberty, and the pursuit of happiness" as core principles for all people in the United States. Euro-Americans have to live with certain contradictions and to build on what is life affirming while recognizing and calling out what is oppressive. Euro-Americans have to recognize that Jefferson is a racist, but we must re-claim his words at this point in history to serve our deeper collective ideals.

Euro-Americans are at a stage where they can take greater responsibility for advocating for such things as life, liberty, and the pursuit of happiness, as well as equity in education and the appreciation of cultural diversity. Such positions take gumption and courage, qualities that are marginalized by deniers and snivelers. Euro-Americans can embrace their history in a way where they could benefit from understanding and appreciating their own culture and history, as well as the culture and history of other people. They can foster mindful wonderment when learning about others. The point here is not about white guilt. It is about Euro-American responsibility for working with all people to create a more just, caring, and learning society. It is about Euro-Americans finding the gumption and courage to confront racism in their own communities and families and making their collective personal space safe for all children, free from snide remarks, racist jokes, and hatred. It is about Euro-Americans learning how to forgive their own historic transgressions and finding the courage to seek greater justice (Luskin, 2002). Courage, gumption, and care for ourselves, our fellow citizens (documented and undocumented), and the environment are what is best in our collective history as citizens of the United States, not greed and exploitation.

The shift to a more just and compassionate society has to be aspirational and rooted in a courage that draws strength from figures like Bruno who spoke his own truth. We might not be burned at the stake, but we might have to stand up to the heat generated by those who have little or no empathy for others. For me, as a Euro-American citizen, it is a matter looking at our history and working toward constructing a more just and vibrant nation that provides opportunities for all and basic support for those in greatest need. It is about creating space where we appreciate and wonder about each others' differences (Marsh et al., 2010).

Having the Courage to Stand Up for Others

If you are in a context where you are the majority culture, there will come a time when you will be challenged to find the courage to stand up and assert that diverse people deserve to be treated with dignity. As a Euro-American, I have stood up and confronted racist remarks, jokes, and other hateful speech. This has not been easy. It means saying something that could make the racist telling the joke or making the comment say something like, "It's only a joke." Hatred and racism is no joke. Your job becomes shedding light on hatred and confronting complicity, silence, and other behaviors that let the racist off the hook. Because, ultimately, silence is complicity. When confronting the racist jokester, you take a position of asserting something like, "Racist jokes are hateful." If you can squeeze it in, go on to talk about how racism dehumanizes the "other" but also dehumanizes the racist. It takes courage to say something because it is likely to cause the racist and those who condone racism to feel uncomfortable about what you say. You might feel alone. You might feel like a wet blanket or a moralist riding for some cause. If so, take a breath, find an ally, or if it is not safe for you to say something, leave the setting.

Generally, confronting others will not get you hugs and recognition from the perpetrator(s). You may get support from others who were not courageous enough to say something or find yourself alone in a group willing to rationalize racism. You might even have to do some work around forgiving yourself before you develop the strength to stand up to your own truth (Luskin, 2002). At the same time, standing up, even when and especially when people of color are not around, means you are stepping up and showing the courage to speak out, even when "they" are not around. You cannot pretend to be color blind; saying things like "we are all the same," or Stephen Colbert's favorite, "I don't see color." Color and cultural differences exist. Racism in the United States is not a white secret; it is principally a Euro-American social disease that must

Bianca and Evelyn, Rolla's nieces

Preston Medina, Elijah Lewis Sok, Austin Medina, Rolla's nephews

be addressed socially and primarily by Euro-Americans.

Sadly, I have ended relationships with acquaintances and family members who continued using racist comments around me, even after I explained that I cannot and will not condone hateful speech about others regarding their race, sexual orientation, or religion. There might come a time when after confronting someone, a friend or relative, who is filled with racist talk that you realize that you can no longer be around that person, and you will make the difficult and saddening choice to cut off that relationship. It is always sad, but it has been necessary in my life to simply say that I cannot condone the behavior of someone who spews hateful speech in my presence, especially after I have talked to them about how offensive I find it to be. Otherwise, my silence would be complicity. If their hateful speech is more important than maintaining a relationship with me, they have made a certain choice. Just as I have a choice when making decisions to break off toxic relationships, even with family members. That is the issue: being silent when there are racist comments or hateful speech normalizes such ways of talking. Silence normalizes what is said in speech and excuses what is said regardless of how hurtful it is. Having the courage to confront racism sheds light on what it really is—verbal hate and verbal violence directed at others. It is a matter of choosing to have the courage to stand up to racism and choosing not to be complicit to racism. Remaining silent is a choice that perpetuates what is being said.

We can recognize and find pathways for transcending racism and learning to appreciate our differences without giving up our own culture and sensibilities. We can forgive ourselves (Luskin, 2002). We can move forward. I have my way, you have your way; maybe together, we can open our hearts to learn from each other, appreciate each others' differences, and love our lives together. That is my path.

QUESTIONS FOR DISCUSSION OR SELF REFLECTION

SELF-AWARENESS

1. Dr. Lewis discusses moving from White Guilt to Euro-American Responsibility. This same concept can be applied to any one of the constructs of power and privilege. What steps are you taking to develop your capacity to enhance your capacity to be in relation with others?

CLIENT WORLDVIEW

2. Describe a time when a life experience has expanded your understanding and appreciation of a worldview different from your own. This does not have to be a huge event. It can be as simple as Dr. Lewis' example of being offered chorizo for breakfast.

COUNSELING RELATIONSHIP

3. Discuss Dr. Lewis' denier and sniveler constructs. How would you add to them or critique their use? How do these orientations impede the counseling relationship?

4. Have you ever been an ally for someone who is from another culture/community? Describe how and what this meant to you? How has this heightened your capacity to serve others across the constructs of power and privilege?

5. Look up Fred Luskin's (2002) work about forgiveness. Explore how you could forgive someone else or yourself regarding a grudge, some hut, or other interpersonal challenge that leaves you still simmering with anger and that could easily be transferred into your relationship with others of a similar background.

COUNSELING AND ADVOCACY INTERVENTIONS

6. What are small or large ways in which to increase positive Cultural Contact in your community?

7. Consider a time when you spoke up on behalf of a person of a different race, religion, background, etc. Who did you speak up for and who was it that you had to address? What was their reaction when you did not participate in the Culture of Silence?

8. Consider a time when you remained silent when something offensive was being said about someone not present at that time. In reflection of this moment, what would you have said or done differently? Role-play the situation with a friend, colleague, or classmate.

NEW CONCEPTS AND VOCABULARY TO REVIEW

Collectivist Ecohumanism:

Individualistic solipsism:

e pluribus unum, out of many, one:

Mindful wonderment:

White guilt:

Euro-American responsibility:

White privilege:

Activity

Dr. Lewis provides one word descriptions under the categories of age, religion, race/ethnicity, and gender. Then, he expands on these words to provide a fuller narrative than what can be captured by one word alone.

Follow his example by beginning with a one word description and then expand on the word. As you reflect on your writing what themes appear from your own life narrative? What factors contribute to the complexity of your life story that would not be evident or captured by the one word categorical description?

Share your findings with a classmate or colleague. How would this more expansive approach change the way in which we perceive ourselves and even how we perceive one another?

References

Ammons, A. R. (1996). *Brink road*. New York: W. W. Norton & Company.

Cooperrider, D. L., & Whitney, D. (1999). *Appreciative inquiry: Collaborating for change*. San Francisco, CA: Barrett-Koehler.

Cupitt, D. (2010). *Theology's strange return*. London: SCM Press.

Cupitt, D. (2009). *Jesus and philosophy*. London: SCM Press.

Fox, M. (1980). *Breakthrough: Meister Eckhart's Creation Spirituality*. New York: Doubleday.

Greason, P. B., & Cashwell, C. S. (2009). Mindfulness and counseling self-efficacy: The mediating role of attention and empathy. *Counselor Education and Supervision, 49 (1)*, 2–19.

Kabat-Zinn, J. (1994). *Wherever you go, there you are*. New York: Hyperion.

Langer, E. J. (1989). *Mindfulness*. Reading, MA: Addison-Wesley.

Lewis, R. E. (2011). Ecohumanism: Integrating humanism with resilience theory. In M. B. Scholl, A. S. McGowan, and J. T. Hansen (Eds.), *Humanistic perspectives on contemporary counseling issues*. New York, NY: Routledge.

Lewis, R. E., Lenski, S. D., Mukhopadhyay, S., Cartwright, C. T. (2010). Mindful wonderment: Using focus groups to frame social justice. *Journal for Social Action in Counseling and Psychology, 3(1)*, 82–105.

Luskin, F. (2002). *Forgive for good: A proven prescription for health and happiness*. New York: HarperCollins.

Marsh, J., Mendoza-Denton, R., & Smith, J. A. (2010). *Are we born racist?: New insights from neuroscience and positive psychology*. Boston, MA: Beacon Press.

Naess, A. (2002). *Life's philosophy: Reason and reeling in a deeper world*. Athens, GA: University of Georgia.

Roszak, T., Gomes, M., & Kanner, A. (Eds.). (1995) *Ecopsychology*. San Francisco, CA: Sierra Club Books.

Sessions, G. (1995). *Deep ecology for the 21st century: Readings in the philosophy and practice of the new environmentalism*. Boston, MA: Shambhala.

Siegel, D. J. (2010). *The mindful therapist: A clinician's guide to mindsight and neural integration*. New York: W. W. Norton.

Taylor, M. C. (2007). *After god*. Chicago: University of Chicago Press.

West, C. (1993). *Keeping faith: Philosophy and race in America*. London: Routledge.

West, C. (2001). *Race matters*. Boston, MA: Beacon Press.

West, C. (2002). *Prophesy deliverance!: An Afro-American revolutionary Christianity*. Louisville, KY: Westminster John Knox Press.

The Mis-Education of the Euro-American Child

"Those are the people they've been shoving down my throat all my life as my heroes! And they're not!"

Euro-American male participant reacting to images of George Washington, Andrew Jackson, Thomas Jefferson, and Christopher Columbus; presentation at the Western Association of Counselor Educators and Supervisors, Palm Springs, CA, November 6, 2008.

I have been told that there are three deaths. The first death takes place when the life force leaves the body. The second death comes when the lifeless body is buried. The third death is the final death; it is when people stop telling the story about the lived life. The person who passed ceases to exist in the memory of those still alive. With these grades of death in mind, I worry that the historical humanists and the many humanists not even touched upon in this book may be on the verge of the final death. The following chronicles the cause for my concern.

Over the years, I have presented curriculum related to the historical subjects of this manuscript in multiple venues throughout the United States. My debut presentation was in Palm Springs, which is when I witnessed, for the first time, the reaction (as noted above) to the content of the curriculum. I was struck by the response of the one male participant to images that were presented along with images of the humanists. Since this first presentation, the same curriculum has been presented in classrooms and conferences in Sacramento, Hayward, Raleigh, New York, and New Brunswick and, while the audiences have been different, the reaction is always the same.

The curriculum is presented through a step-by-step unveiling process in which participants are, initially, shown just the images of the six humanist historical figures, as well as images of the historical figures mentioned above. The participants are asked to write down the names of those that they recognize. They are then provided the names of the people in the images. They tally how many and which images they correctly identified and how many and which images were not identified. They then are asked to write down what they know of the individual once the name of the person in the image has been provided. We go back and ascertain what they know and then tally how many of the people in the images they actually knew once provided the name.

The results are consistent from one presentation to the next. The historical humanists addressed in this book are virtually unknown by sight. Even when the name of the humanist is provided, participants from across this country who have taken part in the presentation have minimal knowledge. The majority of the humanists are unrecognizable by sight and by name. If these results were generalized across the country, the historical humanists would experience the final death. Their life stories and accomplishments would be untold and, subsequently, unknown to future generations.

Another common theme surfaces from these presentations. The participants arrive at the same question that came to me when I stood across the façade of Colonel Shaw and the men of the 54th Regiment in the Boston Common: "How is it that we don't know who these people (the historical humanists) are?" In the discourse that follows, the participants ponder the reasons for their lack of knowledge about the humanists when it is apparent that these lives were significant and had bearing on the trajectory of our nation's development. The participants also recognize how readily they identified the historical figures that history books tout as the "Discoverer of America" and the "Founding Fathers." I ask them to draw from their knowledge base and expand on the people in the images that they readily knew. At first, they offer what they have been told such as "First President," "Signed the Declaration of Independence," "Discovered America" etc. Then there is a point in which the tone of the dialogue takes a turn. Another layer of responses come forth from the participants and are generally offered under their breath or with heads turned to the side. The tone conveys that while what they are saying may be truth, it is, nonetheless, information not commonly shared in a public venue.

What I have learned from presenting this curriculum started with the three Euro-American participants who attended my workshop in Palm Springs. I gained a **phenomenological perspective** that I would not have otherwise understood had I not ventured into a stream of research for the intention of learning ways to evolve the identity development of my own graduate students. The one male member of the group opened my eyes to his reality when he revealed the psychological resistance he has had to exert in the face of ongoing efforts to promote the recognizable historical figures as his "heroes." What I learned from this one man, a white man, is that he feels *expected* to emulate a particular set of historical figures *but he doesn't*.

In presentation after presentation, the responses from participants arrive at the same conclusion, which is best summarized by a statement made many years ago by Frederick Douglass (1994): "The slayers of thousands have been exalted into heroes, and the worship of mere physical force has been considered glorious" (p. 907). Participants, invariably, come to their own conclusions about who and what they know and why their knowledge base is devoid of information pertaining to the humanists. Their responses reveal truths that tell us why the one gentleman in Palm Springs was resistant to claiming these historical figures as his heroes. The following responses are but a partial list of participant reactions to the known historical figures; "owned slaves," "massacred indigenous communities," "responsible for the Trail of Tears," "believed that other races were not equal to them," "started wars," "they were self serving," and "glorified in our history books" (Classroom Presentations, 2009). The public acknowledgement of this information about the commonly touted heroes opens the door to examine why we are not taught about the values and orientations of the historical humanists as well as their impact on our development as a nation. We also begin to critically discuss the consequences of having been taught history from a white male exploitive capitalist perspective.

The Option of Humanistic Models

Euro-Americans' responses to this curriculum consistently reveal an undertone of disassociation with the capitalist historical figures. It is as if the acts of these historical figures are projected onto the whole racial group. In the previous chapter, Dr. Rolla Lewis addressed the feelings of guilt and the "sickness" that comes from the recognition of historic oppression and colonization. The forces of indoctrination, however, attempt to create racial cohesion and identification. Subsequently, if white identity is informed and grounded in a worldview and orientation that values and upholds the behaviors of exploitive capitalistically oriented models, then the ability to perceive racial group membership in a humanistic light can be compromised. The forces that attempt to promote racial group cohesion can also be found in the use of words.

Words have tremendous power. They can communicate a range of emotions and ideas. They can also shape and contextualize our existential reality. Words have the capacity to transmit generalizations contained within our habituated thoughts that can demonize an entire racial group. These words surface particularly when discussing historical events in the United States. For example, it is not uncommon to hear the statement, "White people had slaves" made during classroom discussions or noted in students' journals. It is true that there were white people, just like the Grimké family, who "owned" other people. We can also say that there were circumstances that led to the fact that of those people who participated in the establishment and maintenance of the institution of slavery, the majority were white. Less is known about how at least one Native American tribe that had assimilated United States' *allowable* practices had also adopted the practice of chattel slavery (Halliburton, 1977). What must be noted is that in relation to the vast number of Europeans who came to these shores there were *some* who practiced slavery and their numbers were the minority.

The simplistic statement "White people had slaves" generalizes, unintentionally distorts reality, and implicates an entire group of people associated to a skin color. Coupled with the teaching of history from a capitalistic rather than more balanced perspective that also reflects humanist efforts, such statements limit the possibility of recognizing that there were white people who not only opposed the practice of slavery, but who also were willing to die for the emancipation of people held in bondage. This encapsulated perception has potentially inhibiting implications on white children's capacity to develop what Frankl calls "choice of action" when the only historical white models that they learn are capitalistically driven men who exploited people of color (as well as poor and powerless European immigrants) in their quest for riches. The danger of narrow perceptions and one-sided renderings of our nation's history fuels the divide and rule forces that undermine the evolvement of our society beyond its racialized origins.

Woodson's (2000) ground-breaking book, "The Mis-Education of the Negro," speaks to the crippling forces of Cultural Invasion. He points to how a Euro-centric curriculum instills inferiority

in the African American. His observation of "school" and of the impact of the curriculum on the psyche of African Americans is that it "handicap(s) a student by teaching him that his black face is a curse and that his struggle to change his condition is hopeless is the worst lynching. It kills one's aspirations and dooms him to vagabondage and crime" (p. 3). The socialization enacted by this same curriculum, centric to the "exaltation" and "worship" of capitalistically driven white men, attempts to instill a false sense of superiority in white children. Loewen (1995) states, "Feel-good history for affluent white males inevitably amounts to feel-bad history for everyone else" (p. 301). The aftermath of a mis-education of the Euro-American child in which textbooks attempt to "leave out anything that might reflect badly upon our national character" (p. 13) is a psychological chasm between Euro-American children and their peers of color. This was remarked upon by Elizabeth Cruz when she discussed the cost of friendships lost when learning history from only one perspective.

The price paid for the socialization process enacted upon Euro-Americans has its own set of consequences as the one-sided renditions of history suppress the capacity for positive white identity development. Those who, knowingly or unknowingly, buy into the notion of racial superiority adopt an oppressor mentality. Doing so entails repeating the same psychological adjustment made by Columbus. Sue (2010) states that "To continue in their oppressive ways ... they must engage in denial and live a false reality that allows them to function in good conscience." Within this perception, the white child must accept the disparate realities of his community as a "fixed reality" that is not only unchangeable but, when perceived from the **Helms White Identity Development Model** of the Reintegration Phase, people of color are blamed for their status in society.

Sue further states that "the oppressors' empowered status over marginalized groups may have a corrupting influence in the ability to attune to the plight of marginalized groups" (p. 128). The white child may unconsciously acquiesce to the indoctrination of Divide and Rule forces and by doing so adopts adherence to one's racial group. The price of membership to the exploitive capitalist orientation is that the child then fails to *recognize and see*, whether consciously or unconsciously, the disparities in one's own community. This orientation cripples the capacity of Euro-Americans to engage in, as Dr. Lewis suggests, "constructing a more just and vibrant nation that provides opportunities for all and support for those in greatest need." It also stifles the desire to engage in what Dr. Lewis calls "mindful wonderment."

Racial group loyalty compromises spiritual freedom and choice of action. The Euro-American child is, in essence, spiritually enslaved when relegated to adhere to models that are racially bound to exploitive capitalistically oriented models. She has lost her spiritual freedom and is psychologically enslaved to habituated thoughts that are grounded in the socialization processes that "cause the educated to believe that what America does is right" (Loewen, p. 307). A critical view of the world is unexamined and the chasm of the racial reality gap remains.

The white child who lacks knowledge of white historical humanists is devoid of a counter narrative that the white humanists provide. If the child is raised to value a sense of compassion for those outside their immediate family circle, the humanist models are not only more congruent to the child's value system but these humanists also provide models of behavior to emulate. The possibility for adopting such models of behavior can affirm a way of living that some Euro-Americans may embrace. For example, in a classroom presentation in which students learned about the historical and modern-day humanists, one Euro-American participant, enthusiastically expressed, "I want to be one!" (Classroom Presentation, 2009). Furthermore, a sense of belonging comes from being *in relation* to all people; the historical and modern-day humanists model a positive alternative to divide-and-rule tactics that limit the identification of the white child to just her own racial group. Liberating the Euro-American child from the one-sided forces of implicitly condoned, capitalistically driven values promotes her capacity to be a *subject* of the world rather than the object of indoctrination. The "choice of action" from this liberation promotes the possibility for what Dr. Lewis calls "Euro-American responsibility for working with all people to create a more just, caring, and learning society."

The psychological distress expressed by the gentleman in my Palm Springs workshop can be mitigated by a more balanced teaching of history that provides a range of values and responses from a diverse set of models. The capacity for "choice of action" in responding to social justice issues is enhanced by providing the perspective of humanists rather than just the perspective and orientations of exploitive historical models. The retelling of the stories of the humanists in this manuscript, and the countless other humanists whose stories are not retold here can provide a range of choices in thoughts and action. Otherwise, children are indoctrinated to a generalized perception that projects greed and violence as culturally condoned.

The void in knowledge about white historical humanists exacerbates racial division. The void projects a generalized prejudice to any person in the United States who has white skin by implication to the actions of *some white people*. The rendering of capitalistically driven male models as "heroes," while minimizing or not even mentioning their impact on people of color (as well as poor European immigrants), creates a perception that "white people" are engaged in a "cover up." The historical amnesia also implies that the exploitation is condoned. From a lens of racial cohesion, an impression is subsequently conveyed that implicates all white people in the atrocities committed by a minority group of people who espoused capitalistic gain at the expense of others.

In truth, the values and actions of green-hearted elites in this nation's history prompted a response from red-hearted humanists who were grounded in a different set of values. The one-sided teaching of our nation's history must be considered for the impact it has on children's developmental understanding of how to respond, today, to their reality. As previously mentioned, there is an element of socialization when white children are only given models of human behavior from a capitalistically oriented context. Then, by virtue of protecting these capitalistic figures by not talking about the impact of their action on human beings outside their racial group conveys that their actions are sanctioned. Children are taught, implicitly, that these behaviors are condoned and that the manner in which these so-called heroes behaved during their lifetimes is part of a "fixed reality." This rendering is known as the **"Master Narrative."** The void of alternative models of behavior stymies the development of future agents of social justice who can critically examine injustices in their reality, insert themselves as subjects into this reality, and *change the outcome*.

Learning history from only a white male, capitalistic perspective, white children might understand, or, at very least intuit, the suffering inflicted upon others by *some white people*. If they have not disassociated from their emotions and remain in touch with their *feelings*, as did Angelina Grimké, Sarah Shaw, and John Brown, but have no models of others who resisted the forces of white racial cohesion, then they may internalize feelings of guilt. This can, subsequently, immobilize them. Guilt adopts a burden of shame that disables cross racial relationship building. The capacity to defy the forces of racial group cohesion must be adopted in order for white children to develop habituated thoughts and behaviors that promote being *in relationship* with the world and to develop positive relationships with people outside their own racial group. Our historical and modern-day humanists model this and can provide lessons for the white child to learn how to be fully human in this world without bearing the stigma of complicity for the actions of *some white people*.

Reconstructing the "Founding Fathers" Worldview

Dr. Lewis speaks to "working toward constructing a more just and vibrant nation." He recognizes that this construction is a work in progress and that it has taken hundreds of years since the birth of this nation in 1776 to arrive at where we are. And still, we have not fully arrived. We can begin the process of examining this construction by deconstructing the "Founding Father's" statement that "All Men Are Created Equal." We must acknowledge that from the worldview of the "Founding Fathers," there were limitations in how they perceived "men." They meant only men, white men, men over the age of 35 and men who owned land. Redressing the exclusionary conditions of gender, race, age, and class in the quest for equality has taken massive efforts on behalf of social activists.

So not to fall into a pattern of dichotomous thinking in which we demonize the "Founding Fathers," we need to revisit the world in which these men lived and what templates of governance existed in the nations of their ancestry. Weatherford (1988) states that:

> America's settlers from Europe knew little of democracy. The English came from a nation ruled by monarchs who claimed that God conferred their right to rule and even allowed them to wage wars of extinction against the Irish. Colonists also fled to America from France, which was wandering aimlessly though history under the extravagances of a succession of kings named Louis, most of whom pursued debauched and extravagant reigns that oppressed, exploited, and at times even starved their subjects (p. 134).

We have been told that we must know our history in order not to repeat it. Our ignorance in not knowing the full story, however, impedes our capacity to not stumble upon the same patterns of behavior. Without full knowledge about how social activists responded to their realities, subsequent generations fall into patterns of racial group cohesion, inherent oppositional viewpoints, and disassociation from participation in joint efforts to improve our collective social condition. Then we bemoan the inaction of our youth when national or even local issues arise, and we fault the youth for their disengagement. To revisit and track the ongoing efforts to "construct a more just and vibrant nation," we will return to our "Founding Fathers" and examine the origins and intentions behind a doctrine created to move a new nation toward a democracy. Then we will touch upon the major revisions required over the course of the 250 years from its inception to make it, truly, an inclusive doctrine.

This nation evolved from 13 colonies that acted as separate and sovereign states. The original inhabitants, Native Americans, living on the East Coast were frustrated with regularly having to deal with each and every representative of each of the states. This required more time and energy spent on negotiations and coming to new sets of terms and agreements with states where there was no consistency in policy and administration from one state to the next. Subsequently, the true origins of United States' democracy can be credited to Iroquois Chief Canassatego who, in July 1744, spoke at the Indian-British assembly in Pennsylvania. He lodged his criticism with the multiple colonial administrations and "proposed that the colonies unify themselves" and, furthermore, "told them how they might do it.... As his people had done and form a union like the League of the Iroquois" (Weatherford, p. 135). His intention was to assist the colonists in developing a common voice to represent their interests.

The Constitution of the United States was, subsequently, borrowed from the League of the Iroquois who, between A.D. 1000 and 1450 had created their own constitution called the Great Law of Peace. Further credit can be given to Benjamin Franklin who, as Indian commissioner for the state of Pennsylvania, became familiar with the political culture of the League of the Iroquois, which included their diplomacy. This League consisted of five Indian nations, the Mohawk, Onondaga, Seneca, Oneida, Cayuga, and the Tuscarora. Each nation maintained a council composed of "sachems" that were, essentially, representatives elected by the tribe. These sachems also came together to form the grand Council of the League.

There are 17 articles to the **Great Law of Peace**. The following two articles convey the level of responsibility and the expected character of their elected sachems. Article 24 embodies the nature of service in which they are expected to consider the good of "the people." The article explicitly dictates that sachems must weigh their decisions on what is best not only for the present, but also with a mind for future generations yet born.

> The Lords of the Confederacy of the Five Nations shall be *mentors* of the people for all time. The thickness of their skin shall be seven spans which is to say that they shall be proof against anger, offensive actions and criticism. Their hearts shall be full of peace and good will and their minds filled with a yearning for the welfare of the people of the Confederacy. With endless patience they shall carry out their duty and their firmness shall be tempered with a tenderness for their people. Neither anger nor fury shall find lodgment in their minds and all their words and actions shall be marked by calm deliberation.

The concept of leaders serving as "mentors" and that they be "proof against anger, offensive actions and criticisms" provides an expectation of decorum in the conduct of the representatives. The statement that their hearts be "full of peace and good will" speaks to a way of being in which these representatives were expected to be models of harmony while acknowledging the fact that there may be times in which they must represent with "firmness." Even so, they are still expected to serve with "tenderness for their people," even when difficult decisions were to be made.

Sachems were held accountable and there were repercussions for those who did not conduct themselves according to the standards o their community. This is further explained in Article 25 and demonstrates the role of women in Iroquois Nation governance. Women elected the sachems from their respective nations and were also the ones who held the authority to remove (or impeach) any elected representative who did not consider the interests of the entire people. They would then appoint a new representative.

> If a Lord of the Confederacy should seek to establish any authority independent of the *jurisdiction* of the Confederacy of the Great Peace, which is the Five Nations, he shall be warned three times in open council, first by the women relatives, second by the men relatives and finally by the Lords of the Confederacy of the Nation to which he belongs. If the offending Lord is still obdurate he shall be dismissed by the War Chief of his nation for refusing to conform to the laws of the Great Peace. His nation shall then install the candidate nominated by the female name holders of his family.

When the "Founding Fathers" stated, "All Men Are Created Equal" they had no intention of giving women any role or voice in political affairs. These men were entrenched in a cultural value system that relegated women to subjugated roles. In contrast, the women under the Iroquois Nation participated in governmental affairs through gender-specific systems of checks and balances and were expected, as stipulated under Article 44, to maintain the family and economic structure of the community.

> The lineal descent of the people of the Five Nations shall run in the female line. Women shall be considered the progenitors of the Nation. They shall own the land and the soil. Men and women shall follow the status of the mother.

We then must examine the contrasting and disparate status of Iroquois women within their own nation to Euro-American women in the newly created United States. During this early era in the creation of a new nation, the "Founding Fathers" actively eliminated articles of equality contained in The Great Law of Peace. The worldview of a significant number of the "Founding Fathers" was grounded in a culture defined by subjugation of others. This worldview ingrained itself by doctrine, even as the loosely connected states attempted to create a union. The outcome of the worldview of the "Founding Fathers" meant eliminating any clauses that promoted the equality of women. They also actively engaged in protecting the rights of slave owners to own people.

Upon entering into discussion of how to create a union from 13 separate colonies, slave-holding colonies stipulated conditions for their participation in this new union of states that would be called the "United States." Representatives from slave-holding colonies consented to join this union as long as the newly formed government did not interfere with their right to "own" human beings. They demanded respect to right of property, even if that property included people in bondage. The compromises made to create the union gave further political power to Southern States, where slavery was practiced by counting people in bondage as a three-fifths vote. Though these same people were not accorded the status of full human beings nor could they participate or vote in the electoral process, those who "owned" them gained more power with greater wealth through ownership of human beings (Alexander, 2010).

What does this all mean to us now? The "Founding Fathers," with full intention, embarked upon enacting a "democracy" that was far from democratic. Women and people of color, which at the time of the signing of the Declaration of Independence meant primarily Native Americans and African Americans, had no voice and no representation in the system created by these men. The leaders who were elected in the states in which women and people of color resided were not obligated by any cultural or legal code to consider them as citizens with any rights whatsoever. These groups were excluded from the governmental structure and from its protection. While the Great Law of Peace served as a template for our constitution, it did not serve the self interests of men representing the various states who needed a structure that allowed them to protect their capitalistic interests through the propagation of a racial caste system. The challenge to this worldview came from people whose values and principles eventually moved us to a more just nation.

Constructing a Just and Vibrant Nation via Humanist Narratives

White women who were subjected to the exclusionary dictates of the governmental system created by the "Founding Fathers" did not remain silent. They did not accept their subservient status as a "fixed reality." They understood the nature of their culture from a **problem posing** perspective. They banded, in alliance, with progressive white men and people of color. In 1893, Frederick Douglass' expanded version of his autobiography contained a chapter dedicated to the many people who he came to know once he had escaped from bondage. He entitled this chapter, "Honor to Whom Honor." He pays homage to Lucretia Mott, the Grimké sisters, and a host of people whose names never grace the pages of our history books. Douglass credited women for their role in making the sacrifices that changed the state of affairs for people who were held bondage. He wrote:

> When the true history of the anti-slavery cause shall be written, women will occupy a large space in its pages; for the cause of the slave has been peculiarly woman's cause. Her heart and her conscience have supplied in large degree its motive and mainspring. Her skill, industry, patience, and perseverance have been wonderfully manifest in every trial hour. Not only did her feet run on "willing errands," and her fingers do the work which in large degree supplied the sinews of war, but her deep moral convictions, and her tender human sensibilities, found convincing and persuasive expression by her pen and her voice (Douglass, p. 903).

The rest of his autobiography reveals his evolvement related to his perception of white people that changed with time. He goes on to name woman after woman and, too, many men who evoked this change. He specifically names William Lloyd Garrison as an "acknowledged leader" of a "circle of highly cultivated men and women, banded together for the overthrow of slavery" (p. 901). Sadly, of these people whose individual and collective efforts eventually dismantled the policies that protected the self interests of land-owning (and slave-owning) white men, there is minimal to no record of their names in the books that are utilized to educate our children.

The price paid for this omission and distortive perspective in the teaching of our "his"story is toxic to the development of the Euro-American child. While Angelina Grimké acknowledged her feelings of torment from having witnessed sanctioned atrocities against human beings in her presence, we implicitly "exalt into heroes" the "slayers of thousands" and "glorify" those who benefited from the use of "physical force." The white historical and modern-day humanist models demonstrate that they were clearly in touch with how they felt about what they witnessed in their reality. They refused to succumb to dissociative processes that lead to psychological numbing. And, while children of color have models of social activism from their own communities and promptly name historical figures such as Cesar Chavez, Dr. Martin Luther King, Jr., Dolores Huerta, Fred Korematsu, and Rosa Parks, to name a few of the people that quickly roll off the tongue, white children (and adults) are remiss to name white humanists who refused to succumb to psychological numbing and who, in turn, committed to a life of social activism.

Instead, white children (and adults) are socialized and indoctrinated so they can readily name the historical figures from this nation's past who capitalistically benefited from the willful exploitation of others. These historical figures were psychologically alienated from the people they exploited. They enacted "cognitive dissonance." This modeling of "cutting off" of one's emotions alienates not just the Euro-American child from people of color, but also alienates the Euro-American child from him/herself. The tacit agreement made whenever we teach about the "greatness" of the "Founding Fathers" and the tired tale of the "Discovery of America" implicitly condones a message that achievement and power (at the expense of others) is desirable. Furthermore, any means employed in order to acquire power is allowable regardless of the damage done to others. This trajectory of behavior is not attributable to the Great Law of Peace.

Recognizing that there were white humanists who acted on behalf of others, we can see that they were not the "elected" representatives of their communities nor were they accorded the right to express their humanist values and opinions. They did so anyway. Had they not, we would still be the nation as promoted by the "Founding Fathers" who wrote laws that subjugated people unlike them into subordinate status. Speaking full truths about the "Founding Fathers," as well as highlighting the social evolvement of our society as we examine our "history" from the perspective of our white humanists, casts a wider lens on how human beings have responded to oppression in the past and in the present. It develops our capacity to critically examine our world and enhances our ability to see ourselves as agents of change.

Teaching about "diversity," "cross-cultural communication," and other topics related to the constructs of power and privilege in our nation with people who are grounded in racially bound group orientations has multiple challenges. These discussions can be difficult for white people grounded in a "white development deficiency model," despite invitation by people of color to engage in constructive dialogue in deconstructing our racialized reality. The prominence of this deficiency orientation defaults Euro-American response to a defensive position when they feel blamed for the values and actions of some white people.

Some Euro-Americans employ various means of defense mechanisms to psychologically protect themselves when they are expected to engage in dialogue with people of color about how to undo the aftermath of our racialized origins. Subsequently, those grounded in a lower stage of identity development have difficulty engaging in constructive dialogue with people of color about social justice and oppression if and when they carry the burden of guilt or anger. Disassociation becomes the next logical conclusion in protecting the ego. For this reason, when we ask white people to engage in constructive dialogue in dismantling racism or in stepping up to address micro-aggressions that may occur in our midst, a number of defensive behaviors may manifest themselves. I have witnessed behaviors such as avoidance, inappropriate use of humor, attacking the conveyor of the topic by questioning her motives or intelligence, minimizing the occurrence, or over intellectualizing. These are all defensive responses that attempt to sidestep the discomfort of guilt or anger that surfaces when prompted to engage in issues related to "diversity." These are also responses that impede the path to reaching new and enlightened perspectives across the racial divide.

Addressing the deficiency by providing the models of white historical (and modern-day) humanists develops the capacity of white children and adults to respond from a place of strength and adherence to a non-racialized identity that espouses humanistic principles and responses. In providing the models of white historical and modern-day humanists, a white child can determine that s/he has a "*choice*" in how to *be* in the world and that s/he can be "*conscious*" in making a decision of how to respond to life's realities. If we consider culture as the beliefs, customs, practices, and social behavior of a particular nation or people (Encarta Dictionary), then the shaping of Euro-American culture can be prompted by humanist Euro-American models who defined their identity not by capitalistic but by humanistic terms. The absence of humanist Euro-American models in our social science books promotes a one-sided model of social behavior to future generations of Euro-Americans that may not be their preferred mode of being. Once recognizing the privilege in being white in this society, the white child may develop guilt for having this unearned privilege that was gained through capitalistic structures that promoted white superiority. The introduction of humanist models provides an alternative of choices.

For example, the **counter narrative** provided by the life of Christian Gottlieb Priber (Halliburton, 1977) demonstrates contrasting values that run against the master narrative, yet, knowledge about Priber and his years living amongst the Cherokee Nation remains largely obscure. Priber, a European, settled at Tellico in 1736. He learned the Cherokee language and adopted their customs and dress. He cautioned his hosts against trading with a single country and making land concessions to anyone. Priber soon ingratiated himself with tribal leaders... and (was) appointed as "Prime Minister." Among other utopian goals, the "Empire" was to become a place where runaway slaves, oppressed peoples of Europe, and Indian tribes could obtain sanctuary and happiness. Priber was aware of the "continual flow of runaway slaves finding sanctuary among the Cherokees" and proposed to incorporate them into his utopian communist state. Discrimination would not be tolerated on the basis of race, color, tribal affiliation, title, or wealth. Priber's grandiose plan ended when he was captured by the Creek Indians… and sold to Governor Ogelthorpe of Georgia. He was imprisoned in Frederica prison and remained incarcerated until his death a few years later (p. 10).

Priber's influence during his years with the Cherokee Nation runs in direct opposition to President George Washington's worldview who during his administration, in 1791, negotiated a treaty with the Cherokee Nation at White's Fort. The Treaty of Holston indirectly encouraged the growth of black slavery among the Cherokees. The message imparted by President Washington to the Cherokee Nation was to "stop warring and adopt the white man's ways" (p. 14). At this point in time we have a prominent figure, the President of the United States, assuming a position of being able to speak on behalf of "white" people. We now recognize that there were many "white" people even during this era who would not have agreed with Washington's statement, who would not have appreciated his speaking on their behalf, and who objected to his way of living which included enslavement of people.

The following excerpt from a Counselor Education graduate student, Fiona Arenson, speaks to the transformative potential after learning about the life narratives of historical and modern-day humanists through curriculum presented in her Introduction to Counseling course in Fall 2009.

> As an upper middle class woman with white privilege I was concerned about how this (material presented in class) would be perceived by others. Having emigrated from a country because of the oppression by the white minority over the black majority, I felt complicit in the oppression by virtue of the fact that I was a white individual living in the country. The accompanying guilt I felt has contributed enormously to my passion for doing good deeds for others and for talking up against oppression. Now I feel I have the privilege and the obligation to freely participate in social justice causes to bring about social and political change for minorities who feel powerless and oppressed. I take this responsibility seriously and share the common goals and values with other students who strive to better the lives of others. I hope to use my white privilege and education in a positive way to benefit others whose success might otherwise be limited (Arenson, Fiona).

Arenson speaks to an identity previously affixed to white over black oppression. The "guilt" reveals an understanding of oppression. Her commitment to address the oppression is demonstrated in her redefinition of her identity when she communicates "privilege and obligation to freely participate in social justice causes." This speaks to her evolvement as the burden of guilt diminishes, and she refocuses her purpose in life in a manner that will have positive impact on the lives of others. Adherence to a racialized group identification (deficit model) grounded in capitalist identity would place her in alliance with oppressor group actions and would generate feelings of "complicity." With proficiency in white humanist orientations, Arenson can choose a non-racialized identity to inform her thoughts and actions.

Her country of origin had already, due to its own history, planted a racialized identity. The exposure to curriculum focusing on white humanists provided a vehicle to work toward "common goals and values" that ultimately "better the lives of others." Arenson is free to live by way of a humanistic model that liberates her from the burden of guilt. She is no longer mired in the smog of a useless emotion that would thwart her capacity to speak up and act when needed.

The following excerpt is from another graduate student, Nancy Padrick, who exposes the crippling nature of white guilt and the liberating potential for learning about white historical and modern-day humanists.

> Dr. Borunda's lecture on Euro-American humanists is also based on appreciating strengths. I was amazed at hearing the courage and insight of Euro-American humanists. (A) good friend, a humanist in her own right ... is caring and insightful, ... (though) reluctant to discuss diversity in the past because of the guilt she thought she was supposed to feel. Perhaps many Euro-Americans feel unable to navigate the negativity of "white-guilt" and as a result avoid the issue. I repeated what I had learned about Euro-American humanists to her. After my explanation of the lecture, my friend said, "I needed to hear that," like it was a salve. Examining Euro-American humanists emphasizes the very strengths that our society will need to become more egalitarian. I would like to see these emphasized in schools as children respond well to positive biographies (Padrick, Nancy).

Padrick reveals how many Euro-Americans "avoid the issue" in an effort to sidestep the "white guilt." She suggests that positive biographies may provide the means by which to empower future generations of Euro-American children and adults to move from the sideline of social justice causes to the midst of the efforts to improve conditions for all people. The burden of only having historical figures who committed oppressive acts as models with whom to identify clearly contributes to the defensiveness in being able to talk about "diversity," as well as the immobility to act upon injustices. The models of historical and modern-day humanists provided a sense of healing and evolvement for Padrick's friend. It was the "salve."

Similarly, these models of behavior also serve to bridge the racial divide. One student of color (anonymous contribution) honestly revealed her initial reaction to the images when they were presented in her class. "I automatically had a negative view of these Euro-Americans of history. My thoughts were that they all had something to do with the mistreatment of blacks and that they all supported slavery and the oppression of people of color." Once again, the dispro-portionate attention given to the deeds of capitalist Euro-Americans has painted their behav-ior as the standard and norm for all Euro-Americans. In reality, half the people shown in the images from the curriculum had dedicated and, in some cases, even lost their lives endeavor-ing to change circumstances for people of color. Given what we know about the potential for shifting the habituated thoughts of white Euro-Americans from how they perceive themselves to how they perceive others, let us examine other examples of what processes "mis-educate the Euro-American child."

Color Blindness Blinds

The deficiency of a balanced education that promotes positive identity development of the Euro-American child has far reaching implications on the evolution of our nation. The capacity to participate in constructing a more just and vibrant nation is crippled by a stilted self perception. This capacity is further impaired by well-intended approaches to mitigate the factors that have contributed to a racialized reality for everyone. This brings us back to one of the themes related to white humanists. While they, themselves, were colorblind in their hearts and maintained meaningful relationships with people of color, their capacity to intellectually see racism contributed to their capacity to make strides in creating a more egalitarian society. Their ability to *see* the construction of race changed the trajectory of this nation by acting upon principles that served humanistic rather than exploitive capitalistic orientations.

This theme of being able to *see* injustices that attempt to reinstitute disparate racialized (and genderized) outcomes is evident time and again in the evolvement of the United States. A series of progressive movements since the inception of the proclamation by the "Founding Fathers" that "All Men Are Created Equal" eventually gained civil rights and equal status for people originally excluded. Landmark outcomes attained by people proficient and grounded in their self identity include the Emancipation Proclamation of 1863 that provided immediate freedom to any person who was held in bondage in any state of the Confederate States of America. The Emancipation Proclamation was intended as a means by which to destabilize Southern slave-holding Confederate states during the Civil War by freeing men who would eventually serve in the Union army. The strategy, as we know, worked. Separate state and federal action emancipated people held in bondage in slave-holding Union states of Missouri, Kentucky, West Virginia, Maryland, and Delaware. Progressive abolitionists did not rest here. They remained vigilant and pushed for an end to the practice of slavery, which resulted in the Thirteenth Amendment that actually prohibited slavery and involuntary servitude. This amendment was adopted in 1865.

Oppressive forces grounded in racist ideology do not end with the passage of a law. Habituated thoughts ingrained in our cultural fabric continue to drive a wedge into the efforts of those invested in creating a more just and inclusive society. This is evident time and again throughout the history of this nation. For example, the response by former slave owners to the Thirteenth Amendment was to institute a set of unofficial laws that would, in essence, limit the human rights and civil liberties of recently liberated people and to foment conditions that would reinstitute a form of chattel slavery. Moore (2004) provides a sampling of the laws created, state by state, to restrict the newly acquired freedom gained by virtue of the Civil War and the Thirteenth Amendment:

1. Life in prison for interracial marriage.
2. African American men had to carry a certain amount of money (usually excessive) or they would be declared vagrant and then sentenced to work on a white plantation.
3. Prohibited misspending one's money (decided by the sheriff).

4. It was illegal to walk the street after dark.

5. Children whose parents were impoverished were turned over to the state and hired out on white plantations indefinitely.

6. It was illegal to be unemployed. Punishment was imprisonment of hired out to a white plantation.

7. African American men had to have written proof (from a white person) of housing and employment. (p. 22)

Recall that people in bondage were counted as three-fifths a person but had no voting or civil rights. This was redressed through the Civil Rights Act of 1866, which declared that anyone born in the United States (except certain Native Americans) were full citizens. This was followed by the Fourteenth Amendment, which was intended to override state efforts to return racial relationships to pre-Emancipation status by providing equal protection. In other words, the statement of "All Men Are Created Equal" was finally inclusive of all men (but not yet women). Women did not gain footing on the equation of equality until the Nineteenth Amendment was ratified in 1920.

© 2011 by Michael D Brown. Used under license of Shutterstock, Inc.

The Civil Rights Act of 1875 attempted to secure equal treatment of all people in "public accommodations," such as inns, theaters, water fountains, etc. Though it passed, it was not enforced, and in 1883, it was declared unconstitutional by the Supreme Court. So again, our nation took a step backward. The proliferation of radical white supremacist groups continued to terrorize communities of color, while alliances of people of color and white humanists continued to advocate for laws to gain equality for all people.

One of the major alliances that served to further the values and principles of humanists was the Congress of Racial Equality (CORE), which was open to "anyone who believes that 'all people are created equal' and is willing to work towards the ultimate goal of true equality throughout the world." By 1961, there were 53 chapters in the United States that worked together to desegregate interstate travel and schools, and helped organize events such as the August 28, 1963 march on Washington in which Dr. Martin Luther King made his famous "I Have a Dream Speech." Members of CORE were people of color and they were white. Many people, including William Lewis Moore and Viola Fauver, Gregg Liuzzo (all three white), lost their lives as they faced the violence of extremists. These three named are but a few of the many who paid with the ultimate price to fulfill the hope of "All Men Are Created Equal." http://en.wikipedia.org/wiki/Timeline_of_the_African-American-Civil_Rights-Movement

In today's world, there are many humanists among us; however, the oppression that maintains the racial caste system is not as obvious or as apparent as in the era in which the subjects of this book lived. The many forms in which oppression reinvents itself require vigilance, identification, and concerted response if we are to ensure that we do not regress as a nation. As evidenced in the cursory overview of legal enactments made to create a more just society, there is always a backlash from those invested in maintaining oppression and exploitation. For example, the Emancipation Proclamation was responded to with Jim Crow laws. The Civil Rights Act of 1875 was repealed in 1883. The civil rights movement of the 1960s, which followed the model of peaceful demonstrations and civil disobedience as modeled by Thoreau and Gandhi, faced violent and cowardly reprisals. Subsequently, it is imperative that children *see color*, not in their hearts, but in their minds, so they can "Call 'It' What 'It" Is." The legacy of racism and all the other constructs of power of privilege woven into the fabric of our nation still exist. It just looks different, and agents of change must, first, be able to *see* it if they are, then, going to act upon it.

Michelle Alexander (2010) provides specificity to how racism remanifests itself in our society today. She points to the disparity in incarceration rates for men of color and the contributing factors for this disparity. She states that, "In some states, black men have been admitted to prison on drug charges at rates twenty to fifty times greater than those of white men. And in major cities wracked by the drug war, as many as 80 percent of young African American men now have criminal records and are thus subject to legalized discrimination for the rest of their lives" (p. 7). The zero-tolerance movement created a fast track to imprisonment for youth of color who disproportionately populate our prison system. Release from prison does not grant them a new beginning. Instead, young men who have served their time and "paid their debt to society" are relegated to a growing underclass as they face marginalization from being branded and stigmatized as criminals. Enforced discrimination sustains an underclass status and confronts this population in the areas of "voting, employment, housing, education, public benefits, and jury service" (p. 17). Not being able to *see and identify* the social forces that create such disparities encumbers the possibility for positive change. **Color Blindness** blinds and it incapacitates.

The belief in **meritocracy**, a Euro-American value rising from the legacy of the "American Dream" that drew so many Europeans to these shores, holds that any individual who works hard enough can "pull themselves up by their boot straps" and be successful in this nation. This belief is part of the indoctrination of European immigrants who choose to come to the United States. In the summer of 2011, my husband and I had the privilege of traveling throughout Ireland as we celebrated our 30 year wedding anniversary. We travelled parts of the country with friends that included University of California, Davis professor, Jim McElroy, who was born and raised in Northern Ireland. His daughter, Emma, accompanied us on the trip. While in Dublin, we toured a replica of one of the famine ships. In the hull of the ship was a posting that would have been read by the passengers escaping the brutal and oppressive conditions in their homeland. On their journey they were being conveyed the message that one's success or failure in the United States was directly ascribed to their own ability rather than the social forces or circumstances receiving them. Emma took a picture of the posting which she has provided

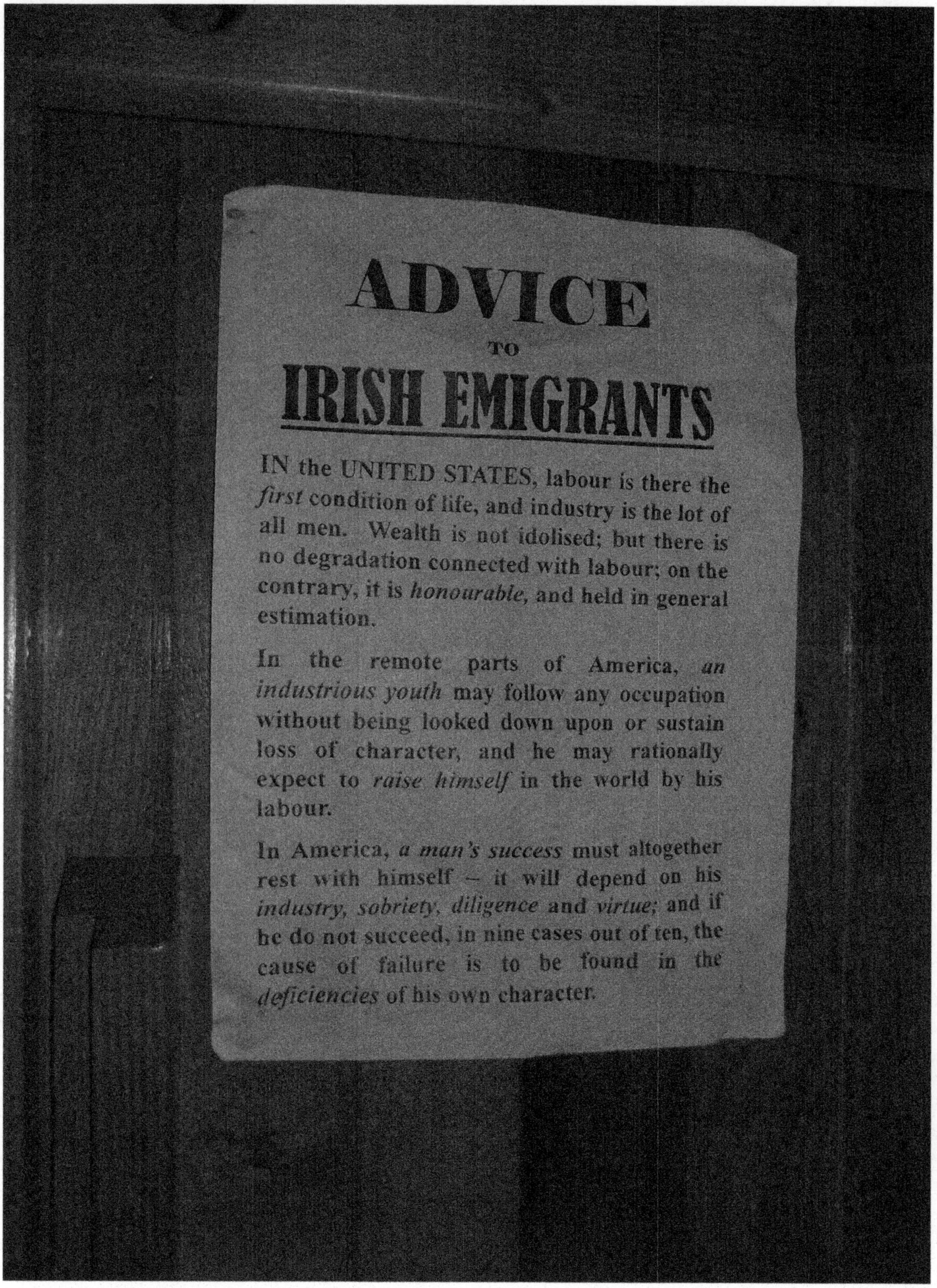

Image courtesy of Jill McEleroy

for this publication: The hope for voluntary immigrants as touted in the "American Dream" is a hope not originally intended for people of color who, rather than being invited to participate in the dream were excluded (and, in many cases, obliterated) for the purposes of those who choose to gain and achieve at any cost. Subsequently, the starting point in today's world for most children differs according to how far down the opportunity structure the child may be born into and whether or not available opportunity structures truly provide strong footing and the ability to move up the structure. Denial of the fact that there are inequitable structures in the areas of access to quality education, technology, health care, employment opportunities, safe neighborhoods, and other conditions that promote a "learning society" is a form of selective blindness. The belief in meritocracy abdicates our role in improving life outcomes for others and, once again, disables our ability to intervene.

Granted, there are many examples of people of color who have gained a firm footing in middle class status, and there are many examples of "exceptional" individuals who have risen to positions of status and prestige in this nation, including the presidency, since emancipation. As a whole, however, our nation is still crippled by differentiated opportunity structures through inadequately funded and staffed schools and economically depressed communities that do not provide sufficient employment and health benefits for those looking to not merely subsist but to thrive. These conditions are not just prevalent in communities of color, but are also a constant challenge to communities in which low-income whites have struggled, generation after generation, to find a foothold on the proverbial ladder toward the American Dream.

The legacy of Jim Crow laws, the erosion of civil rights gains, and the adoption of "Color Blindness" as a way to teach non-racist attitudes has, subsequently, left a whole generation standing on the sidelines with their hands in their pockets. While the intention of "Color Blindness" is to raise children to not discriminate based on skin color, it has impeded children's ability to see the common themes of who is impacted, what is causing the problem and, finally, how to intervene. Our historical and modern-day humanists acknowledged that racism exists. They also understood that it was the negative affixation to skin color and the ever present threat and use of violence employed by others to maintain subjugation. This, they acted upon because though they themselves were not racist, they understood the forces of racism.

Similarly, the many women (and men) who participated in the suffrage movement did so as they recognized that "All Men Are Created Equal" did *not* include them. They were not blind to the fact that the worldview of the "Founding Fathers" was not inclusive of women. They "Called 'It' What 'It' is" and, subsequently, banded together to gain equality of vote for women. It took 144 years after the signing of the Declaration of Independence for women to be legally considered "equal to white men" and 90 years for men of color to be considered equal to white men. The efforts of people since the existence of the historical humanists in this book made strides on our behalf because they saw, clearly, where inequities existed. They did not adhere to the fixed reality of their era. They were color blind in their hearts, but their minds saw clearly through the oppressive smog of racism.

The Three Bridges: Validation, Inclusion, Reciprocity

Our modern-day humanist, Elizabeth Johnson, conveys to her children that they be loving and accepting of all people. She also instills in them the recognition of the privilege that comes with being white and the responsibility to use their privilege to intervene in situations in which people of color are subjected to racism.

> We talk about white privilege so they both know a lot more ... so I try to impart what I've learned to them so they can have more understanding about this and about the racial issues from just the little bit that I know. But the most important part ... I want to do is (that they) ask questions. To be able to understand that when there is a situation at school, don't be color blind, don't ignore the racial issue of whatever is going on because that is a big component and it is generally the white people who say, "This is not an issue. Why do those other people always bring it up?" Be the one to bring it up. Be the white person to bring up the color issue, the racial component of anything (Johnson Interview, March 12, 2007).

The fact that constructs of power and privilege exist is not the doing of those in our generation, so the fact that white people have power and privilege is not cause for shame but rather a call to action. Johnson tells her children to be the one to point out what everyone else may be afraid to say and thereby use the power of their privilege in a positive way.

Dr. Lewis reminds us that "Euro-Americans are at a stage where they can take greater responsibility for advocating for such things as life, liberty, and the pursuit of happiness, as well as equity in education." This means that in whatever construct of power and privilege we may belong to, we, in alliance with those who are objectified in the same construct, can work collaboratively to create positive change in our world. Similarly, the power and privilege of heterosexuals, of men, of adults, of able-bodied, etc., calls us to be responsible with our power and privileges if we are to embrace a humanistic identity that promotes the "shift to a more just and compassionate society." Stories of how people have utilized their status of power and privilege within a wide range of constructs comprise the major body in the final chapter of this book.

The lessons learned from the historical and modern-day humanists teach us it is our responsibility to speak out when we see injustice. This is the first of the three bridges in which we attempt to connect across the racial divide and validate the existential reality of people experiencing oppression. Recall how Angelina Grimké refused to deny her emotions about what she saw. While her journal and her older sister, Sarah, became sources of outlet to vent the torment, she also recognized that her voice, as a white woman, could have tremendous impact on the injustices she witnessed on a regular basis. She validated the experiences of people who were suffering and acted upon the violence by the use of her voice and, eventually, through public written word.

Open **validation** and its power to build bridges across the racial divide were demonstrated in 2007 through the actions of then-Senator Hillary Clinton, and a host of people who reached out when needed. The incredible journey of the Rutgers' women's basketball team to the national championship basketball game in 2007 was almost overshadowed by a derogatory racial comment made by a well-known disc jockey whose hurtful statement made national headlines. Those who know Rutgers' women's basketball, Coach C. Vivian Stringer, know that she has a reputation for fostering championship behavior in her players, on and off the court. The team's response to a spoken word emanating from habituated thoughts grounded in the smog of a racialized reality reveals the grace by which Coach Stringer, her staff, and her players addressed a perception that they do not share. They live above the smog line.

This does not mean, however, that the statements were not hurtful. And, just as Elizabeth Johnson encourages her children to give voice to situations in which racism is occurring and not expect the person of color to carry the burden of having to be the one to respond to such acts, Senator Clinton and countless others, too, gave voice when needed. Coach Stringer's book, *Standing Tall*, speaks to the volume of support received by people from all over the world at the time of the incident. Her statement also speaks to the powerful impact that validation has when people, across the racial divide, demonstrate their support. She wrote:

> Senator Hillary Clinton collected thousands of supportive comments and presented them to me when we met; even now, reading them is almost too much for me to bear. To everyone who took the time to pick up the phone, to write an e-mail, or to put pen to paper in order to let us know that you were behind us, we felt you there, we really did. That outpouring of public support and love told me that we, as a country, are no longer willing to stand idly by when someone drags our best and brightest through the dirt. It told me that we as a nation would no longer tolerate complicity in casual, thoughtless degradation. It told me that the time had indeed come for someone to stand up for what was right (2008, p. 279).

Standing up for what is right means doing so regardless of who has been wronged and who you have to stand up to. This is the courage that Dr. Lewis asks that we demonstrate when we are called to "Call It What It Is," while Johnson encourages us to speak up from that courage and not remain silent. The silence, we know, implies complicity with the act of violence so the importance of validating the reality of those who have been on the receiving end of a micro aggression means that we must openly express that we are abhorred by the act. This is similar to how Angelina Grimké expressed how she abhorred the atrocities that she witnessed. In doing so, we are telling the world that we do not accept this behavior as "normal" nor "acceptable."

The power of **Inclusion** provides another element of bridge building to mitigate the divide and rule forces that continue to define our day-to-day reality. To see the power of inclusionary action, we will examine a common occurrence that happens, even today, but in this instance, it is reported to us by Frederick Douglass.

> Riding from Boston to Albany ... I found myself in a large car, well filled with passengers. The seat next to me was about the only vacant one. At every stopping place we took in new passengers, all of whom, on reaching the seat next to me, cast a disdainful glance upon it, and passed to another car, leaving me in the full enjoyment of a whole form. For a time, I did not know but that my riding there was prejudicial to the interest of the railroad company. A circumstance occurred, however, which gave me an elevated position at once. Among the passengers on this train was Gov. George N. Briggs. I was not acquainted with him, and had no idea that I was known to him ... upon observing me, the governor left his place, and making his way toward me, respectfully asked the privilege of a seat by my side; and upon introducing himself, we entered in to a conversation very pleasant and instructive to me. The despised seat now became honored. His excellency had removed all the prejudice against sitting by the side of a negro; and upon his leaving

it, as he did, on reaching Pittsfield, there were at least one dozen applicants for the place. The governor had, without changing my skin a single shade, made the place respectable which before was despicable (Douglass, p. 396).

Revisiting the definition of racism from Memmi, we can recall that there is first a notation of "difference." Noting difference, in and of itself, does not have to be bad. It is when a negative connotation to difference is affixed that the mistreatment begins to occur. The actions of Governor Briggs provided an alternative response to Douglass. While the other passengers responded from their own negative "habituated thoughts" about a person of color and, subsequently, responded with repulsion which prompted them to not select the open seat next to Douglass, Briggs demonstrated a value to Douglass that negated "difference" altogether. These two men, one black and one white, embarked upon a lovely conversation, and thereby, conducted themselves in a manner that superseded the racialized reality of the rest of the white passengers. The then-governor of Massachusetts used his power and privilege to change the perceived value of skin color from negative to a "non-factor" and enacted inclusionary practices by sitting next to Douglass, who was being subjected to isolation through exclusion. The power of inclusion negated this experiential reality and changed the nature of conduct for those witnessing the positive interaction between Douglass and Briggs.

Levels of comfort are called to question when we examine grades of inclusion. As evolving habituated thoughts and behaviors challenge what has been customary in relation to social distance across racial group lines the proximity of relationship is also challenged. Once a negative association to "difference" has been affixed, grades of inclusion range. For example, Tessler spoke to how her father had to openly oppose the exclusionary tactics by white neighbors who were trying to keep a black family from moving into the neighborhood. While these same neighbors might not protest integrated theaters, restaurants, etc., they sought to maintain a "whites only" neighborhood.

Douglass' life experiences demonstrate the grades of acceptance experienced under Social Distance Theory. After the death of his first wife, Anna Murray, Douglass married Helen Pitts, a white woman. One of Helen Pitts' sisters named a daughter after her. This namesake of Helen Pitts was never called "Helen" by her grandparents, the parents of Frederick Douglass' wife. They choose to, instead, call her "Kitty." Even though Kitty's grandparents were abolitionists, they were ashamed that their daughter had married a man whose father was white and mother was black. It was not until later in life that "Kitty" learned she had been named after another member of the family and then learned the reason why her grandparents refused to call her by her given name, Helen. The marriage lasted 11 years until Douglass' death.

This story is passed down as part of the family lore and communicated by Carol Curinga, granddaughter of Helen (aka "Kitty). With the discovery of this connection to the famous great aunt that had almost been lost due to family shame, the response from Curinga on how she and her generation feel about the famous great aunt and her marriage to Frederick Douglass was very simple. They feel "pride." The family now openly shares this connection with subsequent generations since they have not only embraced their dispossessed ancestor, but have also embraced her famous husband as well (Curinga Personal Interview, March 7, 2011).

These ranges of inclusion become evident as a new social order is created and are revealed in the various levels of bridges binding people across the racial divide. The energy required to build a bridge is not to be negated. It takes conscious effort and a persistence that defies the undermining habituated thoughts and behaviors of others that have persisted for generations. The story shared with Curinga, however, demonstrates that hearts can change with time, with persistence, with contact, and with greater understanding.

The power of **reciprocity** as a bridge building practice is one that has been employed for generations between nations and tribes that have experienced intergroup conflict. Where there has been material exploitation, physical violence or any other perceived mistreatment enacted by one person or group upon another, then the act of reciprocity serves to symbolically mend over time, and can lead to stabilizing a strained relationship. For example, in the summer of 2015, a racially motivated massacre took the lives of nine worshipers at a bible study at Emanuel African Methodist Episcopal Church in Charleston, South Carolina. Rather than allowing this act to polarize the community, the doors remained open to **all** in a sign of racial reconciliation. In reciprocity, a response that demonstrates that this act of violence would not foment further division is evidenced by "Sunday service studded with significant numbers of new, nonblack worshippers" (Sacramento Bee, October 19, 2015). Overt acts or even symbolic gifts serve to strengthen our bonds when relationships are threatened by anything from micro-aggressions to physical violence. This, of course, must be strengthened with egalitarian behavior and treatment between the two parties. Recognizing, first of all, that there has been a breach of relationship and that healing must take place, the active participation in exchange and recognition shows a value in the relationship and demonstrates a desire to work toward what Lewis calls "a more just and compassionate society."

Changing the habituated thoughts and subsequent behavioral patterns that have existed in this nation depends on efforts at various levels. One level will depend on the creation, strengthening, and enforcement of laws that protect civil rights. Another level is in access to quality education that minimizes the different starting points of our children. A third level relates to individual acts committed by people who, day in and day out, think and behave in ways that resist the forces that attempt to enforce racial group loyalty.

In the end, the stories of the white humanists must be retold. Their lives provide a counter-narrative for white Euro-American children to emulate, model, and learn how to be in the world with values and actions that promote equity and harmony. The gentleman whose quote opens this chapter speaks to the need for these models because these humanists could be, for some, the heroes that they would prefer to embrace as their own. We must not let the historical humanists and the values and worldview they possessed experience the final death. That loss would have implications on the very nature and development of all our children, as well as on the soul of this nation.

QUESTIONS FOR DISCUSSION OR SELF REFLECTION

SELF-AWARENESS

1. Who are other humanists from historic or modern times? What values did they embrace and that you would like to emulate?

2. Revisit the Identity Development Model(s) and determine what stage you are at this time? Is your identity situational? In other words, your stage may shift based on who you are with and/or where you are? If so, what factors contribute to this?

CLIENT WORLDVIEW

3. Loewen (1995) states that "Education... encourages students not to think about society but merely to trust that it is good" (p. 308). What are the implications of this as it relates to the wide range of people living in our diverse world?

4. As you observe people around you whether it is people in your own social circle(s), work place, or even public figures, can you identify, based on consistent patterns of behavior and language, their stage of identity development?

COUNSELING RELATIONSHIP

5. What is your internal response when discussions related to any one of the "isms" from our society come up? Are you able to constructively engage in these discussions?

6. What are ways in which to activate the Three Bridges of Validation, Inclusion, and Reciprocity in your day to day living? As part of your practice in your field?

COUNSELING AND ADVOCACY INTERVENTIONS

7. What are opportunities you can identity for teaching from a "counter-narrative" approach?

8. What are ways in which to engage children and youth from a "problem posing" approach in addressing issues in their communities?

NEW CONCEPTS AND VOCABULARY TO REVIEW

Phenomenological perspective:

Helms White Identity Development Model:

Master Narrative

Problem Posing:

Great Law of Peace:

Counter Narrative

Meritocracy:

Color Blindness:

Three Bridges: Validation, Inclusion, Reciprocity:

Activity

1. Conduct further research related to the following:

   a. The names of various humanists are included in this chapter. Who are they? How do their lives reflect the themes addressed earlier in this book?

   b. Identify humanists from this nation as well as other nations who have advocated for marginalized populations. What did they do? What difference did they make in the lives of others? What norms of their culture or society did they defy in order to bring about change?

2. With your colleagues at work, how can you activate the spirit of the MSJCC (Appendix D) and/or the guidelines indicated for Transformational Leaders (Appendix E)?

3. What are historical sources that can be adopted in order to teach U.S. history from a more balanced perspective? How can you provide this information to the greatest number of children, youth, and adults?

References

Alexander, M. (2010). *The new jim crow; mass incarceration in the era of colorblindness.* New York, NY. The New Press.

Douglass, F. (1994). *Douglass autobiographies.* New York, NY: Penguin Books.

Fausset, R. (2015). Recovery slow, painful after S.C. church shooting. New York Times article in Sacramento Bee. October 19, 2015.

Halliburton, Jr., R. (1977). *Red Over Black: Black Slavery among the Cherokee Indians.* Greenwood Press, Westport, CT.

Halliburton, R. (1977). *Red over black.* Westport, CT: Greenwood Press.

http://www.iroquoisdemocracy.pdx.edu/html/greatlaw.html

http://en.wikipedia.org/wiki/Timeline_of_the_African-American-Civil_Rights-Movement

Loewen, J. W. (1995). *Lies my teacher told me.* New York, NY. Touchstone.

Moore, L. (2004). *Voices of successful African American men.* Edwin Mellen Press. Lewiston, NY.

Stringer, C. V. (2008). *Standing tall.* New York, NY. Three Rivers Press.

Sue, D. (2010). *Microaggressions in everyday life.* Hoboken, NJ. John Wiley & Sons.

Prepared by Gerald Murphy (The Cleveland Free-Net - aa300) Distributed by the Cybercasting Services Division of the National Public Telecomputing Network (NPTN). Permission is hereby granted to download, reprint, and/or otherwise redistribute this file, provided appropriate point of origin credit is given to the preparer(s) and the National Public Telecomputing Network. © 1 October 2001, Portland State University.

Weatherford, J. (1988). *Indian givers.* New York, NY. Crown Publishers.

Woodson, C. G. (2000). *The mis-education of the negro.* Chicago, IL. Associated Publishers.

Healing the Soul Wound

Chapter Contribution by Dr. Michael Mobley

In 1991 I was working as a Residence Hall Director at LaSalle University in Philadelphia. During this time, I was responsible for St. Miguel Court, a modern gated townhouse community for upper-class undergraduate students. One Friday evening, I had exited the gated fence of St. Miguel Court and walked toward my car when I noticed a police van driving around the parking lot. Since I was off-duty and in route to a 7:00 p.m. dinner with a close friend, I continued to walk toward my car. While inserting the key into my 1981 Ford station wagon, two police officers quickly approached with their guns drawn, yelling "Put your hands up!" I was absolutely shocked and somewhat paralyzed. I turned to the officers, not raising my hands, and replied: "Officers, there must be a mistake. I'm Michael Mobley, the residential hall staff director for St. Miguel here at LaSalle University." Again, they yelled, "Put your hands up!" Still being shocked and not raising my hands, I responded, "I have my university staff ID in my pocket...." Before I completed my response, an officer had quickly approached and physically pressed me up against my car and demanded that I put my hands behind my back. In reflection, I still "resisted" restating my name and formal position at the university, and stating that my photo ID was in my back pocket. After handcuffing me, the police van drove up and the officer walked me over to the window of the van. Inside was a white female who seemingly shook her head laterally, sideways, indicating "no" and raised her hand laterally over her head indicating "taller." From this, I immediately inferred that she was informing the officer in the van that I was not the African American male who had assaulted her; that particular male was taller. By this time, two LaSalle University campus police officers had arrived. I attempted to communicate with them again, stating my staff position at the university and requesting that they call my supervisor and/or director of residential life. Given this incident occurred during my first month or so at LaSalle, the campus police did not recognize me.

To use the proverbial, "to make a long story short," I was arrested, taken to the police station in Philadelphia, pressured to allow a full body search (which I resisted), and overheard one officer state, "Oh! We have one of these educated 'n***** here," before I was allowed to make a phone call and then placed into a jail for several hours without my shoes. Several months later in January 1992, the night before I had to report to court to defend myself, I observed the Rodney King incident on the 11:00 nightly news. This triggered an immediate flashback and fear in me about my court hearing the next morning. Shockingly, the arresting officer claimed in his police report that I had "physically assaulted him." The judge read this statement out loud and asked, "You telling me that this short, approximately 160 pound young man assaulted you, an approximately 220, 6 foot plus man?" Gratefully, the charges were dismissed by the judge; yet, the racial trauma was emblazed in my psyche. I have since healed from this experience. I do not **"have a chip on my shoulders"** toward Philadelphia police officers.

"Chip on the Shoulder" and "Humanist Models"

During the initial development of this chapter, the title "Chip on the Shoulder" was proposed. What does it mean to have a chip on your shoulder? "A person who has 'a chip on his shoulder' is angry because of something that happened in the past" (http://www.goenglish.com/achiponyourshoulder.asp retrieved November 6, 2010) it's a belligerent attitude or grievance. This term actually was defined in a newspaper article (*Long Island Telegraph*, May 20, 1830): "When two churlish boys were determined to fight, a chip would be placed on the shoulder of one and the other demanded to knock it off at his peril" [early 1800s]. (Ammer, Christine, 2010, The American Heritage Dictionary of Idioms, http://idioms.yourdictionary.com/chip-on-one-s-shoulder retrieved November 6, 2010).

In an interview with Fox News' Greta Van Susteren, right-wing radio host Rush Limbaugh said President Barak Obama was more "passionate" during a news conference about the arrest of his friend, Harvard Professor Henry Louis Gates, than he was about health care. Limbaugh said the reason was clear: Obama is "black" and that as a result, he's "got a chip on his shoulder."

Limbaugh stated:

> I think Obama is largely misunderstood by a lot of people.... We're finding out that this guy's got a chip on his shoulder. He's angry at this country. He's not proud of it. Let's face it, President Obama's black, and I think he's got a chip on his shoulder. I think there are elements in this country he doesn't like and he never has liked. And he's using the power of the presidency to remake the country.

This is the response to President Obama, our leader, attempting to de-escalate a racially charged, volatile, and high-profile situation. It is viewed from the lens of his "blackness" as opposed to the use of his position to bring about change. The behaviors of "the other" will continue to be viewed through the lens of race until we find ways to break the bonds that hold us to a racialized reality. In this book, Dr. Borunda helps us all to bridge the cultural divides.

I am grateful to Dr. Rose Borunda for her invitation to join her and Dr. Rolla E. Lewis on this beautiful journey, *What Color is Your Heart?* I met Rose in February 2010 while attending the

27th Winter Roundtable on Cultural Psychology and Education at Teachers' College at Columbia University in New York City. After delivering my keynote address, I had the pleasure of participating in her workshop entitled, "Hope for Cross-Racial Bridging and Evolving Identity Development: The Power of Presenting Humanist Euro-American Archetypes in Graduate Education." I regret that I arrived late; yet what I learned and experienced from Dr. Borunda's presentation was quite meaningful to my understanding of multiculturalism. As a multicultural scholar, I constantly seek novel ways to engage graduate students in increasing their cultural competence, as well as expand my own cultural competence. From my perspective, it is critical for us all to develop a cultural worldview grounded in understanding "**self-in-relationship-to-others**" (Sue, Ivey & Pedersen, 1996). For me, this tenet espoused within the Multicultural Counseling Theory represents a humanist orientation and way of being in the world.

In her presentation, Dr. Borunda eloquently and passionately introduced me to historical white humanists who advocated for equality on behalf of African Americans in the United States. As a 44-year-old African American gay male with a doctoral degree, I was not familiar with many of these white historical figures. White American historical figures whose values, principles, beliefs, and most of all, **actions** demonstrated their genuine and extremely unique public and private acceptance, respect, and appreciation for "*the other*," called "Negros", "Coloreds," or "Blacks" during their lifetime. To fight actively against slavery, a truly unjust and inhumane form of social order in the United States during such times, captured my mind, heart and spirit.

I recall feeling profoundly moved emotionally and spiritually to hear about such acts of bravery and courage by humanists such as Sarah Shaw and her son, Colonel Robert Gould Shaw, John Brown, William Lloyd Garrison, Angelina Grimké, and Helen Hunt Jackson. The life of these white women and men signify for me the essence of "**a purposeful life**" impassioned by spiritual love for humanity. From its inception, I have been most captured by CNN and Anderson Cooper's annual tribute to heroes, ordinary individuals across the international global landscape who boldly and selfishly act to empower the lives of others, being oppressed. As captured in this program, I hope that Dr. Borunda's project may bear fruit in visual media form as a testament to and honor of white American humanist heroes.

What was it about learning of these white humanists that moved me in such an emotionally and spiritually profound way? Indeed, I feel my eyes swell of tears as I reflect, activate my internalized voice, and type these words. During Dr. Borunda's presentation and presently at this very moment, I am keenly aware that these white humanists were willing to risk their lives (in several cases, two of these men lost their lives) to fight for my ancestors! They put themselves at risk for "Negros," "Coloreds," and "Black" people *who look like me*, or in the case of Helen Hunt Jackson, who advocated for my multi-colored shades of American Indian brothers and sisters. As a spiritual Christian, I am deeply moved spiritually because the courageous acts of social justice undertaken by these white American humanists remind me of Jesus Christ, my Lord and Savior.

As an African American, I have vivid memories of my mother and immediate family members, especially my Aunt Clara, being strongly influenced by the black church. Within the Baptist tradition and faith, I was taught to believe that Jesus died for our (my) sins. Sin is rebellion against God. For me, white American humanists chronicled in *What is the Color of Your Heart?*

were willing to die for the sins of their white brothers and sisters who degraded, devalued, and dehumanized my ancestors through slavery and the period of Jim Crow laws.

On that day in February 2010, I was in a state of awe. For me, I learned and internalized a consciousness that these white humanists valued the lives of my ancestors to the extent that they were willing to confront their family and friends, fellow citizens, and the societal, institutional, and individual levels of racism. In essence, these white humanists were willing to "***carry the cross***." In Christian teachings, the blood of Jesus represents incredible power. As a sacrificial lamb, Jesus gave his blood to cleanse and wipe away our sins. There is power in the blood of Jesus. "God has given blood as the means of atonement by which sins are forgiven." In Leviticus 17:11, he explains: "The life of the flesh *is* in the blood, and I have given it to you upon the altar to make atonement for your souls; for it *is* the blood *that* makes atonement for the soul." Atonement is satisfaction for an offense, resulting in the restoration of a broken relationship. "According to the law almost all things are purified with blood, and without shedding of blood there is no remission" (Hebrews 9:22)

Similar to Jesus, these white humanists were willing to give their blood in the name of social justice for racial equality. Ultimately, for me, these white humanists embody God's love. Their social justice principles and values were selflessly enacted to honor the living human spirit of my ancestors of color. The transformative and transcendent power of these American white humanists serves as a testament to all of us today. A testament of what it means and how one acts to promote a socially just society, wherein we actively fight to end various forms of racism. They were willing to stand up against the potency of racial oppression in its most horrific form, slavery. In learning about their acts of courage, I am struck by their ***conviction***, which is an unshakable belief in the value of all humans regardless of the color of one's skin.

I am equally stuck by their defiance to the racial social order. The behavior of these white humanists was fueled by their intentional contemptuous attitude of the importance to eradicate racial hatred and transgressions. As such, these white humanists reveal the "***color of their hearts***." Within my Christian faith and perspective, the core of my spirit tells me that their heart pulsates with the blood of Jesus, the blood of humanity. In understanding their willingness to be a sacrificial lamb in the name of racial social justice, I instantaneously experience an open spirit and heart to cross the river of racial divide between blacks and whites. Their transformative lives offer hope that contemporary white Americans may demonstrate a similar level of racial consciousness about modern racism that represents oppressive strains of cancer in society. Our search for the cure continues. As evidenced by the choices and decisions of Angeline Grimké and her sister, Sarah, I witness whites who are willing to utilize their white privilege as an instrument of justice, as a voice for the dehumanized and oppressed (Freire, 1998).

For people of color, it is a tremendous challenge to overcome cultural mistrust and healthy paranoia. The varied historical acts of racial trauma are still emblazoned deep within our spiritual souls. Such **Jungian archetypes** serve as unconscious reservoirs of hurt, pain, and historical roots of fear. The fear that "*what if it*" happens again? On most days, our conscious mind assures us of the reality that "*it will not*" happen again. However, there are moments or periods when our conscious mind facilitates a direct hotline to our unconscious Jungian archetype fear. What are modern cultural events that trigger and manifest our unconscious memories of historical trauma? Recall visual and print media reports of the following people and events: the Rodney King beating, the O. J. Simpson trial, James Byrd, Jr., Susan Smith, and the "whites only" shade tree in Jena, Louisiana, from which three colored nooses were hung the day after African American students were granted permission to sit under the tree by school personnel, and African American scholar Henry Louis Gates, Jr., the Alphonse Fletcher University Professor of Harvard, being arrested by a police officer who reported that he was responding to a 911 call about breaking and entering in progress at the Gates' address in Cambridge, Massachusetts. These cultural events particularly affected African Americans.

Similarly, the continued marginalization of First Nations people and the historical racial trauma including murder still presents cultural challenges for Native Americans living on reservations today. The largest single American Indian nation, the Navaho, with a population of 104,565 in 2000, is located primarily in northeastern Arizona. Moreover, in Arizona, there are 22 reservations that have a combined land area of 19.1 million acres; that is 26% of the total state area. In 2000, the nation's third highest Indian population represented 5% of Arizona's total population. In addition, the Latino community continued to be assaulted by the ongoing national call for "English Only" across the United States. Of interest, as of 2005, the total percentage of individuals younger than 25 years of age across racial/ethnic minority groups was 50.2% compared with 29.1% of White non-Hispanics in Arizona. It seems important to understand such cultural demographic data in light of the recent Arizona state law on illegal immigration, which requires police officers to actively identify, prosecute, and deport illegal immigrants. The bias, prejudices, and discrimination have not spared Asian American/Pacific Islanders in the United States. It was during World War II that the United States interned Japanese Americans out of *fear*. Their "difference" marked them as suspicious and untrustworthy. It is important to note that during this same historical period, the same policy was not applied to German Americans.

Almost 30 years ago, African American social scientists identified **cultural mistrust** (Terrell & Terrell, 1981; 1984), which may be considered a healthy form of paranoia (Whaley, 2001) that many blacks hold toward whites as a result of slavery, Jim Crow laws, and modern forms of racism. Terrell & Terrell asserted that cultural mistrust "involves the inclination among blacks to mistrust whites, with mistrust most evident in the areas of education and training, business and work, interpersonal and social relations, politics and law."

Cultural mistrust is connected to the modern phenomenon commonly called "DWB, Driving while Black," among the African American community. DWB has been substantially supported by statistical data for various states such as Maryland and New Jersey. As an African American male who absolutely enjoys driving, I was extremely conscious of DWB when I drove from my home in Columbia, Missouri, to my mother's home in Chester, Pennsylvania. During this travel lasting approximately 17 hours and 36 minutes, mostly along I-70 and I-76, there are only three large major urban/metropolitan centers: St. Louis, Indianapolis, and Columbus, before arriving in the Philadelphia region (the final 26 miles of the approximately, 1,000 mile journey). The interstate journey includes Missouri, Illinois, Indiana, Ohio, West Virginia, and finally, Pennsylvania. My body experienced differential stress levels as I departed large major cities and drove into rural landscapes down the highway.

For many African Americans like me, these physiological bodily reactions are directly linked to what Shawn Utsey and colleagues calls "**Race-related Stress**" (Utsey & Ponterroto, 1996; Utsey, Giesbrecht, Hook, & Stanard, 2008). Race-related stress reflects the result of daily encounters with racism. Repeated experiences of prejudice, bias, harassment, discrimination, and racism have been called "microaggressions" (Sue, 2010). When people of color endure weeks, months, and years of microaggressions, it results in negative physical and mental health effects. Sue (2010) provides four pathways in which the toll of microaggressions is manifested on the well being of marginalized groups. These pathways include biological responses that may include heightened blood pressure and heart rate, cognitive responses that can be found in preoccupation about the

particular event, emotional responses of rage, depression, or some other negative reaction, as well as behavioral responses to the incident that may make the situation worse. I count my blessings that I have encountered few blatant, harsh microaggressions and assaults. Fortunately, and by the grace of God, I have had to live only that one horrible encounter with police officers. As a consequence, I am able to respect police officers, regardless of their race. However, many African American adolescent boys and men, especially in urban communities, may maintain a high level of cultural mistrust and paranoia in the presence of police.

Recognizing the Internal Wounds of Historical Trauma

Both the historical trauma of slavery and modern racism represent forms of oppression experienced by people of color. After repeated exposure to and experiences of oppression, I believe that individuals develop a **latent oppressive identity**, or LOI (Mobley, 2010) and its associated ego status. During the past five years, I have observed this phenomenon within myself and others. LOI is a dormant or hidden part of my distinctive character personality (e.g., self, self-image, sense of self, etc.), which has developed as a result of enduring oppression in various forms (e.g., racism, sexism, heterosexism, homophobia, etc.) and degrees of severity (e.g., subtle taunts, unintended microaggressions, to blatant acts of harassment & discrimination, to cruel, harsh, and tyrannical forms of oppression). "Ego states are the parts of our personality that cause us to act different ways in different situations," and they represent an "organized system of behavior and experience whose elements are bound together by some common principle" (p. 25; Watkins & Watkins, 1997). Oppression serves as the common principle in LOI ego state.

Thus, latent oppressive identity (LOI) ego status reflects an oftentimes unconscious suppressed internalized representation of experiencing unjust and unfair oppressive treatment as a result of one's socio-cultural identity status and group membership. LOI may develop as a result of experiencing various forms of societal oppressions, including racism, sexism, heterosexism/homophobia, anti-semitism, etc., as an internalized process. LOI ego status has its own unique set of behavioral, cognitive, and affective response styles. When an individual's LOI ego status manifests, she/he may experience a range of cognitive and affective responses, including dissonance, silence, anger, dehumanization, guilt, collusion, ignorance, and self-hatred (Pinderhughes, 1989). Equally, individuals may exhibit various LOI behavioral responses, such as stress, lack of reality, horizontal violence, paralysis, confrontational interactions, seclusion, aggression, and violence, as well as internalization of the cycle of oppression (Pinderhughes, 1989).

To understand how LOI ego status affects people of color, it may be helpful to take another look at my internal reactions (thoughts, behaviors, and emotions) to being assaulted by police officers in Philadelphia. When this incident happened, I was a Master's level graduate student studying at Temple University. Being raised less than 30 minutes outside Philly, I understood the high level of drugs, violence, and crime in the city. In fact, in 1990–1991, I was hall director at Temple University in Peabody Hall, which is located in north Philadelphia. Despite being "educated" and aware of social injustices acted upon black boys and men, latent oppressive identity took over when I heard the police officers yell, "Put up your hands!" and I turned and saw their guns drawn. I immediately knew I was being wrongfully accused. I didn't understand why the officers simply didn't approach me and ask, "Young man (or Sir), can we talk with you?" Instead, I was presumed guilty and dangerous based on the color of my skin. Within a few minutes, I lost my conscious capacity to think rationally. I was in a state of disbelief, disoriented, and shocked, not fully in touch with the reality of the situation. In this emotional, mental, and physical state, I was unable to truly act in a manner that would keep me safe and protected. My cognitive thoughts and physical body were not following police orders. Any sudden quick move on my part could have resulted in me being shot. Yet, after being handcuffed, I did my best to remain calm, cool, and collected despite the intense anger and rage I was experiencing in reaction to this unjust treatment.

From my experience, we see that when people of color encounter real or perceived racism in their environment, their LOI ego status associated with their racial identity may be triggered and activated. Past injuries of prejudice, discrimination, and aggressive treatment experienced as a result of one's racial/ethnic minority status are "re-ignited" and LOI ego status surfaces. In fact, we are able to envision LOI ego status and hear its voice as we read the following excerpt shared by an African American male:

> It gets so tiring, you know. It sucks you dry. People don't trust you. From the moment I wake up, I know stepping out the door, that it will be the same, day after day. The bus can be packed, but no one will sit next to you ... I guess it may be a good thing because you always get more room, no one crowds you. You get served last ... when they serve you, they have this phony smile and just want to get rid of you.... You have to show more ID to cash a check, you turn on the TV and there

you always see someone like you, being handcuffed and jailed. They look like you and sometimes you begin to think it is you! You are a plague! You try to hold it in, but sometimes you lose it. Explaining doesn't help. They don't want to hear. Even when they ask, "Why do you have a chip on your shoulder?' Shit ... I just walk away now. It doesn't do any good explaining. (Sue, p. 87, 2010).

In this state of being, it would be a challenge for this African American male to engage in a conversation with whites. At such times during communication, one's mode of functioning and processing may be characterized as "low-mode" (Siegel & Hartzell, 2003). Low-mode of processing involves shutting down our higher processes of the mind, and it leaves us in a state of intense emotions, impulsive reactions, rigid and repetitive responses, and lacking in self-reflection and the consideration of another's point of view. Such cognitive, affective, and behavioral response style is often called the "low road" of processing during communication. In hearing the voice of this African American male, we sense intense frustration, a sense of hopelessness, and despair about not being seen as a "worthy human being" akin to a "*plague*." Essentially, he gives up hope that a meaningful dialogue is possible to bridge the cultural divide.

On the other hand, when processing on the "high road," we are able to access the rational, reflective thought processes of our mind (Siegel & Hartzell, 2003). The high mode of processing supports our ability to reflect on possibilities and consider our choice of action and its consequences. In essence, the high road allows us to make flexible choices during difficult dialogues that support our values in respecting each other on the basis of race and other dimensions of cultural diversity. It does not eliminate racial conflicts and tensions. However, taking the high road gives us an opportunity to be thoughtful and intentional in our communication and choose verbal responses that facilitate bridging cultural divides. It is critical to understand how LOI ego status and low and high modes of processing influence communications between people of color and whites.

Trust, but Verify: A Means to Bridge the Cultural Divide

It is still difficult for many people of color to understand that, in the United States, as a result of a Eurocentric dominant socialization process, many whites may engage in unconscious, **unintentional acts of racism** (Ridley, 1994). Despite the increasing numbers of multicultural pluralistic communities in American society, some whites still live in segregated spaces, such as their predominantly white neighborhoods, schools, churches, and social cliques and clubs. Such lack of exposure and meaningful interaction with culturally diverse racial and ethnic minority individuals during their socialization process leads to unconscious acts of racism.

Often times, people of color struggle to give white people "*the benefit of the doubt*" before characterizing a perceived prejudice, bias, or discriminatory act as racist. For example, some African Americans may be quick to judge and label a white person's verbal and/or nonverbal behavior as *racist*. In a classroom discussion about race, it is not uncommon for some white students to exclaim in exasperation: "Why can't we all just get along," "My parents didn't own slaves," "Why do all People of Color sit together in the cafeteria," "Why does everything has to be about 'race?'" and "I don't see color. We're all humans." During such interactions a domain of LOI ego status commonly called "**white guilt**" tends to surface within many white individuals. As a consequence, many whites may choose to disengage and recoil into silence, which may shut down the communication. Yet, other whites may continue to experience cognitive dissonance, ignorance about race relations and social justice, and/or anger towards people of color for having a "chip on their shoulders" or "playing the race card" (Malveaux, 2002).

On the other hand, the LOI ego status commonly associated with emersion/immersion (Helms, 1990) racial identity tends to surface within many people of color. During such dialogues, African Americans may communicate in a style characterized by intense affective, behavioral, and oral responses. Their tone of voice may become elevated, along with an increased rate of speech, sometimes interrupting a white peer's comments as a way to immediately refute his/her perceived illogically based rationale or perspective (Kochman, 1981). Indeed, because of the manifestation of their LOI ego status, some people of color may experience a range of emotions including frustration, anger, and resentment toward their white peers. In this situation, although the verbal and/or nonverbal behavior of whites reflects a form of racial prejudice or bias, it is oftentimes an unintentional, even unconscious, response based on ignorance. Nonetheless, this style of response on the part of people of color leads to a racial cultural divide in communication and interactions with whites. Unfortunately, many people of color do not recognize how their "emotionally charged" response, particularly when unintentional racism occurs, elicits a defensive posture in whites. Such verbal exchanges are characterized as "confrontational" by whites; thus, the "cultural bridge of communication" falls into deep waters, and neither party may possess the capacity or willingness to jump into the water and re-connect the bridge.

During my doctoral studies, I have a clear memory of when my LOI ego status and emersion/immersion racial identity were triggered. A white peer called me at home to "process" what happened earlier in our assessment class. During this conversation, it was a constant struggle for me to take the "high road" in our conversation. My peer made the following statements during the telephone exchange: "Why don't you talk about multicultural issues in the multicultural class, not the assessment class? If you are going to talk about race/ethnicity, how come you don't also talk about other areas of diversity, such as gender, disability, etc.? In talking about multiculturalism, we don't have enough time to cover all the topics and issues in assessment."

I experienced these comments from my white peer as a form of racial oppression. My emotions were quite intense. I couldn't believe that this peer was calling me, and from my perspective, trying to make me conform to expectations based her/his way of seeing the world and engaging in the classroom. There were several occasions when the "low-road" processing and style of communication took over. Our voices were elevated, we interrupted each other, and at times, we were unable to give enough space and silence to hear each other (Kochman, 1981). Toward the end of the conversation, and certainly more than an hour later, I was able to get back on the "high road" of processing and communicating. I was able to express my opinion and feelings more calmly and directly to my peer. I took time to listen and hear my peer's point of view.

I used the counseling skills (e.g., paraphrasing, reflecting, summarizing, and others) I was being taught to let my peer know that I valued what was being expressed, even if I did not agree with the perspective. I also asked my peer if she/he could understand my view and, in essence, stand in my shoes. Ultimately, I believe we both gained from sticking with a difficult dialogue. We continued to be friends during graduate studies and had both personal and professional interactions many years later. We were able to bridge the cultural divide.

On the other hand, there are times when people of color may simply choose to disengage, disconnect, and become "invisible" during interactions with whites if they perceive one as being racist. In environments characterized as racially tense or hostile climates, many people of color, if forced to occupy such spaces, avoid any sustained meaningful interactions or genuine, real communications with whites. Cultural mistrust is extremely elevated among people of color in such climates. A major racial divide exists, and limited dialogue occurs, except for required formal communications (e.g., within workplace or educational settings among supervisor-employee or faculty-advisor interactions). In some cases, the behavioral response style among people of color may be directed by emersion/immersion ego status espoused within Helms' (1990) racial identity model. As a result of heightened cultural mistrust and perceived racism in the environment, people of color prefer to interact only with others who look like them and avoid white people completely. In this situation, such responses on the part of people of color increase the lack of cultural understanding, maintain the cultural divide, and contribute to racial tensions.

In 1991, it would have been easy for me to adopt this cultural response style (e.g., disengaging, disconnecting, etc.) with a white male who I had been friends with for five years at the time. As we were preparing to enter his car in Philadelphia, he noticed that it had been vandalized. He immediately commented: "My Dad warned me about coming into the city and these n*****!" He quickly caught himself and looked at me and apologized. "I'm sorry. That's how my Dad talks about people in Philly. I didn't mean anything. Of course, I'm not talking about you." My LOI ego status surfaced. I experienced a sense of shock, disbelief, silence, and dissonance. Within seconds, I asked myself a series of questions: "Do I get into his car and go out to the bar? Do I go back to my apartment? How do I talk with him about this? Do I honestly express my feelings of disappointment, sadness, and regret? Is this what all white people are like, deep down inside?"

In this situation, I decided to take the "high road" in our conversation. I expressed my thoughts, feelings, and reactions. I accepted his apology. What helped to heal the racial cultural divide that was created between us was his repeated sincere apology. His openness to recognize that he had internalized stereotypes and beliefs about "inner-city blacks," based on his Dad's prejudice, bias, and racism. For me to take the "high road," I genuinely had to ***feel a sense of "realness"*** in our conversation. Moving beyond my internal emotions, I also had to think about and comprehend that my friend's comment was a form of unintentional racism. Besides, in the previous five years, I had never experienced any form of microaggressions in my interactions with him. Although we are still friends today, we only see each every few years since we live in different cities.

Conclusion

To a large extent, the blatant, historical, overt acts of racism, as witnessed by white American humanists in this book, no longer exist. The experiences of people of color in the United States is still plagued by bias, prejudice, and discrimination in various settings despite one's socioeconomic status, prestige of professional career, or geographic region. As people of color, it is still critical to assess the conditions within any predominantly white environment. In fact, for many African Americans, this cultural scanning of a dominant white environment and its inhabitants is a natural survival mechanism (Jones, 1996). Despite such racial social progress, it is evident that some people of color may still have a "chip on their shoulders" because we have not healed from the historical trauma. Being exposed to the heroic acts of courage of the white American humanists, such as Sarah Shaw and her son, Colonel Robert Gould Shaw, John Brown, William Lloyd Garrison, Angelina Grimké, and Helen Hunt Jackson may foster a willingness to consider or experience more meaningful interactions and genuine, open communication with whites on the part of People of Color.

In our modern times, Tim Wise, who Michael Eric Dyson describes as "one of the most brilliant, articulate and courageous critics of white privilege in the nation," represents a white American humanist who serves as an excellent model for whites and people of color. In a powerful narrative entitled "*White like me: Race and identity through majority eyes*," it is crystal clear to see that Wise (2002) is culturally conscious about racism, discrimination, white privilege, and social injustices adversely impacting the lives of African Americans and people of color in general. It is welcome sense of relief for many people of color to suspend their cultural mistrust when engaged with modern-day, American white humanists such as Wise.

In her compassion, eloquence, and deep commitment to truth, Dr. Borunda asserts that, "The centuries of exploitation and continued denigration leaves much room for healing in the hearts and souls of people of color. Living above the constructions of power and privilege as Humanists do is a difficult place at which to arrive." It is important that all of us, people of color and white individuals, are able to recognize the cultural similarities and differences between us. This perspective affords us an opportunity for continued dialogue and mutual discovery. Such racial understanding will help to bridge the cultural divide that exists. As people of color, we need to call upon our "better angels" to heal the soul wound.

QUESTIONS FOR DISCUSSION OR SELF REFLECTION

SELF-AWARENESS

1. Have you had an incident happen to you where you were targeted for being a woman, a person of color, a gay/lesbian/transgender/bisexual, or in any way as "different"? As a result, do you carry a chip on your shoulder? If so, what are you doing to heal from the incident? If not, how did you work through it?

2. How would you define a Purposeful Life? Is leading such a life of value to you? What factors contribute to the way you live your life?

3. Who do you consider to be a hero? What qualities make that person a hero? What does/did that person do for you to consider them a hero?

CLIENT WORLDVIEW

4. Working as a counselor, social worker, teacher, or administrator, how would you respond to your client(s)/students who are exhibiting signs of having Latent Oppressive Identity ego status?

COUNSELING RELATIONSHIP

5. What implication does the "Jungian Archetype," as discussed in this chapter, have for those endeavoring to enter the fields of counseling, social work, teaching, or educational leadership?

6. If you responded to the first question in this series with a particular incident in mind, did you respond from "high road" or "low road" mode? If you responded from a "low road" mode, can you consider ways in which you could have responded from the "high road"?

COUNSELING AND ADVOCACY INTERVENTIONS

7. What are ways to constructively de-escalate situations that are charged with any one of the "isms"?

8. People often think that heroes have to become extraordinarily famous or have done grandiose acts in order to be recognized, and yet, there are people, in our midst, who commit to purposeful lives every day but will never be recognized on national television. What are ways to promote these accessible individuals from our community as models for our children?

9. In what ways have you used your power and privilege to serve as an "instrument of justice"?

10. What recommendations would you make so that discussions about racism, sexism, classism, etc., can build the cultural bridge of communication rather than fall into the vast racial cultural divide?

NEW CONCEPTS AND VOCABULARY TO REVIEW

A Purposeful Life:

Self-in-relationship-to others:

Jungian Archetype:

Cultural Mistrust:

DWB—Driving While Black (or Brown):

Race-Related Stress:

Latent Oppressive Identity:

"High Road" vs. "Low Road" mode:

Unintentional Racism:

White Guilt:

References

Davison, http://www.oldpaths.com/Archive/Davison/Roy/Allen/1940/blood.html retrieved November 6, 2010.

Freire, P. (1993). *Pedagogy of the oppressed*. New York: Continuum.

Guthrie, R. V. (2004). *Even the rat was white: A historical view of psychology*. Pearson.

Helms, J. E. (1990). *Black and white racial identity: Theory, research, and practice*. New York: Greenwood Press.

Jones, J. M. (1996). *Prejudice and racism*. New York: McGraw-Hill.

Kochman, T. (1981). *Black and white styles in conflict*. Chicago, IL: The University of Chicago Press.

Martin Luther King, Jr. (n.d.). Retrieved November 20, 2010, from BrainyQuote.com: http://www.brainyquote.com/quotes/quotes/m/martinluth164280.html

Malveaux, J. (2002). *Race, rage, and the Ace of Spades*. In B. Singley (Ed.), *When race becomes real: black and white writers confront their personal histories* (pp. 101–110). Chicago, IL: Chicago Review Press/Lawrence Hill Books.

Mobley, M. (2010, March). Latent Oppressive Identity Ego Status: Implications for counselors addressing gender, race/ethnicity, and sexual orientation. Presentation at the American Counseling Association in Pittsburgh, PA.

Pinderhughes, E. (1989). *Understanding race, ethnicity, and power: The key to efficacy in clinical practice*. New York: The Free Press.

Ridley, C. R. (1994). *Overcoming unintentional racism in counseling and therapy: A practitioner's guide to intentional intervention*. Thousands Oaks, CA: Sage Publications, Inc.

Siegel, D. J., & Hartzell, M. (2003). *Parenting from the inside out: How a deeper self-understanding can help you raise children who thrive*. New York: Penguin Putman Inc.

Sue, D. (2010). Microaggressions in everyday life. Hoboken, NJ: John Wiley & Sons, Inc.

Sue, D. W., Ivey, A. E., & Pedersen, P. B. (1996). *Multicultural counseling theory*. Pacific Grove, CA: Brooks-Cole.

Terrell, F., & Terrell, S. L. (1981). An inventory to measure cultural mistrust among Blacks. *Western Journal of Black Studies, 18*, 291–303.

Terrell, F., & Terrell, S. L. (1984). Race of counselor, client sex, cultural mistrust level, and premature termination from counseling among Black clients. *Journal of Counseling Psychology, 31*, 371–375.

Utsey, S. O., Giesbrecht, N., Hook, J. N, & Stanard (2008). Cultural, sociofamilial, and psychological resources that inhibit psychological distress in African Americans exposed to stressful life events and race-related stress. *Journal of Counseling Psychology, 55*, 49–62.

Watkins, J. G., & Watkins, H. H. (1997). *Ego states: Theory and therapy*. New York: NY.

Whaley, A. L. (2001). Cultural mistrust and mental health services for African Americans: A Review and meta-analysis. *The Counseling Psychologist, 29*, 513–531.

Wise, T. (2002). White like me: Race and identity through majority eyes. In B. Singley (Ed.), *When race becomes real: black and white writers confront their personal histories* (pp. 225–240). Chicago, IL: Chicago Review Press/Lawrence Hill Books.

Websites

http://thinkprogress.org/2009/07/24/limbaughs-obama-is-black/

http://www.boston.com/news/local/breaking_news/2009/07/harvard.html retrieved
    November 18, 2010.

http://www.city-data.com/states/Arizona-Ethnic-groups.html retrieved November 6, 2010.

http://www.azdhs.gov/plan/report/dhsag/dhsag05/pdf/purpose.pdf retrieved November 6, 2010.

Grace ... Be the Eagle

CHAPTER 11

I was on the San Francisco Muni Bus, the 31 Balboa line. It travels through a myriad of San Francisco neighborhoods. It starts downtown on Market Street and travels west through various Districts; the Tenderloin/Civic Center, the Fillmore, and the Richmond District before ending at Ocean Beach. Somewhere between Market and Fillmore a woman, who was Asian, boarded the bus and looked around for a seat. I was sitting on the first horizontal pair of seats nearest to the window. I sensed that I was in the seat she wanted. I've learned that these seats are among the most coveted because of the positioning. After looking around at the less desirable seats, she grudgingly sat next to me. A few stops later, the seats in the wheelchair area freed up but were still flipped and configured for wheelchair access. The woman looked at me with disdain and promptly left her seat. Meanwhile, the bus was moving and she displayed poor balance, at best. She tinkered with the folded up seats and couldn't figure out how to pull the release lever down. I pointed out to her the instructional picture above the lever. She more or less ignored me and proceeded to ask a young white couple sitting to my left for help. I had a feeling this would not go well because they were tourists and, indeed, it did not. I saw that she was short of conceding and looking to sit next to someone who looked to be indigent. I left my seat and walked toward her. I pulled up the lever while simultaneously pulling the seats down and three seconds later she sat comfortably. A "thank you" or acknowledgment of any kind seemed like the furthest thing from her mind. I was neither surprised nor particularly upset about it. That sort of thing happens every day. However, I will say, the persistence of such ignorance is a sad but accurate commentary on society.

Personal Communication from Ms. Kisha Beasley

Kisha Beasley is a native of the Sacramento area. She values diversity and the opportunity to live among, as well as serve, people of different backgrounds. Her appreciation for "difference" carried her to Spain, where she spent a semester of her undergraduate years and developed her fluency in Spanish. The acquisition of a second language increases her

capacity to serve more communities and to communicate with people who may be more at ease speaking Spanish.

Ms. Beasley values higher education, as does her mother and her mother's mother, who are both college-educated women. Upon graduation from the University of California, Davis with her bachelor degree, Ms. Beasley served a year-long internship in Washington, D.C. During this time, Ms. Beasley applied to and then received numerous offers of admittance from universities throughout the country to continue her education toward a degree in law. She accepted the admissions offer from the prestigious University of San Francisco, where diversity of community, quality education, and access to family provided the optimal learning experience. This university has also produced a significant number of judges, which is what Ms. Beasley aspires to be. Given that she is now a Deputy Attorney General in the Office of the Attorney General's Department of Justice, State of California, it should not be much longer before she reaches her ultimate goal.

Ms. Beasley is a young, African American woman intent on making a difference in this world and living a purposeful life. From the first time I met her, I was impressed with her determination and her level of focus that enhances her ability to live above the fray of distractions that can derail even the most goal-oriented individuals. For this reason, I have a special nickname for her. I call her "The Eagle." The significance of the eagle feather has been previously discussed. Of all the winged animals, the eagle is the one that flies closest to the Creator. So, too, Ms. Beasley flies above it all. She maintains clear vision and holds high values for herself. This does not mean, however, that she is not spared from having to withstand and experience the clouded and compromised perceptions of others. In her life, she has had to learn how to navigate a world in which her experiential reality may mean being subjected to what Sue, et al., (2007) call **microaggressions**.

The incident communicated by Ms. Beasley reveals how she perceived and responded to a microaggression. She acknowledges that this can "happen every day." In other words, it is not just that incidents such as these are not uncommon, but that she has come to *expect* that she will experience microaggressions as part of her day-to-day reality. Life's experiences have developed in her a sense of healthy paranoia.

Sue, et al., (2007) define microaggressions as "brief and commonplace daily verbal, behavioral, and environmental indignities, whether intentional or unintentional, that communicate hostile, derogatory, or negative racial, gender, sexual-orientation, and religious slights and insults to the target person or group." This chapter examines the impact of microaggressions on people of color, women, gays and lesbians, non-Christians, people from lower socio-economic status, people who are differently abled, etc. More so, this chapter explores the response to these intentional or unintentional slights with the purpose of asserting and expanding upon a vantage that protects and promotes self integrity in the face of hostility and ignorance.

Live Above the Smog Line

Living in a society contaminated by "isms" is like living in smog. When you are in the midst of the smog, you may not be conscious of the effect that the contaminants have on you, even though the pollutants taint everything. You can't necessarily see or feel the contaminants, but the sullied air you breathe, nonetheless, adversely impacts everything from your sinuses to your lungs. Eye rubbing, wheezing, coughing, throat irritation, and chest pains are symptomatic of daily immersion in smog. Your eyes become irritated and compromise your ability to see clearly. Regular contact conditions you to accept these physical warning signs as commonplace to life's existence. Prolonged exposure to smog can have a detrimental impact on your health, yet the causation, as damaging as it is, becomes as *normalized and accepted as the air you breathe.*

The same holds true for a society contaminated by "isms." Living in the United States and surrounded in its culture exposes us to embedded microaggressions that inform our day-to-day reality. Subsequently, those who live in it may develop an unhealthy pathological acceptance to the "isms." We may fail to see or feel the causation to our persistent inter-group tension, even when the causation continuously fuels and pollutes the misperceptions that promote discord. For example, there is still a "Columbus Day," "Columbus Circle," "Columbus Day Sales," and children continue to be taught that Columbus "discovered" America. Not only do we know this to be a lie, but the retelling of lies when we know them to be false is a poignant illustration of the false reality painted for our children who are then expected to adapt to, uphold, and repeat the lie. Of course, children are then told and expected not to lie.

We herald historical figures who committed atrocities in the name of "progress" and then hold them up to young men and women in this nation as models to emulate. This should give us pause. Young men and women develop their value system from many sources; their families, their places of worship, their communities, and from what they learn in school. Young children who might rather identify with models of lives that followed humanistic rather than exploitive capitalistic principles would be hard pressed to find such models in mainstream public education. These young minds and hearts are systematically and seemingly intentionally deprived of the opportunity to learn "history" from a spectrum of perspectives that would enhance their critical thinking and analysis of this nation's development.

Woodson states, "When you control a man's thinking you do not have to worry about his actions" (2000, p. xix). The socialization to which our children are subjected promotes a train of thinking whose behavioral outcome should not surprise us. For example, referring to Europe as the "old world" and the American continent as the "new world" feeds the neurosis. New to whom? Millions of people and for thousands of years have known that the continent now referred to by many as "America" was here. Yet, the smog blinds and distorts our perception of reality. When our contaminants in the air and the "isms" in our day-to-day reality are passively accepted as *normal,* then a natural course of consequences occurs; the discord between people who experience these contaminants differently persists as our relationships with one another are negatively informed by this false reality.

Recognizing the neurosis entails seeing the contaminants that collectively constitute the smog. This requires, first of all, critical thinking and clear perception of one's reality. Then it requires a response to this reality from the place that Dr. Mobley speaks of as the "high road." The capacity to critically examine the subtext in everything that informs our day-to-day reality is vital; the curriculum in our educational systems, who and what gets the lion's share of media attention, the funding for and access to quality education, the safety of work environments, and access to employment opportunities are just a few areas in which the smog resides. Communities that have suffered from generational and chronic poverty will feel hope once the anti-dialogical forces have been identified and a new social order created.

Freire (1998) states, "To surmount the situation of oppression, people must first critically recognize its causes, so that through transforming action they can create a new situation, one which makes possible the pursuit of a fuller humanity. But the struggle to be more fully human has already begun in the authentic struggle to transform the situation" (p. 29). In calling "it" for what "it" is and in responding to the contaminants from the "high road," the oppressed not only attain full humanness but also preserve their health, self dignity, and sanity. The position of seeing a microaggression from above the smog line while perceiving the contaminants in the smog lends itself to self preservation. To see how this operates, we will deconstruct the incident that Ms. Beasley experienced and how she came to call "it" for what "it" is while maintaining her integrity and self respect.

Ms. Beasley identifies behaviors as exhibited by the woman in this encounter as "persistence of such ignorance." She, like the humanists examined in the previous chapters, calls "it" what "it" is. She perceives the woman's behavior from the positional vantage similar to an individual who can discern the pollutants in the smog. Ms. Beasley does not, however, allow the smog to penetrate her own worldview and to adversely affect her. Ms. Beasley's response (high road) to the microaggression demonstrates immunity to the contaminant (ignorance). Ms. Beasley, metaphorically speaking, flies above the smog line so that she is not *poisoned* by the emission of the woman's clouded perceptions.

Ms. Beasley states that she was not "surprised" by the woman's response, which means that Ms. Beasley understands that prejudice, like smog, exists. With this foundational understanding of her reality, she is better prepared to respond to microaggressions when they occur. She is not taken aback or caught off guard. She is able to perceive the situation from a "subjective" experience without becoming "objectified" and allowing the polluted reality of the woman's worldview to penetrate her being. The "subjective" experience of living in a reality polluted with "isms" is further explored as we break down the perceptual realities of Ms. Beasley and of the woman who attempted, at all costs, to not sit by her on the bus.

The encounter between Ms. Beasley and the woman reveals a clash in realities. Ms. Beasley's world is open and holds value for "differences." The woman's world is limited by the disdain she has acquired for "differences." The woman's prejudices inhibit her growth and development, which impedes her capacity to *be* (subjectivity) in the world. Ms. Beasley, on the other hand, remained anchored in her own world, even as she observed the woman's negative response to her: scowling facial expressions, an aversion to close proximity, and an assertion for greater physical distance (social distance theory). Her mounting frustration created a host of behaviors grounded in "habituated thoughts," but Ms. Beasley did not allow the woman's "thoughts or behaviors" to contaminate her own. As she stated, the woman's response did not "particularly upset" her.

Ms. Beasley did, on the other hand, model a transcendent response to the woman's behavior that did not come from a place of anger or hatred. These are not elements of *her* world. She did not enter the woman's polluted world that holds ill-conceived negative perceptions about her, but, instead, remained grounded in her own. She called upon her "Spiritual Freedom" to respond like the candle that illuminates the darkness. This young woman, destined to be a judge, responded from a place of grace. She flies about "it" like the Eagle.

© 2011 by Mike Truchon. Used under license of Shutterstock, Inc.

The Cost of Living in Smog

For people of color, women, anyone not identified as heterosexual, those of us who are differently abled, etc., *being* and *living* above "it" has challenges. Microaggressions can be as common as Ms. Beasley tells us, "every day" and the predictability of these incidents cannot be anticipated, like stop signs in a residential community where we know it is coming and are taught how to correctly respond to its appearance. The deployments of microaggressions can occur randomly and, at times, an incident can be perceivably innocuous so that it leaves one wondering if it really was a microaggression. Nonetheless, the psychological investment of having to determine whether an incident was, indeed, a microaggression stemming from racism, sexism, heterosexism, ablism, etc., can take its toll as valuable energy is expended in attempting to protect oneself from hostile and contaminating perceptions.

Sue (2010) provides insight to the biological impact of exposure to microaggressions by comparing the stress of microaggressions to the **general adaptation syndrome (GAS) model**. Like the effects of smog, there are also bio-psycho consequences to the "isms" that contaminate one's reality. In determining whether one's "integrity or identity is being attacked" (p. 89), the individual goes into what Selye calls the **alarm stage** in which the body's biological defenses are set in motion. These biological defenses may include rapid heartbeat, loss of muscle tone, and decreased temperature and blood pressure. While the target of a microaggression attempts to ascertain whether or not there is cause for alarm, the body utilizes valuable resources as it tries to defend itself. Subsequently, the body's resources are tapped and stressed.

With continued exposure, the next stage, **adaptation or resistance**, compels the body to "defend against, destroy, or coexist with the threat." The biological symptoms in this phase may become more chronic with persistence of exposure which, in turn, compromises and weakens the immune system. This then leads to a range of diseases whose symptoms might be mitigated with treatment while the causes persist. The concurrent psychological symptoms are evident in reactions such as anger, anxiety, guilt, and depression. Over time, exposure to negative social mirroring and society's persistent lowered expectations may result in lowered self esteem.

The final stage, **exhaustion**, is a cumulative symptom of chronic exposure to the stress of microaggression. The individual subjected to toxic doses wears down both physically and psychologically. The exhaustion of having to defend the "self" takes its toll as the body and mind are no longer able to function properly. The diversion of energy from self actualization means that learning, evolvement, and conducting oneself toward healthy relationships can be compromised. These three stages address the biological cost of microaggressions.

Sue (2010) goes on to examine the psychological and social stressors of microaggressions by drawing from De La Fuente's **Crisis Decompensation Model (CDM)**. The stage of **impact** occurs as the incident takes place. The exposure can create confusion and disorientation. The next stage, **attempted resolution**, calls upon the person targeted to draw upon coping strategies and available resources to respond to the situation. In this phase, support from allies and community come to bear. This element of support was modeled in the example discussed in Chapter 9 in which then Senator Hillary Clinton and many people across the world stepped forward to offer their support to members of the Rutgers' women's basketball team. The engagement of community and allies can serve as protective forces to support individual(s) who experience a microaggression so they may successfully resolve the conflict, evolve past the event, and come to a place of internal resolution. The failure or inability to seek resolution may result in the person entering the stage known as **decompensated adjustment**, which may lead to withdrawal, depression, guilt, apathy, anxiety, anger and lead to suffering from chronic biological and physiological consequences (p. 91).

Sue (2010) draws comparisons between the biological and psychological impact of microaggressions to the GAS and CDM models. There are common correlated responses when people are subjected to crisis or threatening situations. Understanding how people respond to natural disasters, as well as being victim to a violent crime provides a perspective by which to deconstruct the aftermath of a microaggression (impact) and to develop healthy psychological responses to protect and promote self integrity and self respect when incidents occur.

No one can, with full certainty, predict the likelihood of experiencing a natural disaster or of being victimized by a violent crime. Similarly, an individual cannot predict the likelihood of when or where and if the next microaggression will occur. Ms. Beasley did not know, in advance, that she would experience a microaggression on this particular bus trip in San Francisco. Given this unpredictability, the individual subjected to such incidents cannot necessarily avoid the impact stage of a microaggression. An individual can, however, draw from her spiritual freedom and employ her "choice of action," as Ms. Beasley demonstrated, in how to respond to others' polluted reality. She chose to stay grounded in her own worldview that is habituated well above the smog line.

Defiance

Living above the smog line is best described by the author of Standing Tall (2009), Coach C. Vivian Stringer. Inducted into the Basketball Hall of Fame in 2009, this is a woman whose individual accomplishments are best measured in her ability to raise the level of performance of the young women she coaches. She is the only women's basketball coach to take three different teams to the Final Four (Cheyney University in 1982, the University of Iowa in 1993, Rutgers University in 2000 and in 2007). This speaks to not only a level of expectation that she holds for her athletes, but also to a level of performance that her athletes achieve.

The Cheyney Team was comprised of 11 non-scholarship athletes who were mostly sophomores. They were the underdog in the 1982 tournament and yet managed to win their way to the championship game. Though they lost the championship to Louisiana Tech, the fact that they overcame such tremendous odds prompted Coach Stringer to remind her team that "it doesn't matter where you come from, but where you're going; it doesn't matter where you start, but where you finish" (p. 19). The challenges they overcame and the run they made to the championship game spoke to a strong collective will.

I, as the author, wanted to know from Coach Stringer what she conveys to her athletes so that they, collectively, can rise to her expectations. Her response was, "Defiance." (Personal Interview with Coach Stringer, February 24, 2011). The will to overcome high odds emanates from the coach's simple but poignant statement that in the defiance of lowered expectations, whether it is on the court or in life, "don't back down."

The acknowledgement that many of our youth do not have mentors or adult figures to guide them was a point I discussed with the coach. Her response continued to revolve around the theme of *team* as she emphasized the importance of sustaining a "lifeline" which was, in essence, her metaphor for the value of interdependence, and the maintenance of associations and connections with supportive people. During my interview with Coach Stringer, she drew diagrams on a white board of how the "lifeline" is enacted on the court. Diagram after diagram, she demonstrated the importance of her basketball players being in proximity to one another on the court. These diagrams communicated the value of being connected to a teammate and that a player should never leave a team member in isolation. The coach's worldview that resides above the smog line reveals another element to how she perceives her athletes:

> … it is my job to develop the whole person, not just the athlete. As I tell every girl who plays for me and every girl I try to recruit: by all means, appreciate the opportunity you have to be involved in sports, but don't let it define you. I'm just not a basketball coach; I'm a woman and a mom and a friend. I love music. I care deeply about politics and social issues, both in my own country and in the world. There's far more to me than simply being a basketball coach; and my girls are far more than just basketball players. (p. 241–242)

The message imparted is that we all possess multiple identities within the context of being a whole person and that nourishing these identities is vital. When the individual is part of a community then the individual is of value to others; family, friends, co-workers, fellow congregation members, etc. People in community matter to one another and show their care for one another. This care can be demonstrated in multiple ways. On the other hand, a person without a network of community lacks the "lifeline" that will enable the individual to receive support and vital nurturance when confronted with the **impact** stage of microaggressions. Resources to resolve the incident are nonexistent. For this reason, studies suggest that immigrants selectively acculturate rather than assimilate to U.S. culture (Portes & Rumbaut, 2001). Maintaining ties to a community that provides nurturing and positive social mirroring strengthens the capacity to resist ill-founded negative perceptions. The vital nature of community is such that Coach Stringer imparts to her athletes that they are to "Care more about their teammates than they care about themselves." The lessons taken from the court to life off the court teach us two valuable lessons: 1) Stay connected with people who will support you, and 2) Develop a sense of accountability and responsibility to one's community.

The coach's lessons promote values that counter Divide and Rule anti-dialogical forces. She asserts that defiance of the negative perceptions (low expectations) and care for one's *team* instills

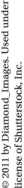

unity, a dialogical force that binds her athletes to one another. When the individual is bound to a whole, then the whole and not just the individual is able to transcend the smog that may attempt to pollute the experiential reality. Contaminants may exist in the realities of others, but they are less likely to penetrate the psyche of a community of people who collectively live above the smog line. The "habituated thoughts" of such a community generate behaviors that are unimpeded and uninformed by the lower expectations. This defiance of the oppressive values and orientation of one's community and society is evident in the lives of humanists.

The reality of living in a contaminated society should not be minimized. The incidents such as that experienced by Ms. Beasley occur, and when they do, members of a supportive community can serve to validate one's experience and to move the person targeted by the microaggression through resolution of the conflict. Without the support of community, the individual targeted by a microaggression may more likely enter the decompensated adjustment stage and experience withdrawal while internalizing the oppression. Presence of a supportive community, on the other hand, allows the targeted individual to synthesize and validate the experience. The strength derived from a circle of people who support us through life's challenges cannot be discounted. Coach Stringer offers:

Life might be unfair; you might be blindsided by bad luck or misfortune. Nobody knows better than a basketball coach that you might not reap the rewards of your hard work, and that you don't always get what you deserve. But with the support of other people, you get through it. We need one another, and if we stick together, we can get through anything (p. 181).

Ms. Beasley and Coach Stringer's athletes fly above the smog line. It is a place of dignity, high expectations, and self respect. It is a place where the smog of other people's polluted realities does not penetrate. The nature of this space above the smog line is further confirmed by Moore's (2004) dissertation study that chronicled the voices of successful African American men. Dr. Moore found consistent themes of how the five men in her qualitative study sustained themselves. Her study revealed that "family, community and friendship bonds are the sources of validation for the successful African American man and that these are also what nourish his resiliency." This is consistent with the message delivered by Coach Stringer, who emphasizes to her athletes that the individual is stronger as part of a *team*. Interdependence is key to survival *and* success.

These values of interdependence, cooperation, and value of one's community seemingly run counter to ideals promoted in the United States of individualism, self promotion, and excessive competition. The gentleman whose comment opened Chapter 9 demonstrates his own psychological resistance to indoctrinating forces. His pronouncement gives hope to "creat(ing) a new situation" and to "be(ing) more fully human." Similarly, Freire tells us that "the situation of oppression is a dehumanized and dehumanizing totality affecting both the oppressors and those whom they oppress, it is the latter who must, from their stifled humanity, wage for both the struggle for a fuller humanity; the oppressor, who is himself dehumanized because he dehumanizes others, is unable to lead this struggle" (p. 29). As people on both sides of the racial cultural divide experience oppression, the efforts to reach and build bridges across the divide are required to create a new reality.

The first step, as previously stated, comes with developing critical awareness of our reality. When members of marginalized communities control their own thinking, they will identify the anti-dialogical forces of Conquest, Cultural Invasion, Manipulation and Divide and Rule. The formation of new habituated thoughts can then replace perceptions rooted in internalized oppression. Habituated behaviors of **horizontal violence** within marginalized communities such as gang affiliation and drug and alcohol dependency can cease. Demonstrating one's power by defying the expectations of self destruction or of annihilating one's communities, which are both highly desired by the oppressor, demonstrates subjectivity and true control of one's life.

As Coach Stringer tells her athletes, "do it right without waiting to have someone else tell you." This is the message imparted to champions. As "whole people," this same message can be applied to marginalized communities in defining the meaning of success, in humanistic terms. The next section delves further into establishing one's capacity to live above the smog line even in the face of microaggressions.

Breaking the Bonds

Dr. Mobley spoke to breaking the bonds of a racialized reality. This is modeled in how Ms. Beasley responded with dignity and grace to a woman who was pushed out of sorts by Ms. Beasley's mere presence. Ms. Beasley cannot control the realities of others, but she does have control over her own response, which was, in this case, illuminant. Had Ms. Beasley responded from what

Dr. Mobley refers to as "low road," which is comparable to responding from the proverbial "chip on the shoulder," she would be succumbing to the contaminants from a polluted racial lens. The "chip on the shoulder" impedes the capacity to clearly *see* and embrace others when diminished by a racialized lens.

Dr. Mobley speaks to being "emotionally and spiritually moved" when learning about white humanists. The acquisition of knowledge related to the historical (and modern-day) white humanists opens the imagination to envisioning an existence for people of all walks of life to exist, more harmoniously, above the smog line. It can be inferred that the gentleman's (from Chapter 9) opening, like our historical and modern-day humanists, would prefer to be *"in relation"* to others, whether or not they are physically or racially *like him*. He would prefer to "construct his own world narrative," as suggested by Dr. Lewis, without having one imposed on him. When people of color and members of other targeted groups allow themselves to be moved by the possibilities of being "in relation" with majority populations, day-to-day interactions are then informed by a more hopeful vision.

The subjects of this book demonstrated that there are people of all walks of life who have chosen to live "purposeful lives" and who have defied the "social order." This is a "truth" not revealed to people of color who are also subjected to the same renditions of "history" and social conditioning processes that expect unquestioning acceptance of the models of exploitive capitalistic men as heroes. Yet the emphasis of teaching about these historical capitalistic models has the unintended consequence of fomenting people of color's prejudices for white people (Borunda & Brown, Unpublished Manuscript, 2011). When people of color acknowledge that there have been and continue to be white humanists who have sought and continue to seek the end to the oppression committed by the elite and the emerging hate groups, then perhaps, like Dr. Mobley suggests, people of color can allow these models of humanism to capture our minds, heart and spirit.

Historical trauma is not to be negated. Collective Trauma informs and clouds the perceptive reality and the nature of cross-racial relationships. The existence of the celebration of Columbus continues to impart **symbolic violence**, which is an attempt to assert power relations in our society (Bourdieu, 2000). The conditions leading to the injustices of the past will only be eradicated, however, by studying it and then creating the "new situation" that promotes cultural proficiency and humanizes the oppressor as well as the oppressed. The role of people of color in this evolvement from a place of cultural distrust is to engage with those who also envision the same communities, as espoused by Dr. Lewis and Coach Stringer. It is a place where all can strive and be successful with clearly accessible and demarcated rungs on the ladder to one's destination.

The engagement of people of color with white people must be, as Dr. Mobley states, on "high road." This capacity is enhanced when people of color are, most likely, in the Integrative Awareness Status of the POC Identity Development (Helms, 1994). "Low road" processing comes from a perceptual cloud of smog and impedes the capacity for people of color to contribute to cross-racial building. From this status of the POC Identity Development Model, the eyes are stinging, the breathing labored, and thinking is not clear. There is an unwillingness to give white people the benefit of the doubt and to provide opportunities for mutual growth and evolvement. The role of people of color in developing cross-racial bridges is further explored as we examine best responses from a "high road" status.

Resist the Culture of Silence

Dr. Mobley states in the previous chapter:

> There are times when People of Color may simply choose to disengage, disconnect, and become "invisible" during interactions with Whites if they perceive one as being racist. In environments characterized as racially tense or hostile climates many People of Color, if forced to occupy such spaces avoid any sustained meaningful interactions or genuine, real communications with Whites. Cultural mistrust is extremely elevated among People of Color in such climates.

There are historical precedents to uncovering the causes to the "shutting down" that transpires when people of color are subjected to circumstances in which the individual feels endangered. These are well documented from the context of collective trauma in which people of color have been enslaved, lynched, mutilated, relocated and dislocated, subjected to genocide, and subjected to forced rape for the purpose of "breeding" and forced sterilization. These are topics not openly talked about in most of our Kindergarten through 12 public education classes. Nonetheless, most people of color and white people know that this level of violence took place. It has informed the context of cross-racial relationships and requires, even today, a mindful and conscious effort to heal as a people and as a nation. This historical context sets the stage for the defense mechanism that prompts the desire for "invisibility" when threatened. We will return to Sue's (2010) contextualization of microaggressions to develop a better understanding of the range of possible responses with the intention of enhancing one's capacity to select the response that does not diminish one's voice.

The various stages of the general adaptation syndrome (GAS) note that the **alarm** stage is triggered when a microaggression takes place, when someone has said or done something that conveys very clearly that the danger of an "ism" exists. Drawing from the three-part definition of racism, recall that the third component of "power" is inflicted onto a target group whose "difference" in skin color has been affixed with a negative value. Historically, the use of power against people of color has taken on many forms, from violence to exclusionary policies to degradation of one's culture and person. Some historical humanists confronted oppressive "power" by employing violence as a means to topple racist structures. This level of response is evident in the work of John Brown, Colonel Shaw, and the revolts of people who were held in bondage and those attempting to protect their homeland from invasion.

Responses to microaggressions in today's world generally will not require the use of violence. The three options that can be taken in responding to the microaggression take place in the **adaptation or resistance** stage. These three options consist of "destroying" or "defending" or "coexisting" with the threat. Brown and Shaw sought to "destroy" the threat and attempted to do so through the use of weaponry. The latter of the three option falls into the path of least resistance in which one tries to perhaps psychologically minimize the incident and then proceeds to avoid contact, to the greatest degree, in the effort to remove oneself from perceived harm. The **alarm** stage prompts fear which, in turn, tells us to protect self. History tells us that "power" is potent, and it has been used and is still used to harm. While each situation must be examined, case by case, the logic to avoidance in engaging in dialogue about the incident must be weighed.

For example, we can deconstruct the incident shared by Dr. Mobley in which his friend made a racist comment upon discovering that his car had been vandalized. Dr. Mobley could have responded violently and ended the relationship. On the other end of the continuum of possible responses, Dr. Mobley could have completely ignored the comment and continued on with the relationship as though nothing had transpired. This would have fueled the Culture of Silence and his friend would not have gained the valuable experience of confronting his internalized prejudices. The constructive dialogue, the "high road" that Dr. Mobley chose to enact led to his friend's reflective exploration and uncovering of where he had internalized negative perceptions of inner-city blacks. Rather than be contaminated by the smog, Dr. Mobley took a subjective stance from the position of the Eagle that empowered him to reach across the racial cultural divide, engage in constructive dialogue, and to challenge and then alter his friend's perceptions. Dr. Mobley humanized his friend by removing the contaminants planted in his heart by the previous generation.

The Power of Unity

We will, next, take Dr. Mobley's lead of responding from the "high road" and incorporate Coach Stringer's value of Community/Team/Unity. This model promotes a capacity to respond to injustices within micro (individual) to macro (systemic) domains that transcends the smog. This is where, as a community built on alliances of like-hearted people, major systemic and cultural shifts are made.

There is no doubt that courage is required in order to step forward and speak to the issues of our time. Often, a humanist who steps forward will not see the outcome of the steps taken in his own lifetime. But, as Coach Stringer's father, Charles Stoner, once told her, "This may not be about you, or for you, but for those who will come after you. You must stand" (p. 284). This sage message compels us to understand that we all belong to a community of people whose collective needs are not only greater than ourselves but that as part of this community, we have a responsibility to lead.

Standing with a community in response to structural "isms" can effect lasting change. John Brown understood this before he embarked upon his attempt to emancipate people held in bondage. Colonel Shaw knew this as he attempted, along with the men of the 54th Regiment, to overtake Fort Wagner. John Brown's life ended with execution by hanging, and Colonel Shaw's life ended with a bullet to the chest. It is evident, however, that their life's work was not in vain. There were other like-minded individuals from the larger community who continued their work and made personal sacrifices to eliminate an oppressive social order.

Using Dr. Mobley's example of "high road" response and Coach Stringer's modeling of "community," we can see how, in this country, positive change and social evolvement is enacted from a micro to a macro level. Thoreau made a "high road" statement by not paying his taxes because he did not support the use of his money to fund a standing army and to have this army fight in a war that he and many others deemed illegal. This was a solitary act of defiance. It, by itself, did not end the war or the employment of soldiers, but it did model nonviolent ways to enact change. Rosa Parks committed a courageous act of defiance to a segregated bus system.

She did not do this alone. A community of people stood with her, in spirit, when she sat in the section of the bus designated "for whites only." The community then physically enacted a bus strike that eventually won the desegregation of the entire bus system. Standing in solidarity with a community of people has enacted major social reforms. This level of response is evident in the work of Gandhi, Martin Luther King, Jr., Cesar Chavez, Dolores Huerta and so many others. The strength of their unity made changes at a macro level.

In essence, targeted groups can choose to adapt, or they can choose to resist to oppression. The models for resistance have been a proud hallmark of oppressed communities throughout the world. The oppressor's fear is greater than the fear felt by the oppressed, which is why the oppressor responds with such virulence. With the power of numbers, however, the oppressed gain momentum not only in liberating the oppressed but in freeing themselves as well.

Standing on the Shoulders of Those Who Came before Us

The starting point and tremendous odds for people in target groups has incredible bearing on the challenges faced in a lifetime. Arbitrary identifiers, such as skin color, gender, sexual identity, socio-economic class, etc., place some who live in a polluted environment at greater risk. This is not to be discounted because we have seen, historically, that these factors subject people to horrific mistreatment. And, it is plausible that many may not have a "lifeline" in place. The vision, however, of a community of people who live above the smog of "isms" still compels the best of human nature to draw from a place of spiritual freedom. This has been modeled by humanists such as Angelina and Sarah Grimké who, despite living amid a culture steeped in racist ideology, they, nonetheless, acted on a set of principles that defied their family, their community, and slave-holding society.

The narratives of historical humanists provide a template for enacting the next level of social justice efforts needed in this society to ensure that the principle of "all men are created equal" also incorporates the acknowledgement that not all men (and women) have an equal starting point. This was evident to the European immigrants who arrived in mass over the span of several hundred years only to find that the streets were not "paved with gold." The realities they encountered proved, for many, not to be the American Dream but more of an American nightmare.

One example of this exploitive reality for newly arrived European immigrants occurred in the early 1900s. New York City garment workers rallied together to acquire better pay and safer work conditions. Their efforts were met with brutal opposition as the police force was deployed to disperse the gatherings. The demands by these women were unheeded until the tragic Triangle Fire of 1911 in the Lower East Side of Manhattan. A fire broke out on the eighth floor and quickly spread to the floors above; 146 people, mostly women from immigrant European families, perished. Many jumped to their deaths rather than be consumed by the fire. Safety regulations would have averted the deaths but with continued lobbying after the tragic fire, safety standards were finally imposed by governmental regulations.

Disasters resulting from the value of profit over the value of human life are a theme evident in many work related deaths. For example, throughout the world many lives have been lost in the mining industry. One of such incident occurred in Jackson, California Argonaut Mine, 1922; forty-seven men lost their lives. In the ensuing investigation and report, Mace (2004) reveals that despite seventeen recommendations to improve safety conditions the section entitled

"Enforcement of Orders did not provide for penalties or punishment for failure to comply" (p. 234). Mace summarizes that "despite the death of forty-seven men in the Argonaut Mine, the government of California had determined that the value of the state's gold mines far exceeded the risk to human life" (p. 235). Value of and appreciation for humanity is often the central point of contention when profit is in question. The devaluation and justification for subjecting humanity to high risk is chronicled in the continued loss of lives in the mining industry that finally resulted in safety acts that would protect workers employed in the mining industry. It took loss of life and concerted action on behalf of mine workers, their families, and advocates to institute changes that protected human life. Yet, years later and in modern times, modern-day humanist Elizabeth Johnson confronted unsafe work conditions and inequitable pay structures at the rice-drying company at which she was employed. This is testament to the fact that the value of capital gain over quality and protection of life persists. Exploitive capitalist orientations continue to be evident in the working conditions of farm workers, coal miners and other forms of industry in which loss of life could be avoided through better work conditions and fair pay structures.

Douglass (1994) states, "to enslave men, successfully and safely, it is necessary to have their minds occupied with thoughts and aspirations short of the liberty of which they are deprived" (p. 290). He goes on to share in his autobiography how people who owned slaves would use the power of manipulation to distract people in bondage from seeking a higher-level engagement with one another. The enactment of "false generosity" is demonstrated by allowing "holidays" and then encouraging participation in "wild and low sports," as well as "plunging them into exhausting depths of drunkenness and dissipation." Douglass expands upon the "cunningness" of the slave master to goad people in bondage to compete in games of drinking, which would leave the multitudes in a stupor. In reflection, Douglass contends that this misuse of one's freedom was "as well to be a slave to *master*, as to be a slave to *rum* and whisky" (p. 292).

The critical consciousness employed by Douglass allows for reflection on how we respond to "limit-situations." Every day, we make choices. Whether or not these choices are from the "high road" or from the "low road" is in the purview of people from marginalized communities to determine. Our choice of response to the smog may come from a range of possibilities. There may be those whose achievement allows for mobility through the social order, but whose internalized image of the oppressor subsequently makes the oppressed into another oppressor. For the individual who has internalized the image of the oppressor, rather than gain a more insightful perspective from having experienced and overcome oppression becomes worse than the oppressor to whom the individual was previously subjected. The heart has become contaminated, and the oppression is passed on and inflicted on other communities. The individual is not capable of change and does not care to offer his shoulders for others to advance. From an existential perspective, the suffering of such people has *no meaning* other than to serve and promote themselves. These individuals no longer see themselves as part of a community, so their disconnection disables their capacity to serve a greater good. Their capacity to value the lives of others is diminished and, at times, completely absent.

The advocacy of white women in the 1800s for those who were enslaved, as well as for those who were being subjected to genocide and relocation, came from a place of empathy. While they recognized that their lot was not at the same level of marginality as those who were in bondage, they, nonetheless, had a context to understand what it *feels like* to be held to a lower standard of value and treatment. They used this understanding of oppression to galvanize others toward the purpose of emancipation, as well as to launch the women's movement. So, too, as people of color, members of the gay, bisexual, lesbian, transgender and intersex communities, and other targeted groups come into positions of power, the lessons from our historical humanists must not be ignored. Others have fought to open the door for marginalized communities, even when not members of those communities. It is only just that those who have benefited from the open doors made for the advancement of marginalized communities also ensure that others from other marginalized groups are provided doors for their passage as well. This means standing on the shoulders of those who have come before us and providing our shoulders for future generations.

Truth has a way of healing wounded hearts, which can subsequently become more resistant to the imbedded contaminants of a society blind to its own pollutants. This book provides a few central characters with references to many others whose lives were lived with purpose. There are incredible models of strength and perseverance from every walk of life in this nation, even though their names are not printed in mainstream discourse of U.S. renditions of "history." Standing Bear's untainted heart took him to the East Coast where he reached out to his white brothers and sisters in an effort to appeal to them for assistance over the plight of his tribe. There, he found Helen Hunt Jackson. They found each other in the space above the smog line. They both envisioned a world that was different than the one in which they existed and did so from the vantage of the eagle.

QUESTIONS FOR DISCUSSION OR SELF REFLECTION

SELF-AWARENESS

1. Who is in your community? What levels of support do you have in shaping the type of reality you would like to live?

2. How do you feel when you are subjected to the proverbial smog of our society?

3. What level of responsibility do you feel for leaving the world better for the generations that follow? What informs your level of responsibility?

CLIENT WORLDVIEW

4. Name examples of holidays or events in U.S. culture that are perceived from diametrically different or varied perspectives. What informs these differences in perspectives?

5. What are examples of symbolic violence you observe in our society?

6. How would the interaction that Ms. Beasley looked like had she drawn from a "low road response?" How would she felt about herself had she done so?

7. What values keep Ms. Beasley above the smog line?

COUNSELING RELATIONSHIP

8. Knowing that strong connections are vital for targeted communities to overcome microaggressions, what would you do, as a counselor, social worker, teacher, or administrator, to build "lifelines" for the people whose lives you touch?

COUNSELING AND ADVOCACY INTERVENTIONS

9. As a counselor, social worker, teacher, or administrator, what are ways in which you can instill the value of accountability and responsibility in a community?

10. How could you employ the concept of a peaceful movement to enact change at a macro level?

NEW CONCEPTS AND VOCABULARY TO REVIEW

Microaggression:

General adaptation syndrome (GAS) model:

Crisis Decompensation Model (CDM):

Horizontal Violence:

Symbolic Violence:

Activity

Ms. Beasley and Coach Stringer are people who live each day with purpose and who inspire others through their life's work. Interview someone from your community who you believe has made a difference in the lives of others and who inspires you. This person can be a teacher, a religious/spiritual figure, a community member, an elder, etc.

1. While you can come up with your own questions here are a few to consider for the interview.

2. Who/What inspires you?

3. What do you value most in life?

4. How do you overcome disappointments?

5. What have been your greatest accomplishments?

6. What advice would you give to others about living in our world today?

References

Bourdieu, P. et al (2000) *Weight of the World: Social Suffering in Contemporary Society*, Stanford University Press.

Borunda, R. & Brown, K. (2011). Building social justice capacity & racial bridges; a work in progress. Unpublished Manuscript.

Douglass, F. (1994). *Douglass autobiographies*. New York, NY: Penguin Books.

Duran, E. (2006). *Healing the soul wound*. New York: Teachers College Press.

Freire, P. (1998). *Pedagogy of the oppressed*. New York, NY: The Continuum Publishing.

Helms, J. E. (1994). *The conceptualization of racial identity and other "racial" constructions*. In E. J. Trickett, R. J. Watts, & D. Birmen (Eds.), Human diversity: Perspectives on people in context (pp. 285–311). San Francisco, CA: Jossey-Bass.

Mace, O. (2004). 47 down; the 1922 Argonaut gold mine disaster. Hoboken, NJ: John Wiley & Sons.

Moore, L. (2004). *Voices of successful African American men*. Lewiston, NY. Edwin Mellen Press.

Portes. A. & Rumbaut, R. (2001). *Legacies*. Berkeley and Los Angeles, CA: University of California.

Stringer, C. V. (2008). *Standing tall*. New York, NY. Three Rivers Press.

Sue, D. (2010). *Microaggressions in everyday life*. Hoboken, NJ. John Wiley & Sons.

Sue, D. W., & Capodilupo, C. M., Torino, G. C., Bucceri, J. M., Holder, A. M. B., Nadal, K. L., et al. (2007). *Racial microaggressions in everyday life: Implications for clinical practice. American Psychologist*, 62, 271–286.

Woodson, C. G. (2000). *The mis-education of the negro*. Chicago, IL. Associated Publishers.

Transcendent Identity: Above the Smog Line

"Though your oppressor might be blind to your importance, you must not be blind to his. Your response, therefore, would be to treat your persecutor as a person of value, giving him a blessing rather than a curse, and loving him rather than hating him" (Reed, 2012, p. 53).

In the summer of 2012, I had the privilege of cofacilitating two focus group meetings with six women who had read the first edition of *What is the Color of Your Heart?* the main text for one of their classes, Power, Privilege and Self Identity. We met during their vacation break on June 8th and August 17th. The two central questions that research assistant Nancy Padrick and I attempted to ascertain from this endeavor was whether there was any change in their identity development or in their perception of others from reading the text.

The transcribed data from the initial focus group meeting was thematically categorized and then situated into a visual model. I recognized the value of creating the visual model as the group participants, even in their communications prior to this meeting, often referred to the "smog." This word became the commonly referenced term that represents the multitude of "isms" in which we navigate in and around each day of our lives. Having common language by which to address "it," the isms, provided a foothold for the group members to constructively discuss our conflictive history and impeded perceptions while doing so in a way that promoted greater understanding. With core concepts that incorporate their thoughts into themes around the proverbial smog, more language was created that facilitated communication and the capacity to address sensitive issues.

At the second meeting, group members provided greater elaboration and detail as they reviewed the content of the thematic categories. This model, visually represented at the end of this chapter, contains four key thematic elements. At the center of the elements lies the following:

- The proverbial smog that contains the various "isms" and that impede our perception of one another

Above and below this smog of isms lie conceptual positions that are not mutually exclusive of one another but as defined allow us to examine where we are in relation to the isms that reside in the smog. The two positions consist of the following:

- The perceptual world of an identity submerged under the proverbial smog line
- The perceptual world of an identity that is situated above the smog line

To the left and the right side of the smog line are lists of factors that promote or impede our capacity to rise above the smog line. These are simply referred to in the following way:

- The obstacles that maintain submersion to rising above the smog line
- The facilitators that promote evolvement above the smog line

This model is referred to as the Transcendent Identity Development Model. In addition to the steady guiding force of research assistant Nancy Padrick—who organized the meetings, transcribed the recordings of the meetings, and hosted one gathering at her home—there were six focus group members who participated in this endeavor: Emilee Hansen, Gabrielle Kolitsos, Kristen Mezger, Latasha Strawder, Cara Wilber, and Beverly Williams.

There had been a six-month lapse since the completion of the semester in which the group members had read the first edition of this text to the date of the first focus group session. Given the time lapse they had had the opportunity to reflect on the application of the material to their lives and to the world around them. What was shared during the sessions was not only encouraging for me as an educator and an author but also inspiring to me as a human being; there was not only evident change in their habituated thinking, but also, more so, transformation in how they perceive themselves *being* in the world. In other words, the evidence spoke to shifts in how they *engaged* with those around them as they began to perceive *themselves*, others, and incidents differently. Segments of their thoughts, stories, and reflections have been captured for the reader as they provide greater context for the four major elements that sit above, below, and on either side of the smog line.

"Isms" Like Cancer

We have already discussed how the construction of race became a rooted element of our social fabric. With an understanding of the factors that impede or that promote our transformation we can also choose to consciously take the path that leads to the deconstruction of this and other isms. This transformation can occur at the micro level, which pertains to each and every one of us as a person, or at the macro level, which means applying what we have learned at a wider scale of action. The humanists and their efforts serve as models for ways of being at the individual level and as well as templates of action to affect change in the world around us.

The mindfulness required of each one of us to enact our own transformation begins with what the group members referred to as "Dual Perception" or even, "Double Mindedness." This means that, like the cancer researcher, one must be able to see the problem, the cancer, though she does not necessarily have to have cancer. Applying this metaphor to our work in deconstructing the isms, our minds must be able to see and understand oppression in order to act upon and uproot it. On the other hand, our hearts must, optimally, be "color blind." This is one of the key elements of being above the smog line and is contained in the Transcendent Identity Development Model.

The data emanating from these focus group discussions provides further explanation to the four elements that are positioned around the smog line. While there is room for development and expansion, the four thematic groupings contain easily identifiable terminology and dispositions that allow us to ascertain where we stand and, more importantly, how we evolve. The thoughts, stories, and reflection from these two focus group discussions has been contextualized so that the reader may further explore the four major elements that exist around the smog line.

Perceptual World of Submerged Identity

One of the topics that emerged from the discussion under the theme of "Perceptual World of Submerged Identity" relates to dichotomous thinking that precludes Mindful Wonderment. Dichotomous thinking does not promote bridge building or allow one to explore different worldviews and the beauty of diversity. This habituated thought pattern is activated whenever difference is encountered, which summarily prompts the categorization of whatever is being evaluated into good or bad.

Kristen prompted this dialogue by sharing a discussion she had the previous fall with several classmates about difference:

> Our group came upon the idea ... when someone's trying new food you either like it, or don't like it. You're not like, "Oh, it's different." You taste something, and you think, "Oh, that's bad" or, "That's good." Applying that to our social context, we've grown up with this black-white issue, good-bad issue, and there's no, "Oh! that's different!"

All of the focus group members are studying to prepare for a career in the field of counseling, so their consideration of this thought focused on how they have had to consider their relationship building with different ethnicities and cultures. Their development as counselors requires a high degree of self-awareness related to multiculturalism. They have developed the awareness of how society shapes self-perceptions as well as how any bias or prejudice brought into a counseling relationship has the potential to harm rather than heal. With this context in mind, Kristen added:

> Let's just say, "We're different." That's all it is. Me and you are different. That's fine. That's not good. That's not bad. We're just different. There's nothing wrong with that. There are differences between people, and that's great. It's a good thing people are different from each other or we'd have the most boring, bland world. We want things to be different. It's just we've been growing up with the mind frame that it has to be good or bad. It can't be a difference that's a positive difference. It's so frustrating when you try to have these conversations; people need to break out of the mold that our education system has us grown up with. It's not a two-sided coin; it is what it is.

In review of the definition of racism, we can recall that the first stage of the definition requires that differences are noted. There is nothing wrong with noting difference in and of itself as long as the evaluation of the difference does not enter the second and third elements, which consist of applying a negative value to the difference and then using power to inflict harm upon the group that holds the trait marking them as different. The focus group members further dissected this habituated thought pattern that is triggered whenever difference is perceived. Beverly expands on Kristen's thoughts and on the implications of this dichotomous thinking:

> You're labeling something that's different as bad. If they can get out of labeling different as bad and just different as something that's just unique, it's just different. You don't have to say it's bad because it's different. And that's what kids are being taught. If something is different, it's bad.

The dichotomous thinking, as reflected upon by the group, has even more insidious outcomes as Emilee chimes in with an emotional element that has greater ramifications on intergroup relationships. She states:

> ... people fear difference ... and when they fear something that will just translate to hate. It's like, "I fear you, so I don't like you." And if you took the time to talk to each other, we would see that maybe there weren't as many differences as we thought. Maybe we're just saying something in a different way, but it means the same thing, or similar thing.

The superficial thought processing that emanates from dichotomous thinking eliminates the possibilities of finding common ground. This habituated thought pattern subsequently becomes a wedge that inhibits relationship building. Emilee elaborates on the possibilities if we were to not judge so quickly: "We all want to love and be loved and we want to take care of our families, whether it's in an individual or collectivistic way; it's a similar outcome. We want to take care of our families."

Emilee explained that she and other classmates had, in the previous semester, participated in an experiential activity conducted by faculty member, Dr. Debby Senna, in her Multicultural Counseling class. They wrote down their values and then compared them with another member of the class to see where the values were similar. Emilee and her classmates uncovered that though the same word was not utilized to name the value, in the end, it still meant the same thing. Initially, there were six values overlooked until they took the time to gain greater understanding about one another. The epiphany from this activity demonstrated to Emilee that while people may be different on the surface, they are also very similar.

In response to Emilee's point, Beverly added this: "Different on the outside, but not the inside. Same as the inside. You still have the same thing on the inside. You just do things in different ways."

Expanding upon the inclination to quickly label difference as good or bad prompted further observation from Kristen:

> Emilee, when you were just talking, you sparked something in my mind where you were saying, "If you just took the time to get to know me." ... our culture, there is no time. We're taught you don't have enough time. We have to rush. We have to go. We develop a coping mechanism of labeling one side or the other; it's either good or bad because you don't have time to explore the difference; you don't have time to

say "there's a difference there." We just have to label it and move on, like you had said. So, I think that we get this good or bad mentality because we probably don't have enough time.

Elements of living in a fast-paced society in the United States can interfere with enacting Mindful Wonderment. Adding to this thematic category is the outcome of efforts to raise a "color blind" generation. The cost of hindering the capacity to notice difference stifles the capacity to respond to difference with an open mind and heart. Subsequently, children's capacity to develop the language or the context by which to discuss difference is impeded. The following story, shared by Cara, demonstrates how this conditioning process occurred for her early in life:

> When I was a little kid, I was in the doctor's office. I saw this African American man walk by. I was in fourth grade. He was the darkest man I'd ever seen and he had a white suit on so the contrast was crazy to me. I turned to my mom, and I was like, "Mom, he was black!" And my mom goes, "Cara!" She gets all mad at me. And I was like, "What did I just say? What did I just do?" To her I said "black," she was like [hand hitting table], "Don't say that around here [hand hitting table], like blah, blah, blah, don't say that at all!" Where, for me, I was fascinated. I thought he was beautiful! So expressing that curiosity, expressing that difference in my life. Wow, look at him! He's so different than me! And I didn't think anything bad.... And I just remember it so clearly. And, of course I remember it even more clearly because Mom slapped me down.

Emilee responded to Cara's experience as being, "Shut down!" which conveys that a person is not supposed to see difference. The unintentional byproduct is that children then learn that there is something wrong with the difference itself. Cara describes the aftermath of the good intention of being raised to be colorblind: "We were taught to stop the exploring at a young age."

Given that difference is generally referred to in our society as bad, then there are not even words by which to enter the discussion that Cara describes "because you might be being racist if you're asking questions. This was passed down by our parents. Even though they want you to be raised with an open mind, if you try to ask a question, it's like, 'Let's not talk about that.'"

Beverly confirmed Cara's sentiments that noticing and talking about differences is taboo. The intention of being raised colorblind fosters a contradictory message that Cara coins as "... telling me one thing, that you want me to have an open mind, but then when I try to explore it, I'm shut down." The lack of opportunity to explore the differences and engage in relationships across the racial divide is one of the factors contributing to submersion.

Elaboration about the perceptual world below the smog line also prompted discussion about ethnocentrism. While having pride in one's origins, ethnicity, and culture was desirable, the topic of exclusionary thinking and behaviors prompted the following dialogue. Cara started the thread of thought:

> The only thing I kind of thought was, under the smog line, adherence to ethnocentrism, separatist reality... I feel like there's a lot of people who are under the smog line not

because they are consciously adhering to ethnocentrism, or, it is something that is not necessarily always what they want or desire. A lot of times it is just something that they're born into ... lack of understanding of histories basically just a lack of understanding of how they're living is actually hurting another without even knowing it. Their own ignorance is something that is detrimental to maybe what they even want. So, I would just say it is all of these things, absolutely, but I don't know how you could say that exactly, because I'm just coming from a feeling right now, and I don't have all of the words, but I'm hoping you can hear what I'm trying to say, as far as just simply that it's not always something that is conscious or desired.

Cara began to formulate several of the concepts that would be incorporated into the model. Beverly responded to Cara, "So it's a fear? Do you think it's a fear of letting go? And a fear of thinking that they'll lose a part of their self or their identity, if they stay ... if they rise above the smog line? Almost like a fear?"

Cara quickly responded to Beverly, "I don't think a lot of them know there is a smog line."

Cara's response speaks to a worldview as presented in Helms (1998) Contact stage of the White Racial Identity Development Model (Appendix C). This level of submersion as well as any of the other stages can shift with concerted effort. We can recall the example of Colonel Shaw whose perceptions changed once he had personal relationships with the men of the 54h Regiment. The danger in not having opportunities to engage in any of the "Facilitators of Evolvement" can result in adhesion to racial group identity. In the second group meeting, Cara shared an incident that had recently transpired and that reflects the extreme end of racial cohesion:

> This happened to my boyfriend.... He's a big tall white guy.... He's balding. So, he's real self conscious about it, so instead of like trimming it he gets a razor and he shaves his head. And he has a real pointy head and he has very intense blue eyes and he always works out, so he's like, in a tank top. So, he looks very scary.

This description provoked laughter from the group members as the visual image came to form. The image collectively captured conveyed a representational stereotype. Knowing she had us all on the same page with this stereotype, Cara went on to fill in the particulars: "He has huge muscles and he doesn't realize how big he is, so he walks around, you know ..."

She trailed off as she had difficulty saying what everyone was already thinking. Finally, she stated, "I do not want to tell ... that he looks like a skin head, you know?"

No one negated the thought but instead laughed at the openly stated confirmation that all arrived at the same stereotypical image. With everyone holding the visual portrayal, Cara went on to describe the content of his character and how he was tested with the forces from below the smog line—racial group cohesion:

> And he is the biggest softy, the biggest kindhearted guy, but he just comes across very, he just looks intense, and he is intense.... The other day he was in the store, and he's very conscious of how people are viewing him. And so, he sees these big tall guys kind of walking past him, and they're all three Euro -American, and they're kind of looking at him. And he's like, "OK, that's weird ... but I don't know what."

He walks around and they see him again and they kind of look at him, and then they go like this [her hand raised in a Heil Hitler salute]. He stops and he looks at them, and he's like, "What the … ? What was that?" The guys were like, "Oh! Well … we thought, we, we …" The guy [her boyfriend] is like, "You fricken thought wrong!" He's [one of the three in the group] like, "Well, white power anyway."

At this point, Cara's boyfriend provided choice words that conveyed to the three young men his feelings about their "power," which then cued them that the conversation was over and that allegiance to racial group cohesion would not be occurring. They took their leave and scrambled off. Cara's reflection on this incident, which took place in a nearby community, revealed her dismay that people could hold such beliefs, but she was also heartened by her boyfriend's outspokenness and capacity to reject engagement to separatist ideologies.

While the existence of white supremacist groups could easily be the one-sided focus of extremes under the thematic category of "living under the smog line," there also took place discussion related to various contexts in which People of Color might also demonstrate behaviors and ideologies that maintain intergroup dissonance. Latasha brought the dialogue to the application of their work as future counselors in which clients might request a counselor of their same race with the assumption that a counselor not of their race would not be able to understand, empathize, and be culturally responsive:

People, in the same racial category, are not the same just because they're in one racial category. For instance, me being an African American woman, there's different trauma that I've experienced as an African American woman, but I've overcome that trauma. It doesn't rule my life, but say, for instance, another African American woman hasn't dealt with trauma in her life, so she probably would want a connection with someone who can identify with her racial experiences. But that's telling me that's different trauma that needs to be addressed, and being able to be dealt with so that she can rise above the smog line.

Latasha applies the concept of Double Mindedness within this example. Agents of change in the fields of counseling, education, social work, or any other arena in which heavy engagement and interaction with people is inherent, must understand varied perceptual worlds. People's life experiences may land them in submersion below the smog line but agents of change must engage mindfully with open hearts while applying an understanding of their worldview.

Beverly provides a reflection on some of the reasons, outside of a therapeutic relationship, why a person of color may hang on to a submerged identity. She expressed that a person may fear losing the identity derived from racial identification. The example Beverly provided meant losing the identity derived from Black Power. The group went on to discuss how Civil Rights movements have made gains by the unity of marginalized groups to challenge and change oppressive laws. The strength of an embraced sense of self-efficacy has enabled many communities to work together and to move our society to more enlightened heights. The positioning, however, of an individual grounded solely in ethnocentric ideologies impedes relationship building across the constructs of power and privilege. The concern for those who cling solely to racial group identification prompted Latasha's reasoning for why a person would fear letting go of this position: "She won't know who she is."

Suddenly, the focus group members found another aspect of submersion. Their dialogue followed a thread of thought, as they were able to finish one another's sentences.

> Beverly responded to Latasha: "Thank you. You get what I'm saying. And that's what I'm starting to see. In different ..."
> Latasha: Individuals
> Beverly: Individuals. It's just like they fear that they're going to lose self-identity.
> Emilee: Hm, hm, and maybe even reject their culture.
> Beverly: Yeah
> Emilee: Like, yeah, on the basis of their background, the people who are below the smog line would be, somehow, looking down upon those, judging those ...
> Latasha: That's what I was talking about ... the learned behavior earlier.

An identity solely comprised of a racial identity that lies in opposition to others perpetuates the divide. It doesn't matter which group a person may identify with but the isolation inherent with ethnocentric identity can be mitigated by participation in the facilitators of evolvement. This requires redefinition of oneself that is not based solely on one's racial group but with the incorporation of elements that lie above the smog line.

Latasha summarized the reasons for the fear of letting go of an identity rooted in separateness. The "victim mindset" is grounded in cohesion to racial identity:

> I feel like it does apply collectively and individually. For instance, a type of power that a person may feel, "It's everyone else is the reason why everything is going wrong." So it's a type of power, "Yeah I'm strong, I'm taken care of. It's everyone else that needs work." Or even, collectively; thinking in terms of reasons why our culture has power, and we don't want that to be taken away. For instance with slavery, there was not any power when it came to African Americans, and so it was a sense of white power. But, that was instilled into the culture at that time. And, so even rising above that, with the Civil Rights movement there was a form of power that they have captured back to themselves to make them feel whole again. So, it's kind of keeping that so that it never reverts back to how it used to be. It's like they're traumatized in a way because they can remember what happened in the past, and they don't want it to be like that in the future ever again. So, it's kind of like the "always and never," the "always or never" mentality. That will never happen to me again. Or this always happens when I go out in public and people look at me this way.

Latasha reveals the perception of people who have been traumatized by historical events. This traumatization leads to the fear of trusting people who look different than them, as they perceive the "other" through a smog-laden lens. Latasha provides a heartfelt understanding of this fear:

> They won't know who they are, if those things don't exist. If they get rid of all of those things below the smog line. It's like, "Who am I going to become? Who am I?" It's like they have to redefine who they are.... That could be the fear, because they don't know, it started from rock bottom.... Victim mindset.

The worldview in which a person holds on to the group identification for need of retaining a sense of power over others was elaborated. Emilee offered that people need to find "a balance between being above [the smog line] and still having that part as your identity, but letting go of the victimization part, or the anger."

Still considered was that people could retain pride in their culture, where they had come from and the obstacles overcome along the way. In merging these two capacities, Latasha presented the idea that one must acknowledge and know about the history of one's cultural group, as well as the history of others. These are facilitators of evolvement. Beverly provided further detail to this orientation so as not to confuse this mindset with people who champion the causes of a community to which they may belong:

> I see some people who are like that. They feel that if they do [rise above the smog line], it's not that they're not advocating for their culture. It's not just advocating for your culture. When you rise above the smog line, you're in harmony with all cultures now. You can see the pain that Indians when through … I can see the pain that Jews went through. I can *feel* those. I can feel it and I can understand it and respect it and don't like that, but not just holding on to, "It's just about my culture," only the pain that my culture endured.

Cara chimed in with, "Also, once you get up here [referring to above the smog line], it doesn't mean you forget the wrongs that have happened."

Facilitators of (and Obstacles to) Evolvement

This is the point at which the focus group members gave words to key elements that lie within the Facilitators of Evolvement and characteristics of Transcendent Identity. First, Beverly further defined a characteristic above the smog line which means being in harmony and knowing the history of other communities, not just one's own. This also constitutes identifying the oppression they have suffered as well as advocating for them.

This reminds me of a journal entry made by another graduate student, Becca Reed, a heterosexual woman, who was already sensitive and responsive to the micro aggressions inflicted upon the gay/lesbian community. She acknowledges that as a Euro-American woman, she must also expand upon her role as advocate when it comes to the construct of race. Prompted by the end-of-chapter question "How do you feel when you are subjected to the proverbial smog of our society?" she responded as follows:

> Honestly, sometimes I may not even notice, especially in the past. If someone was making a joke about a certain race or commenting on a stereotype, I may have not thought anything of it. I now know that there is a smog line in American culture, and in order to live a more fulfilling life I need to live above it. My best friend is homosexual. When people joke about homosexuals, or say things they make that choice for themselves or that God disapproves of their life style, it hurts me because that kind of thing would hurt my friend. I care about him, so I care about the things people say when talking about homosexuals. Perhaps this was me "choking" or "coughing"

because of the smog. I need to learn to detect the smog line involving other human beings as well however, not just homosexuals. (Journal Entry, Fall of 2012).

The focus group discussed that while retaining one's sense of self and engaging with others above the smog line the injustices that transpired in the past must not be forgotten. Becca offers us elements of the transformative identity that includes commitment to the causes of other marginalized groups. The concepts related to addressing the events that have taken place in our history were expanded upon by the focus group. First, Beverly shared her shifts in thinking after having learned about the historical and modern day humanists in the textbook,

> It did make me see people in a whole different way, and treat people based upon how we meet, not because of your skin color. Because, I (had) felt that if you're privileged, that you're just going to be rude to me, because I am of color. I don't think that any more. It's just something that's out of my head. When I meet people, it's just based upon how you receive me. When we see each other, it's reciprocal. If it's not, then I understand you're just on a different page, and I'm going to keep on going.

In juxtaposing Beverly's and Becca's words, we can see two people whose racial group has been framed within the Master Narrative as oppositional to one another. Beverly acknowledged that she had previously perceived that someone from Becca's racial group would be rude to her. Becca, on the other hand, has noted that she must provide the advocacy required to deconstruct racialized behaviors. Both, emerging from the smog, express mutually supporting sentiments in that they have shifted their way of perceiving reality and now have a foothold above the smog line. The potential for relationship between the two is in a more optimal space.

Arriving at this space is not easy. The dialogue by the focus group members revealed elements of disbelief in the fact that the Master Narrative continues to be taught and is still prominent in our public schools. Coming to the place of questioning the reason for this brought up the need for critical thinking about one's education and the information taught. In response to the themes of critical thinking and challenging a curriculum that is not balanced with models that provided the impetus to change our society, Gabby stated the following:

> We're supposed to look up to and learn more about these people, like George Washington and Andrew Jackson so many more, and you're like, "Oh my gosh, this person was horrible in so many ways. They just totally neglect a complete side to them, and they just want to put them up on this pedestal; no, I don't agree with that person, that's not who I look up to. So, it was refreshing to learn about these European American humanists who are just so loving and kind and really put so much out there. And they were so brave for that time. And it's like, "Yay! White people aren't always the bad people" … especially for that time. It was nice to learn about that.

Gabby's statement prompted me to draw from a journal entry she had made when she was enrolled in the class Power, Privilege and Self Identity. What struck me was a sense of knowing self that reflected not only pride in self but that fostered the element of Mindful Wonderment about others. Given racial group existence in the United States, however, she openly rejected cohesion and identification to whiteness as it symbolizes a sense of separateness. This was her response to the end-of-chapter question, "What is your family's place of origin, and how does their history affect you in the here and now? For instance, how do they affect the way you perceive yourself, the way you perceive others?"

> My family's place of origin – well I'm a "mutt," so I'm a mix of French, English, Cajun, Danish, Irish, and Potawatomi and possible Shoshone Indian. Growing up, my mom was always big on knowing our family history and instilled in me and my siblings a pride in knowing our roots. I think today that translates into a curiosity for other people's heritage and where they come from—maybe that is one reason I was drawn to my husband, who is a first generation Greek American. Also, I don't like being called "white." I feel like people who call themselves white don't understand or know their origins. I see white like white noise or some kind of blurred vision where one's origins are just a haze of whiteness. I am not a "melting pot" of origins, but a "soup" with distinctive flavors—and I happen to know the recipe. (Journal Entry, Fall of 2011)

The Facilitators of Evolvement is inclusive of education that examines history from an inclusive orientation. The potential for transformation, which means letting go of an identity grounded in racial group fixation and moving above the smog line, is prompted by the facilitator of having full knowledge of the realities of histories beyond our own identified racial group. Like Gabby, Beverly reflects on the power of having a convergent history that reflects the contributions of all people:

> What promoted me to rethink everything is the information provided in *What is the Color of Your Heart?* It is not taught to us in our early education—the Grimké Sisters, the Secret Six, the people that helped to abolish slavery. And I think me learning that made me rethink a whole different way about privileged people. Because I didn't really know that there were privileged people who were actually trying to help us to overcome slavery. That made me feel good and reevaluate things; that all of the knowledge that had I gained was all wrong. And I had to rethink my process of people because I was taught the wrong way, how to see people of privilege. So, I think for me the education helped me to rethink a lot of things and question a whole bunch of information that I've been taught.

Maintaining one's worldview that resides above the smog line means ongoing engagement in a world still contaminated with the isms. This was readily recognized as the group discussed the strength derived from the counter narratives they had learned. Latasha discussed this point as she recognizes that living above the smog line does not make a person immune to the proverbial smog, "And when we're faced with something, we can reference those stories ... go back and see how it was dealt with ... and how to fit it into our life. It gives me hope and courage. Something outside of myself."

Knowing the positive contributions of all people is vital to developing an identity above the smog line. Absence of this knowledge as perpetuated by the Master Narrative also fosters disconnect across the divides. Having an integrative and convergent rendering of how our histories are all intertwined provides greater cohesion while also providing the impetus to release the burdens that anchor us in a submerged identity. Beverly provides context for this: "I would say one thing for other people of color is understanding your past, and accepting it, and leaving it there where it is supposed to be, and don't carry it into the future."

She goes on to discuss the idea of knowing what transpired in the past but not allowing it to weigh you down:

> Yes, we were discriminated against ... treated bad. Let that go ... because that's not where we're at right now. We understand that there's micro aggression going around as far as with racism, but if you can leave the past in the back, I think it will change you to rise above it, because you left it back there, and you're seeing things in a new light. Yeah, that happened, but that's not me now. Things are different now. And, I think that's one way people of color can rise above the smog. I know that helps me; I just leave that stuff in the past.

Examples of micro aggressions in every construct of power and privilege can be cited every day within our schools, in the media, our communities; yet, the group members recommend a positioning that is demonstrated by Kisha Beasley, the Eagle. From this vantage one recognizes oppression and micro aggressions while also recognizing that the person committing the aggression is submerged. As stated in the opening citation from Pastor Reed, "Treat your persecutor as a person of value, giving him a blessing rather than a curse, and loving him rather than hating him." This vital message communicates that living above the smog line requires the capacity to identify the behaviors emanating from the proverbial smog. These behaviors are not to be ignored. Instead, as we activate Dual Perception we must respond from a place that addresses the wide range of interpersonal violence in a manner that diminishes the smog itself. Conversely, when we perceive the behaviors through the lens of historical burdens our capacity to respond constructively is diminished.

Latasha addresses the power of releasing this burden by stating the following:

> We're all going to have some form of past experience that we feel defines us and who we are today. So it's about overcoming whatever it was that offended you or put you in the state that you're in now. How are you going to keep walking or moving along in life, just carrying that burden on you? People go into the world and they bring all of that with them. And it's like, 'Can you leave that at home?' It's tearing apart relationships or potential relationships when meeting new people.

The power of forgiveness is key to healing. Optimally, our nation could benefit from a healing ceremony that acknowledges and owns the transgressions of the past and then sets an agenda for moving forward. While there have been concerted efforts to this end that have provided footholds toward a more equitable existence, the complexity of our society, the continued encapsulated existence of so many, the systemic disparities that recreate social inequalities and a curriculum that fails to provide convergent perspectives undermines the potential for this collective transformative process. Yet, this does not preclude the possibility of having this transformation happen at the individual level or at a smaller scale in which isms are identified and acted upon within our schools, communities, churches, families, and neighborhoods.

Latasha speaks to this power of one when she stated, "It's forgiving ... it comes to forgiveness. You are never going to be able to fully leave it. But it needs to be forgiven so you can move on. And that could be an experience that you can share with someone else that needs help in that area."

Beverly added this:

> And not only forgiving, also think about the attributes that people contributed to our culture as well. Think about those good things. There's a lot of good things that a lot of African Americans have done, people of color, in every culture, that [have] done to uplift the culture. Think about those things; the first stoplight; the black man that made peanut oil; Frederick Douglass, teaching himself how to read. Think about the good things, and that will uplift you as a person. And just don't always think about the negative; the burden that you've carried from the bad things that did happen.

"Forgiving but not forgetting" was a very strong theme that emerged from the dialogue sessions. Miseducation perpetuates divisiveness but, as discussed by the group members, once they learned about people whose lives ran counter to the commonly touted historical figures, they began to see themselves as well as perceive others in a totally different light. Anti-dialogical forces of cultural invasion—divide and rule, manipulation and conquest—fueled the conditions for collective submerged identity below the smog line. Reconstructing a new identity requires the constructive empowerment of the dialogical force of cultural synthesis, unity, organization, and cooperation (Freire, 1998). Cara offered this thought:

> I think, along with education, also going back to the empowerment ... if your identity's stuck on that burden, you may put it down, but what do you have left to fill it up? Just forgiveness? Well, what can you do? How can you fill it up? If you're only forgiving, what more do you have, basically? So you have to look in our education, when you see ... George Washington, and Abraham Lincoln ... you're also seeing those other people, and so you're seeing actions.... But, you have to know that you are more than the externals. Your skin is also an external. For some people, it's going to be a big rebuild, for others it's going to be like, "Wow, I'm changing my mind about this." And, that's an easier burden to put down. But some people are going to need restructuring, or empowering that says you are way more than your skin color, and you need to know this, and now we're going to build you. And how that, and that's going to make you feel better, you know, and all that.

The Facilitating Factor of Evolvement contained in education that contains knowledge about the contributions of all people also includes the challenges of all populations. While this knowledge contributes, in varying degrees, to factors that prompt evolvement, the absence of this knowledge can also be included on the opposite end of the spectrum related to Obstacles to Evolvement. Beverly summarized this point:

> My experience of being of color altered some things because I was getting treated bad from different people because of who I was on the outside and not because of

my heart, or just me as a person. So, that makes your thinking distorted.... So, I had to, being in this class, it put me back into reality. That you don't have to worry about that. If that's how they are, then that's their ignorance. You have to rise above it, and keep going.

Repeated negative experiences can create distorted perceptions. The result being that the actions of those committing the offenses is projected onto a racial group. This distortion then freezes the person into the static position that Latasha had previously coined as "always and never," in which possibilities for relationship with people of a different racialized group is mitigated by distorted and preconceived notions of "the other." The hope for acting upon a world filled with smog as well as living in state of being that transcends the smog lies within the elements of a Transcendent Identity. While a number of the elements within this category have already been addressed within the dialogue provided and the themes that emanated from the lives of the humanists in this text, the group members provided greater definition to this worldview.

Transcendent Identity

Possessing the capacity for critical thinking is one of the underlying goals in all the classes I teach. As agents of change in the various professions that they are considering for their future, my students will not always find right or wrong answers. They will have to consider multiple perspectives, integrate knowledge from a wide range of sources, and, to a large extent, create higher levels of understanding and knowledge. I ask my students to consider what they have been taught in their education prior to arriving in my class and to question the content as well as the intent of the content. I even ask them to question what I am teaching them and the intent of what I am teaching.

Beverly provided initial thoughts about the process of challenging what she had previously been taught, explicitly and implicitly:

> The only thing we hear about different heritages is when you refer to Africans. They were weak; they couldn't think for themselves.... The Indians were pretty much the same; we had to come and create civilization for them, because they were "uncivilized." So, we just hear bad things about different cultures, but they had their own way of living, and we weren't taught that. The way they lived is the way they were taught, and that's how they grew up and that was civilized to them. Who are you to come over and tell them the way they are living is uncivilized?

The group members came to a common understanding that they question information—its source and its meaning. No longer taking for granted the multiple sound bytes that come their way, Latasha added, "We're thinkers. We're not just accepting stuff. We're thinking about it. We're exploring it and we're analyzing it. We're coming up with different conclusions that aren't considered normal." Arriving at this space in which the group members perceive themselves and one another to be, in relationship, above the smog line reveals a connection with one another that evokes the image of the women of the Boston Anti-Slavery society, black and white, walking with arms linked together into the midst of an enraged mob. Their understanding of unity in a common cause transcends the habituated thoughts mired in the smog. Beverly spoke to the power of knowledge and the consequences of not knowing our collective history:

> The links were not taught. We're all linked together, but instead, in educating our children, they still separate everybody instead of saying that we're all together, some way, somehow, it's not by color, but we're all linked together as one. They don't promote that, they don't teach it. And that's what keeps us where we're below the smog, and not above the smog.

This place of positioning above the smog line promotes looking at people's behavior rather than labeling people according to skin color. As discussed in the chapter entitled, "You Are My Other Me," there was ample evidence provided of how humanists perceive themselves and how they perceive themselves in relationship to others. Latasha provided further evidence to this:

> I look at things in terms of spirituality. I take it with me everywhere I go, just being a Christian. So even going to school, or just my ideology about life, I look at it in terms of sin. So, when I look at the human race, I don't look at it in terms of race, I don't look at in terms of ethnicity, I look at it in terms of; we do good, we do bad, there's evil, there's good. So when I look at things in order to rise above the smog line, it's not pointing fingers, or placing blame on people. It's more so like, that's not right, according to my beliefs. Like that's not how it's supposed to be....They're human beings.... they're going through something. Stop paying attention to their race and how they look, in terms of the problem that's going on. It's more about listening and being there for them. So when I look at different things, and just society, I don't look at it in terms of the small things, I look at it in terms of the broader picture.

The element of Dual Perception frames a more holistic framework in the field of counseling. It is about looking at the whole picture and integrating one's understanding of how people are perceiving, and subsequently inserting themselves within the greater context of their world. The element of seeing with one's heart precludes taking aggressions personally. Seeing with the heart and mind also expands the capacity to understand how the isms contaminate a person's worldview as well as recognize the burden of living in a smog-filled reality. Emilee spoke to this:

> My whole life, I wasn't raised to be racist. I was raised to treat everybody the same. And so, I developed that sense of colorblindness, almost.... Humanists are colorblind in the heart, but not in the head. I think that I almost became colorblind in both. It was like I didn't want to acknowledge differences because I thought maybe that would offend when acknowledging the differences actually validates the experiences. When I don't, I'm minimizing your experiences ... being productive [in these conversations], and deconstructing racism and standing up when I see it.... I had this epiphany!

The capacity that comes from being "double minded" and activating one's dual perception was demonstrated by the following story that Emilee shared. Her emergent self from a position of being conditioned to not acknowledge difference undermined her ability to become an agent of change. Once she was able to confront the immobilizing components of this perception, she was able to then change not just her habituated thoughts but also her habituated behavior. During the course of the first session after she announced she had had an epiphany Emilee opened her copy of *What is the Color of Your Heart?* and read the following portion directly from Chapter 6:

> Fear is real. It can immobilize the kind-hearted and paralyze the courageous. It can grip your tongue and silence you when you know you should be speaking and it can force you to avert your eyes when you should be stepping forward. There may be times when you weigh the level of risk to determine if you are safe enough to speak up. When those risks seem too high, you hold your opinions close and tell yourself, 'I'll say something next time.' (p. 109)

After reading this section Emilee looked up to the members of the group and continued,

> That really hit me because that was me. I would notice it, but I'm like, "Next time I'll do it, next time I'll get the courage." And I think because of living these colorblind ways, it's really just keeping me from moving forward. I had these feelings, but letting them out and participating in the dialogues that are needed with not just my classmates, but others, outside. My epiphany was how much that was holding me back, to take the humanism route … because it came with good intentions … really, really good intentions, but see color with my mind and not in my heart.

Activating change can be difficult. Emilee went on to share her struggle with overcoming fear and then standing up for what she believes. She went on to share how she has taken steps in seeing something occur that did not feel right to her and then saying something. She was completely exuberant when she announced, "Guess what, I'm still here!" In other words, not only had she overcome her fear but she had also discovered that her fears were largely unfounded; there were no dire consequences for being congruent with her beliefs and her actions. The idea of living congruently is another disposition of living above the smog line. The story Emilee shared related to an incident that occurred at a local liquor store in which she went in to buy a cup of coffee. While standing in line, she observed the treatment of the cashier toward an African American woman. Emilee recounted the story for the group:

> There was an African American woman in front of me in line. She paid for something, I don't know what it was and then after she bought it, she realized she wanted change for her twenty-dollar bill, and he (the cashier) was like, "I don't have change." She was like, "What do you mean you don't have change, you just gave me change." And he was like, "No, I'm sorry, I don't." She was like, "What if I buy something else? Then can I have change?" And he was like, "No!" and she walked out. He said, "I hate black people."

Gabby was the first to react to Emilee's experience with a simple "Jeez." With the acknowledgement of the severity of the incident, Emilee then went on to state how she responded to the man. He had expected Emilee to respond with racial alliance and assumed conformity, even by virtue of silence. He was wrong. In going on to describe her reaction we could see, physically, that Emilee was still offended by the incident:

> I'm, "OK?" I was just like, "You know what? I'm not coming here anymore! That was wrong. You know, you don't treat people different like that, or don't treat people poorly like that." And I walked out, and I haven't been back to that liquor store. And, I'm proud of myself. It was short and sweet, and I said it, and I walked away. And I said, "I can do this." It starts small, you know, just with an incident at a liquor store.

Others: Yeah.

It was apparent that witnessing this incident still played out in her mind as the ugliness of the situation repulsed her. The cashier's response continued to haunt her as she recalled his words and shared the aftermath of her rejection of racial cohesion:

> He just kind of looked at me like, "Ugh." He said, "I hate all of them, they're all the same." I was like, "You've got to be kidding me! I'm sorry! That is unacceptable. I'm not comfortable with that … I'm a good paying customer. I come here all of the time for coffee, and I won't come back." And he was just like, "Well, good-bye, like, whatever."

The capacity to move to a place in which we respond to injustice was not previously activated in Emilee. She arrived at the space in which the Grimké Sisters, William Lloyd Garrison, John Brown, and all the other humanists addressed in the textbook had demonstrated by the way they lived. Fine-tuning this concept of Dual Perception recognizes that difference, on the other hand, should not have to produce shame. Cara revisits this concept when she states the following:

> I don't want to see color, I want to see people. But at the same time … there are differences, and they're good, but if you're not aware of them, how can you really connect with people? You know, on a genuine level. Because, you are different, you do have completely different backgrounds. Not to mention people who are coming over here from a completely different country. Seeing the heart of people … like Angelina Grimké, she was a certain personality type … in the midst of her oppressive slave-owning family, woke up, and said, "No, this is ugh!" as a child, you know.

The dialogue then took on another form as the students gave life to the element of acting upon "fixed reality" (Friere, 1998). In other words, it is not just a matter of caring but also a matter of doing. This was what they learned from the lives of those who made a difference in the quality of life for marginalized populations. Beverly brought it to the most basic of human reaction of care: "A person seeing a dog or a cat that got hit outside. A person will go, "Oh, my god!" and be sad.

Beverly then transfers this basic human feeling as applied to humanity, "I think a person with a heart will go, 'That's sad.' She's [referring to Angelina] seeing that and was like, 'I don't like it! It makes me feel uneasy inside to see someone get treated the way they are treated.' She just cared. We all cared about human beings and that's just what it is. You don't have to look at the color, the outside…. You just care for a person.

While the concept of care across all the constructs of power and privilege would seem to be a core condition for anyone endeavoring to enter a field in which one engages with humanity, we hear, too often, of instances in which such care is not evident. Instead, the acceptance of status quo policies, the multiple incidents of hate speech and incidents from politicians, college campuses, and the wide range of sources that reflect the ongoing existence of submergence below the proverbial smog indicate that there is much evolvement needed. Nonetheless, the ideal exists and is reflected when Kristen states the following:

> We're all drawn because we care about people, regardless of ethnicity, regardless of age, regardless of sexual orientation. I think we all mutually share a genuine care for the human being. I think that's why we are all a lot more receptive as a population to this new material, this new way of thinking. Because we all genuinely want to care about people.

A key word in Kristen's statement is *genuine*. If we go back to Cara's statement at the beginning of this chapter. in which she expressed that some people don't realize there is a smog line, we notice that it implies that some individuals lack awareness of their own prejudices about others. The idea that we can always continue learning and growing comes with what Cara later called a "journey to genuineness" and "love for your fellow human," which then prompts a natural curiosity to see how she can connect with people. Latasha referred to this perception as unconditional love. Gabby describes this journey as the following:

> It's kind of a curiosity and wanting to learn more, and just open yourself. It's letting go of any arrogance or ethnocentric kind of viewpoints. Saying, "I'm better. I know everything. I'm set." That's not the kind of person I want to be. When I see a person, I may see some differences, but it's not like in terms of race differences. It's like all of these differences.

The group members went on to address a deficiency in their studies. While all of them have taken many courses in psychology and studied other areas that develop their understanding of people they discussed how, as Cara stated, "Counseling books don't really talk about the 'L word." The focus group members agreed with Cara's observations that "in our language, in our interaction with each another, it's not about being genuine for a scientific way of being.... It's about genuine connection that is encased in "loviness," you know? That sounds fluffy, and it is, but it's also the most powerful thing."

It is fascinating to reflect on the lives of those who, in the past, put everything on the line to help others. Their efforts did not emanate from the extrinsic but rather the intrinsic motivation of genuine love for others. This same motivation prompted Vann to leave a course of study that did not resonate with him; it also provided the inspiration for Fernandez to defy the openly disdainful attitude of her boss and respond to the needs of another human being.

Gabby went on to state the following:

> That's why I was so glad that you had a chapter about spirituality. Because, it's like, in my BA, and everything, in psychology, you couldn't even bring it up. It's just like you were supposed to neglect it. And I felt almost like I was supposed to be

ashamed of having that side to me, you know? That you were only supposed to be like a scientific mind. And, it's like, "No, that's not who I am!"

Others resoundingly agreed with Gabby with a collective, "Yeah!"

There was a differentiated aspect to being solely knowledgeable, scientifically speaking, about humanity and one of being a humanist who works with humanity. The positions between the two were distinguished in the shared observations that followed.

Beverly declared, "That's exactly why I didn't do the masters program in psychology!" To which Gabby disclosed, "Me either, yeah!"

The group went on to shed light to the element of and fostering of love, which they seemed to find absent from various courses of study. Beverly explained it this way:

> Because I felt, disconnected. That's not why I took psychology. I took psychology to try and understand the human being and some aspects. But I also did it because I want to learn to connect with different people. I like what you said about the higher-up love because that's what I have for all humans. I have that higher-up love. If I see you're hurt, I'm not going to walk by and be like, "Oh, she's hurt, and just keep walking." Instead, it's, "Excuse me, can I help you? Is there anything you need?" That's the type of person that I am, and that's why I wanted to counsel.

It is one thing to have knowledge of people. It is another to have knowledge of and care about people. Kristen took the dialogue to the space in which this marriage of the two elements means not only "valuing humanity" but also "willing to engage in self-sacrifice" to help someone else. She indicated that this means going out of your way, even if it means taking an extra step or a small step to help someone.

When I, the researcher, inquired of the group as to what they get out of helping others (though I already know that this means not expecting something in return), they expanded. Beverly started with the following:

> That's just who I am. It makes me feel good on the inside. It makes me feel that I'm an asset to society, helping someone. Just small stuff makes me feel good on the inside. And I've always been a giver of myself. Sometimes that comes back and bites me on the butt, but that's just who I am as a person. I try to be different, but I can't, I'm just a giver, and that's who I am. And it doesn't have to be money. It can be my time.

Hearing Beverly's statement prompted Emilee to piggyback with "It's your purpose." To which I prompted further exploration with one simply worded question, "Purpose?" Emilee drew deeper and made this response:

I just feel like that's what I'm here to do; it's to serve others, and then I end up serving myself. I'm all about growing. I think it's the most important thing to do. You know once I get comfortable with something I know I'm not growing anymore. I'm kind of shy at first, and it's really hard for me to come out of my shell. But I constantly keep putting myself in situations where I have to grow. I force myself to step outside of the box. And, when we're serving people and helping people, we are growing ourselves too. We're constantly bettering ourselves. It's not just like, "Oh,

I feel good, now I can pat myself on the back." It's not about that. It's about improving my life, too, but in that higher level.

The element of intrinsic motivation and living one's life for a purpose is evident in the dialogue that took place. While there were different religious and spiritual orientations represented in the group there appeared to be a common theme of living life for a purpose in serving others. This is another major element of Transcendent Identity. In describing the reasons for doing what they do, the group members were careful to distinguish that serving others was not for the purpose of enhancing one's resume or for seeking accolades. As Emilee went on to explain, "It's not just like, 'Oh, I can write that on my list of things I've done for other people.' It's above and beyond that. It's serving a life purpose. That's how I look at it."

Beverly reaffirmed this worldview: "Yeah, it makes you feel good on the inside. That you did something for somebody and it's not that you like, patting yourself on the back, it just makes you feel good that you gave that person a leg up, to help them out."

Latasha voiced her agreement with Beverly and Emilee by expressing that she serves others out of "obedience to Christ." She further stated, "Most of the times I don't even realize I'm doing something, it just happens. I feel like it is my purpose. I can't say that I don't feel good on the inside, but I can say that I'm really not thinking about myself when I'm doing it. I'm doing it out of pure obedience because that is my purpose, and what I'm supposed to be doing. So, that's kind of like the gift of service."

Gabby chimed in with her own position on serving others and living life with a purpose. While there was an element of self sacrifice in their words there was also a sense of satisfaction from serving others. To this end, Gabby shared the following:

> I wish I could say it was altruistic, but I always get something from it, even when I don't want to get something. It's like, yesterday, my mom called me up and asked me if I could go to her friend's place and take pictures of her face because she fell and totally bruised up her face real bad, and she wanted pictures just as, you know, evidence, in case they needed it later. And, I was so busy with work and everything, and I was so tired, and I just wanted to go home and go to bed, you know? And, it's like, OK, I'll do it. And I went over there and I took the pictures. Afterwards, just seeing how happy her friend was that I did that for her, I was like, now I'm happy! [laughing]

Affirmations came from various group members about the pleasure derived from living a purposeful life and giving to others. Cara summed up the theme with this:

I really relate to what you're saying. I wish you could be all purely altruistic, I kind of feel selfish sometimes because of how good it feels to give of yourself. But it's interesting, I was watching something the other day on Youtube. It was this guy, he goes around and motivates companies to treat each other better. I can't remember his name. But one of the things he talks about is actually, like a biochemical response ... something that is from the heart, produces something that physically makes you feel better. And then, you want to do more because it's almost, not an addictive thing in your body, but it just feels good. So, it kind of, you know, so I just thought that was really neat.

At this point, Kristen revisited a thought. While it is an area that would lie in the obstacles to evolvement, the fact that she was able to recognize this as an area to develop demonstrated her own insights, an understanding of where she resides in the various elements in the Transcendent Identity Model, as well as the areas in which she would like to continue addressing.

> My biggest struggle or kind of like the next step I would work on … I would want to have relationships with and especially people outside of my culture, whether that's ethnic or that's sexual orientation. I desire to have these relationships. And, it's like, I told Emilee before, I totally get friend crushes on people.

This prompted spontaneous laughter from the rest of the group members. Kristen went on to address the area of confidence in establishing relationships outside one's usual circle of friends:

> I'll see someone and think, "Oh, you're so cool! I want to be your friend!" And so, like, figuring out how to bridge that gap without, I mean, without pulling myself in, like, I have a friend crush on you! Like, not being too awkward!

Again came the spontaneous laughter; however. this time Kristen examined how intergroup distrust impedes attempts on her part to establish cross-racial relationships. These interactions can be particularly painful when others have perceived her with the burden of the smog. The aftermath of rejection when attempting to build bridges across the racial divide is real. This topic was openly discussed within the group:

> I think in the past, I've approached people that I really would want to get to know, and there's almost, like, a push factor. Like, "Wait! Why are you asking me questions? Why do you want to me my friend?" And, I feel like I've had that reaction from people, especially of other ethnicities. Like, I have a genuine interest. I want to get to know you and there's almost like that, "Wait . . why?" Like I have mixed motives. I feel like, in our culture, growing up with racism, a lot of people have this negative reaction, like there has to be another reason why. And it's like, "No, I just want to get to know you." I know that a lot of people, would be receptive to it if I'm persistent. But it's hard for me to have the confidence to be persistent and persistently pursue a relationship after like that first kind of pushback. You have to build the rapport, and you have to build the trust. And, I understand that's just on my part, having the confidence to continue to pursue that and convince that person that I genuinely just want to get to know them.

Similar to Beverly, who is African American and reflected on how she learned to not project the micro aggressions that she has experienced by some to a whole racial group, Kristen, who is Euro-American, processes the understanding that intergroup distrust is evident and plays itself out when she attempts to genuinely start a relationship with someone across the racial divide. She explained that the rejection makes her feel hurt when the distrust is projected onto her. She goes on to state that she understand that it is not anything personal and concluded that building friendships is something she is learning to "ease into." Yet, she admitted to, at times, "pushing the relationship a bit faster than other people are used to." This, once again, prompted laughter from everyone in the group as they gave their full attention to Kristen, who shared the impact of this awkward and painful experience.

Emilee confirmed with Kristen that she was not alone in having to navigate this reality and stated, "It worked for me!" Again, the group laughed at the dynamics of having to live in and around the smog. This smog is also cloaked in a façade in which people may enter fields in which they are supposed to be helping others but lack the genuineness required to fully serve. Having this level of understanding is similar to the different positions that Angelina Grimké and Catherine Beecher had related to emancipation. While both agreed that slavery was wrong, Grimké believed immediate emancipation and incorporation of emancipated people into society because she cared for and loved those held in bondage. Beecher, on the other hand, believed in gradual emancipation but then stood on a position that the people held in bondage would never be able to stand on equal ground, so the best option was to send people, once emancipated, back to Africa. This position lacked personalized care and love. Grimké appreciated the common ground; however, she saw how the outcome of lack of genuine care ultimately marginalized the people whose mistreatment was grounded in prejudice and racism. If people from her era were to have acted solely from a position of exclusion and exile, we would be even less evolved as a nation today. Having the critical thinking to decipher this is a must as expressed by Beverly:

> I feel that everybody's good ... until I learn the real person, and then when I learn of the real person I feel a disconnect. I don't know how to explain to that person that "me and you are not on the same page. I'm sorry, I tried, but we're not on the same page." So, what I do is I get quiet, and I don't talk to that person anymore. Because, I trust everybody, and I'm learning now, you can't, I know I'm this old, you can't do that. You can't trust everybody and have an open heart with everybody because everybody is not the same as who I am. So, that's one of my things that I'm working on, too, that you got to learn slowly and build that trust because a lot of people put on a façade. And I seen that a lot this ... that genuineness was not real, it was fake.

The discussion took a turn and went to the dynamic of seeing the intentions of others. Latasha reflected on the intentions of her own classmates who are all preparing to enter the field of counseling field:

> [to] maybe to help themselves, or to get some underlying, I don't know what it is. But I'm starting to notice that, too, because we're in a cohort, so I think it's really important because you start realizing different character flaws, character issues, or just who people truly are. So, it is the like spirit thing that Angela Grimké speaks of, because it's just really rare. Well, for me, in my experience, I get so overjoyed! You're a great person! Because it's rare that you find people who have something in common with you or similar spirits. So, it's really refreshing for me. I get overly excited.

Coping mechanisms related to living in a world where people exist with varied levels of awareness of their own positioning around the smog line were further explored. The group members talked about their pain when trying to build bridges and being rejected, having to unlearn assuming that others were apt to inflict pain due to their experiences, endeavoring to find other people of like spirit, and then approaching life from a guarded orientation. Cara gave life to this last coping mechanism:

> It's funny, it's like I'm more opposite than you guys in that way. It's like I've got my walls, and I'll throw over big nuggets of honesty and on the heart level with people. I do stay pretty guarded because I have been hurt a lot. I guess I've taken it. So, you know, I guess there's just that fear. And, I'm looking for like spirits, too. I just have a different way of doing it.

The group participants discussed the multiple worlds in which they exist—family, school, work, greater society. The context of their environment had major bearing on how cautious they are as they engage in a world that may reflect different realities within these contexts. While their work contexts may force them to be particularly attentive, their choice to maintain personal relationships with "like spirits" was related to the effort to protect themselves from the toxicity that comes from the behaviors inherent in a smog-derived worldview. Additionally, they had to address their role in addressing the contaminants of the smog line as living "in congruence" and demonstrating courage as they overcome fear whenever they have to intervene and act upon the isms. Cara offered this thought:

> I love what you said.... I can't be a victim inside of myself.... So, we all have it in some way or another. And I think, wow, I've got to be congruent with myself. Wow, I've got to talk down, write down and live down this prejudice, this situation, whatever it is. And, living from that fear, you know, you're not being true to yourself, you're not being true to those around you who need an advocate. And, this is just one instance in my life. And I'm thinking, oh, two years down the road, that's when it will start, you know? When I become an official therapist. You have to it practice it now, like you're saying. I have to get up, tell it to shut up, and get out and go in the morning. And, so I think it's just choosing to be brave, choosing to not give into that fear, in our very specific, purpose-filled situations that we step up and say no to that fear and say yes to being congruent with yourself and say no to being that victim of your own self and the supposed people that you're going to disappoint.

Emilee immediately responded with, "I love that! Say no to yourself and yes to being congruent." Kristen inserted, "It should be a T-shirt!" Someone else chimed in, "Bumper sticker!" Beverly added to the way in which we all need to acknowledge the fear but also incorporate it into an aspect of engaging the word differently from what we have been accustomed to doing:

> I like how we talk about fear, and I think with the fear it's like you said, getting comfortable with the uncomfortable. And that's what the hardest part is, is trying to get comfortable with the uncomfortable, and that brings about a lot of fear within all of us.

For those who endeavor to live above the smog line, it means having to live congruently, which calls for acting upon and responding to incidents that they witness. Not doing so means being in conflict with oneself. Latasha stated the following:

> You can't live the lie. And it just healed me. And I was like, I can't ignore stuff, I can't, I can't sweep things under the rug, I can't do what's wrong, I have to do what's right. And it's because I cannot lie to myself, I just can't do it. So I had to, like just speak up, just like Angela Grimké and the Grimké sisters, I feel the same way. And just with counseling, I feel like, I have to be transparent, I'm a transparent person, I don't care how it makes me look. And, it's just, I can't live the lie, I just won't do it.

As the researcher, I asked these six individuals how they would feel if they did not respond to incidents around them. To this, Emilee, who had previously admitted to not being able to respond to such incidents but who had made major shifts in her thoughts and behaviors, shared the following:

> I would have felt awful. But there have been so many times before that I haven't. And that's what my whole 220 and the color of blindness and really working through standing up for what's right, and seeing those things. Obviously I would have seen that because that was very covert form of racism. But noticing even the micro aggressions now. Even before that [the incident at the liquor store] I had noticed that I was treated differently when I came in, than when people of color [came in]. And, I obviously hadn't said anything at that point, but just taking notice, I wouldn't have taken notice to those small micro aggressions before, only if it was overt racism ... out in the open, I would notice. And that one obviously was. The fact that I'm picking up on things before that I was just really naive to, I think is huge progress. I'm not saying that I going to have the courage to do that every time, but the fact that I did that time shows me . . I'm still OK. I'm here, you know? And what am I still afraid of?

Emilee spoke to her new positioning on the Transcendent Identity Development Model. Defying the fear so she cannot only identify but act upon micro aggressions was a major sign of progress. She never assumed a position of racial cohesion, but her silence to incidents in the past would make her appear to be in allegiance. She recognized this. Latasha, on the other hand, had a different response to my prompt:

> It's hard, internally.... I fight with myself. I argue and I try to and my soul won't allow me to do it. I think mine is kind of opposite of yours [addressing Emilee], but it's getting back to being yours. Because when I hear things that aren't right, I'm like, no I addressed it. I'm not afraid of confrontation. I do what's right. But then I start noticing how people stop calling or stop wanting to be around me. I was like, "OK, maybe I shouldn't have said it that way." So then I start being more covert. I stopped saying what was in me, but then that anxiety, like I need to get this out. And now when I was trying to just hold it in, and that's the time I had the breakdown, because I was holding all of this in, that I'm usually letting this out, but

then when I had that revelation, I can't live the lie, it made me feel comfortable, for me to go back to confronting the situation, but definitely out of love, instead of being just very passionate about it.

Latasha offered a state of being that affirms, once again, Pastor Reed's statement of "treat your persecutor as a person of value, giving him a blessing rather than a curse, and loving him rather than hating him." Latasha explained her struggle with having to learn to be honest with herself, living congruently, and more so, enacting what she calls her "spiritual walk." Doing so meant learning how to engage people from a heartfelt place in which she responds "with grace" and has found more "peace" within herself as she has come to learn "who Tasha is again."

The group members then turned the dialogue to being socially excluded, a consequence from living in congruence. They shared stories and instances in which they had spoken up when a relative or a friend had made a racist comment only to be rejected and avoided. They elaborated on how this can be hurtful, but, as Emilee reflected about this matter, "It's going to piss people off sometimes, and just being able to deal with that [is a necessary] consequence." Acknowledging that people will not always accept their well-intended interventions meant developing a worldview that embraces coping with the pain. Cara offered the group her coping mechanism:

> This thing just popped into my head! I will embrace the collateral heart that is involved with living from my heart, and living with honesty and not giving in to the lie, which so many people in that situation, and in other ways, give in to … that whole idea of embracing the collateral heart. I'd take this hurt any day because it's worth it. It's like, getting to that point is very hard, but it's so worth it.

This, truly, is the point at which the group members entertained the idea that they had to engage with the isms despite the negative feelings that come with it. They discussed how they could not sidestep issues or incidents that made them feel uncomfortable but, instead, must openly interject themselves so they could, as Kristen stated, "Feel the pain of the world!"

Avoidance of anything that makes us feel uncomfortable is natural. What the focus group members distinguished for us at this point, however, was that to be actively engaged as humanists in the world they had to confront the negativity, despite how it makes them feel, and process the residue of emotions later. Kristen offered her own experience with allowing herself to *feel* "it":

> Sometimes I'll break down crying! Everybody's like, "What is wrong?" I'm like, "I just feel sad, like this world sometimes just feels sad." And sometimes I just have to let it sit there and consume me and kind of just feel it for a little bit. And then go out to my wailing wall and just let it out, and then come back in, and be like, "OK, now I can keep going." But just having the capacity and the willingness to just feel those sad feelings and just feel this injustice around us, and not push it away … let it sink in and feel it for a little bit.

At the end, research assistant Nancy Padrick recognized that there appeared to be a multigenerational theme to the path of living above the smog line. In other words, similar to the Seven Generations given to us by the Iroquois Nation, we must consider one's actions today as they will have impact on the next seven generations. With this concept in mind, the group understood that their words and actions may not have impact immediately. Cara reinforced this concept by stating the following:

> I love to view things in this way, to where what you do now is not just about you and the person sitting across from you, it's about my children, it's about their children, it's about their children. And so, in the same say, Angela Grimké wrote so many things that we just quoted today. So that action though it was writing on a piece of paper, and maybe in and of itself, didn't change the entire scope of the south, they, you know what I mean, it still does something today. That action still has ramifications, good ramifications today. So I think, just in anyway, whatever you can do, you may not be able to say the right thing, but you said something. You may not have the wherewithal within you to say something right there. But either way it's an action that will do something, maybe not then, maybe it's not about you and right now maybe it's about them way down there.

The group members shared, with full heart, their thoughts and experiences. Their stories provide inspiration as they model behaviors that are congruent with their heart. The fact that they openly shared and discussed their own reflections of growth and transformation speaks to shifts in how they perceive themselves in the world. Without doubt, they are already making a positive difference in the world and while their impact may not always be evident in their lifetime they have positioned themselves from an unimpeded standpoint—their vision is clear; they reside above the smog line.

Dialogical Forces at Work

The difficult work of not only seeing the smog but of deconstructing it requires that we ask ourselves very difficult questions. First of all, how and for what purpose was the construct created? In other words, how are the polarities created? Who constructs them and what purpose does the construct serve by keeping them?

The long-term impact that the dialogical forces have had on our society related to race are apparent through the many disparities that still exist and the prevalent micro aggressions reported. Yet, the many other constructs to consider must be questioned and challenged. For example, Maggie Daugherty's dissertation, "Redefining Normal: The Path to Self-attainment for People with Neurodiversities: How Do People from the Neurodiverse Spectrum Define Self-fulfillment?" challenges us to question who defines normal and how, as a society have we behaved toward people not defined as normal. In the opening page of her dissertation, Daugherty (2013) states the following:

> The history of individuals with disabilities is filled with pernicious injustice. Throughout history, people with disabilities have been murdered, abused, institutionalized, segregated, ignored, thrown away, labeled, judged, and mistreated (MNDDC, 2010; Chupik & Wright, 2006). They have been viewed as less than, not good enough, and deficient. They were often mocked and belittled by atrocious nicknames such as retard, gimp, cripple, dimwit, imbecile, lame, moron, mental and diseased. When people are told they are nothing, how can they believe anything else?

There is a pervasive mindset about people with "disabilities." Their differences have been viewed as a disease, a disorder, or a deficit. This negative perception has led to atrocities toward individuals considered "abnormal." (p. 1)

Daugherty goes on to cite the Nazi regime's extermination of people deemed as "undesirable" and outside the "norm." While it would be easy to point fingers to such barbaric behavior that occurred overseas, Daugherty provides countless examples of how, in our own society, we have perpetuated violence, by virtue of laws and policy against anyone deemed "abnormal." Changing habituated thoughts and mindsets that have been rooted in the fabric of our society takes time. Daugherty takes on the construct of ablism as she adds,

> Ultimately, the acceptance of differences will change the prejudicial perspective directed at individuals with neurodiversities, and help them overcome the oppression placed on them by societal imagery of disease-based disorders that need preventions, cures, and treatments. Removing the negative labels associated with disabilities and transforming the mindset in which individuals are perceived as diverse may foster the capacity of moving people with neurodiversities through the spectrum of inclusion and achieve self-actualization. (p. 12)

Acceptance, in an operational sense, requires compassion. Yet, we live in a time in which cruelty underscores the lack of empathy in our society. The heightened level of mistreatment and the number of ways in which cruelty is enacted has been such that many of our children have selected death rather than be subjected to the torture of living in this world. Valinda Frost's dissertation, "The Effects of Educational Policy on Criminal Peer Abuse," takes on the rampant bullying in our schools and in our society along with the fatal outcome leading to suicide for those subjected to baseless torment.

While we could easily focus on attention on those who commit and seemingly take delight in committing acts of torment, Frost (2013) reveals another element of behavior that supports the relational (as well as physical) violence associated with bullying:

> Bystanders watched and did nothing or worse, joined the "fun" or actually recorded the violence. Sadly, most bullies are never held accountable for their abusive behavior even after their victims have taken their own lives and most bystanders do not acknowledge the possibility of their roles in instigating and behaving in ways that keep peer abuse happening over and over again (Insoo & Hazler, 2009).

I have no doubt as to how John Brown or Angelina Grimké would respond to the pleas of children and youth subjected to the mistreatment of their peers. Nonetheless, it has been apparent that there have been many instances in which the pleas fell on deaf ears as those with power and privilege that are in the position to respond upon the acts of cruelty did little or did nothing to make the abuse end. Despite the fact that we have countless laws and policies to protect our children from abuse, there is an arbitrary nature to who is afforded protection and who is not. Frost's dissertation study included the interview of a parent, Lisa Ford Berry, who lost her son, Michael, to suicide after not only suffering the torment of his peers but of also having his pleas for help minimized and unheeded. In reflecting upon the lack of response to her son's attempts to seek intervention, Ford Berry states the following:

> A lot of times, common sense gets left at the front door. From zero tolerance to willful disobedience, should you choose to follow the Ed code or Seth's law, the problem is there are no consequences for failure to comply. You can just willfully disregard student behavior. "Willful disregard" is the dumping ground for everything (Frost, 2013).

The notion of "willful disregard" stayed with me as I read Frost's dissertation. I could not help but to reflect on the words of the focus group members related to living congruently. In other words, while we do have laws and policies to dictate behaviors and how we treat one another, having the moral courage to address injustice and mistreatment in all its forms is vital. Yet, the price that we pay for not acting upon such behavior means suffering and enduring rather than living in a society that has yet to enforce mutual standards of respect for all humanity.

As these two researchers confront and question our world of today, there are forces that compel us to recapture the vitality of ourselves as human beings in this world. Defining the essence of our true selves rather than the dictates of the way others pigeonhole us is critical in healing the trauma resulting from the anti-dialogical forces in this nation's history. Crystal Martinez (2013) examines the generational trauma inflicted upon Native Americans in the United States in her dissertation titled "The Perceptions of Tribal Leadership and the Impact of Education and Cultural Knowledge: Examining Tribal Leadership and Education within California Native American Communities." For the First Nations of this land to still feel the impact of conquest, genocide. and dislocation, culturally responsive leadership requires a tremendous amount of compassion.

The focus group participants discuss that what has transpired must not be forgotten. From a state of Transcendent Identity we must understand the histories of all people and ascertain how to intervene upon what many would regard as 'fixed realities.' Martinez states the following:

> Due to the lack of research that examines tribal leadership, there are few tribal leadership programs and educational models to emulate. Without examples of cultural integration within the funds of knowledge, it can be very difficult for tribes to establish educational programs that incorporate language, culture, and history of the tribal leadership process. Developing the next generation of leaders is a critical challenge facing American Indians today (Nichols, 2008). The Census bureau reported that a little over one percent of the total U.S population was American Indian (Census, 2000). As the population continues to grow so do the challenges that impact the community. According to Nichols (2008), today's tribal communities are faced with a multitude of challenges which include the nation's highest rates of poverty, substance abuse, heart disease, diabetes and teen suicide. (p. 9)

While these three doctoral students enter the final stages of writing and defending their dissertations, we are left with many but yet very pointed questions: How and for what purpose was the construct created? How were the polarities created? Who constructed them and what purpose do the constructs serve by keeping them? The final question is, "How will you respond next time you bear witness to acts of aggression that harm and can have an effect for generations?" As we move into the next chapter, we continue the theme of care and demonstrate the care enacted by those who care enough to ensure that not all act with willful disregard.

Transcendent Identity

Dual Perception: 1) Heart: Differences Are Appreciated. 2) Mind: Recognizes How "Differences"
Are Perceived Below the Smog Line & Able to Identify Micro Aggressions
Care for and Love for **All** Humanity: Rejecting Racial Group Cohesion
Understanding of the Collective History of All People and How We Are All Linked
Able to Recognize the Pain and Challenges of All People
Seeks Relationships with Like-spirited People
Being and Acting in Congruence
Recognizing That Being Disliked or Hurting Is Not to Be Avoided: Distress Is Inevitable
Altruism: Self-Sacrificing for Benefit of Others
Critical Thinking Applied to Understanding of the World
Actively Seeking Positive Purpose in Life
Defying Fear When Enacting Change
Recognizing the Long Range Vision in One's Work: Multigenerational Impact
Mindful Wonderment

Obstacles to Evolvement

Perceptual Distortions
Acquiescing to Judgment of Others
Rejection
Lacking Confidence to Engage in
Relationships with People Who Are
"Different"

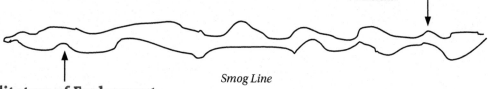

Smog Line

Facilitators of Evolvement

Models of Humanists
Education: Full Knowledge of Realities of All People
Forgiving but Not Forgetting
Knowing Positive Contributions of All People
Confronting "Heroification" of Exploitive Historical Figures
Recognizing How "Silence" Maintains Separateness, Inequities & Social Structures.
Identifying and Then Applying Ways to Change One's Patterns of Behavior; Self evaluating
Reconstruction of an Identity That Is Grounded in Purpose/Cause Committed to Improving the World

Perceptual World of Submerged Identity

Adherence to Exclusionary Ethnocentrism & Cultural Encapsulation
Lacking Understanding of Convergence of Collective Histories
Quick to Label "Differences" without Knowing Anything about the Source/Origin
Dichotomous Thinking: Everything Is Labeled as "Good" or "Bad"
Superficial Relationships Based on Minimum Standards of "Similarity"
Conscious or Unconscious Adherence to Racial Group Identity
Conditioned Patterns of Behavior That Are Exclusionary
Fear of Others; Anything or Anyone Who Is "Different"
Use of Racial Identity to Hold Power over Others: Fomenting Fear/Guilt
Adherence to an Identity Submerged in Domination/Victimization/Traumatization

Note: Transcendent Identity Development Model developed by Focus Group (2012): Research Assistant, Nancy Padrick, and M.S. in
Counselor Ed Graduate Students: Cara Wilber, Gabrielle Kolitsos, Beverly Williams, Emilee Hansen, Latasha Strawder, Kristen Mezger.

QUESTIONS FOR DISCUSSION OR SELF REFLECTION

SELF-AWARENESS

1. At this time in your life, do you perceive yourself to be mostly above or below the Smog Line?

2. Do you find that there are situations or factors that contribute to keeping you in a Submerged Identity?

CLIENT WORLDVIEW

3. In observing behaviors that stem from the Perceptual World of Submerged Identity, what are the factors that you can identify that anchor someone in this submerged state?

COUNSELING RELATIONSHIP

4. In working with an individual whose perception is clearly falls in the Submerged Identity, what would be your response should they make a statement that is offensive to you and to others.

COUNSELING AND ADVOCACY INTERVENTIONS

5. Review the Facilitators of Evolvement and discuss ways in which to enact positive evolvement at the following levels: intrapersonal, interpersonal, institutional, community, public policy, and international/global levels.

Activity

Write a Self-Identity paper and give an oral presentation. Include the following:

a. A brief description of what major forces/events affected the previous 6 generations of your family. You are the seventh generation. If you are unable to uncover anything about your family background, describe the major historical events that impacted people of your ethnic background. For example, look up the names of your grandparents to determine where they came from and what was occurring, historically, during their lifetime. Did your ancestors immigrate (voluntarily or involuntarily) to this part of the world? If so, when did they arrive and what were the forces behind their coming? Include the people and events of major impact to you as you grew up. This could include family behaviors such as alcohol or drug abuse, violence, poverty, emotional detachment, divorce, etc.

b. Your cultural heritage: Customs related to major life events (births, weddings, deaths, etc.) How are they celebrated? Core Values (what is most important to people of your cultural heritage? What do you and they value most? What foods are eaten almost daily? Anything else you identify as practices that comprise your cultural heritage.

If there are other people in the class with the same cultural background, you may want to divide up cultural elements so that each presents on something different—for example, one could talk about births, another about funerals, etc.

c. An analysis of your own growth and identity development (on the identity development scale).If you wish, you may bring in traditional clothing, artwork, a short film or video clip, or a sample of typical food that provide a positive visual image of your culture and increase interest. You may supplement your presentation with a handout(s).

d. Discuss where you are on the Transcendent Identity Model and what efforts you are making to reach and maintain a Transcendent Identity.

References

Chupik, J., & Wright, D. (2006). Treating the "idiot" child in early 20th-century Ontario. *Disability & Society, 21(1)*, 77–90. doi:10.1080/09687590500375481

Daugherty, M. (2013). Redefining Normal: The path to self-attainment for people with neurodiversities: *How do people from the neurodiverse spectrum define self-fulfillment?* Unpublished doctoral dissertation, California State University, Sacramento.

Freire, P. (1998). *Pedagogy of the oppressed*. New York: The Continuum Publishing Company.

Frost, V. (2013). The effects of educational policy on criminal peer abuse. Unpublished doctoral dissertation. California State University, Sacramento.

Insoo, O., & Hazler, R. J. (2009). Contributions of personal and situational factors to bystanders' reactions to school bullying. *School Psychology International*, 291–310.

Martinez, C. (2013). The perceptions of tribal leadership and the impact of education and cultural knowledge: Examining tribal leadership and education within California Native American communities. Unpublished doctoral dissertation. California State University, Sacramento.

MMDDC–The Minnesota Governor's Council on Developmental Disabilities. (2010). Parallels in time: A history of developmental disabilities. Retrieved from http:www.mnddc.org/parallels.

Nichols, T. (2008). Culture is key to developing Native American leaders. *Agricultural Education Magazine, 1*, 14–18.

Reed, D. (2012). *God is a gift*. Eureka Springs, Arkansas; Thorncrown Press.

U.S. Census Bureau. (2000). We the people American Indians and Alaska natives in the United States. Special Reports. Issued date (2006): 1–23.

When We Care

I think one of the questions people ask me is "Why do you even care?" "Why do you care?" My response is,

"Because when I see human beings who are not happy, who are not reaching their potential and I see more in them than what they are seeing at the moment and if I see hurt then I have enough compassion to care." And you can go through life, "Tell me what I need to do to earn money. What's my job? What's my hours? I did my job. I did what I was paid to do" and they somehow can make it through there and my response to them is, "I'm more curious as to why you DON'T care? How can you go through life so callously? How can you get through life and see all that around you and not want to do something to make it better for other people? That's the part that I think is more puzzling than why I care. It's why don't you care." (Tessler Interview, April 10, 2007)

And there it is. How much do you really care? The humanist models presented in this book activated their humanistic principles knowing, quite often, that their actions would be viewed as unpopular and they would, most likely, face aggressive and even violent opposition. In some cases, they understood that they would not live to see the monumental outcomes that were generated from their actions that were in alignment with other like-minded people. Certainly, Colonel Shaw knew he was facing imminent death as he charged Fort Wagner. He did not live to see the end to legalized slavery in the United States that was enacted in 1865. He did, however, bear witness to and contribute to the undoing of prejudices against African Americans. This was his contribution to building the bridges that heal our racial cultural divide.

Sacrifices are made every day by people who commit courageous acts, small and large. Collectively and individually, these acts demonstrate the Color of the Heart. Acts of humanism speak volumes to those whose suffering is alleviated when we call upon our "better angels." The acts serve to humanize us all as they heal the soul and seek to remedy the generations of cultural mistrust and undo the larger body of dissonance created by the social constructions of racism, sexism, ablism, heterosexism, classism, etc.

Acts of humanism do not have to shake the foundation of a nation like John Brown's actions did. They do not have to end in a self-sacrificing and heroic death like the Colonel's did. In fact, the models of humanism have taught us that the use of rifles and muskets are not the only way of changing our reality. Nonetheless, words do not have to stir the opposition into a riotous frenzy like the words of Angelina Grimké. The printed word does not have to gain wide audience like the published words of Helen Hunt Jackson and William Lloyd Garrison, but *you* can still speak, you can write, and you can act. There are people who do so every day and who, like Sarah Shaw, raise the next generation to not only care, but to care enough to continue building bridges that heal.

What follows are contributions to this manuscript from individuals who choose to act upon their humanistic principles, as well as stories that I have inserted from observations of humanists in action. As you read the stories, consider the dialogical forces employed and the challenges that they face. Note the capacity for these individuals to perceive the reality of their world, which Freire (1998) calls "naming the world." As we have read about the lives of six historical and two modern-day humanists, there were five common themes that emanated from their lives. As you read through the stories that follow, see if you can recognize the same themes. In some cases, the theme may not be evident. If this is the case, then use the narrative as a way to discuss how you would create the conditions for greater success in activating humanist principles. The common themes are provided below in a format that will guide your reading and application to the stories.

1. What is the "it" that is being addressed in each story? In other words, what is the "ism" that the subject in the story is addressing? What type of micro-aggression is being committed?

2. Identify if there are any alliances drawn upon by the subject, and if none are evident, who would most likely be called upon to serve in this capacity?

3. What is the specific "action" enacted by the subject in the story to cause a different outcome?

4. What were some of the emotional/physical costs for enacting humanist action?

5. How does the subject perceive those who she/he is advocating for, and how do their perceptions demonstrate a positioning in which they "fly above the smog line?"

6. If you are oriented toward the helping professions, such as counseling or social work, how do the efforts in the story meet the Multicultural and Social Justice Competencies (Appendix D) delineated for the counseling profession?

7. From the orientation of a leader, what elements of a Transformational Leader (Appendix E) are evident in the stories that follow?

8. Apply the Framework of the Transcendent Identity Development Model and discuss what elements of the framework are present in the stories that follow.

As you read through each story, begin to utilize the language and concepts presented throughout the previous chapters. Having the words to "name the world" will provide the capacity for you to be a subject in the world. Consider the greater socio-political context regarding who is being targeted and why the activism was needed. The subjects in these stories recognize their position of power and privilege and employed it to make a difference. Consider the implications if the humanist in the story had not interceded. What would the lives of those in the story look like without humanist intervention? Think about the "low road" responses that could have been made in each of these cases and how the outcome would have turned out differently if this approach had been taken.

These are stories contributed for the purpose of seeing the many ways and settings in which humanism can be activated. They provide *inspiration for future generations.*

Small and Large Acts of Courage

Yes, You Can!

Contributed by Dannah Nielsen, M.S.
Dannah.nielsen@hotmail.com

I began my counseling internship at a rural high school known for its farming and agriculture and was asked to work with the freshman class, seeing as the other high school counselors had their hands tied with getting the upperclassmen to graduate on time. The first step I took was going to each of the freshmen health classes and introducing myself. During this, I had asked each student to write down on a piece of paper a question they would ask if they had a few uninterrupted minutes of my time. While I was well aware of the migrant population in this farming community, I felt hesitant on how to meet the needs of these students. I hoped that my introduction would help pave this path. And it did.

Halfway through my day I came across several classrooms that were filled with what appeared to be predominately Latino students. I asked if there would be a student volunteer to help translate what I was saying. I also told the students they could write down their question for me in Spanish. While I am not fluent in speaking, I can easily translate what is written. In came the slips of paper, and in came the questions. "Why should I care about school? I can't go to college." "I'm not a citizen, what choices do I have?" And there were even statements. "I gave up. I can't go to college. I can't get a job." "Don't bother with me. I'll work in the fields."

At the same time, the Health Teacher invited me to come back and help present to the Freshmen on how to be successful in, and make the best out of High School. She gave me the slides to review and welcomed me to make any additions or corrections. Using my collection of unanswered questions, I went to work. Immediately I noticed there was nothing in this presentation that spoke to undocumented students, and an image flashed in my head of these students ignoring the presentation, falling asleep, or even feeling desperate or depressed with the situation they were in.

I knew there were options, but it was obvious these students did not. I created slides that gave information on how, why, and where undocumented students could go to college. It was brief, but the biggest message that needs to be driven into their minds is "YES, YOU CAN." And their attention to their education needs to start TODAY.

The Health Teacher was honest, and helpful. She admitted she was just recently learning more about this group of students. During our conversation she kept referring to the students as "illegal" and I felt unsure how to correct her, and the opportunity didn't seem to present itself for me to address it. Shortly after our presentation to the classes, she sent out an email to staff acknowledging my efforts and my inclusion on information to "illegal" students. While I knew her email was well-intended, I felt embarrassed that the impression was given that I, too, was referring to these students as "illegal." How was I going to politely correct this? Equally important was, how many other teaching staff did not understand the implications of using terminology that was potentially offensive or demeaning?

Around the same time I was contemplating my response, two seniors at the high school wanted to present during the faculty meeting regarding their own struggles as migrant students who were now on their way to college. As I sat there listening I realized this was all falling into place perfectly. The next day I sent a mass email response citing the courageousness of these seniors, and emphasizing what they presented. I included my own experiences already working with the freshmen and included links to websites that promoted the opportunities for undocumented students. And equally important, I noted in my e-mail the importance of using the correct terminology—undocumented—when encouraging these students to consider college and other dreams they might have thought weren't possible.

It sounds simple enough, but as an intern I was incredibly nervous about e-mailing the entire high school staff with my thoughts. I wasn't sure the response I would get. I wasn't sure if it would be well received, if it would be ignored or if it would invite an unwanted political debate. But at the same time, I knew it was important, and I feel my commitment is first to the students I work with, regardless of their situation.

The Digital Divide: The Emotional Cost of the Technological Revolution

Contributed by Dr. Samer Batarseh (Samer.m.batarseh@gmail.com)
Full-time Employee of a High Technology Company and an Adjunct Community
College Instructor at Sacramento City College

According to Atkinson, Black, and Curtis (2008), the digital divide is defined as "the gap between people who have access to information and communication technologies (ICT) and those who do not, and is an issue of significant social justice" (Atkinson, Black, ... Curtis, 2008).

Sacramento is the Capital of California and is located 128 miles northeast of Silicon Valley the global technology engine that powers the world's need for information and communication technologies (ICT). The demographic composition at Sacramento City College includes

58% female students, 38% first generation college students, 69% minority students, 15% over 40 years of age, and 68% attending as part time students.

As an adjunct faculty member at Sacramento City College (SCC), I am aware of the demographic composition of SCC. Usually, I am assigned high level courses that are part of certificates, degrees, or transfer requirements. Nonetheless, a few years ago I was assigned to teach a "Computer Familiarization" course which is a non-transferable and non-degree course designed to introduce students to personal computers.

I was aware of the digital divide as a symptom of social injustices related also to income, race, and education but that did not prepare me for the first question in my first computer familiarization course that came from an older female minority student when I started my lecture by explaining that a mouse is an important input and pointing device to interact with computers. The lady casually stated: "What do mice have to do with computers?" I continued with my lecture by pulling the mouse from the back of the computer and showing it to students.

After the class, I casually asked the student about her experience with computers and the student explained that the reason she is taking the course is that "kids these days are not into writing pen and paper letters anymore and that her grandkids have stopped writing for the past few years." Her motive in learning how to use a personal computer was to be able to use e-mail in order to stay in touch with her children and grandchildren. As a worker in a hi-tech company and as college instructor, I have always viewed technology as a valuable asset that transformed all our lives to the better. I have never thought that these innocent digital devices that are turning the world into a tiny village would also create barriers and break families apart forcing a grandmother to attend a computer class on a walker. From a humanist approach, the information revolution has shaken the foundations of this woman's social, emotional, and family structure. She longed for the days of waiting to hear the noisy engine of the small jeep delivering the mail, getting up from her comfortable seat on the porch, and walking over to the mailbox to open letters from loved ones. She no longer is able to leave pieces of old mail on her night stand or next to the telephone or on top of her television set for frequent reviews. The touch of paper and smell of ink awakened her senses and made her feel closer to her children and grandchildren. But alas, the paper letters stopped coming and she is now on a mission, at this advanced stage in life, to learn new skills in order to stay accounted for as one of many recipients on a massive e-mail distribution list.

As a high-tech worker and a part time college instructor, this experience has transformed my views on access and equity when it comes to information and technology. I am now more determined to ensure that technology becomes a path to equal access and knowledge and not a tool to marginalize members of our society.

Work Cited:

Atkinson, J., Black, R., & Curtis, A. (2008). Exploring the Digital Divide in an Australian Regional City: a case study of Albury. *Australian Geographer, 39* (4), pp. 479–493.

The Power of a Counselor: Jerry Black, and a Simple Button

I had the fortune of working, for seven years, as a high school counselor under an incredible head counselor, Jerry Black. He led our department with a quiet force. When I arrived at this campus gang affiliation, a by-product of horizontal violence, was derailing the success of many of our Mexican American students. They were undermining their own and each other's capacity of acquiring an education and securing a promising future, which is the very reason why many of their families migrated to this country.

Intent on starting dialogue between the two rival gangs, Sureños and Norteños, I brought together natural leaders from this student population. They discussed having goals of wanting to do something with their lives, and, in some cases, expressed the desire of pursuing higher education. They recognized, however, that the violence and antagonism created by the ongoing strife between the two rival gangs had to end. It was hurting everybody. In response, they created a movement called, "Latinos Unidos." This movement was intended to unite the polarized Mexican American community, create peace on campus, and provide a culture of academic excellence. Sounds like good intentions, but there were people from the dominant community opposed to the concept. Unity (like education) is threatening. There were vocal members from the dominant community who, although opposed to the gang violence, they also did not want to see the youth engaged in gangs become student body presidents, homecoming queens, etc. I received open opposition. I was called "Malcolm X." (Curiously, I didn't realize it was intended as an insult. At the time, I thought I was being complimented.) My work was considered "radical" and threatening, even though I thought I was doing the "right thing."

As a by-product of the ongoing discussions between members of the rival gangs, the respective leaders indicated that they were willing to "drop their colors." Mexican American students were swept up and excited about the potential for peace within their community. The optimism in perceiving hopeful possibilities for their future, however, was undercut by the "vocal and reputable" members of the larger community who held adverse feelings about "Latinos Unidos." I was instructed to shut down the movement. I was heartbroken and angry. I wanted to walk away from my job and, out of frustration, choose instead to consult with two mentors, Rick Melgoza, a counselor from a nearby district, and Paul Ramirez, an EOP Counselor for University of California, Davis at the time. Their words of wisdom gave me the strength to stay and to do whatever good I could, even though the forces of power and privilege in this community were working against me. What I came to understand was that the high visibility and power of "Latinos Unidos" was a threat to the existing power structure, and I'd have to find another way to end the violence.

Bruised but still functioning, I went about my work as a school counselor. One day, I walked into Jerry's office to consult with him about a student matter, and there at the bottom of his computer monitor, facing every individual who sat in his office, was a button. The button read, "Latinos Unidos." Now I knew why the students in his case load, *all* the students including those who were Mexican American, never requested to be switched to another counselor. And, despite language, cultural, socioeconomic differences, the Mexican American students assigned to Jerry choose to stay with him. The button he proudly displayed, so simple an act, spoke volumes. It was his quiet act of defiance that demonstrated his alliance with a marginalized community. His success in working with the youth from this community was motivated by his own movement in supporting their hopes and dreams.

First Client, First Impact

Contributed by Amanda Mangurten, M.S.

As I took my first steps toward the small office that would serve as my counseling space for my first semester of field study, my heart began to race. I was leading my first client into our first session. Jessica (a pseudonym), a freshman, followed me obediently. She had been referred by her eighth-grade counselor regarding a "deeply personal problem" she had reported to him the previous year. "Deeply personal" was vague enough to terrify me. The range of experiences that could be described as "deeply personal" floated through my mind. Would I hear of violence experienced or witnessed as a child that, half-remembered, left her waking, shaking, every night from recurring nightmares? Or did she have a crush on a boy or a girl and didn't know how to approach them? Or would she tell me anything at all?

Who was I to assume that she would even care to share with me? Me, a young, educated, white, native English-speaking, middle-class woman, who had been placed at this extremely diverse school in a poverty- and violence-ridden area of South Sacramento for my first unsupervised counseling experience. Gender was one of the few demographics Jessica, a working class, second-generation, bilingual Latina high-school student, and I shared. Would she be willing to reach through the cloud of power and privilege that separated us and share her concerns?

She was willing. In our first session, we talked a little bit about what counseling is, about confidentiality, and about what we would be doing in our time together. I offered that I knew why she had been referred, and asked if she would like to share her concern with me now or at another time. "Next time," she declared carefully, waiting for approval. I acknowledged her decision, and asked what she would like to share with me in the time we had this session. I learned that Jessica loves to cook, enjoys school, and has a supportive family. I ended our first meeting by asking if she had any questions for me.

A week later, I called for Jessica again, still nervous about what I would learn about her. After making some "small talk" about her week and how school was going, I returned to the referring concern. Jessica was willing to share with me this time. Carefully maintaining composure, she recounted in great detail how her white, male P.E. teacher had groped her after class when she attended seventh grade at a school district in Los Angeles County before moving to Sacramento, and how her report of the incident had gone unheeded at the school. After what she had said settled in, I let her know how angry I was that this had happened to her. Frankly, I was livid. As I sit here now writing this, my face turns red. How damaging such an event could be to a young woman of Color, already facing an uphill battle in society as it is and how unjust it was that her school further marginalized her by brushing aside her accusation left me with a deep disquiet.

After disclosing to Jessica that this would be one of the times that I would have to break confidentiality—which she fully understood—I proceeded straight to my supervisor. I knew considerable time and distance stood between her report and the event, but I also knew that there must be something to be done. My supervisor, herself a middle-class, white woman, agreed, and together we negotiated the system in order to bring Jessica's report to whom it needed to go. Our first audience was with two male sheriff's officers assigned to our district, one of whom dismissed Jessica as a fabricator. Neither my supervisor nor I were satisfied with this, and we further pursued the issue. After many phone calls, the other school district and the Los Angeles County Sheriff's department were contacted, and Jessica's report finally made it to sensitive ears and caring hearts. She continued to see me for counseling during my semester there, as well as receiving additional support from a licensed therapist who visited the school from a local agency.

I left my internship knowing that I had made a difference in the life of this beautiful young woman, and that if both of us hadn't the courage to reach across the gap that divided us, she would never have received the validation and support that she so clearly deserved.

A Principal Shapes his Community

In 2003, I was honored by my hometown as a Graduate of Distinction. A few years later, I got to share a ride in a convertible with another recipient of this honor, Bill Bristow, in the annual homecoming parade. I had known Bill since I was a child. He had been principal of the middle school I attended. He eventually became superintendent of our school district and then the junior high that my daughter attended was named after him.

It was a beautiful autumn evening. Crisp air, elongating shadows, and a highly spirited crowd along the parade route framed this event. As we slowly wound our way through the streets of our home town, waving at the crowds, Bill took the occasion to tell me a story. He shared an incident that occurred during his earliest appointment as a school principal in a nearby, smaller school district. The incident he shared had occurred when I was still a child.

Bill told me how he spent some time with a man who was considering moving his family to this community. The man had asked Bill to walk him around the campus and tell him about the community. As they were walking the hallways and the playground, the demographics of the community were evident. In the faces of the children, there was a strong presence of Mexican Americans. This man, a white man, told Bill, who is also white, that "these children" brought down the quality of the community. Bill disagreed with this man and told him so. He also told this man that it was people like him that brought down the quality of the community and that it was best that he not move his family to Bill's town.

I am sure this had happened some 30 years or more before that shared ride in a homecoming parade. I knew that Bill, himself, was son of migrant farm workers; survivors of the Oklahoma Dust Bowl and that he had worked alongside Mexican Americans in the field as a child. What I didn't know is that he had unceremoniously taken on these encounters to create a community in which a child, like myself, was valued and respected.

The parade route ended after we passed in front of the football stands and were announced to a cheering crowd. At the end of the route, he helped me get out of the convertible, I recommended some natural healing remedies for his cancer, we gave parting words, and he disappeared into the darkening far reaches of the stadium. I never saw Bill again. He passed away a few years later. Many people valued and respected Bill. They came to his funeral that was standing room only. Many of them were Mexican American reciprocating Bill's humanist care.

Spiritual Leader Moves the Circle

There was an overlap of several years in which I worked as adjunct faculty at the tribal college and had started my tenure track faculty position at California State University, Sacramento. During this period, I had the opportunity to set up cross-cultural experiences for students in my multicultural counseling courses to meet the students from the tribal college. In one cultural encounter, I had arranged for the presence of our community's spiritual leader, Angelbertha Cobb. A descendent of the Mexica tribe, Mama Cobb, as we affectionately call her, was one of the main individuals who have taught the dances and traditions of her tribe to many of us who would, otherwise, not have a direct connection.

In preparing my students from the university to meet with the students from the tribal college, I had to demonstrate the proper way of greeting Mama Cobb in the manner accorded to someone of her stature. There were well over 40 students from the university arranging to meet with approximately 50 students from the tribal college. The logistics were arranged to use the large ceremonial hall where ceremonies and pow-wows were held and directions disseminated to ensure that everyone from the university arrived safely and on time. One of my university students was hearing impaired and engaged in class discussions with the assistance of a transcriber who typed everything said in class for the student to read. In ensuring that this student would be able to participate in what I anticipated to be a rather large circle with so many people attending this one gathering, I advised the transcriber to bring an extension cord so she could sit, in the circle, with access to the electrical outlets from the nearest wall.

The day of the gathering, all arrived on time. My university students gathered outside the hall and awaited word to enter the hall, where they would ceremoniously enter and meet Mama Cobb and then individually greet every student from the tribal college who were already awaiting them in the circle. At the moment in which the students were to begin their entry, the transcriber notified me that she had forgotten to bring an electric cord. I was mortified. I had 90 people waiting for my cue, and the building in which I might be able to find a chord was a 10-minute walk. As the facilitator of the gathering, I felt that I could not leave and detain everyone while in search of a chord. I told the transcriber to do the best she could.

The entry began. My university students greeted Mama Cobb as they were instructed, as well as greeting my students from the tribal college. We started a dialogue session in which students from both campuses could come to know one another and engage in a process of true "discovery." A few minutes into the dialogue, however, Mama Cobb stopped our discussion, turned to me, and said, "Why are those two women sitting outside the circle?" Certainly, there was my student and the transcriber, sitting close to the nearest wall with an outlet, but outside the circle. I felt horrible. This was totally out of our cultural norms. It was exclusionary. I meekly replied to Mama Cobb, "We did not secure an extension cord, and she needs to have access to an electrical outlet." At that moment, Mama Cobb turned to everyone in the circle and said, "Everybody, pick up your chairs and we will shift the circle toward the wall." And, that is what we did. It took all of 30 seconds to shift the circle. No one was put out and, in the end, everyone was in the circle. I suppose that is why Mama Cobb is called a "Spiritual Leader."

The Abled Unlearn Ablism

It was the mid 1980s in New Jersey. Dr. Barbara Metelsky was director of a nonprofit organization that provided services to people with developmental disabilities. New Jersey was in the process of deinstitutionalization, which meant moving people with developmental disabilities from state institutions to live in community settings such as group homes and other supportive living settings. Nonprofit agencies from across the state that served people with developmental disabilities and their families recognized the need to share best practices and, more importantly, to advocate for quality services. Dr. Metelsky joined the board of directors of this organization.

The New Jersey Division of Mental Retardation (DMR) deinstitutionalization process required the development of individual service plans for each person who was moving out of the institution to a new life in the community. Teams of professionals led by a DMR caseworker were charged with developing these plans. Some of these professionals had provided services to the individual in the institution, while others had little to no contact with the person. These professionals were making critical life decisions about the future of the people being deinstitutionalized by deciding their living arrangements, the type of work or day program the individual should attend, what other services the person needed, and where the person should live. Essentially, a bunch of strangers sat in a room and made major life decisions for people they didn't know, while the person with the disability and his loved ones had little or no input into the decision making. They were objectified.

Some of these professionals believed it was wrong to not include the people most affected by deinstitutionalization and not allow them to have a voice in their own major life decisions, such as where they wanted to live, what supports they needed to transition successfully to life outside an institution, and what training they needed to live as independently as possible. This contingency of professionals worked with the population experiencing deinstitutionalization and their families to advocate on their own behalf to affect a change in public policy. Their goal was to have a new process by which the people being deinstitutionalized and their families could participate in the team in developing their transition plans.

Dr. Metelsky chaired a committee of this association that researched how transitions were handled in other states, obtained input from individuals and their families about how they wanted to be included in the process, and developed recommendations for how New Jersey could change its policy to give individuals and their families a voice and an opportunity for decision making. This contingency, the individuals and their families, and member organizations collaborated to advocate for the policy change and were successful! The policy was changed. Future work involved not only implementing the policy, but also ensuring that the process was truly collaborative and simply not given lip service. While the goal was to deinstitutionalize people with disabilities, it was those with the most abilities who learned a valuable lesson to be mindful in remembering to humanize those they are charged with serving and include them as subjects in their lives.

Strength in the Face of Hostility

North Carolina State University maintains a full-time diversity director whose purpose is to create an inclusive environment in the College of Natural Resources. The director, Dr. Thomas Easley, has promoted a number of initiatives that reached out and targeted a range of populations, including women, African Americans, Asian Pacific Islanders, Native Americans, Latinos, and people with different abilities. His intentions are always to broaden the diversity of the College of Natural Resources and to not only attract a diverse student population, but also to provide a safety net and supportive environment in which students from all walks of life can endeavor to secure a degree from his college. After graduation they enter the pipeline into a range of careers that include forestry, environmental science, paper science, recreation, and tourism, to name a few. These initial events were widely accepted and attended in the college, as well as the university. Director Easley enjoyed wide success and drew full support for these events at all levels but had a different experience when he extended his advocacy efforts on behalf of a population that he had not reached out to before: the gay, lesbian, bisexual, transgender, queer and intersex (GLBTQI) community. In his effort to reach out to this community, Dr. Easley endeavored to host a panel of students identified from this community so a dialogue could begin on how to make the environment in their college more welcoming. The hope was that this venue would educate members from the college community to the particular needs of this population so they could meet their overall goal of promotion and retention of a diverse student body without their students having to do so in a hostile environment.

A poster was made to publicize the event and was posted on a Thursday. The next day, the poster was torn down. For the next two weeks, the tone of the college changed. All the way from the dean's office to the hallways, the tension could be felt. The general question was, "Why are *we* being involved in anything like this?" The poster went back up on Friday, and this time was tied up so no one could tear it down. On Monday afternoon, the poster was cut down. Dr. Easley put it right back up. On Tuesday, the poster was gone. Another was made and posted again. People were quiet in the hallways, but Dr. Easley started receiving e-mails while others popped in to his office and expressed their entitlement. They felt it was wrong to be holding the panel and that God would not honor this outreach effort.

The following Tuesday, it got even uglier. A flurry of e-mails, phone calls and traffic to Dr. Easley's office pummeled this director with accusations of "not being a good Christian." His sexuality was questioned for having advocated on behalf of this community. It was intonated that his job status and reputation would be ruined as a result. On Wednesday, the day of the event, the heat turned up and Dr. Easley had people in his face as they continued to challenge him on what they perceived to be a slight on the reputation of the college. Walking down the hallways, Dr. Easley was ignored by students and colleagues alike. People he had had lunch with just the week before now gave him the cold shoulder.

The event, despite all the challenges, was attended by members of the university community but only a handful from the college itself. Afterward, Dr. Easley made two calls. One was to the provost who told Dr. Easley, "Because people are acting this way; this is a sign that what you are doing is right." This was validation that he was on the right track. His next call was to his mother, who was an ardent civil rights activist and freedom fighter even now. She told him, "You don't deserve to be treated like that, but now you know a little bit of how people from this community feel. They have to live it every day. Now you don't have to provide any anecdotal stories about how bad people can be, and now you know what it is like to feel ostracized and isolated. You need to keep doing what you're doing." Her statement made Dr. Easley stronger.

People continued to express themselves to Dr. Easley belligerently. The strength derived from his mother's statement provided the empowerment to stand up and fight back. Dr. Easley did not allow himself to be yelled at and victimized by the homophobia. He encouraged those who challenged him for his advocacy to revisit their beliefs and understanding of Jesus, whose life Dr. Easley, as a deacon, had studied extensively. This was in October 2006. Since then,

Dr. Easley has held this panel every year, as well as teaching about this issue in his classes. The event, "Everyone Welcome Here," has become a regular occurrence within the annual programming. Dr. Easley and his assistant have participated in Project SAFE training that promotes the role of allies for the GLBTQI community. The sticker outside his office and that of his assistant clearly states their alliance with this community and that members of this community are safe with them. Overt resistance is now minimal. Dr. Easley engaged the new dean who not only understood the role of allies, but also volunteered to send out all publicity regarding the event for this population directly from his office. Dr. Easley expanded the circle of allies for this community, pulled from the strength of his elders, and is no longer walking alone in his path to create an inclusive environment.

Stories from Recreation Program Planning Course

Contributed by Annette Moore, North Carolina State University
Dept. of Parks, Recreation & Tourism Management
Annette_Moore@ncsu.edu

"Ms. Moore, if we weren't here, this agency would have hired people to do what we did. If you're going to have students volunteer to run events in the community, have them run programs that wouldn't otherwise be offered."

I teach a recreation program planning course to undergraduates at a state university. Often, my students are the ones teaching me. I had required my class to assist with the planning and delivery of a special event run by our local public recreation department. It seemed like a great way to give students a deeper understanding of course material by engaging in practical experience. While it did serve the purpose of having students learn by doing, the more profound lesson was that students recognize the value of providing services to groups that are traditionally underserved. As students serve populations that are unfamiliar to them, they have the potential to learn lessons that extend beyond course material.

Having learned this lesson from my students, I regularly have a group of my service-learning students partnered with a learning center located in a public housing community. In addition to tutoring one afternoon a week, students plan and deliver two recreation programs for the youth at the center. When one student began the service partnership, he verbalized and demonstrated by his demeanor that he did not see the value of having to work at the learning center, particularly because he intended to be a professional in the golf industry upon graduation. He disengaged himself from his group and from the youth at the center. Through his group's first program, however, his attitude changed. As a closing activity to their field day event, two students in the group sat with a cluster of middle and high school students to debrief the event. In the course of their conversation, the youth were asked what they aspired to be. My student was shocked to learn he was sitting with future doctors, lawyers, teachers and business professionals. Their aspirations coincided with his high school buddies' career goals. It struck him, however, that the youth in this public housing community will have to work harder to realize these same dreams. After that revelation, my reluctant student became the group leader, championing the group's efforts to provide quality service to the youth. Another student who had partnered there a different semester summarized his learning, saying, "I was brought up believing that in America, anyone who works hard enough can pull himself up by the bootstraps, and succeed in life. After working at the learning center this semester, I realized it's not these kids' faults that they are poor and live in public housing."

Service-learning is a powerful vehicle for learning course material by applying it in the community. When the service is provided to people who might not otherwise receive these recreation opportunities, students have the potential to learn profound life lessons that equip them for their futures as recreation professionals and as caring citizens in our communities.

High School Teacher Educates Counselor

Contributed by Kandy Aldana, Liberty High School

"No blue, little sis. No blue." Those were the words my student, Gloria (pseudonym) grew up hearing almost daily. Her entire family wore RED, only red, signifying their gang allegiance as Norteños for life. Gloria, however, developed a different plan for herself as she got older. When she reached 9th grade, she was inspired by an amazing Spanish teacher who did not tolerate her disrespectful attitude, held her accountable for her actions, and pushed her towards excellence. The fact that he cared so much, made her start to care for the first time. Once she started to succeed, she never looked back.

By the time Gloria was a Senior in my English class, she was earning good grades, going to all of her classes, actively involved in clubs and holding leadership positions. She was working as a Teacher-Intern, teaching a beginning Spanish class 4 mornings each week at our high school. I observed her teaching and was very impressed!

A few months into her Senior year, Gloria came to me in tears, mascara running down her cheeks, confusion and sadness clouding her beautiful green eyes. When I asked her what was wrong, she explained. "Ms. Aldana, my counselor just told me I should not apply to Saint Mary's College, that I should just go to a community college. My counselor told me I shouldn't bother applying to any 4-year colleges." My response was, "Oh, really? She said that to you?" I managed to calm myself down internally in order to assuage Gloria's fears. I was shocked and enraged by this insult to my student. Inside, my blood was boiling. What counselor *discourages* a student from applying to college? And, why? Was it because her family claimed "red"? Was it because she was a Mexican female? I needed to find out and set this counselor straight.

I explained to Gloria about the "High Potential" program that Saint Mary's College offers to students whose grades or test scores don't reveal their true potential. It is a competitive process to be accepted into the program, but I knew without a doubt that Gloria would be accepted. She was a brilliant, natural leader, pulling herself through high school despite extreme pressure to continue the family gang legacy. Gloria was strong, intelligent, passionate, and teachable. I was determined to write letters of recommendation and make phone calls, even go to the college and meet with the director in person in order to get the college to give her a chance.

I discussed the options Gloria had with her, my confidence in her flowed, and I convinced her that she should still apply. Then, I went to speak to Gloria's counselor, not only to advocate on Gloria's behalf, but also to educate this counselor on the many options Gloria had. If there was a D on Gloria's transcript, she could go to night school to get it replaced with a higher grade. The counselor was taken aback, but also humbled by what she learned that day. She was unaware of the "High Potential Program." It is my hope that she will never tell another student not to apply to a 4 year college. Where there's a will, there's a way. There are always options.

At the time this story was originally written Gloria was a sophomore at Saint Mary's College, earning over a 3.5 grade point average. All of her tuition and expenses were paid in full through a combination of grants and scholarships (totaling over $50,000 per year). Clearly, the college saw that Gloria's potential was worth a large investment as she just graduated with her Bachelor's Degree! I just wish her counselor would have seen that potential, too.

Drama Teacher Reclaims the Stage

Extracted from Interview with Courtenay Tessler

At the end of that year in which the Youth In Focus group was enacting strategies to change the racialized school culture, the drama teacher, Gwyneth Bruch, approached Courtenay while they were in a meeting and said, "We never get any minorities to be in our plays. Why is that?" An Asian student had approached Mrs. Bruch and said, "That's because we are told that we can't apply to be in a play." Mrs. Bruch said, "What? I don't say that." Gwyn was perplexed. This drama teacher has an advisory board for her drama department and, at the time, it consisted of all white students. One of these advisory board students had conveyed to the Asian student, "When we have a play, certainly you wouldn't expect to be the lead role, right? It would have to be a white girl." Apparently, the students on the advisory board were telling the black students, the Chicano/Latino students, the Asian students, "You wouldn't apply because these are white roles." Courtenay explained that the drama teacher knew nothing about this and she was devastated. And, rather than allow the exclusionary practices persist, she was inspired to write a play with another teacher, Mr. Lee, and a range of students from the campus community. They wrote the musical that was dynamite and incredible. It was simply, a day at Davis High School. In the musical you saw all the little groups (cliques) and what was going on between them and at the end of it they danced together and they started befriending one another. There were beautiful songs and then they did another thing, "Songs of Ourselves." Each group brought in something from their culture. It was usually a song, a dance or a fairy tale. They put together this program and then when it was done, the next year, some of the girls said, "Well, now that we've let them do this now we can get back to what we do which is the white plays." Gwyn stood her ground and said, "I don't think you understand. This is the way we are going to do it from now on. There is no more white plays." So that ended that. It takes a lot of people to step up and make change and Gwyn did it on the stage for all to see.

Landed in an Unexpected Land, but Found a Way to Thrive

Contributed by Dr. EunMi Cho
EunMiCho@csus.edu
Professor, CSU, Sacramento; Coordinator of the One Mind Group

"I felt a spring shower fall all over my body and now I feel better!"
"I think I can handle it!"

A young mother looked relieved from the fear and pain she had carried to the mother's monthly gathering. It was a beautiful Saturday morning in March at a restaurant in Vacaville,

California, where a group of Korean-speaking mothers gathered together for their time away to provide some much-needed healing for their souls. The bright lights of the fine spring morning and the special connection between these mothers blended into a cohesive unit to empower this young mother in her journey with a recently diagnosed son with autism.

The Korean-speaking mothers share two commonalities. They immigrated to the United States and also raise children with disabilities in this new country. After the major upheaval of moving to this country, the mothers had to take another move. This second move made them feel reluctantly pushed to relocate into an unknown land. It was as if they woke up one day and found themselves in an unfamiliar land that required its citizens to take a specially designed obstacle course to navigate.

This second move is the land for parents of children with disabilities. While trying to find their way amidst fear and uneasiness, the parents learned that there are some necessary steps to make themselves feel comfortable in this new land of disabilities. Initially, they experience denial that they have become citizens of this land. The internal struggle continues. However, the level of their struggles lightens as they begin receiving guidance and support from other mothers who have become more acclimated. As time passes, they become more comfortable raising their children with disabilities and gain new insights regarding life in the new land. They also learn to acknowledge and appreciate their children's uniqueness. The children's accomplishments, however imperfect, become sources of true joy for the mothers.

During a brunch gathering, another mom with a 26-year-old son with autism encouraged the young mother to hold a color-coded rope tight while explaining the meaning of each different colored knob of the rope. Each knob represents the different stages of the child's life. The red knob may represent an emergency trip to a hospital due to a seizure. The yellow knob may signify the importance of taking family trips to recuperate everyone's physical and emotional strengths. The green knob may represent the triumphant moments of a child with disabilities with even the smallest accomplishment. More colors would continually be added to the rope with each learning experience until they would leave the land or continue to live there in comfort.

The brunch gathering of mothers is one of several activities organized by the One Mind Group which is a support group for Korean-speaking parents of children with disabilities in northern California. Through these gatherings, the mothers convert their sorrows and frustration into a source of rejuvenation and understanding. They also develop assertive attitudes to obtain appropriate special education and related services for their children with disabilities.

Parenting a child with a developmental disability, like autism, is an ongoing and exhausting endeavor. This is especially true for mothers, since they are more involved with the child's care-giving and education. Coping with their extremely high stress levels starts with the acceptance of the fact that their child has a disability and raising him or her with unconditional love, patience, passion, and proper advocacy skills which are not easy. This process requires parents to continually take steps in an invisible and unpredictable direction. It was found that mothers of children with disabilities experience more stress than mothers of typically developing children. These mothers tend to cope with the difficulties in a variety of methods, both positive and negative, by seeking social support, escaping, avoiding, or by positively reappraising the situation more frequently than mothers of typically developing children (Vidyasagar & Koshy, 2010).

The mothers came to a new land, unsure and often lost, but they either found a way out from the land or continue to live there by supporting each other. Their time away to soothe both their wounded minds and souls is an opportunity to regain their strength and convictions.

Vidyasagar, N. & Koshy, S. (July, 2010). Stress and coping in mothers of autistic children, *Journal of the Indian Academy of Applied Psychology, 36* (2), 245–248.

"Never seek validation from the oppressor"—Parham

Contributed by Dr. Dana Harley, MSW, LISW-S Ph.D. Candidate

As I reflect on navigating the often turbulent waters of my doctoral voyage, I am reminded of two incidents that affirmed my minority status at a predominately white university. As a second year doctoral student, I was eager to engage in various activities offered by my academic department and the university. One such activity involved an informal meeting with an employee (white male) of my particular academic department. A fellow colleague contacted me and requested that I join her at this meeting, as she was the only student scheduled to attend. I agreed to participate in the meeting to support my colleague, but was regretful for accepting the invitation soon after our discourse began. The first half of the meeting was spent discussing our research interests, experiences in the doctoral program and our recent accomplishments. The departmental employee seemed rather disinterested in the discussion and proceeded to his "agenda" for the remainder of the meeting. Apparently, he wanted my colleague (also an African American woman) and I to understand that we were indeed minorities, and this status might negatively impact our futures in academia. The departmental employee went on to discuss the "problem" with minority faculty based on his perceptions and experiences. The knockout punch came when he stated, "minorities can't expect the bar to be lowered." After his comment, no rebuttal was necessary or offered by myself or my colleague.

Following the meeting, my colleague and I waited for the elevator silently. Our unspoken hurt was evident; all I could manage to utter was, "wow." My late grandmother's words of wisdom comforted me as I thought to myself, "You have to work twice as hard, to get half as far." Ironically, I was somewhat relieved that the departmental employee revealed his feelings of bigotry and prejudice openly. No longer would I have to assume that diversity was appreciated by this individual. As I grappled with the reality that I had been insulted and berated, I knew that I had something to prove, not to him, but to myself. Perhaps my minority status in society prepared me for such a moment as this; encountering daily racial microaggressions have helped me to "never seek validation from the oppressor."

On another note, I recall an incident that I am still trying to gauge. It was shortly after administering a midterm exam that I made my way to the university's testing center to submit my scantron forms for grading. The white gentleman behind the desk politely looked up and asked, "what do you need done today?" I simply replied, "I need to submit these scantrons for grading." Without looking up the gentleman began typing on his keyboard and said, "Let's see how he wants these graded." It was apparent that the gentleman assumed that I was submitting scantrons on behalf of a male faculty member or instructor. He proceeded to ask for the name of the instructor. I gave him my last name. The gentleman replied, "I don't have him on file. Has he submitted scantrons before?" I then explained that I was the person being referred to as "he" and I probably was not in the system as this was my first time submitting scantrons. His response was, "Oh, I didn't know they were yours." This experience was unique. I wondered about his assumptions that led him to conclude that I was not the course instructor. Was it my race, gender, or age? Maybe it was my brown skin, or womanly features. I would like to think it was my strikingly youthful appearance.

Grappling with the Unpleasant: Critical Consciousness, Racial Identity, and the Discovery of Humanist Role Models

Dr. Diane Carlson

Folsom Lake College

I teach several racial and ethnic inequality courses each semester in a community college region that is largely middle class (or wealthier), largely segregated, and largely white. Identifying as white and middle-class myself, I feel a great deal of responsibility in this setting to use my power and privilege to facilitate understanding of personal and structural transformation in whatever way possible. However, no matter how much I work for our class time to be "dialogical" (Freire, 1974) and collaborative, becoming a humanist (Borunda, 2011) and an ally often require relearning or even unlearning preconceived ideas. My power to shape this process is significant and cannot be taken lightly. I am reminded each semester how little many students know about the experiences of various peoples in the United States because they are so culturally encapsulated, and *they don't know that they don't know.*

Much of the curricular work I do at the beginning of each semester involves encouraging students to reconsider what they *think* they know. This is not easily done as they have spent their lifetimes being engulfed by stereotype narratives and seeing them reinforced in the media. They have spent their lifetimes living segregated lives and so have no format in which to challenge these stereotypes and ideas. They have had no access to white anti-racist role models, and they have no idea how institutional inequality privileges them in any way. Their worldview at this point parallels Helms' (1995) Contact stage of racial identity development in which many students have a minimal understanding of racism and tend to think of themselves as "colorblind." I only have one semester. It has taken me decades of praxis—action, learning, and reflection—to develop and become confident in my own anti-racist identity. How much can I possibly do for my students in one semester? As daunting as it may seem sometimes and as personally exhausting a process as it can be through the course, I have to remind myself that measuring "how much" is not nearly as important as having the power to open a door or light a way.

One of the ways I use my power to *empower* and open up dialogue is to give "permission" for students to be uncomfortable with the material. When I first started teaching the course, I discovered that students did not know it was "okay" to be uncomfortable and ask questions—just as they would in another course in which material was new to them. The norms they brought told them that talking about racism is scary and that it is best not to talk about it so as not to be misunderstood. Students still bring these norms and prior knowledge with them, but when I tell them that these thoughts are common and understandable—we all start where we are—many more feel some relief that we may be able to create a classroom space that is safe enough to ask hard questions and have difficult conversations. I now have a small but consistent stream of students that come to me toward the middle of every semester with relieved smiles on their faces and who tell me in one way or another, "You're right, I hate your class!" Some students are by this point in the prickly spot of Helms' Disintegration stage—conflicting feelings of recognizing that racism exists, perhaps coupled with some guilt, but not recognizing personal biases or privileges.

Of course, I still have students who feel there is "blame" of whites in our discussion of racism and privilege and may have even passed into the Reintegration stage—regressing into an "easier" place to avoid issues of racism and expressing fear and anger toward folks of color. However, based on our class dialogues and the many assessments throughout the course, many more students now open themselves up to working through and *with* what feels uncomfortable, moving themselves into anti-racist identities and abandoning beliefs in white superiority. I do see students move into Pseudo-Independence, recognizing their privilege even if they are not sure what to do about it. Their learning happens *because* they grapple with the unpleasant.

Until recently, I considered that, because the course involved talking about racism, students would get to practice working through their discomfort and would slog through their own issues at their own rate and we would get through it. Other students are often part of this process and play a particularly significant role in offering alternative models for how to respond to fears and uneasiness. I never know who will enter my class and play that role, but without fail I have had at least one student, and sometimes many, every semester who offers some counterpoint and alternative ways of responding that are more powerful than what I can suggest as an instructor. Often it is a response like, "Wow! I didn't realize I had that kind of privilege! What do I do now that I know?" that presents an alternative model to defensiveness or guilt and may open doors to other conversations. Students themselves become the anti-racist models for their peers as their Freirian critical consciousness (*conscientizacao*) awakens.

I had initially opted out of addressing racial identity development in the curriculum of the course. There is so much material to cover in a semester that I chose to focus more on the institutional inequality aspects of racism, such as justice system sentencing and residential and educational segregation, and less on the social psychological aspects related to identity development. However, racial identity development is nevertheless happening. Students are coming in contact with their core beliefs, their own contexts that have influenced who they are, impacting their development of self, and they are bumping up against their racial identity even if they have no language to describe it. When we are addressing their fears and discomfort in the class, we are often actually talking about their racial identity. This epiphany compelled me to bring this discussion overtly into our course. Previously we had no language to talk about what is happening as students are believing what they believe, feeling what they feel. Providing a framework, a context of language, that would enable them to see themselves as part of a process and would offer words for that process could actually help them see where they could go, especially if they want to work toward becoming humanists and allies.

An important part of seeing what is possible and moving to the active, anti-racist identities of Immersion and Autonomy is also discovering those humanist models out there in the world and what it *means* to be an ally. I ask my students to name some white Civil Rights activists. Silence. I ask them to name *one* white Civil Rights activist. Silence. How does a white person, maybe one of my white students, adopt an alternative, anti-racist identity when we have no idea that such people exist? What might the work of Virginia Durr and Tim Wise and Morris Dees and Anne Braden and Howard Zinn and Peggy McIntosh tell us about what is possible? Encouraging this exploration and offering space to do so in this course is another step in working through the unpleasant. Perhaps, then, after all that we will be able to move on to working through the dreadful.

Borunda, R. (2011). *What Color is Your Heart? A Humanist Approach to Diversity.* Dubuque, IA: Kendall Hunt.

Freire, P. (1974). *Pedagogy of the Oppressed.* New York: Seabury.

Helms, J. (1995). An update of Helms's White and People of Color racial identity models. In J. G. Ponterotto, J.M. Casas, L.A. Suzuki, & C.M. Alexander (Eds.), *Handbook of multicultural counseling* (pp. 181–198). Thousand Oaks, CA: Sage.

"It's Never Too Late to Advocate"

Elisabeth E. Liles, Ph.D.
Associate Professor
California State University, Sacramento

Historically, there has been a disproportionate number of students of color in special education programs. Unfortunately, this phenomenon still occurs, despite efforts to more accurately identify students who qualify for these services. It is not uncommon for a student to be placed in special education when there is not an actual learning disability but, rather, a language barrier. Knowing this, many educators have taken native language into consideration when identifying students for special education. As a high school counselor, I experienced an unusual circumstance in which language became a different type of barrier—a barrier to actually receiving services.

I first met Jocelyn (pseudonym) during her sophomore year in high school. At the time, we offered a lower-level math class that divided the content of Algebra 1-2 into two separate years. Jocelyn had barely passed the first year of the sequence, and she was now enrolled in the second year. As a new counselor, I was meeting with all of the students on my caseload in order to introduce myself to them and to address any concerns. When I met with Jocelyn, she disclosed that she was struggling with math and had struggled since elementary school.

My first instinct was to check Jocelyn's file to determine if she had ever been tested for a learning disability. I found that she had not. Instead, she had been repeatedly tested for language services. Jocelyn was Filipino, yet she did not speak Tagalog. English was her first language and the language spoken in the home. However, educators for the past ten years had all assumed her difficulties were due to a language barrier. Perhaps they were so afraid of mislabeling Jocelyn's difficulty as a learning problem due to her ethnicity that they, indeed, did mislabel her difficulty *based on* her ethnicity.

The school where I was working had recently adopted the Response to Intervention (RTI) model, so I initiated a team meeting to address Jocelyn's math struggles. At the meeting, we met with her father, who reiterated that English was Jocelyn's first language. It became clear that Jocelyn's father came from a culture of trusting the school system to have his child's best interests addressed. He needed someone who could advocate for his daughter since he was not aware that there were services for which she might be eligible. He and Jocelyn had both fallen victim to the fear of educators who were worried they may be viewed as prejudiced for recommending assessment for Jocelyn for special education eligibility. Their fear of acting prejudiced led them to activate the bias that all students of color experience a language barrier. In this case, individuals assumed that English was not Jocelyn's first language, which resulted in their failure to accurately assess her needs.

The RTI team immediately instituted interventions in Jocelyn's math class, including one-on-one tutoring and group study sessions during lunch. After a few weeks of measuring Jocelyn's progress, it became evident that the interventions were not making a significant impact. I advocated at this time to assess Jocelyn for a learning disability. Her father agreed, and the school psychologist arranged for testing as soon as possible. It came as no surprise that the tests revealed that Jocelyn not only had a mathematics learning disability, but it was severe. She scored almost two standard deviations below her IQ in achievement. Jocelyn immediately began receiving special education services.

To this day, I am still appalled that Jocelyn's learning disability was not identified until she was fifteen and almost through high school. She had struggled needlessly for ten years, and it took a team who was willing to address the elephant in the room to help her begin to thrive in school. I do not want to imagine what Jocelyn's future may have been if she did not begin receiving appropriate services. She has since graduated from high school and attends a community college where she continues to receive the appropriate support she needs to succeed.

This experience with Jocelyn reminded me of many things to consider when working with children. First, it is imperative that counselors view children holistically. Jocelyn was viewed from one framework until our RTI team met with her. It was only then that a team of educators considered the entire child and not just one element of her. Culture is often viewed as indicating only an individual's ethnicity. However, culture encompasses the entire person, including ability. This experience also reiterates one of the important roles that counselors have: to advocate. As a school counselor, it is essential to advocate not only *for* children but also *with* them. We must include children in the decision-making process and help inform them and their families of the services and resources that are available. Jocelyn's father had trusted educators to advocate for his child, yet he had not been included in this process until her sophomore year in high school. Only when the entire team, including Jocelyn and her father, collaborated were this child's needs met

Using the Power of Privilege to Transform and Heal in the Speech Classroom: Spitting in the Face of a Culture of Silence

Dr. Scott Kirchner

"Suddenly, as if hit by a hammer, I lost my focus and the world itself had come to a violent start. I was reminded of the old days, that feeling I'd get when so intoxicated that it felt as though I was riding in somebody else's body. Who is this ass who feels it necessary to stand in front of a group of unsuspecting folks and inform them of the horrors this world might just contain?

"You have just read the opening paragraph of a paper crafted by one my Community College Public Speaking students to reflect upon the performance he gave while delivering his informative speech. Geoffrey picked the topic of childhood sexual abuse and, as a statement of credibility, self-identified as a survivor.

As the old bearded white dude sitting in the back of the classroom, one of the privileges I am afforded is that of facilitating the learning experience of my students. The term meta-curriculum, or "incidental learning," is used to describe knowledge that may be transferred within the learning environment and that is not overtly identified within the objectives of the course. Certainly, "to experience emotional healing" is not a student learning objective identified within any community college public speaking courses that I know of; however, given the right combination of variables, it can become a "learning of incident."

According to Freire (1993), the system of dominant social relations creates a culture of silence that instills a negative, silenced, and suppressed self-image into the oppressed. The learner must develop a critical consciousness in order to recognize that this culture of silence is created to oppress. Also, a culture of silence can cause the "dominated individuals [to] lose the means by which to critically respond to the culture that is forced on them by a dominant culture." In mainstream American culture, men don't talk about having been molested as children, nor are they aware of or do they acknowledge the effect such an experience may have on their sense of self.

As a social scientist (and an old bearded white dude), my ego would have me believe that I know what is needed by my students to "become more human." The process of human construction is personal and there is "no single narrative or way of describing humanism (Borunda, 2011). My personal path to humanism is through a perpetual process of learning who I really and truly am, and embracing where I am in my becoming in any given moment. The truth is, I don't know what others need in their process because I am not "them" and I don't live in their skin. All I can do is to provide an environment that may facilitate the types of risks and support needed for transformation through the process of *praxis,* a blending of reflection and action.

Geoffrey goes on to write: "One of the byproducts of society's dirty secret is standing in front of innocent people who shouldn't be taxed by such horrible burdens. Put in short, that very byproduct is desirous of revenge and standing before them, spewing out the vitriolic truth, is enough to light some fires."Maslow's (1943) original hierarchy of needs identifies self-actualization as the highest need on his pyramid. Newer versions of the pyramid indicate transcendence as a higher level need than self-actualization. Transcendence is where the individual is moved to facilitate the self-actualization of others. Through Geoffrey's writing he indicates a desire to transcend, catalyzing the growth of others by "lighting some fires."

Geoffrey gives more: "I was one of the lucky ones. *I survived beyond my third birthday and somehow lived into my mid-twenties. I'm the luckiest bastard in the world. I'm standing in front of thirty or so people and telling them that this brief existence we live is so incredibly beautiful. Yes, that sounds cheesy because it is cheesy. I don't much care how it sounds, though. Looking back now on the speech, I'm so incredibly happy at how well I did in comparison to what I thought I had done. You see, I thought I had let my family win. Their perversions once more crawled into my mind and took from me the sovereignty I so viciously fought for. As a psychology major, though, I am being taught to question everything. So then I am curious if that was the subconscious whispers of past memories brought back to torment me or if I'm using them as a reminder to myself and maybe, if they're paying close enough attention, the people around me. A reminder that this beautiful world can be so Goddamned ugly sometimes."*

On its face, this paper is about the use of privilege by an old bearded white dude to facilitate growth in his students, but really it is about my personal healing. I, too, am a survivor of childhood sexual abuse, and old bearded white dudes just don't talk about that stuff. Geoffrey is not the only student who has dragged out this or some equally provocative topic, and each time a student touches one of my (sometimes very) personal experiences, I reciprocate in front of the class by disclosing that I, too, have had that experience. Generally, on the faces of the students I see degrees of shock; on the face of the speaker I see gratitude. The ripples in the pond expand as more students perceive "permission" to disclose. The norm of reciprocity is alive and well!

As I craft this paper using the words of my former student, now friend and colleague, I am moved to tears. I think back now to formal and informal mentors that I have had over the years and how they helped me in my process of becoming more human, and I look forward to those in the future who will be cleverly disguised as students.

"You Speak So Well for a Black Person"

Dr. Lisa William-White
California State University Sacramento

Freshly off the heels of earning my baccalaureate degree in Journalism (Public Relations), I entered a fledgling job market in the San Francisco Bay Area in 1992. California was still reeling after the 1990–91 recession, and employment prospects were limited for many, particularly for a recent college graduate who was competing with many other would-be-hopefuls seeking employment in a paltry job market. Yet, I was optimistic that things would fall into place once I relocated from my former college town.

Thus, filled with anticipation on the road to landing my first post-college job in a major cosmopolitan city, I sent out hundreds of cover letters and resumes that presented my newly conferred degree from Humboldt State University, my experiences and skills with technical and editorial writing, and my knowledge as someone with a broad-based liberal arts education.

In response to my effort, a major non-profit organization contacted me for an immediate interview. This agency sought prospective hires that possessed strong oral and written communication skills to work as administrative support for upper-level managers. Consequently, in preparation for my upcoming interview, I researched the company's history and mission. I acquired knowledge about the company's most recent projects and broader humanitarian and philanthropic efforts in the community. But, most importantly, I bubbled with enthusiasm about the prospects of working for this company, which had an outstanding reputation and boasted many opportunities for professional growth and advancement.

On the day of my interview, I arrived fifteen minutes early and was warmly greeted by the young brunette receptionist. She then picked up the phone receiver to announce that I had arrived. Shortly thereafter, a petite, stern, middle-aged Asian woman appeared and greeted me with a formal business salutation. The woman, Ms. Chan,[1] extended a firm handshake and then directed me to follow her to the small conference room where my interview was to be held.

[1] pseudonym

After a brief introduction, Ms. Chan's questions ensued: "Tell me about yourself and your educational background...? Why you are seeking employment with our company...? What knowledge do you possess about our organization's mission...? What professional experiences have you had that relates to this position...? Why do you believe that you are well-suited for employment with...?"

As I responded to each of her queries, she smiled and nodded affirmatively. Ms. Chan's eyes were affixed on me, and her non-verbal communication appeared to suggest that my answers were acceptable and appropriate for the deluge of questions. The pace, tone, and tenor of the interview hummed along pleasantly, and, as the interview evolved, Ms. Chan's formal, business disposition softened. There was even a jovial quality present in the exchange that made me feel quite comfortable.

I was in the midst of a response to a question when I suddenly heard, "Wait; stop!" The unforeseen interruption actually startled me, so much so that I instantly wondered if I had said something wrong. At that juncture, Ms. Chan then quizzically exclaimed: "I just have to ask you, where are *you* from?

"Of all the questions asked so far, this question was the most curious. *Had she not read my cover letter and resume? Had I expressed something that was inconsistent with my written qualifications or my earlier narrative?* I searched for some indicator in Ms. Chan's face to clarify the intent of her question, while trying to recount what I might have articulated that would cause her to interrupt me.

"Where am I from?" I found the question odd, but I obliged: "I am originally from Buffalo, New York; however, my family moved to the Bay Area in 1979, and we settled in East Palo Alto, California, in 1981...."

Ms. Chan suddenly became quite animated, gesticulating in a manner to signal astonishment or disbelief.

She then asserted: "The reason why I ask where you are from is, you *don't* speak like *most Black people*! You speak so *well*. My goodness! I just had to ask because you are so *articulate*."

I was speechless. I sat there not knowing how to respond or what to say next.

Not losing her momentum, she continued further: "I just have to tell you, Lisa. You have this journalism background, and you are very bright ..."

I sat, waiting for the other shoe to drop.

"Let me give you some advice, Lisa. This is *not* the job for you! You're young, well-spoken, and attractive. You know, I could really see someone like you in front of the camera on television news. Plus, you are so engaging and interesting to listen to!"

I was amazed at what I was hearing.

Ms. Chan continued further: "You know what you should do? You should apply for a job as a news reporter at a television news station. And even if you have to sweep floors for the next five years, you should do just that and work your way up to eventually get a broadcast news job because I think you'd be great on TV!

"Suddenly, Ms. Chan stood up. "It was such a pleasure meeting you, Lisa!" She extended her handshake to me at that moment and ended our interview.

At once, I felt both confusion and anger. *Did she really think that she had just paid me a compliment by telling me that I "do not speak like most Black people"? And to add insult to injury, did she really think she was doing me some favor by providing me professional advice, which began with doing physical labor for a potential hypothetical employer to work my way up to a potential hypothetical broadcast job that I was not seeking?* I was reeling. I felt heat rising up the small of my back, the type of physiological response that occurs when I am confronted with some challenge or threat that I must immediately meet. This "race-related stress" was my body's fight or flight response (Mobley, as cited in Borunda, 2011, p. 198). And by nature, I am one who fights (figuratively). But, rather than tell Ms. Chan all the thoughts that were dancing in my twenty-two-year-old brain at that very moment, I sat on them. Instead, I extended my right hand to shake hers, and with my left hand, I reached down to pick up my attaché case.

Truthfully, I wanted to explode and tell Ms. Chan all the things that polite company would not articulate. Moreover as my mind raced, I recounted all my preparation for that interview. I purchased a navy blue power suit to look "the part." I had straightened and feathered my long, Afro-textured hair to create the corporate-assimilationist look that many African Americans understood as being necessary to even be considered as a prospective hire in a largely Eurocentric corporate environment. And, I prepared myself for all the possible questions that would be asked of me. But nothing had prepared me for the outcome of this exchange.

Dazed, I walked out the conference room. I then walked past the receptionist greeting area, and toward the front exit of the building.

All the while, I could not help but ask myself: "*What in the hell had just happened to me? This was a metropolitan city in California, 1992, not Mississippi, 1952!*"

The discrimination here was so apparent. Ms. Chan violated federal equal employment opportunity laws. But most importantly, Ms. Chan's stereotypical perceptions also violated my humanity—they was peppered with the intersecting forces of linguicism and racism. Her biases reflected pejorative views that permeate American society about many ethnic and linguistic minority populations who are assumed to speak *only* nonstandard speech varieties.

Language is a chief vehicle for deploying power, whether constructively or destructively. Language is a kind of social asset...[it] is often used to benefit the privileged and disenfranchise the powerless (Diaz-Rico, 2008, p. 29).

"You speak so well for a *Black* person!" That statement played over and over in my head as I drove home, anxious to share with my family the humiliation that I had just endured.

Those words, spoken over twenty years ago, still echo through my mind, but the assault from *that* microinsult—a form of "dysconscious" racism—does not hold the sting it once did (William-White and White, 2012). In fact, I have recounted this story to my students a million times since, as I share examples of the varied ways that oppression and "microaggressions" operate in American culture from a systems perspective (Pierce, 1974; Pierce 1995; Sue et al, 2007; Sue, 2010). Ms. Chan's individual prejudice was operationalized on a systems level, as she functioned in a position of power to influence hiring practices in a company. This is a prime example of the insidious nature of prejudice.

As an educator today, I am uniquely positioned to engage my students in deep examination of, and reflection on, how we *all* have been "constructed and produced by our environments"

(William-White, Muccular, Muccular, and Brown, 2013), particularly prejudice. Being born into, or naturalized in, a country and culture whose foundation is indispensable from racialized oppression (amongst other isms) mandates that one examines how one's experiences have been shaped by such historic and systemic forces. Thus, I have been privileged to hold a position in which I am empowered to create spaces for such discourses. Overall, it is imperative that those of us who desire to work in the helping professions deconstruct our own lives in tandem with intense examination of macro and micro systems, revealing and simultaneously unlearning the unexamined biases we hold.

Mindfully Responding to Each and Every Client, Every Time

Dr. Chris Knisely

Entering the field of behavioral health is quite trying. For many, myself included, you are called upon to enter the non-profit realm with an environment that comes with high caseloads, low pay, heavy responsibility, and a training manual entitled, "Sink or Swim." These challenges are interlaced with your self-questioning ability to perform behavioral and emotional transformations, often with your biggest fans, e.g. parents and teachers, also being your biggest barriers. I, like many who enter this world start out with a mint master's degree, limited experience, a balance between being happy to have your first job in the field and the belief that you will "rescue" all your clients. Then, you encounter the harsh "reality" that you are not sound with your theory, interventions, or documentation (which is a rather large piece of the counseling pie) and the realization that your clients are not transforming to the perfect little angels that you had envisioned. This often leads to self-reflection, a.k.a., the belief that you are not a "counselor," and your best bet would be to seek out a position that requires little to no contact with "the humans."

However, if one is lucky, you will be privileged to work with a family that makes one of those miraculous transformations. What is interesting about these "treatment-successes" is that the young, aspiring clinician takes far too much credit for the change, and while that may be a concern for clinical supervisors (like myself), it also may keep clinicians from burning out. During one such episode of "counselor winning," a Latino male adolescent client, and his first generation immigrant father, and mother joined my caseload. The adolescent youth had cryptic case notes presenting him as an oppositional defiant, angry, aggressive individual, with no respect for authority, parents included, and responsibilities.

Despite the picture this vision conjures up, the primary issue, were parents who were mostly traditional in their cultural/life practices, and the son who was becoming more and more "Americanized." The "oppositional" behavior included arguing with his parents and going to meet with friends/a girlfriend without the permission of his parents. For the parents, these behaviors were overwhelming, and nothing they had experienced in their home country. However, for the youth, observing peers who processed freedoms above his childhood comprehension, he felt trapped in his parents' web of "tradition." While providing education around acculturation, both in peer-culture, and parenting styles, the family started to build a bridge of understanding of the other's perception. They were able to communicate again, without resentment, and restart a relationship with rules/boundaries, an understanding of roles, and an initial foundation of trust. Connecting with the family's commonalities, the youth was allowed to seek out employment, an endeavor that the father took great pride in, and the mother tolerated in part because the deal was the youth had to maintain a certain grade point level.

While I did not add in the complexities of the case, those inevitable pitfalls that each case places at the perfect time to humble a young clinician during their time of optimism, I can honestly say that I do not recall them. It is one of the great benefits of telling "your story," in that the false-narrative one presents is often leaning toward the thoughts, feelings and beliefs you connect to the story. The client, per a former colleague and an individual familiar with the family, would later become a doctor. I would later on attempt to recreate the magic experienced in this case with other cases, only to fall victim to the next step in my development, the need to not "cookie-cutter" my counseling, and to meet the client(s) unique challenges and perspectives with unique goals and interventions.

Looking back at this case, a case that is roughly a decade old, it was one of those rolls of the dice that young clinicians attempt, in the hopes of something sticking. The beautiful thing for this once young clinician, is that what did stick was the need to thoroughly assess each client(s) perspective on culture, and to present goals/interventions that take culture into consideration. I would impress upon those who are entering or have recently entered the field, to please consider this story as an opportunity to not have to roll the dice, and rather, to take my experience into account, and to begin immediately to support culturally appropriate counseling techniques, trainings, and consultation from individuals who share cultural insights and awareness. It is a brand of counseling that has been emphasized since my start in counseling roughly a decade ago, and yet, is still underutilized as an orientation to this day.

References

Borunda, R. (2011). *What is the color of your heart? a humanist approach to diversity.* Dubuque, IA: Kendall Hunt.

Diaz-Rico, L. T. (2008). *Strategies for teaching English learners.* (2nd ed.) Boston: Pearson Education.

Pierce, C. (1974). Psychiatric problems of the black minority. In S. Arieti, (Ed.),

In American handbook of psychiatry (pp. 512–523). New York: Basic Books.

Pierce, C. (1995). Stress analogs of racism and sexism: Terrorism, torture, and disaster.

In Charles Willie, P. Rieker, B.Kramer, & B. Brown, (Eds.), *In mental health, racism, and sexism* (pp. 277–293). Pittsburgh, PA: University of Pittsburgh Press.

Sue, D. W. (2010). *Racial microaggressions in everyday life: Race, gender, and sexual orientation.* New York: John Wiley.

Sue, D. W., Capodilupo, C. N., Torino, G. C., Bucceri, J. M., Holder, A. M. B., Nadal, K. L.,

& Esquilin, M. E. (2007). Racial microaggressions in everyday life: Implications for clinical practice. *American Psychologist, 62J,* 271–286.

William-White, L., & White, J. (2011). Color marks the site/sight of social

difference: Dysconscious racism in the "age of Obama," *Qualitative Inquiry, 17(9),* 837–853.

William-White, L., Muccular, D., Muccular, G., & Brown, A. (in press). Critical consciousness in curricular research: Stories from the field. New York: Peter Lang Publishers.

Conclusion; Micro-Level Humanism

Making the familiar strange can be difficult. The values and messages from our family, our religious upbringing, our friends, our culture, and our society become an embedded part of our reality, even without our consent. The potential for "choice of action" within this reality allows us to determine whether the values we embrace, our "habituated thoughts," are truly the values we want to live by, our "habituated behaviors." The concept of mindful wonderment provides a way of perceiving the world as though we were seeing it for the first time and viewing each and every human being who passes our way as a work of art ... and yet, as we all are; a work in progress.

The concept of "high road" responses to situations that are uncomfortable and very possibly, confrontational, may take practice. Apply the concepts of visualizing yourself as "the eagle" and position yourself above the situation. From this vantage, above the smog line you will see more clearly. Determine what can be said or done that will make a *positive* difference in shaping the world and in evolving the way we perceive one another.

Applying the concept of "making the familiar strange" came up for me as I was writing this book. I recognized the power and potency of each written word as I re-read several passages. There were sections that forced me to return to them and change my word selection. For example, in writing about the institution of slavery, I found that referring to the people who were enslaved as simply, "slaves," tended to objectify and depersonalize human beings who were subjected to extreme mistreatment and subjected to a dehumanizing practice. The use of the term "slave" affixed a term to a people as though their enslavement was a "fixed reality." It is similar to saying "white people owned slaves" verses *"some* white people owned slaves." The former generalizes a behavior to all white people. The latter specifies the behavior so as not to affix a behavior to a whole group. By saying "people who were enslaved" we can now humanize people and separate them from their condition which did not have to be permanent and static. It was easier to put a face on people when using the phrase, "people who were enslaved" rather than affixing a status to people by referring to them as merely, "slaves."

Another concept to consider is not only how we respond to situational acts of microaggressions but also the choice of words that we use every day. Word usage in the United States is wrought with terms that hold violent origins. The continued use of them in our word choice normalizes the violence without our even knowing it. The following being a short list of terms to consider, "beat the tar out of ...," "bullet statements," "shoot from the hip," "best bang for your buck," "hold your feet to the fire," "kill two birds with one stone," " fit to be tied," "whip them into shape," "bite the bullet," "kick the bucket," "bleed like a stuck pig," "black sheep," and "in the crosshairs" are just a few commonly used expressions to consider.

Word usage may be considered inconsequential to some yet it is important to note that words reflect our culture and our values. With conscious word selection derived from humanist principles, we can choose to employ words that shape a more egalitarian reality. The commitment to owning our individual responsibility in how we shape this reality means owning our subjectivity, acknowledging the power and privilege we possess, and determining how we choose to use it. Perhaps, up until this time, you have contained your sense of healthy outrage over what you see in our world today and are now willing to use your power and privilege in ways that carve out a more just world for others. If so, then perhaps you too will be inspired to be as bold as the humanists in this manuscript and reveal the true Color of Your Heart.

QUESTIONS FOR DISCUSSION OR SELF REFLECTION

SELF-AWARENESS

1. Do you have a story in which you demonstrated strength/courage in the face of hostility?

2. Consciously follow your choice of words and determine how many times you use a phrase that has violent meaning. Determine if you want to keep using the term and, if not, how can you substitute the phrase? For instance, instead of "killing two birds with one stone" use "light two candles with one match."

CLIENT WORLDVIEW

3. Ask a classmate about a time they have witnessed or been subjected to a micro aggression. Use validating and empathic responses as well as open ended questions.

COUNSELING RELATIONSHIP

4. What would a "low road" response to the same situation have looked like? What would have been other "high road" responses that could have been enacted?

COUNSELING AND ADVOCACY INTERVENTIONS

5. How do the actions of the humanists cited in the stories align with the dialogical forces of Cooperation, Unity, Organization and Cultural Synthesis?

6. From a Transformational Leader perspective, what are other ways in which you would have responded to the situation?

Activity

1. Revisit the stories in this chapter and brainstorm responses and strategies that address the various domains of MSJCC socioecological model; intrapersonal, interpersonal, institutional, community, public policy and international/global levels.

2. Watch the movie "Glory" and trace Colonel Shaw's identity development and the factors that contribute to his evolvement. Concurrently, examine the various responses and reactions of the men of the 54th Regiment as they are subjected to racism. What were "low road" and "high road" responses?

In Relation: Developing Cross Cultural Competence

Perceiving our world from the top level of the Transcendent Identity Model requires ongoing praxis. Similarly, the development of cross cultural competence from the highest realm of this Identity model is imperative so that we understand *and* respond to the needs of others in a manner that is congruent with their values and orientation. It calls for us to develop the capacity to be *in relation* within different cultural contexts. Requisite to this engagement that builds upon awareness and knowledge is development of the skills by which to engage within the cross cultural sacred space that is grounded on the tenet of unconditional positive regard. To this goal, we will expand our understanding of terms and concepts relevant to the acquisition of cross cultural competency skills.

One primary concept, "**Culture**," is defined as, "the knowledge, attitudes, and behavior associated with a group of people" (Cavanaugh and Kail, 2013, p. 8). It has also been defined as "an ambiguous concept that defies definition, can in a broad sense be thought of as "things a stranger needs to know to behave appropriately in a particular setting" (Pederson, 1988, p. viii). If we consider that our profession(s) require us to "do no harm" then we are ethically bound to provide a "culture-centered" approach that ensures that our interactions and interventions "recognize culture as central and not marginal, fundamental and not exotic" (Pederson, 2008, p. 5). For this reason, we must be aware of how our own cultural values inform our perceptions as we engage our clients' in the sacred space of counseling, teaching, and other realms in which we look to serve a range of people in our multicultural world.

Counseling, Teaching, and Engaging

In applying praxis to the developmental process of cross cultural competence from a Transcendent Identity framework, I reintroduce Dr. Anna Kato who relates in Chapter 3's section, 'White Humanist Resistance to Education as a Weapon,' a series of oppressive incidents and circumstances from early in her career. She offers the following reflection on this time in her life,

> Some of the experiences that I have had in my professional life provide me with "lessons" that teach me over time. When I taught Navajo children at Tuba City Boarding School over forty years ago one such experience in particular continues to inform my work as an educator. When my fellow white colleague asked a Diné third grader,

"When are you going to learn to tell time? Are you going to be a dumb Indian all your life?" Her questions chilled me to the bone and do, still. Racist, in essence, the questions were an utter denigration of the child's identity. At the time, I did not think of her questions as racist because concepts like racism, concepts rooted in the philosophical perspectives of multicultural education, were not part of my awareness. I characterized my colleague's questions as hurtful, disrespectful, and mean.

Now, after retiring from my full time lecturer position in Teacher Education at University of California, Davis in which I taught for 23 years, I now teach in the Counselor Education program at California State University, Sacramento, as an adjunct professor. One course I teach is entitled "Power, Privilege and Self-Identity," and the book I select for the course is this one, What is the Color of Your Heart? Recently, after a student read my story about teaching on the Navajo Reservation, she asked me what I would do now, looking back on that experience when the child was the recipient of such demeaning words. I replied that I would engage the child immediately, sit on the floor with him while we took turns moving the hands on the toy clock he held with his small fingers so that I could affirm his knowledge and nurture his spirit. I said that I wish I had known then how to listen to him tell me about the various ways he knew of telling time. And, I wonder how this boy felt. I wonder what he remembers of this moment. Lauret Savoy writes in her book, Trace (2015) "How is the past remembered and told? Who owns memory?"

From Dr. Kato's reaction to the incident it is evident that she rejects *racial cohesion*. She also names her colleague's words as weapons of *dominance and culturcide*, a term that captures the essence of cultural invasion. The mistreatment inflicted on the child related to "differences" and has the potential of planting seeds of *internalized oppression*, especially when the abuse is normalized in a system that promotes institutional racism or "ism" of any kind.

This particular incident occurred in a cross cultural context in which the child, belonging to an ethnic group that falls under the *Involuntary Immigrant* classification, was subjected to abuse that fueled the experiential reality of **historical trauma** which is defined as the "cumulative trauma…fueled by centuries of incurable diseases, massacres, forced relocation, unemployment, despair, poverty, forced removal of children to boarding schools, abuse, racism, loss of traditional lands, unscrupulous land mongering, betrayal, broken treaties-the list goes on" (Gonzalez, J. and Trimble, J., 2008, p. 93). Dr. Kato's colleague projects an orientation known as the **deficit model** which perceives anyone who is "different" as being inherently inferior. This viewpoint does not recognize the strengths and assets of people who are culturally different from her. It also neglects to acknowledge sociohistorical factors and deficiencies in the institutional realm that negatively impact humanity. Instead, the *deficit model* promotes "at risk" rather than "at promise" thinking. Subsequently, incidents such as that experienced by Dr. Kato will continue if not acted upon.

With heightened awareness and knowledge to the multiple ways in which discrimination and oppression manifest in thoughts, words, actions, and policy, the capacity to not only validate the experiential reality of people being mistreated but to intervene is enhanced. Dr. Kato lays out how this is done from a socioecological perspective when she states that she would "engage the child" and "affirm his knowledge and nurture his spirit." The domain of "Intrapersonal" is attended to when she indicates that she would respond in an age-appropriate manner to the child in an effort to mitigate the damage of the words inflicted by the teacher and to acknowledge his funds of knowledge. This validation of experience is one of the tenets of cross cultural competence and what has been previously referred to as bridge building. What is critical in cross cultural competency from a multicultural social justice framework, however, requires more of us than validating the experiential reality of people we serve. Dr. Kato expands upon this in her ongoing reflection.

> At the time I taught at the boarding school, the philosophical construct of multicultural education was not part of my awareness. When I was a student teacher in the early seventies, instructional methods of multicultural education were not among the required courses. Later, in the mid-seventies when I was a graduate student working on my Master of Science degree in counseling, and concurrently earning a second teaching credential in bilingual education, research on the relationship between identity and language were just beginning to be introduced in my classes. Faculty in the Bilingual Teaching Credential Program introduced me to Paulo Freire's work while a humanistic perspective among the faculty in the Counseling Program shaped my view on counseling.

> Currently, there are state standards that guide the training of counselors. One standard includes the requirement that students "Understand counselor and consultant characteristics and behaviors that influence helping processes, including age, gender, and ethnic differences, socioeconomic status, verbal and nonverbal behaviors, and personal characteristics, orientations and skills." Now, too, available to any counselor are resources provided through The National Association for Multicultural Education. The Association's website provides definitions of multicultural education that includes, "Multicultural education advocates the belief that students and their life histories and experiences should be placed at the center of the teaching and learning process and that pedagogy should occur in a context that is familiar to students and that addresses multiple ways of thinking. In addition, teachers and students must critically analyze oppression and power relations in their communities, society and the world."

Even though Dr. Kato recoiled to the enacted and systemic violence upon the children at the Navajo Reservation, she did not have the skills, at that time, by which to respond to the situation in a way that made the outcome or the experience any better for the children and families living under conditions that sought to strip them of their culture; **culturcide**. Dr. Kato's expanding awareness in the area of social advocacy was precipitated by what she was learning in the environments provided in her counselor and teacher preparation programs.

Cultural Confrontation in the Sacred Space

From the framework of the Transcendent Identity Model, the "Facilitators of Evolvement" points to Dr. Kato possessing an "identity that is grounded in purpose/cause" and that she is "committed to improving the world." With further training, her enhanced awareness strengthens her capacity to "Know ways in which to Activate Change and then changing one's patterns of behavior." Her inherent

Mindful Wonderment brought her to this cross cultural context early in her career but, in present day and in response to her student's question of "what would she do now" we follow Dr. Kato's journey as we revisit another "Facilitator of Evolvement".... "Education: Full Knowledge of Realities of All People."

I know, now, different from my knowledge at the beginning of my career, that concepts inherent in multicultural education can assist us to identify behaviors and concepts that are related to "isms," and to help us to identify our biases that can interfere with being effective counselors or teachers. Since my earlier experience in working at the Navajo reservation I have learned from Indigenous educator, Vincent Werito, who contributed a chapter to the book, Honoring our children: Culturally appropriate approaches for teaching indigenous students (2013). He interviewed nine Navajo people about their perspectives on schooling and identity. With respect to one Navajo woman's realizations about race he writes that she knows that race is a social construct: "...while a racial identity is not real, its consequences and outcomes can be dangerous. This is an important lesson not only for students but educators who need to be able to address these issues in their teaching and in how they interact with students." I believe that counselors, as well as teachers, must heed Werito's words.

Furthermore, reading about multicultural education in university courses and participating in subsequent class discussions are important ways to learn about who we are as diverse groups of people. However, unless we engage with others through a combination of talking and listening to one another, our knowledge about the precepts inherent in the concept, multiculturalism, may remain solely at an academic level of our understanding. Academic knowledge without personal connection may result in the objectification of one another. For example, without connecting with one another on a very human level we can continue to make statements like "they" do such and such, or "they" hold certain beliefs, or "those people" like to wear that sort of clothing. We can unwittingly define people as "the other" and we can remain culturally encapsulated but "well educated." In contrast, the lesson that I derived from my experience with Navajo children reminds me that talking with one another, and listening deeply, provides a way for us to reach out to one another, to care about one another despite differences in belief, or gender, or ethnic background, or social class, or primary language.

Upon reflection, I realize that my early work on the Navajo reservation taught me that it is essential to engage with each other with both mind and heart. The intersection of mind and heart occur when we allow ourselves to be vulnerable to one another. It is in this way we approach a state of empathy defined by Carl Rogers (1980): "He appreciates what my experience feels like to me." Genuine, open interaction with one another combined with tenets of multicultural education offer us the potential to be whole people, to live as Borunda (2013) writes, as people "in relation" with one another, people who create bridges to effective human relationships constructed of caring, hope, courage, and possibility.

Finally, the answer to the student's question of "what would you do now" comes with years of experience, training, and reflection that Dr. Kato is able to offer a thoughtful response to how she would respond at this point in her life. This is where the Transcendent Identity Development Model component of "Defying Fear when Enacting Change" becomes an active and vibrant practice as we engage the world with Mindful Wonderment. Dr. Kato addresses social justice as an essential practice of being an effective and culturally competent educator and counselor. Her further reflection on what she would have done differently now takes her beyond the Intrapersonal domain which is her intervention with the child but also to the domains of Interpersonal as she discusses confronting and educating her colleague, the institution and its' guidelines for the evaluation of teachers, and finally, the community realm in which she reaches out to the Navajo Nation.

I have learned a great deal about advocacy and about the behaviors that promote social justice since I taught at the boarding school so many years ago. Now, besides engaging with the third grader I would meet with my colleague to tell her that I was floored by her questions and that the implicit meaning in the questions told the child that he needed to "be white," to *assimilate*, to deny his identity. I would tell her that what she said to the boy had the potential to erode his self-esteem and his confidence for many years, perhaps, leaving permanent emotional and spiritual scars. I would tell her that the words she used told that child that he was "dumb" and that Indian people are innately lacking in intelligence. I would ask her if that is what she intended. I would state that we teachers hold enormous authority and power over children. I would ask her if her destructive words were congruent with her beliefs about teaching and learning. And, I would know that, by speaking up, I would risk a confrontation, and the chance that I would be ostracized by the majority of teachers on the staff once word got out that I dared to question a more senior teacher.

At this point in my career I also have the skills to challenge the person who was our supervisor at the school and to confront the principal as well in order to ask for the guidelines that our supervisors used for the evaluation of teachers. I would find out if the guidelines, probably published by the Bureau of Indian Affairs, included something about demonstrable behaviors that communicated respect for the children and their families and for children's primary language and cultural traditions. I would say that the culture at the school promoted racism and I would give the example of my colleague's questions. I would find out if, at that time, the Navajo Nation had a mission statement about education. I would read it and implement its principles. I would ask parents or elders if I could learn about ways in which they themselves taught their children and what they would hope from me in order to be an effective teacher of their children. To do less than this would be to continue the destructive culture of silence, to sustain an environment that thwarted the well-being of everyone at the school on every level. Finally, I would do more to extend myself to the only Navajo teacher at the school in order to ask if she would be willing to mentor me so that I could develop the skills to be a teacher of Navajo children (Kato, 2016).

Dr. Kato addresses key elements related to Multicultural and Social Justice Counseling Competences (Appendix D). First of all, she conveys how she would activate her skill of "enriching her understanding of clients' worldview, assumptions, attitudes, values, beliefs, biases, social identities, social group statuses, and experiences with power, privilege, and oppression." By seeking out the mentorship from the Navajo Nation she enhances her understanding of how to better serve the community and builds cross cultural bridges. While enhancing her cultural competence she acknowledges there are "within-group differences and between group similarities and differences among privileged and marginalized clients" so that she does not, subsequently, group ALL Navajo people into one monolithic group.

The difficulty with assuming a client's **Group identification** (GI) is that it fails to recognize intragroup differences as well as variances in **Personal Identity** (PI). Failure to be holistic in our approach to counseling and teaching can be as damaging as not recognizing variances at all. This applies to all and any cultural group. For example, Alessandria (2005) challenges the "assumptions that all Whites are alike" (p. 58) and recommends that "One needs to look at clients in the context of their lives and attempt to understand their whole beings.... by assuming that European American clients are all alike, counselors are not attending to the whole client" (p. 60). The intragroup variances that include Group as well as Personal Identity are deciphered by careful exploration with the client who is their own expert.

Dr. Kato, in her reflection, indicates how she would expand on her role as an agent of change at the Institutional Level by "ask(ing) for the guidelines... used for the evaluation of teachers... find out if the guidelines... included something about demonstrable behaviors that communicated respect for the children and their families and for children's primary language and cultural traditions." Lastly, Dr. Kato addresses the teacher's behavior, the Interpersonal domain, and how she would have employed what is referred to in the counseling profession as "**Cultural Confrontation.**" This competency consists of two phases, Critical Examination and Supportive Challenge. The first phase encompasses an evaluation of the person's values to determine if there is connection between these values and self-defeating behaviors which in this case is markedly dysfunctional and harmful to the children.

The second phase of Cultural Confrontation consists of allowing for exploration of how belief systems lead to negative consequences while seeking resolution (Ethington, L. et al, 2006). In a counseling relationship, counselors are in the position to hold up the mirror for the client to see themselves. This is vital for self-examination. Acquiring and employing this advanced level of skill must be preceded with foundational trust in the relationship; the risk weighed with each situation when one dares to challenge a client or a system. Similarly, when we refuse to accept and adjust to differences in cultural contexts, the damage can be just as harmful as lacking knowledge altogether. If Dr. Kato was in a counseling relationship with her colleague, the subsequent interaction would have led to pointing out whether there was congruence with the teacher's values and behavior, and with the subsequent impact and outcome on the children.

We are fortunate to have Dr. Kato's reflective and insightful analysis of an event which happened early in her career. Her story provides a model by which to examine one interaction from the socioecological model. As we come to understand how our statuses of Privileged and Marginalized engage within varied relationships we can also apply our skills within the various levels of intrapersonal, interpersonal, institutional, community, public policy and international/global levels, we can begin to embrace our capacity to enact *positive change* in our world today. Yet, as Dr. Kato states very clearly is the danger of choosing not to say or do anything... and fomenting the "destructive culture of silence."

Learning to Respect and Engage in Different Contexts

After living in the college town of Davis, California for eleven years, my husband and I relocated to an area where we could enjoy country living. Our search for a new home resulted in a move to the Sierra Foothills where a seasonal river and ancient rock formations dominate the view in our back yard. I have never lived in such a rural setting where we co-exist with coyotes, deer, mountain lions, raccoons, skunks and other four-leggeds. My closest two legged neighbors are Sue Kendall, a retired educator, and her husband, Rich. Their home is situated on the hill that overlooks our property.

After we moved into our home, Sue observed me cleaning the property of layers of accumulated weeds and leaves from the cottonwoods and oak trees. In doing so, I have to reach in crevices between boulders and rock formations that have been on the land for thousands of years. My goal is to restore ancient trails but I do so delicately so as not to harm the rocks. Additionally, I seek to clear the path of an ancient river that cuts through the property. Dams built during the gold mining era disrupt the year round flow but when the rains return, the flowing waters restore the life of the river and all is, once again, *in relation*. One evening while visiting my neighbors Sue offered sage advice, "Rose, be sure you look where you are reaching. Rattlesnakes rest in cool places in between rocks. If you startle them, you can get bit."

I am reminded of Pederson's definition of culture, "things a stranger needs to know to behave appropriately in a particular setting." Sue apprised me of what I needed to know if I wanted to live in harmony with rattle snakes. This left me a choice of accepting and applying her advice or behaving as I did in all the places in which I lived before. The former requires adjusting my behavior and the latter means not being mindful that I am engaging in a different context and running the risk of not just a negative encounter but, in this case, a painful one. Given the options, during the warmer seasons of the year I not only look where I am reaching while working in my yard but I also announce my coming by tapping the ground ahead of me with a rake. The rattle snakes, in return, will from time to time send warning of their own presence with a shake of their rattle. We do our best to avoid startling one another and, when possible, to live in harmony.

Many lessons can be derived from this story as it relates to cross cultural competence; the lesson learned and applied is to be mindful when entering a different cultural context in our relationships. While the rattle snake will, in most cases, give a "verbal" warning, in many cases when working with our clients and in the community, non-verbal cues are just as important to read. Failure to respond in a culturally congruent manner can result in termination of the relationship. This means in the counseling context that the client does not return and in education, the student shuts down and fails to learn, or a family or community becomes oppositional. Additionally, being responsive to differences in cultural values requires, as Dr. Kato suggested, that we consult with members of the community. In other words, seek to understand the values and orientation of the people being served to as to not only foster a sacred space for learning and counseling but also to avoid offending. Expanding one's rapport with a client, a student, or a community calls upon careful observation and tapping into not just what we are told, but what we observe.

Mindful Engagement and Exploration

As related to mental health, the price for not acknowledging and accepting the cultural context of one's client may mean early termination, and subsequently, the client does not receive proper assistance. D.W. Sue and Sue (2002) promote "three primary goals for culturally competent helping professionals. The first goal (awareness) is an active process on the part of the helping professionals to gain awareness of their own values and beliefs, their societal systems, and the differences that exist between them and their clients. The second goal (knowledge) is that of understanding the worldview of the culturally different client. And the third goal (skills) is the process of actively developing and practicing appropriate, relevant, and sensitive intervention strategies and skills in working with a culturally different client." Yet, in relation to ethnic minorities there is "consistent findings on mental health underuse (which) suggests that current mental health practices such as talking to a counselor, psychologist, or psychiatrist may be inadequate in meeting the needs of these groups" (Arora, A. et al. 2004). Subsequently, learning values and practices that are congruent with the client's worldview requires not only awareness and knowledge but also culturally congruent consulting, collaboration, and advocacy skills. Our willingness to accept guidance and apply what we have learned that expands our capacity to engage in multiple cultural contexts becomes not only foundational but holistic.

Learning by What is Not Openly Stated

The practice of observing and asking questions when entering a cultural context different from one's own was apparent to me when I invited my friend, Carol Gamble, to the Big Time gathering hosted by the Northern Sierra Miwok at Grinding Rock Park in Pine Grove. This is a major event in which many tribal nations gather to dance in the sacred Round House. It is also the one event in which non-tribally affiliated two-leggeds are invited to enter the Round House. Having attended many Native American ceremonies and non-Native American services and ceremonies, I recognize the diversity in the way people express their religiosity and spirituality. Generally, there are not rules of conduct posted when entering the wide range of contexts in which people worship. And, there is not always a neighbor like Sue to provide direction on how to behave so as not to offend and face the repercussions.

Given minimal prompts from me, Carol and her two grandchildren were observant of how people entered the Round House and subsequently mindful as to the manner in which a person entered and conducted themselves once they were inside. They were cognizant of the vocabulary to name what the dancers were wearing which is referred to as "regalia" and came to understand that dancing in this context is a form of prayer and is not to be regarded as a form of entertainment. This means that clapping in the Round House is not appropriate. Carol and her grandchildren carefully observed, asked questions, and accepted the guidance as how to engage while entering this cross cultural context. They asked questions so that they could behave in a culturally competent manner, and then, lastly, applied their knowledge (skill). In most cases, we will not experience being "bit" when we fail to adjust our thinking and our behavior but when we become aware and are knowledgeable of the differences, we can enter the sacred space of another cultural group and demonstrate our capacity to walk in harmony within this cross cultural context; the sacred space. We then build bridges and inclusion becomes the norm. Such is the case with my friend, Carol, and with two of my colleagues whose story follows.

Collectivism and Individualism

At the end of last semester, I had the opportunity of having lunch with two friends and colleagues, Dr. EunMi Cho (contributor in previous chapter) and Dr. Ana Garcia-Nevarez, Chair of our College of Education's Undergraduate Branch. I was explaining to my friends how I was in the midst of translating a document from English to Spanish and the challenges that come with translating terms or concepts that don't have a direct translation due to different cultural context. My friend, EunMi, who is originally from South Korean, communicated that she understood this challenge by providing a specific example from her culture that defies a clean translation. She introduced us to the term **Jeong**. She provided context by explaining that the term relates to how the three of us share a "sisterhood" but that the term encapsulates more than that; it is a feeling and emotion that extends beyond oneself.

I was intrigued by this term and its' relevance to counseling so located an article (Cho & Chung) that explained how "*Jeong* seems located not only inside of our hearts but also outside. In other words the location of *jeong* is between individuals... related to the idea of collective emotion." While terms such as "feeling, love, etc..." provided some substance to the term, they do not, in and of themselves, provide full definition of a term in which "Interdependency and collectivism are highly valued, rather than autonomy, independency, privacy, and individualism" (p. 1). This term seemed to be rooted in cultural values similar to that of other collectivist cultures. The article went on to state that "Korean-Americans will often say that their lives in America are dry because of *jeong* deficiency" (p. 2). This conveys a degree of **Acculturation Stress** which examines the psychological adjustments and physical health changes associated with relocation and living in two cultural contexts, the home culture and the host culture.

Further exploration of this term brought me to how Korea and other East Asian regions have been strongly influenced by Confucian values. In modern times it has become evident that "modified Confucian values are still deeply saturated in the consciousness of the Korean people and embedded in every aspect of daily life and the way of thinking of individuals who then transmit these values to the next generation" (Cervero, R. and Ryu, K., 2011, p. 140). I then learned that the Chinese and Japanese have a concept relevant to *jeong*, but there are inherent differences. I wondered how closely aligned this term is to the Sacred Space and the extent of culture shock for the many people of different cultures living in the United States.

In Conclusion

During the rainy seasons the ancient river in my back yard flows, once again. It pains me to think of the distress on this beautiful site when many of the existing rock formations were blown up during the Gold Rush Era for the purpose of building a dam. As the clouds burst water upon the surrounding hills, rivulets from greater heights converge to forge the river's original path. I identify where blasted rocks left in the wake of detonated dynamite impede the flow and I do my best to restore the movement that was once familiar to the spirit of the river. As in working with people who can find themselves disconnected from others and often, even from themselves, my goal of being *in relation* sometimes means simply restoring.

Similarly, as we navigate and engage in a diverse world, we seek awareness, knowledge and skill. Being *in relation* calls us to help our clients identify what impedes their well-being and undermines their capacity to attain *jeong*. This, I believe, is what our historical humanists sought, fought, and died for. This is what our modern day humanists continue to do. We identify and eliminate the obstructions that keep us from being *in relation* with one another. In doing so, we strengthen the capacity to teach and learn, to develop therapeutic and healing alliances, to build bridges across traumatic and conflictive histories, and ultimately, restore our human connections with one another.

QUESTIONS FOR DISCUSSION OR SELF REFLECTION

The stories in the previous chapter hold many imbedded concepts discussed in this chapter. Understanding the application of these concepts to the experiential reality as applied to Dr. Kato's experience serves to build one's competence in the realm of multicultural competency. From the lens of a cross-cultural orientation, we can gain greater insight to the development of a culturally responsive therapeutic relationship.

SELF-AWARENESS

1. In what context might your own cultural values be incongruent with those of an individual or community you are serving?

CLIENT WORLDVIEW

2. What are the cultural values inherent in each of the case studies provided in Chapter 13?

COUNSELING RELATIONSHIP

3. If you were the protagonist in the story, how would the relationship or outcome of the interaction be different given your Privileged or Marginalized status?

COUNSELING AND ADVOCACY INTERVENTIONS

4. Similar to Dr. Kato's reflection in which she expanded upon how she would respond differently to an event that occurred at the Navajo Boarding School 40 years ago, what are additional strategies, from a socioecological model, that you would employ if you were working with the individual(s) and their families within these case studies? Consider all the levels from the Multicultural and Social Justice Counseling Competencies of intrapersonal, interpersonal, institutional, community, public policy and international/global levels.

NEW CONCEPTS AND VOCABULARY TO REVIEW

Acculturation Stress

Culture

Culturcide

Historical Trauma

Group Identification

Personal Identification

Cultural Confrontation

Deficit Model

Jeong

Activity

Meet with an individual from a culture that is distinctly different from your own. Interview the individual using the Twelve Aspects of Culture or Ethnicity (Appendix A) to gain greater understanding about his/her belief systems, values, history, spirituality/religiosity, family patterns, etc. Discuss your career path with this individual, and ask what he/she would recommend in your development of culturally responsive practices. 1) Incorporate how the information you gather from this interview is informed by the theories discussed. 2) Discuss how this interview has either affirmed or changed your perspective/knowledge/understanding of working with people from this particular culture. 3) What will you take from this interview as you begin your career?

References

Alessandria, K. (2002). Acknowledging white ethnic groups in multicultural counseling. *The Family Journal: Counseling and Therapy for Couples and Families, 10* (1), 57–60.

Arora, A., et al. (2004). Indigenous and interdependent perspectives of healing: Implications for counseling and research. *Journal of Counseling and Development, 82.*

Borunda, R. (2013). *What is the color of your heart: A humanist approach to diversity* (2nd ed.). Dubuque, IA: Kendall Hunt.

Cavanaugh, J., & Kail, R. (2013). *Human development. A life span view.* Belmont, CA: Wadsworth, Cengage Learning.

Cervero, R., & Ryu, K. (2011). The role of Confucian values and politics in planning educational programs for adults in Korea. *Adult Education Quarterly, 61* (2), 139–160.

Cho, S., & Chung, C. (n.d.). Significance of "Jeong" in Korean Culture and Psychotherapy. Retrieved from http://www.prcp.org/publications/sig.pdf

Ethington, L., Heppner, P., & Ridley, C. (2008). Cultural confrontation, a skill of advanced cultural empathy. In P. B. Pederson, J. G. Draguns, W. J. Lonner, & J. E. Trimble (Eds.), *Counseling across cultures* (6th ed., pp. 5–20). Thousand Oaks, CA: Sage.

Gonzalez, J., & Trimble, J. (2008) Cultural considerations and perspectives for providing psychological counseling for Native American Indians. In P. B. Pederson, J. G. Draguns, W. J. Lonner, & J. E. Trimble (Eds.), *Counseling across cultures* (6th ed., pp. 5–20). Thousand Oaks, CA: Sage.

Definitions of Multicultural Education. (n.d.). Retrieved from http://www.nameorg.org/definitions_of_multicultural_e.php

Pederson, P. (1988). *A handbook for developing multicultural awareness.* Alexandria, VA: American Association for Counseling and Development.

Pedersen, P. (2008). Ethics, competence, and professional issues in cross-cultural counseling. In P. B. Pederson, J. G. Draguns, W. J. Lonner, & J. E. Trimble (Eds.), *Counseling across cultures* (6th ed., pp. 5–20). Thousand Oaks, CA: Sage.

Rogers, C. (1980). *A way of being.* New York, NY: Houghton Mifflin Company.

Savoy, L. (2015). *Trace: Memory, history, race, and the American landscape. Berkeley, CA:* Counterpoint Press.

Sue, D. W., & Sue, D. (2002). *Counseling the culturally diverse: Theory and practice* (4th ed.). New York, NY: Wiley.

Werito, V. (2013). Diné youth and identity in ducation. In J. Reyhner, L. L. Martin, & W. S. Gilbert (Eds.), *Honoring our children: Culturally appropriate approaches for teaching indigenous students* (pp. 53–64). Flagstaff, AZ: Northern Arizona University.

Twelve Aspects of Culture or Ethnicity

1. **History:** A written or oral history that refers to the account of a particular group's collective experience in a geographic place and time. The time period and conditions under which groups immigrated or migrated is significant when we consider that these factors influence their subsequent opportunities.

2. **Social Status Factors:** Refers to one's social position, or "class," in society's hierarchy based on education, occupation, and income. This aspect of culture hinges on the nature of economic, political, education institutions of the society. In the United States it is uncommon for many people to consciously recognize social class because of the pervasive belief in meritocracy, the conviction that the United States is a fair, color- and gender-blind society. The ideology of meritocracy serves to mask recognition of institutionalized inequalities.

3. **Social Group Interaction Patterns** (within-group relations) and Intergroup (between-group relations)
   Intragroup relations are among members within the same group. These relations are influenced by age, gender, color, religion, education, socioeconomic background, sexual orientation, language or dialect spoken, and culture change (acculturation) processes, which can include culture shock and intergenerational conflict.
   Intergroup relations are between members of different groups. Social status and political-economic power is relevant here. Are relations cooperative and friendly or conflict ridden? Is there economic and political exploitation with widespread stereotyping and institutional discrimination?

4. **Value Orientations** are the deep subjective ideals and standards by which members of a culture judge their personal actions and those of others. Individualism, competition, and consumerism are three values common to U.S. mainstream national culture.

5. **Language and Communication: Verbal and Nonverbal** are composed of two components. *Verbal communication*, or language, includes the verbal categories and language structure (grammar and syntax) for the perception of reality and for communication. *Nonverbal communication* refers to everything else that conveys meaning but primarily remains unconscious. Tone of voice, gestures, facial expression, touching, body smell, and time orientation are aspects of communication that convey meaning directly without the use of words. The experience of time is elusive and depends on the culture's time orientation of which we are a member.

6. **Family Life Processes** encompass gender, family, and occupational roles. Gender roles become an essential part of this aspect of culture in considering the spoken and unspoken rules for male and female behavior that vary greatly among the different cultures of the world. Also, occupation, education, marriage customs, divorce, and parenting beliefs and practices are included here. Family structure is relevant as well. *Nuclear family* is the term for father, mother, and children living in the same household. *Extended family* refers to a mix of relatives under the same roof. *Augmented family and recombined families* are terms to describe households in which one or both parents were previously divorced or widowed (Parkin & Stone, 2004; Stone, 2001)

7. **Healing Beliefs and Practices** refer to the assumptions, attitudes, beliefs, and practices people possess regarding health, their bodies, determinants of disease, pain, death, and health practices and practitioners (Anderson, 1996; Culhane-Pera et al., 2003; Kleinman, 1988; Nebelkopf & Phillips, 2004; Spector, 2000).

8. **Religion** corresponds to the myriad spiritual beliefs and practices of human cultures (Bowie, 2000; Lessa & Vogt, 2000; Pandian, 2002).

9. **Art and Expressive Forms** involves the creative use of imagination in interpreting, understanding, and enjoying life. These forms include visual art, myth, ritual, stories, proverbs, poetry, ballads, legends, music, and performance art.

10. **Diet/Foods** are the preferred foods eaten by groups and their members. To many people, this aspect of culture is a quality-of-life issue.

11. **Recreation** refers to pastimes, activities, and sports for leisure and enjoyment.

12. **Clothing** are the types, styles, and extent of body coverings.

The four skills of cultural diversity competence: a process for understanding and practice by HOGAN-GARCIA MIKEL. Reproduced with permission of THOMAS BROOKS/COLE in the format Republish in a book via Copyright Clearance Center.

APPENDIX B

White Racial Identity Development Model

1. **Contact**: People in this status are oblivious to racism, lack an understanding of racism, have minimal experiences with Black people, and may profess to be color-blind. Societal influence in perpetuating stereotypes and the superior/inferior dichotomy associated between Blacks and Whites are not noticed, but accepted unconsciously or consciously without critical thought or analysis. Racial and cultural differences are considered unimportant and these individuals seldom perceive themselves as "dominant" group members, or having biases and prejudices.

2. **Disintegration**: In this stage, the person becomes conflicted over unresolvable racial moral dilemmas that are frequently perceived as polar opposites: believing one is nonracist, yet not wanting one's son or daughter to marry a minority group member; believing that "all men are created equal," yet society treating Blacks as second class citizens; and not acknowledging that oppression exists while witnessing it (à la the beating of Rodney King in Los Angeles). The person becomes increasingly conscious of his or her Whiteness and may experience dissonance and conflict between choosing between own-group loyalty and humanism.

3. **Reintegration**: Because of the tremendous influence that societal ideology exerts, initial resolution of dissonance often moves in the direction of the dominant ideology associated with race and one's own socioracial group identity. This stage may be characterized as a regression, for the tendency is to idealize one's socioracial group and to be intolerant of other minority groups. There is a firmer and more conscious belief in White racial superiority and racial/ethnic minorities are blamed for their own problems.

4. **Pscudo-Independence**: A person is likely to move into this phase due to a painful or insightful encounter or event, which jars the person from Reintegration status. The person begins to attempt an understanding of racial, cultural, and sexual orientation differences and may reach out to interact with minority group members. The choice of minority individuals, however, is based on how "similar" they are to him or her, and the primary mechanism used to understand racial issues is intellectual and conceptual. An attempt to understand has not reached the experiential and affective domains. In other words, understanding Euro-American White privilege, the sociopolitical aspects of race, and issues of bias, prejudice, and discrimination tend to be more an intellectual exercise.

5. **Immersion/Emersion**: If the person is reinforced to continue a personal exploration of himself or herself as a racial being, questions become focused on what it means to be White. Helms states that the person searches for an understanding of the personal meaning of racism and the ways by which one benefits from White privilege. There is an increasing willingness to truly confront one's own biases, to redefine Whiteness, and to become more activistic in directly combating racism and oppression. This stage is marked with increasing experiential and affective understanding that were lacking in the previous status.

6. **Autonomy**: Increasing awareness of one's own Whiteness, reduced feelings of guilt, acceptance of one's own role in perpetuating racism, renewed determination to abandon White entitlement leads to an autonomy status. The person is knowledgeable about racial, ethnic and cultural differences, values the diversity, and is no longer fearful, intimidated, or uncomfortable with the experiential reality of race. Development of a nonracist white identity becomes increasingly strong.

Helms (1995) from Sue, et al. (1998). *Multicultural Counseling Competencies: Individual and Organizational Development.* Sage Productions. Thousand Oaks, CA.

People of Color Racial Identity Development Model

1. **Conformity Status:** This status is characterized by a de-emphasis on or denigration of being a person of color.
   Example: "I am not Asian American; I am an American."

2. **Dissonance Status:** This denotes the period where circumstances create confusion about what it means to be a person of color; the individual has the opportunity to reinterpret his or her worldview differently as a result of an experience, or to maintain the conformity status.
   Example: "The security guard in the store wasn't really following me; he just happened to be in the area that I as in and might have been watching someone else."

3. **Immersion/Emersion Status:** For many at this point, there emerges an us-versus-them mentality where whites are seen as the enemy and one's racial group is seen as good.
   Example: "I don't want to attend that function; there's isn't going to be anyone there who looks like me and I don't like being around white people."

4. **Internalization Status:** This status is characterized by an individual who has an identity that is not exclusionary; the person is able to see that all groups have positive attributes and that all groups have individuals that discriminate.
   Example: "While I felt that I was stopped because of the color of my skin, I do know that not all white officers are racist and that some officers of color are not immune from stopping people of color."

5. **Integrative Awareness Status:** The individual is able to accept his or her multiple identities and has successfully managed the dissonance resulting from the previous statuses.
   Example: "I love going to my church, where all speak the same language and for the most part are of the same race; however, what I enjoy more is going to my daughter's school, where I get to interact with parents of all races. I feel I learn more in a multiracial group setting than when I am just with others from my own race."

Helms, J. E. (1994). The conceptualization of racial identity and other "racial" constructions. In E. J. Trickett, R. J. Watts, & D. Birmen (Eds.), *Human diversity: Perspectives on people in context* (pp. 285–311). San Francisco: Jossey-Bass.

Multicultural and Social Justice Counseling Competencies

Counselor Self-Awareness

Privileged and marginalized counselors develop self-awareness, so that they may explore their attitudes and beliefs, develop knowledge, skills, and action relative to their self-awareness and worldview.

1. **Attitudes and beliefs:** Privileged and marginalized counselors are aware of their social identities, social group statuses, power, privilege, oppression, strengths, limitations, assumptions, attitudes, values, beliefs, and biases.

   Multicultural and social justice competent counselors:

   - Acknowledge their assumptions, worldviews, values, beliefs, and biases as members of privileged and marginalized groups.

   - Acknowledge their privileged and marginalized status in society.

   - Acknowledge their privileged and marginalized status influences their worldview.

   - Acknowledge their privileged and marginalized status provides advantages and disadvantages in society.

   - Acknowledge openness to learning about their cultural background as well as their privileged and marginalized status.

2. **Knowledge:** Privileged and marginalized counselors possess an understanding of their social identities, social group statuses, power, privilege, oppression, strengths, limitations, assumptions, attitudes, values, beliefs, and biases.

   Multicultural and social justice competent counselors:

   - Develop knowledge of resources to become aware of their assumptions, worldviews, values, beliefs, biases, and privileged and marginalized status.

   - Develop knowledge about the history and events that shape their privileged and marginalized status.

   - Develop knowledge of theories that explain how their privileged and marginalized status influences their experiences and worldview.

   - Develop knowledge of how their privileged and marginalized status leads to advantages and disadvantages in society.

3. **Skills:** Privileged and marginalized counselors possess skills that enrich their understanding of their social identities, social group statuses, power, privilege, oppression, limitations, assumptions, attitudes, values, beliefs, and biases.

Multicultural and social justice competent counselors:

- Acquire reflective and critical thinking skills to gain insight into their assumptions, worldviews, values, beliefs, biases, and privileged and marginalized status.
- Acquire communication skills to explain how their privileged and marginalized status influences their worldview and experiences.
- Acquire application skills to interpret knowledge of their privileged and marginalized status in personal and professional settings.
- Acquire analytical skills to compare and contrast their privileged and marginalized status and experiences to others.
- Acquire evaluation skills to assess the degree to which their privileged and marginalized status influences their personal and professional experiences.

4. **Action:** Privileged and marginalized counselors take action to increase self-awareness of their social identities, social group statuses, power, privilege, oppression, strengths, limitations, assumptions, attitudes, values, beliefs, and biases.

Multicultural and social justice competent counselors:

- Take action to learn about their assumptions, worldviews, values, beliefs, biases, and culture as a member of a privileged and marginalized group.
- Take action to seek out professional development opportunities to learn more about themselves as a member of a privileged or marginalized group.
- Take action to immerse themselves in their community to learn about how power, privilege, and oppression influence their privileged and marginalized experiences.
- Take action to learn about how their communication style is influenced by their privileged and marginalized status.

Client Worldview

Privileged and marginalized counselors are aware, knowledgeable, skilled, and action-oriented in understanding clients' worldview.

1. **Attitudes and beliefs:** Privileged and marginalized counselors are aware of clients' worldview, assumptions, attitudes, values, beliefs, biases, social identities, social group statuses, and experiences with power, privilege, and oppression.

Multicultural and social justice competent counselors:

- Acknowledge a need to possess a curiosity for privileged and marginalized clients' history, worldview, cultural background, values, beliefs, biases, and experiences.

- Acknowledge that identity development influences the worldviews and lived experiences of privileged and marginalized clients.
- Acknowledge their strengths and limitations in working with clients from privileged and marginalized groups.
- Acknowledge that learning about privileged and marginalized clients may sometimes be an uncomfortable or unfamiliar experience.
- Acknowledge that learning about clients' privileged and marginalized status is a lifelong endeavor.
- Acknowledge the importance of reflecting on the attitudes, beliefs, prejudices, and biases they hold about privileged and marginalized clients.
- Acknowledge that there are within-group differences and between group similarities and differences among privileged and marginalized clients.
- Acknowledge clients' communication style is influenced by their privileged and marginalized status.

2. **Knowledge:** Privileged and marginalized counselors possess knowledge of clients' worldview, assumptions, attitudes, values, beliefs, biases, social identities, social group statuses, and experiences with power, privilege, and oppression.

Multicultural and social justice competent counselors:

- Develop knowledge of historical events and current issues that shape the worldview, cultural background, values, beliefs, biases, and experiences of privileged and marginalized clients.
- Develop knowledge of how stereotypes, discrimination, power, privilege, and oppression influence privileged and marginalized clients.
- Develop knowledge of multicultural and social justice theories, identity development models, and research pertaining to the worldview, culture, and life experiences of privileged and marginalized clients.
- Develop knowledge of their strengths and limitations in working with clients from privileged and marginalized groups.
- Develop knowledge of how to work through the discomfort that comes with learning about privileged and marginalized clients.
- Develop a lifelong plan to acquire knowledge of clients' privileged and marginalized status.
- Develop knowledge of the attitudes, beliefs, prejudices, and biases they hold about privileged and marginalized clients.
- Develop knowledge of the individual, group, and universal dimensions of human existence of their privileged and marginalized clients.
- Develop knowledge of the communication style of their privileged and marginalized client (e.g., high context vs. low context communication, eye contact, orientation to time and space, etc.).

3. **Skills:** Privileged and marginalized counselors possess skills that enrich their understanding of clients' worldview, assumptions, attitudes, values, beliefs, biases, social identities, social group statuses, and experiences with power, privilege, and oppression.

Multicultural and social justice competent counselors:

- Acquire culturally responsive evaluation skills to analyze how historical events and current issues shape the worldview, cultural background, values, beliefs, biases, and experiences of privileged and marginalized clients.

- Acquire culturally responsive critical thinking skills to gain insight into how stereotypes, discrimination, power, privilege, and oppression influence privileged and marginalized clients.

- Acquire culturally responsive application skills to apply knowledge of multicultural and social justice theories, identity development models, and research to one's work with privileged and marginalized clients.

- Acquire culturally responsive assessment skills to identify limitations and strengths when working with privileged and marginalized clients.

- Acquire culturally responsive reflection skills needed to work through the discomfort that comes with learning about privileged and marginalized clients.

- Acquire culturally responsive conceptualization skills to explain how clients' privileged and marginalized status influence their culture, worldview, experiences, and presenting problem.

- Acquire culturally responsive analytical skills to interpret the attitudes, beliefs, prejudices, and biases they hold about privileged and marginalized clients.

- Acquire culturally responsive conceptualization skills to identify the individual, group, and universal dimensions of human existence of privileged and marginalized clients.

- Acquire culturally responsive cross-cultural communication skills to interact with privileged and marginalized clients.

4. **Action:** Privileged and marginalized counselors take action to increase self-awareness of clients' worldview, assumptions, attitudes, values, beliefs, biases, social identities, social group statuses, and experiences with power, privilege, and oppression.

Multicultural and social justice competent counselors:

- Take action by seeking out formal and informal opportunities to engage in discourse about historical events and current issues that shape the worldview, cultural background, values, beliefs, biases, and experiences of privileged and marginalized clients.

- Take action by attending professional development trainings to learn how stereotypes, discrimination, power, privilege, and oppression influence privileged and marginalized clients.

- Take action by applying multicultural and social justice theories, identity development models, and research to one's work with privileged and marginalized clients.

- Take action by assessing ones limitations and strengths when working with privileged and marginalized clients on a consistent basis.
- Take action by immersing oneself in the communities in which privileged and marginalized clients reside to work through the discomfort that comes with learning about privileged and marginalized clients.
- Take action by using language to explain how clients' privileged and marginalized status influence their culture, worldview, experiences, and presenting problem.
- Take action by pursuing culturally responsive counseling to explore the attitudes, beliefs, prejudices, and biases they hold about privileged and marginalized clients.
- Take action by collaborating with clients to identify the individual, group, and universal dimensions of human existence that shape the identities of privileged and marginalized clients.
- Take action by consistently demonstrating cross-cultural communication skills required to effectively interact with privileged and marginalized clients.

Counseling Relationship

Privileged and marginalized counselors are aware, knowledgeable, skilled, and action-oriented in understanding how client and counselor privileged and marginalized statuses influence the counseling relationship.

1. **Attitudes and beliefs:** Privileged and marginalized counselors are aware of how client and counselor worldviews, assumptions, attitudes, values, beliefs, biases, social identities, social group statuses, and experiences with power, privilege, and oppression influence the counseling relationship.

   Multicultural and social justice competent counselors:

   - Acknowledge that the worldviews, values, beliefs and biases held by privileged and marginalized counselors and clients will positively or negatively influence the counseling relationship.
   - Acknowledge that counselor and client identity development shapes the counseling relationship to varying degrees for privileged and marginalized clients.
   - Acknowledge that the privileged and marginalized status of counselors and clients will influence the counseling relationship to varying degrees.
   - Acknowledge that culture, stereotypes, discrimination, power, privilege, and oppression influence the counseling relationship with privileged and marginalized group clients.
   - Acknowledge that the counseling relationship may extend beyond the traditional office setting and into the community.
   - Acknowledge that cross-cultural communication is key to connecting with privileged and marginalized clients.

2. **Knowledge:** Privileged and marginalized counselors possess knowledge of how client and counselor worldviews, assumptions, attitudes, values, beliefs, biases, social identities, social group statuses, and experiences with power, privilege, and oppression influence the counseling relationship.

Multicultural and social justice competent counselors:

- Develop knowledge of the worldviews, values, beliefs and biases held by privileged and marginalized counselors and clients and its influence on the counseling relationship.
- Develop knowledge of identity development theories and how they influence the counseling relationship with privileged and marginalized clients.
- Develop knowledge of theories explaining how counselor and clients' privileged and marginalized statuses influence the counseling relationship.
- Develop knowledge of how culture, stereotypes, discrimination, power, privilege, and oppression strengthen and hinder the counseling relationship with privileged and marginalized clients.
- Develop knowledge of when to use individual counseling and when to use systems advocacy with privileged and marginalized clients.
- Develop knowledge of cross-cultural communication theories when working with privileged and marginalized clients.

3. **Skills:** Privileged and marginalized counselors possess skills to engage in discussions with clients about how client and counselor worldviews, assumptions, attitudes, values, beliefs, biases, social identities, social group statuses, power, privilege, and oppression influence the counseling relationship.

Multicultural and social justice competent counselors:

- Acquire assessment skills to determine how the worldviews, values, beliefs and biases held by privileged and marginalized counselors and clients influence the counseling relationship.
- Acquire analytical skills to identify how the identity development of counselors and clients influence the counseling relationship.
- Acquire application skills to apply knowledge of theories explaining how counselor and clients' privileged and marginalized statuses influence the counseling relationship.
- Acquire assessment skills regarding how culture, stereotypes, prejudice, discrimination, power, privilege, and oppression influence the counseling relationship with privileged and marginalized clients.
- Acquire evaluation skills to determine when individual counseling or systems advocacy is needed with privileged and marginalized clients.
- Acquire cross-cultural communication skills to connect with privileged and marginalized clients.

4. **Action:** Privileged and marginalized counselors take action to increase their understanding of how client and counselor worldviews, assumptions, attitudes, values, beliefs, biases, social identities, social group statuses, and experiences with power, privilege, and oppression influence the counseling relationship.

Multicultural and social justice competent counselors:

- Take action by initiating conversations to determine how the worldviews, values, beliefs and biases held by privileged and marginalized counselors and clients influence the counseling relationship.

- Take action by collaborating with clients to identify the ways that privileged and marginalized counselor and client identity development influence the counseling relationship.

- Take action by exploring how counselor and clients' privileged and marginalized statuses influence the counseling relationship.

- Take action by inviting conversations about how culture, stereotypes, prejudice, discrimination, power, privilege, and oppression influence the counseling relationship with privileged and marginalized clients.

- Take action by collaborating with clients to determine whether individual counseling or systems advocacy is needed with privileged and marginalized clients.

- Take action by using cross-communication skills to connect with privileged and marginalized clients.

Counseling and Advocacy Interventions

Privileged and marginalized counselors intervene with, and on behalf, of clients at the intrapersonal, interpersonal, institutional, community, public policy, and international/global levels.

A. **Intrapersonal:** The individual characteristics of a person such as knowledge, attitudes, behavior, self-concept, skills, and developmental history.

Intrapersonal Interventions: Privileged and marginalized counselors address the intrapersonal processes that impact privileged and marginalized clients.

Multicultural and social justice competent counselors:

- Employ empowerment-based theories to address internalized privilege experienced by privileged clients and internalized oppression experienced by marginalized clients.

- Assist privileged and marginalized clients develop critical consciousness by understanding their situation in context of living in an oppressive society.

- Assist privileged and marginalized clients in unlearning their privilege and oppression.

- Assess the degree to which historical events, current issues, and power, privilege and oppression contribute to the presenting problems expressed by privileged and marginalized clients.

- Work in communities to better understand the attitudes, beliefs, prejudices, and biases held by privileged and marginalized clients.

- Assist privileged and marginalized clients with developing self-advocacy skills that promote multiculturalism and social justice.

- Employ quantitative and qualitative research to highlight inequities present in current counseling literature and practices in order to advocate for systemic changes to the profession.

B. **Interpersonal:** The interpersonal processes and/or groups that provide individuals with identity and support (i.e. family, friends, and peers).

Interpersonal Interventions: Privileged and marginalized counselors address the interpersonal processes that affect privileged and marginalized clients.

Multicultural and social justice competent counselors:

- Employs advocacy to address the historical events and persons that shape and influence privileged and marginalized client's developmental history.

- Examines the relationships privileged and marginalized clients have with family, friends, and peers that may be sources of support or non-support.

- Assist privileged and marginalized clients understand that the relationships they have with others may be influenced by their privileged and marginalized status.

- Assist privileged and marginalized clients with fostering relationships with family, friends, and peers from the same privileged and marginalized group.

- Reach out to collaborate with family, friends, and peers who will be a source of support for privileged and marginalized clients.

- Assist privileged and marginalized clients in developing communication skills to discuss issues of power, privilege, and oppression with family, friends, peers, and colleagues.

- Employ evidenced-based interventions that align with the cultural background and worldview of privileged and marginalized clients.

C. **Institutional:** Represents the social institutions in society such as schools, churches, community organizations.

Institutional Interventions: Privileged and marginalized counselors address inequities at the institutional level.

Multicultural and social justice competent counselors:

- Explore with privileged and marginalized clients the extent to which social institutions are supportive.

- Connect privileged and marginalized clients with supportive individuals within social institutions (e.g., schools, businesses, church, etc.) who are able to help alter inequities influencing marginalized clients.
- Collaborate with social institutions to address issues of power, privilege, and oppression impacting privilege and marginalized clients.
- Employ social advocacy to remove systemic barriers experienced by marginalized clients within social institutions.
- Employ social advocacy to remove systemic barriers that promote privilege that benefit privileged clients.
- Balance individual counseling with systems level social advocacy to address inequities that social institutions create that impede on human growth and development.
- Conduct multicultural and social justice based research to highlight the inequities that social institutions have on marginalized clients and that benefit privileged clients.

D. **Community:** The community as a whole represents the spoken and unspoken norms, value, and regulations that are embedded in society. The norms, values, and regulations of a community may either be empowering or oppressive to human growth and development.

Community Interventions: Privileged and marginalized address community norms, values, and regulations that impede on the development of individuals, groups, and communities.

Multicultural and social justice competent counselors:
- Take initiative to explore with privileged and marginalized clients regarding how community norms, values, and regulations embedded in society that hinder and contribute to their growth and development.
- Conduct qualitative and quantitative research to evaluate the degree to which community norms, values, and regulations influence privileged and marginalized clients.
- Employ social advocacy to address community norms, values, and regulations embedded in society that hinder the growth and development of privileged and marginalized clients.
- Utilize the norms, values and regulations of the marginalized client to shape the community norms, values, and regulations of the privileged client.

E. **Public Policy:** Public policy reflects the local, state, and federal laws and policies that regulate or influence client human growth and development.

Public Policy Interventions: Privileged and marginalized counselors address public policy issues that impede on client development with, and on behalf of clients.

Multicultural and social justice competent counselors:
- Initiate discussions with privileged and marginalized clients regarding how they shape and are shaped by local, state, and federal laws and policies.

- Conduct research to examine how local, state, and federal laws and policies contribute to or hinder the growth and development of privileged and marginalized clients.

- Engage in social action to alter the local, state, and federal laws and policies that benefit privileged clients at the expense of marginalized clients.

- Employ social advocacy to ensure that local, state, and federal laws and policies are equitable toward privileged and marginalized clients.

- Employ social advocacy outside the office setting to address local, state, and federal laws and policies that hinder equitable access to employment, healthcare, and education for privileged and marginalized clients.

- Assist with creating local, state, and federal laws and policies that promote multiculturalism and social justice.

- Seek out opportunities to collaborate with privileged and marginalized clients to shape local, state, and federal laws and policies.

F. **International and Global Affairs:** International and global concerns reflect the events, affairs, and policies that influence psychological health and well-being.

International and Global Affairs Interventions: Privileged and marginalized counselors address international and global events, affairs and polices that impede on client development with, and on behalf of, clients.

Multicultural and social justice competent counselors:

- Stay current on international and world politics and events.

- Seek out professional development to learn about how privileged and marginalized clients influence, and are influenced by, international and global affairs.

- Acquire knowledgeable of historical and current international and global affairs that are supportive and unsupportive of privileged and marginalized clients.

- Learn about the global politics, policies, laws, and theories that influence privileged and marginalized clients.

- Utilize technology to interact and collaborate with international and global leaders on issues influencing privileged and marginalized clients.

- Take initiative to address international and global affairs to promote multicultural and social justice issues.

- Utilize research to examine how international and global affairs impact privileged and marginalized clients.

APPENDIX E

What is a Transformational Leader?

Transformational Leadership is the act of empowering individuals to fulfill their contractual obligations, meet the need of the organization and go beyond the "call of duty" for the betterment of the institution. Leaders inspire, motivate, and appeal to followers through an array of skills and behaviors which communicate:

1. Their value to the institution.
2. The potential of their contribution.
3. High expectations in accordance with a supportive environment.

Transformational leaders also serve as role models to others, emulating the characteristics, behaviors, actions which they seek from all members of the organization … guid(ing) constituents towards individual and institutional success, beyond what is expected of them.

There are Three Major Elements to being a Transformational Leader:

1. Team Approach
2. Emphasis on follower empowerment
3. A comprehension of change within oneself and in the organization.

There are Three Primary Aspects of a Transformational Leader:

1. They are Motivational: They inspire those around them to achieve the highest standards possible.
2. Intellectually challenge themselves and others in envisioning an organization that surpasses its current form.
3. Provide individualized attention and support to each member of the institution.

Nevarez, C. & Wood, J. L. (2010). Community college leadership and administration: theory, practice, and change. New York, NY: Peter Lang Publishing, Inc.

CPSIA information can be obtained
at www.ICGtesting.com
Printed in the USA
LVOW02s0335030616

490704LV00002B/6/P